FUNDAMENTAL SKILLS
FOR MENTAL HEALTH PROFESSIONALS

FUNDAMENTAL SKILLS FOR MENTAL HEALTH PROFESSIONALS

LINDA SELIGMAN
Walden University, Faculty Member
Johns Hopkins University—Faculty Associate
George Mason University—Professor Emeritus

Merrill
is an imprint of

Upper Saddle River, New Jersey
Columbus, Ohio

Library of Congress Cataloging-in-Publication Data

Seligman, Linda.
   Fundamental skills for mental health professionals / Linda Seligman.
     p. ; cm.
   Includes bibliographical references and index.
   ISBN-13: 978-0-13-229231-3
   ISBN-10: 0-13-229231-9
  1. Mental health personnel.   2. Mental health personnel—Training of.   3. Clinical competence.
4. Mental health personnel and patient.
   [DNLM: 1. Psychiatry—methods.   2. Clinical Competence.   3. Mental Disorders–therapy.
4. Professional-Patient Relations.   5. Psychotherapy—methods.
   WM 21 S465f 2009] I. Title.
   RC454.4.S4568 2009
   616.89′023—dc22

2007048115

Vice President and Executive Publisher: Jeffery W. Johnston
Editor: Meredith D. Fossel
Director of Marketing: Quinn Perkson
Marketing Manager: Kris Ellis-Levy
Marketing Coordinator: Brian Mounts
Production Manager: Wanda Rockwell
Creative Director: Jayne Conte
Cover Design: Bruce Kenselaar
Cover Illustration/Photo: Getty Images, Inc.
Image Permission Coordinator: Lori Whitley
Full-Service Project Management/Composition: Puneet Lamba/Aptara, Inc.
Printer/Binder: R. R. Donnelly/Harrisonburg

Credits and acknowledgments borrowed from other sources and reproduced, with permission, in this textbook appear on appropriate page within text (or on page 383).
Portions of this book originally appeared in *Technical and Conceptual Skills for Mental Health Professionals*, by Linda Seligman, copyright © 2004 by Pearson Education, Inc.

Pearson Education Ltd., London
Pearson Education Singapore, Pte. Ltd
Pearson Education Canada, Inc.
Pearson Education–Japan

Pearson Education Australia PTY, Limited
Pearson Education North Asia Ltd., Hong Kong
Pearson Educación de Mexico, S.A. de C.V.
Pearson Education Malaysia, Pte. Ltd.
Pearson Education Upper Saddle River, New Jersey

Merrill
is an imprint of

10 9 8 7 6 5 4 3 2 1
ISBN-13: 978-0-13-229231-3
ISBN-10:   0-13-229231-9

For my husband
Bob Zeskind

PREFACE

This book is intended to help students and novice clinicians as well as more experienced clinicians in the mental health professions of counseling, psychology, social work, psychiatric nursing, and others to develop competence in the fundamental skills of their profession. With a solid grounding in such skills as effective use of questions, reflection of feelings, eliciting and modifying dysfunctional thoughts, and behavioral change strategies, clinicians can acquire a sound understanding of their clients and also develop strong helping skills, leading to successful treatment outcomes.

ORGANIZING FRAMEWORKS

Several organizing frameworks are used to give a clear and useful structure to this book. These include the BETA framework, the presentation of both general and specific skills, and many descriptions, examples, case studies, and learning opportunities.

BETA Framework

The leading theories of counseling and psychotherapy, along with their associated strategies and skills, can be organized into four broad categories that reflect their particular emphasis. This organizational framework, represented by the acronym BETA (standing for **B**ackground, **E**motions, **T**houghts, and **A**ctions) includes the following theories:

- **Background:** Sigmund Freud and psychoanalysis, Alfred Adler and individual psychology, Carl Jung and Jungian analytical psychology, transactional analysis, brief psychodynamic therapy, and other developmental and psychodynamic treatment systems
- **Emotions:** Carl Rogers and person-centered counseling, existential therapy, Gestalt therapy
- **Thoughts:** Aaron Beck and cognitive therapy, Albert Ellis and rational emotive behavior therapy
- **Actions:** behavior therapy, cognitive behavior therapy, reality therapy, brief solution-based therapy

The BETA framework was originally used to organize treatment theories in *Theories of Counseling and Psychotherapy: Systems, Strategies, and Skills* (2nd edition)

(Seligman, 2006) and also was used to organize the presentation of advanced clinical skills in *Conceptual Skills for Mental Health Professionals* (2008). This framework has been used in this text as well, but here the emphasis is on skills rather than theories of counseling and psychotherapy.

The use of this organizing framework in all three books facilitates understanding of the broad range of treatment approaches and skills available to clinicians. Although each book is separate and is designed to be used by itself, any two or three of these books can easily be combined in instruction that is part of a graduate training program or other educational program. Following the same organizing framework allows these books to build on each other and provides learners with a comprehensive understanding of theories of counseling and psychotherapy, fundamental skills, and conceptual skills.

Most clinical skills can be logically connected to one of the elements of the BETA framework more than to one of the other three. For example, reflection of feeling is most strongly associated with treatment theories that emphasize emotions; modification of distorted cognitions is most strongly associated with theories emphasizing thoughts; and contracting is most strongly associated with approaches emphasizing actions. However, readers should keep in mind that most clinicians today use a broad range of interventions and do not limit themselves to those most strongly linked to their theoretical orientations. Similarly, as readers develop their own clinical styles, they should feel free to draw on all skills presented throughout this book.

General and Specific Skills

Chapters 3 through 10 of this book focus on the four elements in the BETA format: Chapters 3 and 4 address skills to elicit clients' background information; Chapters 5 and 6 hone in on identifying and enhancing clients' expression and management of emotions; Chapters 7 and 8 provide information on modification of clients' dysfunctional thoughts; and Chapters 9 and 10 provide strategies to help them change unrewarding actions.

The first chapter of each of these four pairs focuses on the most general and fundamental skills, whereas the second chapter of each pair helps readers acquire more specific and advanced skills. For example, Chapters 5 and 6 both target emotions, but Chapter 5 presents information on such basic skills as tracking and effective use of encouragers and reflections of feeling, whereas Chapter 6 discusses strength-based reflections of feeling, solution-focused language, nonverbal expression of emotions, and rational emotive imagery. General skills are used by nearly all clinicians, whereas specific skills are those that most clinicians use only occasionally in the treatment of certain clients, problems, and disorders.

Descriptions, Examples, Case Studies, and Learning Opportunities

People learn in different ways, and this text offers a variety of approaches to maximize learning for everyone. When a skill is first presented in this book, a description of the skill is provided along with available and important research on the value of that skill and the appropriate use of that skill. Examples and case studies then are provided to illustrate the use of the skill in practice. Finally, at the end of each chapter, exercises allow readers to apply the learning they have gained. These exercises include

- Written exercises
- Discussion questions
- A role-play exercise
- An Assessment of Progress form that enables readers to describe and evaluate their learning and skill application
- Personal journal questions that allow readers to apply the material to themselves and their own lives, personalizing and making more meaningful use of the skills presented in the chapter

OVERVIEW OF CHAPTERS

Organized according to the frameworks described previously, the 11 chapters of this book highlight the following topics and skills.

Chapter 1, Becoming an Effective Clinician, provides an introduction. It discusses the process of becoming a successful mental health professional; emphasizes the importance of theory; provides historical and descriptive information on the fields of psychology, social work, and counseling; and provides information on making effective use of this book. Also presented is information on the use of feedback from colleagues and supervisors, leading to continuous professional development.

Chapter 2, Antecedents to Effective Skill Development, provides information that is essential for all mental health professionals and that serves as the foundation for skills development. This chapter ensures that readers become knowledgeable about the ethical standards of the mental health professions, theories of counseling and psychotherapy, multicultural understanding and competence, social justice and advocacy, the mind–body–spirit integration, and other important areas of nearly all of the mental health professions.

Chapter 3, Using Questions Effectively to Gather Information and Understand Background, begins the presentation of fundamental skills, focusing on those interventions that are especially important in obtaining background information. Skills presented in Chapter 3 include the importance of having a purpose before making an intervention, the effective use of open and closed questions, and conducting an intake interview. Eileen Carter, a client who is featured throughout this book to illustrate many of the skills, is introduced via an intake interview.

Chapter 4, Additional Skills Used to Gather Information and Understand Background, presents more specific skills for clinicians to use in eliciting and making good use of clients' histories. Described in this chapter are ways to structure an initial session, helping people identify and build on strengths, and the use of early recollections, genograms, and lifelines.

Chapter 5, Using Fundamental Skills to Elicit and Clarify Emotions, shifts attention from background to emotions. This chapter, as well as Chapter 6, focuses on useful skills to help people express, identify, manage, and change their emotions. Skills presented in this chapter stress the importance of attending and following and include information on eliciting and understanding emotions, using verbal encouragers to promote accurate listening (accents, restatements, paraphrases, and summarizing), communicating accurate empathy, and reflection of feeling.

Chapter 6, Using Fundamental Skills to Contain and Change Emotions, includes information on positive psychology and strength-based reflection of feeling. Specific skills described and illustrated in this chapter include using effective openings to elicit emotions, using language to promote expression of emotions, silence and brevity, analysis, imagery, new perspectives, focusing, Gestalt, and other strategies. Chapter 6 also includes information on nonverbal expression of emotions, clinicians' use of their own emotions, and helping clients contain and change emotions.

Chapter 7, Using Fundamental Skills to Elicit, Identify, Assess, and Modify Thoughts and Accompanying Emotions and Actions, focuses on improving clients' cognitions. This chapter presents skills that clinicians can use to help their clients identify, evaluate, and modify their thoughts. Skills described and illustrated in this chapter include a structured format for eliciting, assessing, and modifying thoughts.

Chapter 8, Additional Skills Used to Elicit, Identify, Assess, and Modify Thoughts, continues the focus on helping people maximize their helpful thoughts and change their dysfunctional ones. Included in this chapter is information on reflection of meaning, identifying focal concerns, problem solving and decision making, information giving, self-talk and affirmations, anchoring, reframing, thought stopping, meditation and mindfulness, journal writing, and mind mapping.

Chapter 9, Using Fundamental Skills to Identify, Assess, and Change Actions and Behaviors, introduces skills that are especially helpful when clients want to make changes in their actions and behavior. Important skills included in this chapter are developing behavioral change plans, establishing a baseline, goal setting, contracting, and making effective use of rewards and consequences.

Chapter 10, Additional Skills Used to Identify, Assess, and Change Actions and Behaviors, continues the focus on helping people modify unhelpful actions. Skills included in this chapter are the use of between-session tasks, empowerment, challenge and caring confrontation, visualization, behavioral rehearsal, modeling, skill development, relaxation, systematic desensitization, and others. Guidelines for promoting behavioral change, as well as ways to eliminate barriers to change, also are included in this chapter.

Finally, Chapter 11, Reviewing, Integrating, and Reinforcing Learning, affords readers the opportunity to apply much of what they have learned throughout this book and to evaluate the learning they have gained, as well as their strengths as clinicians. This chapter provides an intake interview, and readers are then given a series of exercises to apply to this case, reflecting their newly honed skills. This chapter also includes all of the Assessment of Progress forms that have been presented throughout this book. This offers a comprehensive picture of all of the skills that have been learned and gives readers a final opportunity to practice, review, and rate themselves on these skills, increasing awareness of the progress and learning they have achieved.

Uses of This Book

Many ways are available to make productive and effective use of the material in this book.

1. This book is ideally suited to a skill development course, extending over either one or two semesters or quarters. If its use is spread over more than one semester, then instructors might alternate weeks, using the first of each pair of classes for lectures and in-class demonstrations and discussions and the second of each pair of classes for the practice group exercises.

2. This book can be combined with either my book on theories of counseling and psychotherapy (*Theories of Counseling and Psychotherapy: Systems, Strategies, and Skills*) (Seligman, 2006) or with another theory book to integrate the teaching of both skills and theories.

3. This book can be combined with my book *Conceptual Skills for Mental Health Professionals* (2009) to teach an even broader and deeper array of skills. If this combining is done, the learning experience should extend over two semesters or quarters with the first focusing on acquisition of fundamental skills and the second focusing on the conceptual skills such as case conceptualization, diagnosis, and treatment planning.

4. This book can be used as a textbook for students in practicum and internship who have already had course work in basic skill development. This book could provide a review of the fundamental skills they have already learned and serve as a vehicle for helping them develop more advanced skills.

5. Practicing clinicians in mental health, school, or other settings could use this book on their own to review and refine their skills. Almost all clinicians can learn new skills from this book and will deepen their understanding of their clients and the treatment process as they use this text.

6. Units of this book could be selected to teach one or a group of skills in a special seminar or could be incorporated into a variety of courses. The following are a few examples:
   - The information on ethics might be included in a course or unit on ethical standards in the helping professions.
   - The information on the development of multicultural counseling competencies, social justice, advocacy, and positive psychology might be included in a unit on new developments in the mental health professions.
   - The information on the effective use of questions, encouragers, reflections of feeling, and reflections of meaning might be used in a unit on basic clinical skills.

Feel free to innovate and experiment in your use of this book!

ACKNOWLEDGMENTS

I am grateful for all of the personal and professional support I received while writing this book. The following people made a particularly important contribution to this book:

- My virtual assistant, Terri Karol, carefully checked my references, created the table of contents, and proofread much of the manuscript. Although working against a tight deadline, she continued to exercise care and thoroughness.

- Diane Tuininga, Ph.D., helped me to update the research for this book and made sure that both classic and new references reflected current thinking on the topics in the book.

- Shantel Edmonds, graduate student at George Mason University, generously offered her time to conduct some additional research for this book. Her eagerness to learn and become more involved in her profession was reflected in the high quality of her work.

- Lynn Field, Ph.D., LPC, psychotherapist in private practice in Fairfax, Virginia, was deeply involved in the first edition of this book. As my graduate assistant at George Mason University, she unfailingly provided excellent research and editing skills as well as good judgment, clear feedback, and encouragement.

- Diana Gibb, Ph.D., faculty member at George Mason University and counselor in private practice also made an important contribution to the first edition of this book. Dr. Gibb carefully reviewed the book manuscript and provided knowledgeable, helpful, and detailed feedback. Her understanding of graduate students and beginning clinicians helped me shape this book.

- I thank the administrators at George Mason University who provided me a study leave during which I wrote the first iteration of this book. In addition, the faculty, administrators, and staff of the Graduate School of Education at George Mason University, particularly Associate Dean Martin Ford, Dr. Gerald Wallace, and Janet Holmes, provided time and support that facilitated my work on this book.

- I am also grateful to the many students and clients I have met over the years and from whom I have learned so much.

- This book would not have happened without Kevin Davis, Assistant Vice President and Publisher at Pearson Education, who invited me to write this book as well as *Theories of Counseling and Psychotherapy: Systems, Strategies, and*

Skills (2006). He and his staff facilitated the development of this book in many ways. I am appreciative of all their assistance along the way.

- Meredith Fossel, Editor, Counseling and Introduction/Foundations of Education, at Pearson Education, offered information and assistance during my writing of the second edition of this book.
- Special thanks are due to my family and friends who have remained supportive through the pressures of this, my fourteenth book. My husband Dr. Robert M. Zeskind, Gerri Eastment, Terri Karol, and my dear friend Bettie Young have been especially important to me during this time, as always, in ensuring that I have some balance in my life.

ABOUT THE AUTHOR

Dr. Linda Seligman received a Ph.D. in Counseling Psychology from Columbia University. Her primary research interests included diagnosis and treatment planning as well as counseling people with chronic and life-threatening illnesses. During her lifetime, she authored 14 books, including *Theories of Counseling and Psychotherapy: Systems, Strategies, and Skills; Selecting Effective Treatments; Diagnosis and Treatment Planning in Counseling; Developmental Career Counseling and Assessment;* and *Promoting a Fighting Spirit: Psychotherapy for Cancer Patients, Survivors, and Their Families.* She also wrote more than 80 professional articles and book chapters. In addition, she has lectured throughout the United States as well as internationally on diagnosis and treatment planning and was recognized for her expertise on that subject.

Dr. Seligman was a professor in the Graduate School of Education at George Mason University in Fairfax, Virginia, for 25 years. She served as co-director of the Doctoral Program in Education, coordinator of the Counseling and Development Program, Associate Chair of the School of Education, and head of the Community Agency Counseling Program. She was later named professor emeritus at George Mason University. Dr. Seligman also served as associate at Johns Hopkins University and a faculty member in counseling psychology at Walden University, an on-line university.

Dr. Seligman was known for her extensive clinical experience in a broad range of mental health settings, including drug and alcohol treatment programs, university counseling settings, psychiatric hospitals, correctional facilities, and treatment programs for children and adolescents. She kept private practice in Bethesda, Maryland, where she provided therapy, supervision, coaching, and consultation.

Dr. Seligman served as editor of the *Journal of Mental Health Counseling* and as president of the Virginia Association of Mental Health Counselors. In 1986, her colleagues at George Mason University selected her as a Distinguished Professor, and in 1990, the American Mental Health Counselors Association designated her as Researcher of the Year. In 2007, the American Mental Health Counselors Association honored her with the title of Counselor Educator of the Year.

BRIEF CONTENTS

PART 5: USING FUNDAMENTAL SKILLS TO IDENTIFY, ASSESS, AND CHANGE ACTIONS AND BEHAVIORS

PART 6: SOLIDIFYING FUNDAMENTAL SKILLS

CONTENTS

PART 2: USING FUNDAMENTAL SKILLS TO UNDERSTAND AND ADDRESS BACKGROUND

Chapter 3
Using Questions Effectively to Gather Information and Understand Background

PART 3: USING FUNDAMENTAL SKILLS TO ELICIT AND MODIFY EMOTIONS

Chapter 5
Using Fundamental Skills to Elicit and Clarify Emotions   **134**

PART 4: USING FUNDAMENTAL SKILLS TO ELICIT, IDENTIFY, ASSESS, AND MODIFY THOUGHTS

Chapter 8
Additional Skills Used to Elicit, Identify, Assess, and Modify Thoughts   **257**

PART 5: USING FUNDAMENTAL SKILLS TO IDENTIFY, ASSESS, AND CHANGE ACTIONS AND BEHAVIORS

PART 6: SOLIDIFYING FUNDAMENTAL SKILLS

Chapter 11
Reviewing, Integrating, and Reinforcing Learning   355

FUNDAMENTAL SKILLS
FOR MENTAL HEALTH PROFESSIONALS

PART 1

Chapter 1

BECOMING AN EFFECTIVE CLINICIAN

ENTERING THE WORLD OF THE CLINICIAN

Who are you and why are you reading this book? You have probably begun to read this book because you are taking a course designed to teach skills you will need as a counselor, psychologist, social worker, or psychiatric nurse. You may well be a graduate student, en route to a career in one of these professions, or you may be an undergraduate student seeking to understand and develop a strong background in the helping skills. If you are an undergraduate, you may not yet have decided on your major or future career, but you probably have an interest in learning more about one of the helping professions. On the other hand, you might be a practicing clinician in a mental health profession who is reading this book to improve your skills or—because you recognize that the mental health professions are constantly evolving fields—you want to continue honing and expanding your skills.

A more important question is this: "What is drawing you toward the mental health professions and what qualities do you see in yourself that will enable you to succeed as a clinician?" (Because this book is directed toward people from a variety of helping professions, I will use the neutral term *clinician* rather than *counselor, psychologist,* or *social worker.*) Before we proceed any further, jot down two reasons why you have decided or might decide to enter a helping profession:

1. _____

2. _____

1

Individuals enter the helping profession for a variety of reasons

During my many years as a clinician and faculty member teaching graduate students in psychology, counseling, and social work, I have heard many answers to the preceding question. Some make me hopeful that I am talking to someone who will be a credit to their profession and will make important contributions to the people who seek his or her help as well as to our society. Other answers make me worry that the person I am talking with may be making an unwise choice because of misinformation or compelling personal issues.

Motives for Entering a Helping Profession

People enter the fields of counseling, psychology, psychiatric nursing, and social work for a wide variety of reasons. Of course, most of them want to help people. However, other motives may also be present. The following are some of the common reasons that people enter these professions:

- They are altruistic; they want to help others and make a contribution to society.
- They are seeking a vehicle for their need to take care of others.
- They want to be important to others.
- They are following in the footsteps of their own therapists and want to share with others the benefits they derived from therapy.
- They received little help with their own difficulties while they were growing up and do not want others to suffer the pain and lack of support they experienced.
- They had a disappointing experience in counseling and believe they can improve the profession so that others will get more help than they did.
- They believe they have the skills needed to become fine clinicians.

- They believe that becoming a clinician will enable them to resolve their own difficulties.
- They have a need for status, control, and power that they believe they can meet by advising others on how to lead more rewarding lives.
- They view themselves as good listeners and helpful friends and want to use those skills in their work.
- They are psychologically minded and enjoy learning about and trying to understand others.
- They are concerned with cultural, political, or societal issues and want to address those broad problems through clinical work.
- They view the helping professions as offering many extrinsic and intrinsic rewards such as desirable salaries, hours, working conditions, and prestige.
- They want to leave teaching or another profession and view counseling as easier, more flexible, and more rewarding.
- They have been in professions that afforded them little opportunity to interact with and help others; they have decided that those professions are unfulfilling and are seeking a better match for their skills and values.
- They feel a spiritual calling to help others.

How do the reasons you listed for considering a helping profession compare with these? Do your reasons appear in this list or do you have different reasons for your interest in helping others? Perhaps the list of frequently heard reasons gave you a different perspective and made you aware of other or additional reasons that make one of the helping professions an appealing career choice for you. If so, list those additional reasons below:

3. _____

4. _____

Assessing Your Motivation for Becoming a Helping Professional

An important initial step for you as an aspiring or relatively new clinician is assessing your own motivation for becoming a counselor, social worker, psychiatric nurse, or psychologist and developing a clear awareness of what you expect those professions to be like. You will probably benefit from thinking about your image of the practicing clinician, including where your vision of the profession came from, how you picture the work of the clinician, and what sort of relationships you expect to have with your clients. Being aware of your preconceptions can help you identify discrepancies between your images and the reality of the clinician's role, as presented in this book.

Let's take a closer look at your interest in possibly entering a helping profession. Ask yourself the following questions about your reasons for considering a career in the mental health field:

- Are your reasons based on reading, volunteer work, course work, conversations with mental health professionals, and other sources of information that have given you a sound understanding of the helping professions and of the role of clinicians?

- Are you primarily moving toward an appealing and potentially rewarding future career choice rather than primarily moving away from an unsuccessful or unsatisfying current career choice?
- Do you see in yourself skills and characteristics that suggest you have the potential to be a skilled clinician?

Have you answered "yes" to all three of these questions? This chapter will help you further gauge the wisdom of your choice by giving you additional information about the helping professions, the skills of effective leaders and clinicians in those professions, and your own strengths and characteristics. The exercises at the end of this chapter will offer you the opportunity to respond to the previous three questions in writing using the added knowledge you will gain from this chapter.

CHARACTERISTICS OF THE EFFECTIVE CLINICIAN

Research has been accumulating for more than 20 years to indicate that success rates in treatment have more to do with the skills and personal characteristics of the clinician than they do with the setting or the interventions used (Luborsky, McLellan, Woody, O'Brien, & Auerbach, 1985; Luborsky et al., 1984). Clinicians bring with them personal and interpersonal characteristics, attitudes, and behaviors that greatly influence their success in their work. Professional training and experience will build on those qualities, but having the basic characteristics of effective clinicians goes a long way toward determining clinicians' effectiveness and satisfaction with their work.

Research, as well as my own professional experience as clinician, professor, and supervisor, suggests that effective clinicians have a cluster of desirable characteristics and attitudes. Careful and honest self-assessment helps clinicians identify and build on their strengths and reduce or eliminate some of their weaknesses. Think about the qualities and skills you currently have as you review this section of the book.

Jennings and Skovholt (1999) conducted a study of peer-nominated outstanding therapists and found that these clinicians were characterized by nine qualities:

1. They are eager learners.
2. They draw heavily on their extensive experience.
3. They value and can deal with ambiguity and complex concepts.
4. They can recognize and accept people's emotions.
5. They are emotionally healthy and nurture their own emotional well-being.
6. They are self-aware and can assess the impact their own emotional health has on their work.
7. They have strong interpersonal skills.
8. They believe in the importance and value of the therapeutic alliance.
9. They can use their good interpersonal skills to develop a positive therapeutic alliance.

Although counseling and friendship are very different processes, many of the same qualities that make someone a good friend and capable of healthy interpersonal relationships can also make that person an effective clinician. Research has shown that personal qualities such as being responsible, ethical, sensitive to and respectful of individual differences, open minded, objective, stable, well adjusted, and optimistic are more important in determining a clinician's efficacy than are factors such as age, gender, or cultural background (Sexton & Whiston, 1991).

Characteristics of Leaders in Mental Health

Perhaps you are aspiring not only to become a skilled and effective clinician, but also a leader in your profession, someone who serves as a role model for others, has an impact on the mental health field, and even improves social justice and the prizing of individual differences in our world. What qualities are needed to become a leader in the profession? Black and Magnuson (2005) interviewed the protégés of 10 leading women in the counseling field to determine those characteristics that made the women effective leaders. This research identified six terms that described these influential women (p. 339):

- *Authentic.* They are ethical, trustworthy, and self-aware; They have a realistic sense of themselves; and they live their lives in a way that reflects who they are and their spiritual beliefs.
- *Passionate and tenacious.* They have a mission and work hard to achieve it, energizing and motivating others, setting high standards for themselves and others, and effectively addressing problems and barriers that get in their way.
- *Compassionate.* They are caring, perceptive of the needs of others, and willing and available to help them.
- *Empowering.* They are role models, inspiring others to better themselves, to work harder, and to accomplish more; they encourage, teach, challenge, and support others in their efforts, valuing their diverse attributes and abilities.
- *Visionary.* They can see the big picture and focus their work on making a positive difference; they are hopeful, optimistic, and encouraging, collaborating with others to promote healing and growth.
- *Intentional.* They are deliberate and purposeful and have clear goals in sight as well as a plan to achieve those goals. They can set priorities, express and assert themselves as needed, and develop effective strategies to achieve their goals.

Self-Assessment

The following checklist encompasses many of the desirable qualities of clinicians. I suggest you use this checklist to assess yourself. Mark your strengths with a plus (+). Put a minus (−) by each item you view as a weakness or a quality you have not yet developed. If you are uncertain whether an item describes you, mark it with a question mark (?). You might also ask a trusted friend, colleague, or family member to identify those items on the list that he or she perceives as your strengths.

Checklist of Clinician Strengths

_____ Able to ask for help
_____ Able to deal with ambiguity and complexity
_____ Able to express oneself clearly, both orally and in writing
_____ Able to give credit to others for their accomplishments
_____ Aware of own political, spiritual, interpersonal, and other values
_____ Can draw on and learn from past experience
_____ Can see details as well as the big picture
_____ Caring
_____ Comfortable with networking and collaboration
_____ Creative
_____ Emotionally stable
_____ Empathic and able to identify emotions in self and others
_____ Ethical and respectful of laws, rules, standards, and boundaries but also able to exert efforts to change harmful standards
_____ Flexible and resourceful
_____ Hard working
_____ High frustration tolerance
_____ Insightful and psychologically minded
_____ Intelligent
_____ Interested, curious; an eager learner
_____ Maintains balance in own life
_____ Maintains own physical and emotional health
_____ Manifests good interpersonal skills and has some close relationships
_____ May have own concerns, but is addressing them and does not impose them on others
_____ Objective
_____ Open minded
_____ Respectful and appreciative of others and their differences
_____ Self-aware and honest with oneself
_____ Serves as a role model and inspiration to others
_____ Sound capacity for attention and concentration
_____ Willing to listen to feedback and make changes as needed

Summarizing Your Self-Assessment   Now that you have completed the checklist, think about how this information can help you progress toward becoming an effective clinician. List what you see as the three strengths that are most likely to help you succeed as a mental health professional:

1. _____

2. _____

3. _____

Now write down three steps you can take to minimize your weaknesses, build on your strengths, and get to know yourself better. This might include such activities as practicing asking others for help, developing your spiritual interests and activities to bring greater balance into your life, and seeking some counseling for your tendency to become angry when others challenge you.

1. _____

2. _____

3. _____

Now let's look at your potential for leadership. Using the +, −, and ? symbols again, assess yourself in terms of the six characteristics of outstanding leadership identified by Black and Magnuson (2005). Following each word, write briefly about how that word applies to you.

Checklist of Leadership Skills

_____ Authentic
_____ Passionate/tenacious
_____ Compassionate
_____ Empowering
_____ Visionary
_____ Intentional

Seeing Yourself Clearly as a Mental Health Professional

What have you learned from the preceding self-assessment exercises? My guess is that you have identified many strengths in yourself and some compelling reasons to pursue your interest in the mental health professions, but you have also identified some areas that need improvement. View this learning in light of some of the key messages of the mental health professions of the 21st century:

- Be honest and genuine with yourself, your colleagues, and your clients.
- Identify and emphasize strengths and assets.
- Growth and development are lifelong processes that can be rewarding and empowering.

Incorporate these messages into your own life by being honest and straightforward with yourself, emphasizing your assets and also acknowledging areas needing improvement, and developing clear goals and plans to continue meaningful and purposeful growth and development.

Although the effectiveness of the clinician is central to the success of treatment, the therapeutic process actually includes three ingredients: the clinician, the client, and the context of treatment. These combine to create the therapeutic alliance. Each of these elements almost always plays an important role in determining the success or failure of the treatment process.

The Client

People seeking treatment, of course, are not blank slates; they bring with them the following:

- *Background.* A history of relationships, experiences, disappointments, successes, and perhaps traumas has shaped who they are. Their families and their spiritual and cultural backgrounds contribute greatly to their development.
- *Emotions.* Depression and anxiety are people's most common presenting concerns. Many other emotions arise and need attention during treatment such as low self-esteem, rage, suicidal ideation, and terror. Positive emotions such as pride, love, and self-confidence should receive attention too, and can serve as the foundation for positive change.
- *Thoughts.* Each person has his or her own views of the world, expectations about people and events, and an individual way of reasoning, thinking, and making decisions. People's inner experiences as well as their experiences with people and events are filtered through these lenses. Most current approaches to mental health treatment take a phenomenological perspective, seeking to understand how each person perceives and makes sense of the world.
- *Actions.* People's actions both reflect and shape their emotions and thoughts. How much they study in school, how they choose a partner, where they decide to live, what jobs they hold, and how they spend their money and leisure time are only a few of the many important actions that shape people's lives.
- *Problems, goals, and expectations.* People usually seek treatment because they are dissatisfied or unhappy or in pain and want to make some changes or because another person has encouraged or required them to obtain help. When people enter treatment, they may be optimistic or pessimistic, enthusiastic or reluctant about the treatment process. They have preconceptions and expectations about what will happen in treatment. They probably have goals that they hope to accomplish through treatment. These may be realistic, such as improving their mood or changing their eating habits, or they may be unrealistic, such as finding a way to prevent a husband from having affairs or never again feeling shy or fearful.

In general, people who benefit most from treatment are those who have a realistic view of that process, are motivated to make changes, and can take some responsibility for their difficulties. They have reasonably good ego strength, have had some rewarding relationships, and are psychologically minded (Lambert & Cattani-Thompson, 1996).

Of course, many people do not fit this profile of the ideal client. This book will help you to get to know and understand your clients better, to maximize the strengths they bring with them to the treatment process, and to reduce the barriers that can impede their progress.

Context of Treatment

The treatment context is the setting in which counseling or psychotherapy takes place. The location and size of the office, level of privacy, décor, temperature, parking, support staff, and even the magazines in the waiting room combine with the clinician's initial response to the client's request for help to create that person's first impression of the treatment process. Whether the context is a private practice, a school counseling office, a community mental health center, or a residential treatment program, the treatment context ideally should be

- Easily accessible to all, including people with disabilities;
- Comfortable and welcoming;
- Able to maintain privacy of both client and confidential records; and
- Responsive to client needs, including promptly returning e-mails and telephone calls and dealing with billing and third-party payers.

Although more attention will be paid in this book to the clinician and the client, the importance of the clinical setting should not be overlooked when mental health services are provided.

The Therapeutic Alliance

The therapeutic alliance, that is, the working relationship between the client and the clinician, has been shown in study after study to be the best predictor of treatment outcome (Lambert & Cattani-Thompson, 1996; Sexton, 1995; Walborn, 1996). In addition, when clients identify what they found most helpful about their mental health treatment, the item that ranks first is the clinician's facilitative interpersonal style (Paulson, Truscott, & Stuart, 1999). This means that having a clinician who is supportive, caring, personable, attentive, and understanding has great importance in the development of a positive therapeutic alliance. In addition, role induction, the process of teaching people to be successful clients, can greatly enhance treatment outcome. More information will be provided throughout this book about developing a sound and therapeutic alliance.

This book will help you to assess the essential ingredients of the treatment process: the context, the client, the clinician, and the therapeutic alliance. In addition, it will provide you with strategies to maximize the strengths of these ingredients and address barriers or areas of difficulty that may limit treatment success.

IMPORTANCE OF THEORIES OF COUNSELING AND PSYCHOTHERAPY

Although this book is not designed to teach theories of counseling, social work, and psychotherapy, knowledge of the established treatment systems and approaches available to clinicians is another important element in the treatment process. Without that information, it is unlikely that clinicians can develop successful treatment plans and determine interventions that are likely to be effective with a particular person.

More than 75% of today's clinicians describe their theoretical orientation as eclectic or integrated (Walborn, 1996). For these treatment providers, in particular, familiarity with a broad range of clinical theories and interventions is essential. That knowledge gives them the ability to select ingredients from several theoretical approaches and logically develop an integrative treatment plan designed to meet the needs of a given client.

Research suggests that 60% or more of the reasons for clients' progress in treatment can be attributed to the treatment theories and strategies used by the clinician (Seligman, 2001). Not only do treatment systems make a difference through the way the client's difficulties are conceptualized and through the particular interventions and strategies used, but also through the power of the treatment system to promote a positive therapeutic alliance and to engender hope and optimism in clients.

Having a clear and clinically appropriate theoretical framework for any treatment provided is also important in demonstrating accountability. Clinicians are increasingly being asked to justify their work to their clients, their employers, and third-party payers. Knowledge of treatment approaches and their effective use enables clinicians to plan successful treatments and to explain their reasons for selecting particular approaches or interventions. In addition, although malpractice suits against mental health professionals are uncommon, clinicians are sometimes sued by angry or disappointed clients who believe they were harmed by their treatment. Here, too, information on the research supporting a given treatment system and its application is a clinician's best defense in the event of a lawsuit.

Having a solid grounding in treatment systems and theories of counseling and psychotherapy is expected to become even more important in the next 5 to 10 years in light of the increasing use of evidence-based and manualized treatment programs. Evidence-based treatment approaches whose effectiveness has been demonstrated through empirical research are increasingly being emphasized. The fields of counseling, social work, and psychology are witnessing a rapid growth in treatment protocols and manuals that have been developed and proven effective in ameliorating the symptoms of a particular mental disorder (Chambless et al., 1998). Manuals have been developed and empirically validated for the treatment of anxiety disorders, behavioral difficulties, mood disorders, some eating disorders, borderline personality disorder, and other emotional disorders. To use these treatment protocols and incorporate them into their work, clinicians once again will need to have their therapeutic efforts solidly grounded in a broad and deep understanding of treatment systems.

MAKING THE TRANSITION FROM THEORY TO TREATMENT

Determining which theoretical framework is most appropriate for a particular client and which interventions are most likely to be helpful involves having a sense of purpose or direction. Only when we know what we want to accomplish and what our desired destination is can we determine the best way to get there. Treatment is likely to be most successful if clinicians have a sense of purpose at each level of treatment: the overall therapeutic process, the individual session, and the specific intervention. If asked, skilled clinicians should be able to

- Explain what they hoped to accomplish with each intervention and each session.
- Assess whether and how their goals have been met.
- Modify the treatment process as needed to achieve their desired outcomes.

The BETA Format

This book and the following table of examples of treatment goals have been organized according to the BETA framework. BETA is an acronym that reflects the four primary emphases of treatment approaches:

B: Background
E: Emotions
T: Thoughts
A: Actions

Although treatment approaches have many common ingredients and considerable overlap, each treatment approach typically emphasizes one of the four elements in the BETA framework more than it does the other three. You will learn more about the BETA framework as you continue reading this book.

Desired outcomes that frequently arise during treatment can be categorized according to the BETA format and according to whether the desired outcome is a large-scale goal to be accomplished in one or more sessions or a small-scale goal to be accomplished in one or more interventions. Table 1-1 presents typical treatment goals.

Additional information will be presented later in this text on goal setting and determining interventions that target particular goals.

TABLE 1-1   Typical Treatment Goals Organized According to the BETA Framework

	Background	Emotions	Thoughts	Actions
Small-scale goals	Obtain information.	Reflect feelings.	Orient to treatment.	Identify target behaviors.
	Make an interpretation.	Promote awareness of emotions.	Promote awareness of meaning.	Establish a contract.
		Promote expression of emotions.	Elicit thoughts.	Set limits.
		Increase motivation.	Dispute dysfunctional cognitions.	Give homework and directives.
		Provide support and encouragement.	Obtain clarification.	Change the focus of the session.
		Enhance the therapeutic alliance.	Provide information, advice.	Reinforce gains.
Large-scale goals	Promote insight.	Improve ability to manage emotions.	Modify thinking patterns.	Change dysfunctional behaviors.
	Take a history.	Improve ability to identify and express emotions.	Promote sense of responsibility and ownership.	Prevent relapse.
	Conduct an assessment.			Empower.
	Make the unconscious conscious.	Reduce painful emotions.		Develop skills.
	Facilitate working through past issues.	Increase positive emotions.		Promote self-control.

UNDERSTANDING THE HELPING PROFESSIONS

Readers of this book are most likely to be students in counseling, psychology, or social work. You might also be engaged in training for psychiatric nursing or psychiatry but, because those professions rely strongly on medical intervention, they will not be a prominent focus of this book.

Students and prospective students in the programs in which I teach often ask me about the differences among counseling, psychology, and social work. Their question is a good one, because teasing out their differences can be a challenge. I believe that these three mental health professions have more similarities than differences and, over time, have become increasingly alike with differences being attributed more to a specific graduate training program, a school or agency's use of their employees, or the way a specific person has designed his or her training and subsequent work activities rather than to basic differences among the three professions.

All three professions require graduate training, typically the equivalent of 2 years for training at the master's degree level and 5 or more years for the doctorate in any of these fields. Social workers and counselors can be licensed in the states in which they practice if they have a master's degree in their field, appropriate course work, sufficient credits (usually 60 semester hours) and the requisite postgraduate supervised experience (usually the equivalent of 2 years). Psychologists, however, generally cannot receive state licensure without a doctorate as well as the required postgraduate supervised experience. (Some states do license school psychologists for independent practice at the master's degree level.)

People in all three professions study and use in their work information on human development, abnormal psychology and the diagnosis of mental disorders, the sound therapeutic alliance, theories and strategies of intervention, and group and family dynamics. Professionals in all three usually are trained to provide individual and group counseling and usually learn strategies for helping couples and families make positive changes. In addition, all three professions emphasize multicultural competence and have similar ethical standards that are integral to the effective practice of the profession.

Although social work has always paid considerable attention to social justice, counseling and psychology have paid increasing attention to effecting change at community and societal levels. All three professions value empirical research and publish journals to disseminate research and advance the profession. All three have professional membership associations that are designed to promote the profession, help clinicians develop their skills and knowledge, and offer a source of professional identity. For counselors, this organization is the American Counseling Association; for psychologists, the American Psychological Association; and for social workers, the National Association of Social Workers.

Professional Roles

Although private practice is a popular career option for people in all three professions, each profession has its own distinctive areas of specialization. Social workers, for example, often work in hospitals and other medical settings, have an important role in many school systems, and seem more likely than counselors or psychologists to work at the program level, dealing with nonprofit and governmental programs to help people who are facing poverty, abuse, disability, and other challenges. Social workers typically make less use of assessment tools than do counselors and psychologists and typically have little or no specific training in career development.

Counselors, historically emphasizing school counseling, rehabilitation, and career counseling, continue to be the helping professionals most likely to be employed in those settings. However, mental health counseling and family counseling have become increasingly popular options for counselors. Counseling in college and university settings is another well-established specialization for counselors. The roots of counseling emphasize prevention and encouragement of healthy development and those continue to be important areas of focus for counselors. However, counselors are now well established in private practice, community mental health centers, and other settings that emphasize treatment of emotional disorders and symptoms.

Because the field of psychology views the doctoral degree as the standard for practice and usually requires a dissertation as part of that degree, the training of psychologists usually emphasizes research as well as development of clinical skills.

Emphasis on empirically supported treatments has become central to the practice of psychology. Unlike counseling, psychology has its roots in the diagnosis and treatment of mental disorders, and psychologists have typically been well-accepted treatment providers in both inpatient and outpatient settings. However, like counseling, the role of the psychologist has broadened over the years. Many psychologists are now working collaboratively with school counselors and physicians, becoming involved in organizational change and consulting, expanding their reach and impact via community psychology, and becoming more involved in positive psychology, prevention programs, and social change efforts. Psychologists have historically made considerable use of assessment tools, especially projective tests. Although testing is no longer a prominent part of the role of most psychologists, they can be distinguished from the majority of counselors and social workers by their training in projective tests. Social workers and counselors often refer clients to psychologists for assessment of learning skills, intelligence, and personality and that consulting role is an important one for many psychologists.

Other Helping Professionals

In addition to psychologists, social workers, and counselors, other helping professionals include psychiatrists and psychiatric nurses. Both usually have a strong background in understanding physiology, physical illnesses, and the role of medication in treating mental disorders. In addition, they also are educated in theories of psychotherapy and the interventions skills of psychologists, social workers, and counselors. As a practicing clinician, you may often collaborate with these professionals.

Your Perceptions of the Mental Health Professions

Now that you have read a brief description of the similarities and differences among social workers, counselors, and psychologists, you can take a closer look at your own knowledge and impressions of these professions. Just as people have a variety of motives behind their interest in entering the fields of counseling, social work, or psychology, so do they have a broad range of ideas about the nature of these fields. Some people have the misconception that counseling involves telling people what choices or actions would be best for them. Many enter training for a mental health profession with little awareness of the differences between helping a troubled friend and helping a troubled client. Some expect high salaries and flexible hours, not recognizing the limited budgets of most educational and social service agencies and forgetting that people often need evening, weekend, or emergency appointments. Fortunately, many people do have an accurate understanding of the counseling process, gained through reading, through conversations with clinicians or people who have received mental health treatment, or through their own experiences.

Having learned about the characteristics of effective clinicians, your personal strengths and motivations, and the professional of psychology, counseling, and social work, respond to the following questions, either for yourself or for class discussion:

- Think back to your earliest images of the mental health professions. List one or two misconceptions you had about those professions:
    1. _____
    2. _____

- List three statements you believe to be accurate about the mental health professions that reflect the appeal these professions hold for you:
    1. _____
    2. _____
    3. _____

Information on the mental health professions, the roles of client and clinician, and the treatment process will be presented throughout the rest of this book. That information will help ensure that you have a realistic understanding of these professions and your interest in them. In addition, questions and checklists will help you relate that information to yourself and facilitate your own development as a helping professional.

HISTORICAL OVERVIEW

Understanding the historical development of the mental health professions can enhance and deepen your knowledge of those professions. The three professions of social work, psychology, and counseling have different origins but seem to converge on a common ground.

Social Work

Social work as a profession began in the early 19th century, primarily in England and the United States. Acting in a missionary-like role, the early social workers used prayer, along with provision of food and shelter, to help the poor. Social justice has always been an integral part of social work, and history suggests that social workers played a helping role in nearly every significant problem in U.S. history. They worked with emancipated slaves following the Civil War, assisted immigrants of all nationalities to establish themselves in the United States, helped people impoverished by the economic depression of the 1930s and by worker strikes, and played an important part in early efforts to help people in what were then called mental asylums.

The settlement movement of the late 19th and early 20th centuries increased awareness of the important role of social workers, and the work of Jane Addams at Hull House established the reputation of the profession. Focusing on social causes, social workers of the first half of the 20th century paid particular attention to children and families. They often collaborated with psychiatrists who provided medication and psychotherapy, while the social workers addressed family concerns through therapy and other interventions.

By the 1960s, social work was well established as a profession, generally requiring graduate training. It had made a place for itself in many settings including hospitals and social welfare agencies. During the last quarter of the 20th century and the early years of this century, social workers further expanded their areas of specialization. Although they continued their emphasis on social justice as well as their role in medical and social service settings, social workers were increasingly employed in schools, community mental health centers, private practice, and other venues. Although therapy provided during the early years of the social work profession generally followed the guidelines of Freudian thinking, today's social workers have diversified and broadened their theoretical orientation and skills. Some have continued the profession's tradition of providing direct service, whereas others have joined psychologists and mental health counselors in a broad range of clinical settings.

Psychology

Although the emergence of psychology as a profession gradually occurred throughout the 19th century, the work of Freud and his associates led to subsequent rapid growth of the field. Freud laid the groundwork for psychologists to move into private practice settings, but early psychologists were often employed by child guidance centers, psychiatric hospitals, the military, and even business and industry. Their roles included not only treatment of symptoms and mental disorders, but also screening, assessment, and placement.

The theoretical perspectives and interventions used by psychologists were greatly influenced by the ideas of a series of prominent researchers, theoreticians, and practitioners. Freud probably had the greatest initial impact. However, from the 1920s through the 1960s, psychologists discovered behavior therapy through the work of such innovative thinkers as Ivan Pavlov, B. F. Skinner, Joseph Wolpe, Albert Bandura, John Dollard, Neal Miller, and others. This offered psychologists a radical alternative to the unstructured work of psychoanalysis.

The 1960s and 1970s witnessed the emergence of two more compelling treatment approaches: person-centered therapy, developed by Carl Rogers, and Gestalt therapy, developed by Fritz and Laura Perls. These treatment approaches added an emphasis on emotions to the focus on background promoted by the psychodynamic theorists and the importance of behavior, encouraged by the behaviorists. Now psychologists recognized the importance of feelings as well as background and behavior, and skills such as empathy and reflection of feeling and meaning became essential tools of the clinician.

Cognitive therapy emerged as a powerful force in the 1970s, 1980s, and 1990s, influenced primarily by the work of Albert Ellis and Aaron Beck. Now attention to thoughts, and the many interventions emerging from the work of the cognitive therapists, enhanced psychologists' work.

The 21st century, sometimes referred to as the postmodern era in psychology, is characterized by major shifts in the profession. Multiculturalism and social justice, discussed in the next chapter, are essential elements of the psychologist's role, and new treatment approaches integrate multiple theoretical approaches. Narrative therapy, feminist therapy, and constructivist therapy take a phenomenological stance, underscoring the importance of eliciting people's perceptions, stories, and contexts. Interventions such as eye movement desensitization and reprocessing, as well as the energy therapies, remind us of the powerful influence of biology on the mind. Preventive work, psychological education, positive psychology, and social change now are part of the work of many psychologists.

Counseling

When the field of counseling began in the early 1900s, the role of the counselor was a circumscribed one that focused primarily on helping people make occupational choices by matching person to job. Although many counselors do embrace the ideas of Freud and his associates, the early counselors were not much influenced by psychoanalysis. In this they differed from the social workers and psychologists. Both the behaviorists and Carl Rogers's person-centered therapy, however, had a profound impact on counselors. These approaches were particularly useful to counselors, as they moved beyond career counseling and into rehabilitation counseling and school counseling during the 1940s and 1950s. Gestalt therapy, as well as existential treatment approaches, also influenced the counselors' work.

With the passage of the Community Mental Health Centers Act in 1963, doors opened for counselors to move into clinical work. The American Mental Health Counselors Association, founded in 1976, facilitated counselors' efforts to find employment in mental health centers, while the concurrent initiation of licensure for counselors enabled them to join the social workers and psychologists in independent practice. Although counselors have preserved their emphasis on prevention, holistic understanding of their clients, and attention to diversity and have expanded their areas of specialization, they have also developed more commonalities with social workers and psychologists during the past 50 years.

Evolution of the Mental Health Professions

During the past 50 years, the fields of social work, counseling, and psychology have evolved and deepened. Before the middle of the 20th century, treatment of emotional difficulties focused primarily on disorders involving a loss of contact with reality (psychotic disorders) and disorders characterized by disabling depression or anxiety (then called neurotic disorders). Psychiatry and psychoanalysis dominated the mental health field, and treatment usually entailed medication and lengthy, intensive psychodynamic treatment. Clinicians paid relatively little attention to problems of adjustment and life circumstance, to relationship difficulties, and even to the treatment of people with drug and alcohol problems. Understanding of problems and disorders such as physical and sexual abuse, attention-deficit/hyperactivity disorder, and borderline personality disorder was almost nonexistent.

Counselors and social workers played a limited role in mental health treatment up to the middle of the last century. Counseling was just beginning to develop as a

profession. Counselors, at that time, focused primarily on school and vocational counseling. Social workers, too, had a limited role, focusing their efforts on helping the poor
and people with disabilities and working with the families of people treated by psychiatrists. Psychologists had a relatively broader role but they, like the psychiatrists, largely
practiced psychodynamic therapy and treated a limited range of emotional difficulties.

Prior to the 1950s, much of the mental health literature was in the theoretical
realm, making the transition to practice and application a difficult one. The writings of Freud, Jung, Adler, and their followers dominated the field. Case studies and
their own therapy, as well as supervised practice, gave clinicians some understanding of the dynamics of mental disorders and the theoretical underpinnings of their
treatment. However, little attention was paid to helping clinicians make sense of a
particular client (conceptual skills) and to helping them determine the interventions that were most likely to help (fundamental skills).

Carl Rogers's writings (1951, 1967) in the 1950s and 1960s were among the
first to call attention to the specific words and interventions (fundamental skills)
clinicians used and the great impact those strategies could have on the treatment
process. Allen Ivey's (1971) development of microcounseling skills, described by
Ivey in the 1970s, enhanced clinicians' awareness of the importance of choosing
their interventions carefully and deliberately. The rapid development of cognitive
and behavioral approaches to treatment during the 1980s and 1990s (Beck, 1995)
accelerated the movement toward clinical competence.

Training in Fundamental and Conceptual Skills

Courses and programs to develop clinicians' skills have become an essential part of
nearly every graduate and undergraduate program for mental health professionals.
Many studies supported the importance and value of such training. For example,
Little, Packman, Smaby, and Maddux (2005) concluded, "Recent studies have indicated that systematic skills-based counselor training has resulted in trainees' improved learning of group and individual counseling skills when compared with
trainees who have not received skills-based training" (p. 189). The recognition of
the importance of skills-based training for mental health professionals was followed
by an awareness that, to develop fully functioning mental health professionals, their
training must encompass not only the teaching of intervention strategies and skills
but also the conceptual and cognitive skills required for effective practice. Fong,
Borders, Ethington, and Pitts (1997), for example, concluded, "Results suggest a
need to emphasize student cognitive development as strongly as skills development
in graduate programs" (p. 100). Fong et al. also identified three levels of thinking
that needed attention and development as part of clinical training:

1. *Cognitive events or discrete thoughts.* These include clinicians' decisions on use
   of skills and interventions (for example, how to reinforce a client's gains,
   when to communicate empathy, and whether to confront a discrepancy between the client's values and actions).
2. *Cognitive processes.* These involve more complex conceptual thinking skills
   such as those involved in clinicians' efforts to help clients solve problems or

make decisions. For example, a clinician may plan a series of interventions to help a woman overcome her fear of snakes or to help an adolescent improve his social skills.

3. *Cognitive structures or schemas.* These encompass broad systems of organizing perceptions and are the skills that enable clinicians to understand the dynamics of a client's difficulties, formulate a diagnosis, and develop a treatment plan that is likely to be effective. For example, a clinician may recognize and address the impact of a woman's birth order and upbringing on the current problems in her career and her marriage. Perhaps the woman is still trying to win the love of her parents by making choices that meet with their approval but is not recognizing that those choices do not mesh well with her own abilities and interests. Having this in-depth understanding of a person enables clinicians to promote clients' own self-awareness and develop a treatment plan that will enhance their strengths and ameliorate their difficulties.

Whiston and Coker's (2000) findings support the conclusions of Fong et al. (1997). Whiston and Coker determined that "research findings suggest a significant link between counselor skillfulness and counseling outcomes" (p. 233). As a result, Whiston and Coker stated, "We also advocate that the reconstruction of clinical training focus more on increasing students' levels of cognitive complexity" (p. 233).

Fong et al. (1997), Whiston and Coker (2000), and many other educators, clinicians, and researchers agree that mental health training programs must teach skills, strategies, and interventions, and must also help students develop conceptual skills. The treatment process should be solidly grounded in theory and in a clear conceptual model for understanding and helping a person with emotional difficulties.

PURPOSE OF THIS BOOK

The purpose of this book, *Fundamental Skills for Mental Health Professionals,* is to help clinicians improve and refine the skills and interventions they need to be effective in their work. Not only does this book pay attention to promoting clinicians' skillful and purposeful use of specific techniques and interventions, but it also provides research, information, examples, and exercises to promote and reinforce learning. The skills are linked to theoretical models, as well as to the treatment process, which will help readers choose interventions based on thought and purpose.

This book focuses primarily on the first two stages of Fong et al.'s (1997) model, cognitive events and cognitive processes. This book can be used alone in beginning or intermediate courses in development of clinical skills or it can be used before or along with its companion volume, *Conceptual Skills for Mental Health Professionals* (Seligman, 2008). That book builds on knowledge of fundamental skills and interventions and integrates that knowledge with development of cognitive structures or schemas—Fong et al.'s third stage. These encompass broad systems of organizing perceptions. I encourage advanced clinicians and those seeking to develop their conceptual skills to consult that text for additional information.

This book focuses on fundamental skills and interventions. Whiston and Coker (2000) defined these skills as ". . . those basic interviewing or counselor interpersonal skills that facilitate the general purposes of counseling" (p. 234). These are the building blocks of the treatment process, the tools that clinicians use to accomplish their goals. Knowledge of fundamental skills, as presented in this book, provides clinicians with a repertoire of interventions they can use to join with and help their clients. It enables clinicians to make statements and use language that demonstrate sound listening; that help clients become more aware of their emotions, thoughts, and actions; and that help them to acquire the knowledge and skills they need to resolve their issues. Two organizing frameworks provide the structure for this book. The *first organizing framework* for this book, mentioned earlier in this chapter, entails the grouping of clinical skills into **four broad categories,** represented by the acronym BETA, described in detail in my book *Theories of Counseling and Psychotherapy: Systems, Strategies, and Skills* (Seligman, 2006):

B: Background

E: Emotions

T: Thoughts

A: Actions

This grouping is based on five premises:

Premise 1:
Treatment approaches are more alike than they are different. All approaches to counseling and psychotherapy pay some attention to all four elements in the BETA model: background, emotions, thoughts, and actions. These are universal ingredients in all treatment processes.

Increasing evidence is accumulating in the literature to demonstrate that all approaches to counseling and psychotherapy have underlying commonalities and that many of these shared ingredients in treatment are associated with positive outcomes (Lambert & Bergin, 1994). Individual clinicians and treatment approaches differ in terms of how they conceptualize cases, the proportion of time they devote to each of the four elements in the BETA framework, and the way they elaborate on each of these elements during the treatment process. However, whether clinicians adhere strictly to one theoretical approach or use an integrative approach to treatment; whether they work with children or adults; whether they work in schools or mental health agencies; whether they are counselors, psychologists, social workers, or psychiatric nurses—all mental health treatment providers use the basic ingredients or general skills that are presented in this book.

In addition, as integrative and eclectic approaches to treatment increasingly become the norm, clinicians find they can combine strategies from apparently incompatible treatment theories. For example, the clinician who describes her theoretical orientation as primarily a person-centered one may pay attention to background factors when working with a young woman who was sexually abused in childhood. Similarly, the clinician who emphasizes humanistic strategies in his work may rely on reflections of feeling, paraphrases, and encouragement when working with an angry and skeptical client.

In light of the flexible boundaries between treatment approaches and the underlying commonalities among clinicians, this book uses a variety of terms interchangeably, including *clinician* and *counselor,* and *psychotherapy* and *counseling*. Today's clinicians, whether they are counselors, social workers, or psychologists, are more alike than they are different, sharing diagnostic systems, conceptions of mental health, treatment theories, strategies of intervention, and belief in the importance of ethical, culturally sensitive, and socially conscious treatment.

Premise 2:

Treatment theories, strategies, and skills can be categorized and distinguished according to whether their primary emphasis is on understanding and changing the impact of past experiences (background), current feelings and sensations (emotions), thoughts and cognitions, or actions and behaviors.

Although this book is not designed to educate readers about theories of counseling and psychotherapy, the skills presented in this book are drawn from and organized according to the treatment approaches represented by the BETA model. Therefore, readers should familiarize themselves with the following list, which reflects the way treatment systems are grouped in this model, to better understand the corresponding grouping of skills.

Treatment Systems Emphasizing Background

- Sigmund Freud and psychoanalysis
- Alfred Adler and individual psychology
- Carl Jung and Jungian analytical psychology
- Freudian revisionists (ego psychologists, object relations theorists, self psychologists, and others including Helene Deutsch, Karen Horney, Harry Stack Sullivan, Anna Freud, and Heinz Kohut)
- Brief psychodynamic therapy

Treatment Systems Emphasizing Emotions

- Carl Rogers and person-centered counseling
- Existential therapy
- Gestalt therapy
- Emerging/postmodern approaches emphasizing emotions (narrative therapy, constructivist therapy, feminist therapy, transpersonal therapy)

Treatment Systems Emphasizing Thoughts

- Aaron Beck and cognitive therapy
- Albert Ellis and rational emotive behavior therapy
- Emerging approaches emphasizing thoughts (eye movement desensitization and reprocessing, neuro-linguistic programming, thought field therapy, emotional freedom techniques, and others)

Treatment Systems Emphasizing Actions

- Behavior therapy
- Cognitive-behavioral therapy
- Reality therapy
- Solution-focused brief therapies

Premise 3:

Each of the broad categories of treatment approaches (those focusing on background, emotions, thoughts, and actions) encompasses both basic or general skills and specific skills.

The basic skills are integral to the particular group of treatment approaches and are widely used, not only by those practicing the treatment approaches with which they are most strongly associated, but also by nearly all clinicians. An example of this is open questions, discussed in detail in Chapter 3. These are essential in obtaining background information, but I cannot imagine a clinician who does not make some use of questions in order to better understand many aspects of his or her clients.

Specific skills used to elicit background information include such interventions as development of a lifeline and construction of a genogram. These specific skills and others are discussed in Chapter 4. Specific skills are used much more selectively than the basic or general skills. They would only be used when they seem appropriate for a specific client or problem.

Description of Table 1-2

Table 1-2 presents a list of some of the most important clinical skills, both fundamental and conceptual and general and specific, organized according to the BETA format. Of course, the organization is not as definitive as Table 1-2 may imply. Each skill is most strongly associated with the element in the BETA format under which it is listed, but also is used by a wide range of clinicians to treat a variety of clients and concerns.

The fundamental skills listed in Table 1-2 are presented in this book. The list of conceptual skills completes the picture and encompasses those skills included in the companion volume *Conceptual Skills for Mental Health Professionals* (Seligman, 2008).

TABLE 1-2 Fundamental and Conceptual Skills Organized According to the BETA Framework

Fundamental Skills General Skills	Background General Skills	Emotions General Skills	Thoughts General Skills	Actions General Skills
	• Open questions	• Attending	• Reflection of meaning	• Contracting
	• Closed questions	• Encouragers	• Modifying cognitions	• Goal setting
	• Intake interviews	• Reflections of feeling/empathy	• Problem solving	• Advice giving
		• Identifying and managing emotions	• Decision making	• Challenging/ confronting
		• Nonverbal communication	• Information giving	
	Specific Skills	**Specific Skills**	**Specific Skills**	**Specific Skills**
	• Earliest recollection	• Imagery	• Affirmations	• Empowerment
	• Lifeline	• Focusing	• Anchoring	• Systematic desensitization
	• Genogram	• New perspectives	• Reframing	• Relaxation
		• Reassurance/ support	• Thought stopping	• Modeling/ role-playing
		• Distraction	• Journaling	
		• Body language	• Mind mapping	
Conceptual Skills	• Understanding context	• Establishing a therapeutic alliance	• Assessment	• Referral
	• Initiating treatment	• Role induction	• Testing	• Collaboration
	• Organizing background information	• Core conditions	• Mental status exam	• Structuring sessions
		• Providing support	• Defining the problem	• Critical incidents
	• Addressing transference and countertransference	• Values and judgments	• Case conceptualization	• Assessment of progress
		• Crisis intervention	• Diagnosis	• Session notes
	• Multicultural counseling competencies	• Handling strong emotions	• Treatment planning	• Generating solutions
		• Addressing reluctance		• Termination
	• Interpretation	• Clinician self-disclosure		

> **Premise 4:**
>
> Counseling and therapy progress according to predictable stages, although shifting back and forth between stages is common as some issues are resolved and new issues surface and as people strive to deal with new and challenging information, skills, and changes.

STAGES OF THE TREATMENT PROCESS

The treatment process typically consists of four broad stages:

1. *Establishing the foundation for effective treatment.* People are oriented to the treatment process and given information on ethical standards, the role of the client, the role of the clinician, and other relevant policies and guidelines.

2a. *Information gathering.* The clinician elicits information from the client on presenting concerns, relevant history, coping skills, strengths and challenges, and more. This enables the clinician to formulate a preliminary understanding of the client's difficulties and what resources and interventions can help to ameliorate those difficulties and promote personal growth. Questions are the primary intervention used to gather information, although effective clinicians integrate questions with reflections, encouragers, and other types of interventions to smooth the dialogue, demonstrate accurate listening, and increase comfort and rapport.

2b. *Developing the therapeutic alliance.* The relationship of the clinician and the client probably is the most important determinant of treatment outcome. Although that alliance evolves throughout the treatment process, the first few sessions are particularly important in launching treatment in a positive direction and promoting a collaborative working relationship between client and clinician. Attending skills, including tracking, verbal encouragers, accents and restatements, paraphrases, reflections of feeling, and summarization, are the skills that seem to contribute most to the development of the therapeutic alliance. They enable the clinician to partner with the client in the healing process and communicate caring, involvement, and acceptance to the client. Nonverbal messages further contribute to the nature of the therapeutic alliance.

3. *Effecting change and enhancing strengths.* This is the heart of the treatment process. By this point in the treatment, clinicians should have gathered enough information on people's difficulties and strengths, their contexts, and their backgrounds so that the clinicians can determine a treatment plan and collaborate with their clients to help them make positive changes. Clearly stated goals, developed and agreed to by both client and clinician, can facilitate the process. Essential to the success of the change process is a positive therapeutic alliance in which the clinician has joined or partnered with the client and the two become a team, working to help the client achieve better emotional health and a more rewarding life.

4. *Consolidation and termination.* Although premature termination does sometimes occur, ideally termination occurs when clients have achieved their goals to

their satisfaction and feel ready to implement what they have learned through their treatment. Termination is a planned stage in the treatment process. Client and clinician review progress, reinforce and consolidate gains, and complete treatment for the foreseeable future. Relapse prevention often will be a part of this process, helping people become aware of warning signs of difficulties and identify ways they can maintain the gains they have achieved.

Understanding and being able to recognize these predictable stages, as well as their variations, is an important clinical skill. It helps clinicians to plan the treatment process and to recognize when it is proceeding smoothly and when the process may be getting derailed.

IDENTIFYING PEOPLE'S AREAS OF DIFFICULTY

People who seek counseling or therapy generally have difficulties in four areas:

- *Emotions*. They may experience little joy in their lives and a great deal of depression, anxiety, loneliness, anger, and other negative emotions that are painful and interfere with their relationships and functioning. People with emotional difficulties also often report having difficulty managing their emotions; they may lose control and rage at others or avoid potentially pleasant activities and interactions out of fear of failure or rejection.
- *Thoughts*. Many clinicians believe that it is our thoughts that determine our emotions and actions. People who think of themselves as failures and believe that they do not have the ability to help themselves are likely to feel discouraged and hopeless, avoiding constructive actions that might enhance their lives. Distorted and unhelpful thoughts tend to further entrench themselves as people allow their negative perceptions to become their reality.
- *Actions*. People who seek counseling often have difficulty identifying steps they can take to help themselves. Instead, they persist in self-destructive and ineffectual actions that contribute to their negative emotions and distorted thoughts. They may repeat unsuccessful efforts to change or may engage in self-destructive behaviors such as harmful use of drugs and alcohol, dysfunctional eating, and acting in aggressive and disruptive ways.
- *Background*. Typically plays an important part in all three areas of difficulty. Problems typically have their origins in early messages and experiences, although the present may have an even more important role in perpetuating and exacerbating early difficulties.

Example

Let's look at Jeff, who has long-standing intertwined difficulties in emotions, thoughts, and behaviors. Jeff's parents were unhappy together and worked in unrewarding jobs that barely enabled them to support their family. They gave their children the message that life is difficult and painful, that happiness is unattainable, and that the best you can hope for is to earn an adequate living. Although Jeff found a job he enjoyed after completing high school, his parents convinced him that, for economic reasons, he must go to college. Jeff studied accounting in college because he believed it was a well-paying field, but his distaste for his studies led him to have an un-rewarding experience in college; he cut classes frequently, did as little work as possible while still passing his courses, avoided involvement in extracurricular activities, and longed for the job he had enjoyed. After graduating from college with a low C average, Jeff obtained a job as an accountant and stayed with that job for many years, although he was bored and disinterested in his work and, as in college, did as little as he could on the job. Jeff sought treatment after he was fired from his job, presenting concerns in all four areas:

- *Emotions.* He was depressed and discouraged, anxious about his ability to support himself, angry at the advice his parents had given him, and full of self-hatred.
- *Thoughts.* Jeff believed it was impossible for him to find a rewarding job or rewarding relationships. He thought of himself as an incompetent failure who had no good options.
- *Actions.* Jeff became withdrawn and isolated. He made no constructive efforts to seek employment, rarely left his apartment, and ate poorly. His primary activity was watching television.
- *Background.* Jeff was driven by the discouraging messages he had heard throughout his youth and that sapped him of motivation to seek a more rewarding life. The clinician working with Jeff first sought to build a therapeutic alliance with him, which was a challenge because of his hopelessness, his mistrust of others, and his lack of experience with rewarding relationships. At the same time, the clinician gathered information on the context and background of Jeff's difficulties, seeking not to undo the past but to use information from the past, as well as Jeff's strengths, such as his intelligence and his persistence, to inform treatment focused on Jeff's current concerns. Efforts to help Jeff began immediately, but a few sessions were needed before the clinician thought she had enough information to develop a treatment plan that was likely to be effective.

PLANNING THE TREATMENT

Like most clients, Jeff's concerns showed up in his emotions, his thoughts, and his actions, and clearly stemmed from his family background and early messages. Where to focus the treatment and what approaches to use are important decisions. Answers to those questions are determined by many factors including these:

- Which of the three areas reflects the most prominent or troubling symptoms
- Which of the three areas reflects the symptoms that are most amenable to change
- The client's preferred mode of relating to the world
- The clinician's theoretical orientation

Parts 2, 3, 4, and 5 of this book will help you determine whether a person's treatment should focus primarily on background, emotions, thoughts, or actions. Those parts will help you determine which of the broad approaches to treatment is most compatible with who you are, both personally and professionally, and will help you choose your preferred treatment approach. In addition, as indicated in Table 1-2, presented earlier in this chapter, you will learn skills associated with each area of focus (background, emotions, thoughts, and actions) and will have the opportunity to hone your skills through role-plays, written exercises, and other learning experiences.

Many clinicians today prefer a treatment approach that is integrative, rather than reflective of only one treatment model. Integrative treatment approaches are not just a haphazard array of therapeutic techniques; rather, they are carefully chosen based on the clinician's vision of pathology, emotional health, and ways to promote positive change.

In working with Jeff, the clinician decided to pay some attention to background but to use a primarily cognitive approach to help Jeff modify his self-destructive thinking. A lifeline, discussed later in this book, also helped Jeff recognize his long-standing pattern of self-destructive choices and helped him find new and more rewarding ways to make decisions. Although understanding Jeff's family background shed light on ways to help Jeff, his clinician did not want to overemphasize background lest that further entrench Jeff's tendency to blame his parents for all his difficulties.

STRUCTURE OF THIS BOOK

This book presents both general skills and some specific skills for each of the four areas in the BETA model (background, emotions, thoughts, actions). Two chapters are devoted to each of the four areas in this model. The first of each pair of chapters focuses on the basic skills essential to all clinicians, and most strongly associated with one of the four areas. The second of each pair of chapters presents some specific skills that clinicians can use to enrich and empower their work.

Premise 5:

Clinicians who know themselves well, have positive and realistic self-esteem, have a sound understanding of the helping professions and their own professional goals, and are motivated to improve their clinical skills are more likely to achieve professional success than those who lack these attributes.

Learning the skills of counseling and psychotherapy is essential to the development of all mental health professionals. However, also important is clinicians' personal growth. This book is designed to facilitate the personal and professional development of clinicians. Discussion questions, role-play exercises, and personal journal questions at the end of each chapter have been crafted to promote that development. This process will be facilitated if you take a truthful look at yourself as you move through this book. Particularly important is awareness of your motives for entering a helping profession, the relationship between your own personal characteristics and those of the effective clinician, and an understanding of the transitions you are likely to encounter as you progress in your field.

By now, you have probably realized that becoming an effective clinician is a process that involves hard work, considerable thought, learning, and change. It can be a rewarding process or it can be fraught with obstacles and disappointments.

How This Book Will Contribute to Your Skill Development

Effective clinicians not only have many personal strengths, but they also have developed a broad array of fundamental and conceptual skills that enable them to help their clients meet their goals. As a result of this book, you should be able to acquire the following skills:

- Launching the treatment process.
- Gathering important information about your clients' life experiences, resources, strengths, and difficulties (Chapters 3 and 4—eliciting background and other client information).
- Identifying and respond in helpful ways to clients' strong feelings (Chapters 5 and 6—fundamental skills focused on emotions).
- Promoting client learning and change in dysfunctional cognitions (Chapters 7 and 8—fundamental skills focused on thoughts).
- Using contracts, suggestions, and challenge to promote positive change (Chapters 9 and 10—fundamental skills focused on actions).

Learning these skills should enhance your efforts to become an effective clinician. In addition, exercises throughout this book will continue to enhance and strengthen your self-awareness and other personal characteristics that can contribute to your professional success.

Using This Book Effectively

This chapter and Chapter 2 give you the foundation you need for making sound use of this book and developing your fundamental skills. They are also designed to increase your understanding of the mental health professions.

Chapter 1

As you have read Chapter 1 includes information on

- The mental health professions, especially psychology, counseling, and social work;
- The importance of both fundamental and conceptual skills;
- The BETA (background, emotions, thoughts, actions) framework for organizing treatment approaches and interventions as well as the skills presented in this book;
- Characteristics of effective clinicians;
- The essential ingredients of the treatment process, including the context, the client, the clinician, and the therapeutic relationship;
- The importance of having a solid grounding in treatment approaches; and
- The four stages in the treatment process.

The rest of this chapter orients you to the ways in which this book will promote the development of your fundamental and conceptual skills. Information on understanding how to participate fully and constructively in the practice exercises presented throughout this book is especially important. Whether you are in the role of client, clinician, or observer and whether you are giving or receiving feedback, your listening and communication skills and your involvement in the exercises determine how much you and the other members of your group will learn from the exercises.

Chapter 2

Chapter 2 provides information that forms the backdrop for effective treatment. This includes information on

- Ethical guidelines for the mental health professions;
- Human development;
- Theories and strategies of counseling and psychotherapy;
- Multicultural competence, and the criteria for becoming a clinician who has multicultural sensitivity and awareness and manifests that knowledge through clinical work;
- Social justice and its importance to clinicians;
- The mind–body–spirit connection; and
- Additional areas of importance and specialization.

PROMOTING SKILL DEVELOPMENT

This book is designed to promote your learning in a variety of ways. Each of Chapters 3 through 10 introduces a group of skills that have common threads:

- All are fundamental skills.
- All are linked to the same element in the BETA framework (background, emotions, thoughts, or actions).
- All are either general skills that will be used by nearly all clinicians with all clients or they are more specific skills, used to accomplish particular goals with certain clients.

When a skill is initially presented, I generally provide you with a description of that skill, along with information on what research, case studies, and experience have taught us about the appropriate use of that skill. Illustrations of the appropriate use of the skill enhance your understanding of the skill. Exercises are presented to enable you to try out and practice the skill. Feedback on the exercises should help you develop facility with the skill and learn ways to use it constructively during treatment. For example, questioning, presented in Chapter 3, is one of the most important skills for clinicians. The section of Chapter 3 on effective use of questions will provide background information on types of questions, their appropriate and inappropriate use, and when they are likely to be most helpful. Examples will help to make this information meaningful to you. A series of exercises, gradually building your questioning skills, will help you learn the skill so that you can both describe and demonstrate effective use of questions.

The Learning Opportunities section at the end of each chapter affords you many additional opportunities to review and practice the skills presented in that chapter. Discussion questions will help you talk about the skills with your classmates or colleagues. Written exercises give you practice in using and integrating that chapter's skills. In addition, a group activity will help you apply the skills via role-plays and obtain useful feedback from others. Forms and checklists provided in each chapter help you track your learning, assess your progress, and refine your goals so that you continue to improve your skills. Finally, topics are provided for you to write about in a personal journal. This affords you one more opportunity to deepen and consolidate the learning you gained from the chapter.

PRACTICE GROUP EXERCISES

You will probably find that, as a developing clinician, your most valuable learning experiences will come from the practice group exercises suggested throughout this book. These experiences provide you the opportunity to try out new skills, build on skills already learned, give and receive feedback, and demonstrate improvement.

Receiving and providing supervision, as well as engaging in demonstrations and observing role-plays, have been important in my own professional development. Those experiences have enhanced my work as a counselor and psychologist, as well as my teaching. I anticipate that you, too, will enhance your clinical skills by

Group exercises provide students with the opportunity for valuable learning experiences

participating in role-plays, observing the work of your colleagues, and finding ways to give them both reinforcement and helpful suggestions.

The practice group sessions can be rewarding experiences, involving shared learning and professional growth, facilitated by useful and meaningful feedback. Group members frequently develop strong and supportive relationships and benefit both personally and professionally from the practice group sessions.

On the other hand, the practice sessions can be anxiety-provoking experiences in which people feel attacked and belittled. Our apprehensions and self-doubts may get in the way of our listening carefully to feedback and understanding it fully. We might interrupt to defend or explain ourselves and may become more concerned with being right than with learning from the feedback.

Maximizing Learning from the Practice Groups

To maximize the benefit you obtain from the practice group exercises, I suggest the following strategies:

- Participate fully in the group exercises.
- Tape record an entire practice group session and review the tape before the next group session, listening for ways in which you might improve both your clinical skills and your participation in the group. Write down, for yourself, one or two changes you want to work on in that next practice session and keep them in mind as you play the role of the clinician.
- Adhere to the guidelines that follow for giving and receiving feedback.
- Complete the Assessment of Progress form at the end of each chapter, beginning with the form at the end of this chapter.
- Practice what you are learning between class meetings. Use your daily interactions as an opportunity to observe how you communicate with others and consciously use what you have learned to improve your communication.

Constructing the Practice Groups

I suggest the class be divided into groups of three or four people. The composition of these groups should change no more than once, if at all, over the course of a quarter, semester, or other training unit. Continuity allows participants to build rapport and trust, become familiar with each other's styles of interaction, see development and improvement in skills, and foster positive change based on the feedback that has been shared in the group.

During the exercises presented throughout this book, one or two members of the practice group will serve as observers, depending on whether the group has three or four members. Their task is to take careful notes on the role-play, using the

Assessment of Progress forms as guides. One of the observers also should assume the role of timekeeper, gently reminding the group when only 2 to 3 minutes remain in the role-play and then letting the group know when the allotted time has elapsed.

The other two members will engage in a role-play, with one assuming the role of client and the other, the role of clinician. The clinician's task, described specifically in each chapter, is to demonstrate the skills highlighted in the exercise, in the context of sound overall counseling.

The group member in the client's seat also has a challenging and potentially growth-promoting role. The client has the choice of either presenting actual concerns or role-playing a hypothetical client. More will be said on this choice and on the client role later in this chapter.

Practice Group Sessions

To maximize your learning, I recommend that your practice group sessions adopt the steps that follow. Once this pattern becomes familiar to you, your group will be able to move efficiently through the steps:

1. The practice group members review the exercise to be sure they have a clear and shared understanding of the nature and purpose of the experience. Any uncertainty about the nature of the exercise is clarified within the group or with the help of the instructor.
2. Practice group members review the Assessment of Progress forms to remind themselves of their goals.
3. If this is not the first practice session, group members review, either individually or as a group, their progress thus far and identify areas that need attention. For example, if a group member had difficulty asking helpful questions in a previous session, the group member should focus on both the new skill to be practiced and previous skills that need some improvement.
4. Determine group members' initial roles. Think about the three or four possible roles in terms of a sequence and progress through all roles in the first meeting:

   • Clinician
   • Observer 1/timekeeper
   • Client
   • Observer 2 (for groups with four members)

   For each subsequent group session, assume the role in the sequence that comes next after the one you first took in the previous session. In other words, if you began the first practice group session in the role of clinician, you should begin the second session as observer 1, then become the client, then observer 2 (for four-member groups), and finally the clinician again. This rotation ensures that the same person will not repeatedly be the clinician either first or last (both of which have advantages and disadvantages) and that each person will have approximately the same amount of time in each of the three or four roles over the course of the practice group's meetings. This rotation also ensures that, for four-person groups, you will not have to assume client and clinician roles back to back, a potentially stressful sequence. Sufficient time should be allowed for each exercise so that group members have the opportunity to assume all four roles.

5. Practice group engages in the first iteration of the skill development exercise.

6. Feedback begins with the person in the clinician role, describing and assessing his or her own performance. That person addresses the following

   - Brief overview of the exercise;
   - Strengths of clinician and session;
   - Assessment of clinician's ability to demonstrate the skills highlighted in the exercise as well as overall skills. Specific details and examples facilitate understanding of feedback and self-assessment;
   - Identification of areas needing improvement or causing the clinician discomfort or concern; and
   - Questions the clinician might have for the group on his or her skill development.

7. The person in the client role should provide feedback next, addressing the following

   - Overall reaction to the experience;
   - Helpful elements in the session. Attention should be paid to verbal interventions as well as nonverbal communication;
   - Clinician's ability to demonstrate the skills highlighted in the exercise as well as overall skills; and
   - Ways the role-played session could have been even more helpful.

8. The one or two people in the observer roles should provide feedback last, addressing the following

   - Overall perceptions of the experience;
   - Helpful elements in the session. Attention should be paid to verbal interventions as well as nonverbal communication;
   - Clinician's ability to demonstrate the skills highlighted in the exercise as well as overall skills; and
   - Ways to improve the role-play.

9. While receiving feedback, the clinician makes sure he or she has a clear understanding of the feedback and takes notes on important points on the Assessment of Progress form. The clinician's role is to understand, not to defend or argue.

10. The clinician then summarizes the group feedback, checking out with the group members their understanding of the feedback provided and identifying specific areas of strength and areas that need improvement.
11. Practice group members then change roles, moving on to the next role in the sequence as described previously, and these steps are repeated.

The Nature and Importance of Helpful Feedback

One of the most important determinants of the nature and value of the practice group sessions is how group members give and receive feedback. Giving feedback is a learning experience, as is receiving feedback. Giving and receiving feedback can be a challenge but also is an art that can be mastered and that can contribute greatly to clinicians' skill development.

To provide feedback effectively, avoid dominating the group and allow ample time for others to contribute their perceptions and ideas. Share feedback in a way that is empowering rather than demoralizing and offer suggestions that can be easily understood and implemented. Giving and receiving feedback effectively can greatly enhance the value of the groups. These skills also can be productively used in many other personal and professional settings.

Giving Feedback   The following are two examples of feedback given to clinicians:

> **Unhelpful feedback:** I just didn't like the way you interacted with the client. You looked like you would rather be having lunch than talking to the client.
> **Helpful feedback:** "Your eye contact seemed much better this week; you didn't look down the way you had in the last session. I did notice that you crossed your arms when Ginger started to cry. It seemed like you were putting a barrier between the two of you. What is your recollection of that part of the session? Perhaps next time you could try to assume a more open posture so that you communicate acceptance throughout the session.

The differences between the two examples are probably clear to you. The clinician in the first example speaks in vague and critical terms without offering specific examples or suggestions. The focus is on the clinician rather than the interventions. In addition, the language seems insulting and unprofessional.

On the other hand, the second speaker begins with positive feedback, is specific, focuses on interventions rather than the person, asks for the recipient's reactions to the feedback, and suggests specific ways to improve. The feedback is respectful and professional, yet it points out areas that might benefit from change.

The following guidelines will help you to provide useful feedback:

- Feedback should be gentle, supportive, respectful, and professional.
- Feedback should focus on strengths first and then address areas that need improvement.

- All feedback should be specific so that the recipient can readily grasp the information. Pinpoint the times in the session when the clinician made particularly effective or noticeably weak interventions.
- Feedback should focus on the behavior and interventions, not the person.
- Feedback should focus on a few important areas; do not inundate the clinician with information.
- Feedback should include specific but tentative suggestions for improvement.
- Feedback should be linked to goals and previous skill development exercises and experiences.
- The effect and understanding of feedback should be checked out with the recipient, and discussion should be invited.

Receiving Feedback Listening to feedback and making good use of helpful suggestions are at least as difficult as giving sound feedback, especially for novice clinicians who may doubt and devalue their abilities. At the same time, hearing objective and useful feedback is one of the best ways to learn new skills and improve your effectiveness as a clinician. Over the course of your training, you will receive feedback from other students, from your professors, from yourself, and perhaps from colleagues, supervisors, and more advanced graduate students. The following information will help you make good use of the information you receive about your skills from others.

Let's look at some additional examples of feedback and some common types of responses to the feedback.

Feedback 1: You really heard the client's underlying anger. However, when the client said she wished she could "just disappear," you shifted the topic back to her work conflict. You might have missed some very strong feelings, perhaps even suicidal ideation. Maybe you could have reflected her feelings there. What do you think?

Response 1: I was going to address her statement as soon as I was clear on the nature of her work conflict.
Response 2: She always gets melodramatic whenever we discuss substantive issues. I didn't want her to get off the track again.
Response 3: Thank you for pointing that out.
Response 4: It didn't occur to me that she might be feeling suicidal. What made you think about that?
Response 5: That's a good point. Maybe I was scared by what she said. How might I have reflected her feelings?

The feedback here reflects several helpful strategies. It is supportive and respectful, it is specific, it suggests a way to improve the intervention, and it invites a reply from the recipient.

Despite the high quality of the feedback, the five respondents have very different reactions. The first two people seem more concerned with defending their interventions than they are with acquiring new learning. The second respondent even blames and disparages the client. Response 3 is a neutral one; it is hard to determine whether that person really absorbed and thought about the feedback. The fourth respondent is having difficulty understanding the feedback, and that is not an unusual reaction. Asking for clarification is appropriate and can help the clinician decide whether the feedback is meaningful and useful. Respondent 5 seems most likely to benefit from the feedback; that person has clearly heard the feedback, tries to understand what led him to overlook the client's strong statement, and then seeks to learn even more by asking for additional help. Responding to feedback in that way is most likely to promote skill development.

Let's look at another type of feedback, followed again by some responses.

Feedback 2: I can't believe you missed the statement that she wished she could "just disappear!" She's practically telling you that she wants to kill herself and you just keep talking about her work problems!

Response 1:   I guess that really was a dumb mistake. I do need to be more careful. I wonder if I really have what it takes to be a good clinician.

Response 2:   We can't pick up on everything. Remember when your client said she'd been throwing up again and you didn't stop to explore that?

Response 3:   OK. Anybody have any comments on anything else?

Response 4:   You probably have a good point, but the way you're talking to me isn't helpful. It just makes me feel angry and put down. Can we come at this in a different way?

Although the person providing feedback here may be on the right track, the delivery is far from growth promoting and is likely to elicit self-blame and defensiveness from the recipient. Response 1 reflects those feelings of self-blame, while response 2 is a defensive and attacking one. Response 3 is probably the most common reaction to the type of feedback illustrated in this example. The person may well have some strong reactions to the attack but pushes those feelings away, at least temporarily, and changes the subject. Making a response like the fourth one is not easy; it calls for courage, honesty, and the ability to take a risk. However, the fourth response is most likely to promote skill development and personal growth for both giver and receiver of feedback.

The following guidelines for responding to feedback will help you maximize the learning you receive from that process:

- *Be aware of and address any discomfort you experience when hearing negative feedback.* Negative feedback can contribute to your own self-doubts and even make you question your career choices. Novice clinicians are particularly susceptible to placing too much weight on criticism of their work and ignoring praise. Try to put critical feedback into perspective, balancing it with all of the positive feedback you have received. Also, be sure you are clear on the substance of the feedback. You might be doing what Albert Ellis calls "awfulizing," magnifying a minor or occasional error or omission.

- *Avoid being defensive and attacking in response to negative feedback.* If your reactions to feedback are getting in the way of understanding the feedback, using it constructively, or feeling good about your successes, work on changing the self-talk underlying those reactions. Discussing your reactions with a faculty member, supervisor, or colleague might be helpful.

- *Write down the feedback you receive.* Sometimes the pressure of the moment makes it difficult to absorb feedback when it is received. Later, you may not be able to recall the feedback well enough to determine whether or not it provides useful information, or you may recall the criticism much more clearly than you can remember the praise. Writing down the feedback you receive can help you obtain a balanced and accurate picture of the feedback. Having a written record of the feedback affords you the opportunity to think it over, assess its value, and, if necessary, obtain more information later to help you understand and use the feedback in helpful ways.

- Remember that if you believe the delivery of feedback is confusing, harsh, or attacking, be courageous and *state how the delivery or content of the feedback could have been made more helpful.*

- *Be aware of and address any discomfort you experience when hearing positive feedback.* Positive feedback, too, can be hard to hear. Our own self-doubts might lead us to believe that people are just praising our work to avoid hurting our feelings or we might feel like an impostor, concealing our shortcomings from others. We might even feel that we cannot live up to the positive images people have of us and might experience considerable pressure when others are impressed by our skills. These are all common responses to positive feedback, especially for novice clinicians. Making a written record of the feedback you receive can help you appreciate your strengths and identify areas needing improvement.

- *Be sure you have a clear understanding of both the positive feedback you receive and the suggestions for improvement.* Restate the feedback you receive to be sure you have heard it correctly. Ask for examples and elaboration of people's reactions to your work so that you know exactly what they mean. If they have not offered specific ways for you to improve your skills, ask them what you might have done differently or how you might improve on your work.

- *Keep track of your goals and the progress you make toward those goals.* The Assessment of Progress forms provided in each chapter will help you accomplish that. Seeing yourself moving forward can be empowering and rewarding and can encourage further improvement.

- *Focus on your strengths and improvements, but continue to set realistic goals for yourself.* One of the exciting aspects of becoming a counselor or therapist is that the possibility for new learning and professional growth is limitless. Our field is stimulating but can also be intimidating and overwhelming. You will probably feel successful and satisfied in this field if challenge and growth seem like exciting prospects to you and if you continue to promote your own learning and development in realistic ways.

Role-Playing a Client

Just as there are skills and strategies that help you succeed in the clinician role, so are there skills that will help you enjoy and learn from the client role. These skills also will enable you to help the other learners in your practice group when you are in the client role.

As a client, you will be talking about concerns or issues with which you would like help. When you are in the client role, you can choose whether to present concerns that you are experiencing or have experienced in your own life, or to assume a persona and talk about problems that are not really your own. You might role-play one of your clients, someone you know, or a client created out of your imagination. You might even take on the role of someone in a novel, film, or television program who is familiar to you, or you might enact a famous figure in history. Of course, if you portray a real person, you must change any identifying information to protect the confidentiality and privacy of the person who is the model for your role-play. In addition, taking on the role of a well-known historical figure or media personality runs the risk that the role-play will become silly; that could happen if, for example, you take on the body language and attitude of Elvis Presley or Bill Clinton. Both choices—role-playing yourself or role-playing a hypothetical client—have benefits and drawbacks.

Role-Playing a Hypothetical Client

Benefits

- The risk is low that the person in the client role will become hurt or upset.
- The client can feel free to present more severe issues and concerns.
- The group members can observe and discuss freely how a clinician might treat a problem or client such as that which was role-played.

Drawbacks

- The person in the client role might not be able to provide a realistic presentation of the client.
- The clinician might not take the problem or person seriously.
- The group members might become more involved with the intricacies of a melodramatic story than they are with their skill development.
- The clinician will not have the opportunity to see the interventions actually make a difference in the client's life.

Presenting One's Actual Concerns

Benefits

- This will make the exercise more realistic.
- The person in the client role may experience some personal growth as a result of this process.
- Clinicians can assess the impact of their interventions by looking at changes in the targeted concerns over time.

Drawbacks

- Clinicians might find themselves dealing with issues that are too challenging for them.
- Clinicians might be reluctant to ask personal questions of the person in the client role.
- Clients might become upset or hurt during this process.
- If students present their own serious concerns, that may affect how others in the group view them and can interfere with the development of trust and rapport in the practice groups.
- The presentation of serious personal concerns by a group member also can create dilemmas for the other members. Should they share this information with the professor? Do they have an obligation to help the person outside of class? Do they need to avoid giving critical feedback to a group member who is in crisis?

Selecting Appropriate Client Concerns   I have observed many practice groups in my classes over the years. Although most students used sound judgment in the issues they chose to present, this has not always been the case. One student disclosed that he was consuming large quantities of alcohol and another described symptoms that indicated she had a severe eating disorder. In both cases, group members wisely encouraged the "clients" to inform me of these difficulties so that I could assist them in finding some help and that did happen. However, I expect that these disclosures were disturbing to the group members and may have led them to perceive the "clients" negatively.

Instructors might want to recommend whether people in the client role present their own concerns or those of a hypothetical client. If instructors choose to leave this decision up to the individual group members, the decision should be made with care and deliberation. People who choose to present their own concerns in the practice group sessions can minimize the risks of that decision through careful selection of the types of issues they present.

Selecting appropriate concerns to present when you are in the client role is crucial to the success of the learning process. The following guidelines can facilitate the selection process:

- Select concerns that focus on the client rather than on another person, that seem amenable to change, and that are not painful or difficult to discuss. Present concerns that are specific, meaningful, and important but that are not likely to feel overwhelming, either to you or to the clinician. Focus on current issues, rather than past wounds. Avoid bringing up difficulties that reflect serious emotional upset or that you are addressing in therapy. Instead, bring up concerns or decisions that are common, that are likely to be shared by some of the other group members, and that you would not mind becoming public information.
- For example, instead of discussing your abuse by one of your parents, focus on the difficulty you experience when encouraging your child to do her homework.

- Instead of discussing your long-standing depression, discuss your disappointment with your performance in a class.
- Instead of discussing your unhealthy use of drugs, discuss your wish to eat a healthier diet.
- Instead of complaining about a teacher you dislike, ask for help in making the most of courses that are not as interesting as you would like them to be.
- Instead of addressing your fear of death, present your concerns about helping an elderly parent remain as independent as possible.
- Instead of discussing the rape you experienced in college, ask for help in figuring out how to build a healthy friendship with a new colleague.

Suggested Concerns for Clients to Present   The following are categories of concerns that might be suitable for discussion in the practice group sessions. Examples are provided for each category.

- *Professional goals and direction.* Deciding whether to pursue doctoral study, whether to change jobs, whether to become a school counselor or a mental health counselor; determining how to ask your supervisor for a salary increase or promotion, how to make the transition from being a lawyer to being a psychologist.
- *Finding more balance in your life.* Balancing family and professional responsibilities, maintaining a leisure life while being a graduate student, finding time to be alone with your partner while rearing five children, dealing with your tendency to spend too much time or too little time on one aspect of your life.
- *Current relationships.* Improving your relationship with your best friend, achieving more closeness in a family relationship, getting to know other students, dealing successfully with supervisors or professors, identifying the strengths you bring to relationships, talking with a friend who has disappointed you, ending a friendship that is no longer rewarding.
- *Changing habits or behaviors.* Stopping smoking, developing an exercise routine, getting clutter under control, improving study habits, eating more nutritionally, developing new leisure activities.
- *Enhancing interpersonal skills.* Improving parenting skills, becoming more assertive, managing anger, becoming less critical of others, initiating conversations, expressing more positive feelings toward others.
- *Coping with current issues.* Dealing with a parent's illness, developing new friends and interests after a divorce, deciding whether a romantic relationship should be continued, developing a realistic budget, planning a special but anxiety-provoking event, deciding whether to buy a new car or have the old one repaired.
- *Dealing with disappointments and fears.* Reducing fear of cats, disappointment over your failure to receive a promotion, apprehension about meeting new people, sadness over the loss of a job opportunity or promotion, rejection by another graduate school or program, loss of contact with an old friend.

Suggested Concerns to Avoid   The following are concerns that probably should *not* be the focus of your client role plays in the practice group:

- Serious drug or alcohol problems
- Suicidal ideation
- Severe depression or anxiety
- Traumatic experiences
- Issues that date back to childhood
- Your own life-threatening illness
- Loss of contact with reality
- Uncontrollable anger
- Sexual or physical abuse
- Conflicts with professors or students who may be known to others in the group

Identifying Topics for Client Role-Plays   After reviewing these lists, identify two or three topics that you would feel comfortable discussing in your practice group and that reflect the guidelines presented. Remember that you are in control of yourself; you can reveal as much or as little as you choose. Although I assume you want to be helpful to the other group members, you, like all clients, should collaborate with the clinician in setting the agenda for the sessions, and you have the right to let the clinician know that you choose not to discuss certain areas of your life. Be sure to take care of yourself so that your experience as a client is a rewarding one.

Topics I Might Discuss in the Practice Group:

1. _____
2. _____
3. _____

Confidentiality

Maintaining the confidentiality of the practice group is essential. This needs to be clearly stated as a ground rule for the group. Only if group members can trust that information about their lives or their performance in the practice group will not be shared inappropriately can they feel comfortable engaging in the exercises in such a way as to promote personal and professional growth.

Exceptions to the guideline of confidentiality may exist, and these should be stated and explained before the first practice session. Professors or supervisors responsible for this learning experience may want group members to provide written or oral feedback on their own performance in the group and on that of their colleagues. Emphasis should be placed on people's self-evaluations rather than how others evaluate them. The practice groups should provide a learning experience rather than one that may promote feelings of competition and vulnerability, and I encourage instructors to take that perspective. Although I suggest that group members present concerns that are not highly charged, the direction of a session is unpredictable. Unanticipated issues may arise. As in the real world of counseling, social work, and psychology, clinicians are permitted to break confidentiality if clients present a danger to themselves or to others. However, this is not a decision to be made lightly; breaking confidentiality usually should only be done after careful thought and consultation with a colleague or supervisor in which you conceal the identity of the person under discussion. If you believe that someone in your practice group presents a danger or if you believe that the concerns presented by a group member are serious enough to require professional help, you should discuss this matter with the group member and then with your professor or supervisor. This guideline, too, should be clearly stated before the group begins its role-plays so that all participants understand the circumstances under which confidentiality may need to be broken.

LEARNING OPPORTUNITIES

Selecting the Most Useful Exercises and Questions

This book contains a great many exercises and questions. You are not expected to respond to all of these but rather to select those that are most meaningful to you and most likely to help you achieve your learning and skill development goals. If you are using this book in conjunction with a course or a training experience, your supervisor or instructor will probably tell you which questions and exercises to address. Of course, feel free to respond to any additional items that seem important to you and your professional growth. The personal journal questions are especially likely to promote your self-awareness and development.

Written or Discussion Questions

1. On page **5** six characteristics of influential women in the mental health professions were listed. What additional characteristics would you add to this list? What do you think would be the six essential characteristics of influential men in the mental health field?
2. The BETA model (background, emotions, thoughts, and actions) is used in this book as a framework to organize treatment interventions and skills of counseling and psychotherapy. What are your reactions to this framework? What are some ways in which you can use the BETA framework to help you develop your knowledge and skills?
3. Research suggests that theories of counseling and psychotherapy have more commonalities than they do differences. Do you find this surprising? Why or why not? What do you think are the most important commonalities?
4. What steps can you take to ensure that you are paying enough attention to your client's context and worldview?

5. This chapter described the nature and history of three mental health professions: social work, psychology, and counseling. What is your understanding of the differences and similarities among these professions? This chapter has described the practice groups that you will be using to improve your skills. What are your initial reactions to these groups? What do you see as their advantages? Their drawbacks?

6. Discuss the differences between helpful and unhelpful feedback. Develop three examples of helpful feedback and three examples of unhelpful feedback.

Assessment of Progress Forms

An Assessment of Progress form appears at the end of each chapter, with sections included in each form to reflect the salient skills that have been targeted in that chapter. A complete set of Assessment of Progress forms is included in Chapter 11. Complete each chapter's Assessment of Progress form as you finish the reading, exercises, and practice group experiences associated with that chapter. When you have finished this book, the complete set of Assessment of Progress forms in Chapter 11 will afford you the opportunity to assess the overall progress you have made. The Assessment of Progress form that follows will enable you to make an initial assessment of your clinical strengths and areas needing improvement. This will give you a sort of baseline for your perceptions of yourself as a clinician.

Assessment of Progress Form 1

Name : _____

Date : _____

1. List three clinical skills that you believe are strengths for you:
   a. _____
   b. _____
   c. _____
   d. _____

2. List three clinical skills that you believe you need to develop or improve:
   a. _____
   b. _____
   c. _____
   d. _____

The Personal Journal

One of the learning tools you will be using in conjunction with this book is the personal journal. You might obtain a blank book that will be used for this journal or you might prefer to create a journal on your computer. The primary purpose of the personal journal is to provide you the opportunity to think about some of the issues raised in this book, to apply them to yourself, and to enable you to become more aware of yourself as a developing clinician.

The personal journal, like the rest of this book, is designed to be used flexibly and to be adapted to the needs of a particular learning environment. When I use the journal as part of my teaching, I do not grade the students' journals because I want to encourage them to think and express themselves freely about important personal and professional issues. Rather, I briefly review the journals at the end of the semester to be sure they have been completed as directed. Instructors may follow this format, they may choose to put students on their honor to complete the journal assignments, or they may decide to grade the journals as an assignment. Whatever choice is made, students should be advised at the beginning of the course who will read their personal journals and if and how that material will be evaluated.

Personal Journal Questions

The following are the personal journal questions for this chapter:

1. This chapter discussed three mental health fields: counseling, psychology, and social work. Is one of these your chosen field? If so, what led you to choose that one over the other two? If not, which of these appeals to you most and why?
2. Before you began your training, what did you think it would be like to become a counselor or psychotherapist? How have your ideas changed as a result of your training?
3. The characteristics of effective clinicians are listed on page **4**. If you have not already done so, rate yourself on those characteristics as directed in the instructions that precede the list. Then, based on your self-evaluations, describe in your journal three ways in which you could build on your strengths, develop your self-awareness, and minimize your weaknesses.
4. Do you currently have a treatment system or theory of counseling and psychotherapy that you prefer to use in your clinical work? What attracts you to that particular approach?
5. A list of six qualities of women who have become leaders in the mental health professions is given on page **5**. Which of these six qualities do you see in yourself? What are qualities that you would like to develop?
6. The practice groups include three roles: clinician, client, and observer. Describe what you think it will be like for you to take on each of the three roles.
7. List two or three concerns that you have which would be appropriate to discuss in the practice groups. List two or three concerns that you have which would not be appropriate to discuss in the practice groups. What do you see as the differences between the two groups of concerns?
8. Table 1-2 (page **23**) presents a list of skills, organized according to the BETA format. In your journal, list up to five of those skills that you view as strengths and up to five of those skills that you want to improve.

SUMMARY

This chapter began to establish the groundwork for you to learn and apply the fundamental skills of the mental health professional. It included information on characteristics of effective clinicians and leaders in the mental health field; the context of treatment; the importance of theories of treatment; the professions of psychology, counseling, and social work and their historical development, the BETA (background, emotions, thoughts, actions) model, and the four stages in treatment. The chapter also described the structure of this book and ways to make good use of the practice groups.

Chapter 2 will complete the process of establishing the groundwork for skill development. Included in that chapter is information on multicultural competence, ethics, the importance of social justice in the clinician's role, and strength-based treatment.

Chapter 2

ANTECEDENTS TO EFFECTIVE SKILL DEVELOPMENT: MULTICULTURAL COMPETENCE, ETHICAL UNDERSTANDING, SOCIAL JUSTICE, AND OTHERS

PAVING THE WAY FOR SKILL DEVELOPMENT

Before we turn our attention to developing the fundamental skills of effective clinicians, we must look at the groundwork or infrastructure that supports and underlies our use of these skills. As we discussed in the previous chapter, most people providing counseling and psychotherapy today have been trained in one of three fields: psychology, counseling, or social work. Each of these fields has its own history and its own training programs. However, when we look at their understanding of human development and multiculturalism, their approaches to helping people and making contributions to the welfare of our world, their ethical standards, and their goals and values, the three fields have far more in common than they do to distinguish them. This chapter will provide a brief overview of these topics in order to put the process of skill development in context and to familiarize you with the underlying concepts and information that all mental health professionals should keep in mind, regardless of their discipline, their specialization, and their theoretical orientation.

LEARNING GOALS

This chapter is designed to provide readers with a basic understanding of important learning and skills that serve as the groundwork for all of the mental health professions. Acquiring knowledge of these areas before or while developing your clinical and helping skills is essential to effective application of those skills. These areas include

- Ethical standards
- Human development

- Theories and strategies to promote change
- Multicultural understanding and competence
- Social justice and advocacy
- The mind–body–spirit connection
- Additional areas of importance and specialization

This chapter also provides a brief overview of additional and more specialized areas of learning that you will probably study after you have achieved some mastery of the fundamental skills presented in this book.

ETHICAL STANDARDS

Each of the mental health professions has its own ethical standards and guidelines. The American Counseling Association has the ACA Code of Ethics and Standards of Practice, revised in 2005; The American Psychological Association developed the Ethical Principles of Psychologists, revised in 2003; and the National Association of Social Workers has its code of ethics. In addition, many of the specializations and divisions of these three umbrella organizations also have ethical guidelines. For example, the American Association for Marriage and Family Therapy expects its members to abide by the Code of Ethical Principles for Marriage and Family Therapists, whereas school counselors are guided by the Ethical Standards for School Counselors. At the time this book was written, the major codes of ethics could be accessed online as follows:

- American Counseling Association: http://www.counseling.org/resources/ethics
- American Psychological Association: http://www2.apa.org/ethics/code2002/doc
- National Association of Social Workers: http://www.socialworkers.org/pubs/code/code.asp

The revision of ethical standards is a significant undertaking for a professional association. Committees are formed, information is solicited from the membership, drafts are written for review and then further revised, and finally a new code of ethics is published and disseminated to the members of the organization. Because of this, 5 or more years may elapse between revisions, but leaders of these organizations are constantly gathering information on necessary changes in ethical standards so that they can provide up-to-date advice and prepare for the next revision of the association's ethical standards.

Importance of Ethical Standards

Ethical standards are important not only for the members of a professional association, but also for consumers and the general public. Ethical standards shape the image that people have of the mental health professions, give structure to these professions, and guide individual, legal, and professional decisions on appropriate behavior of those in the mental health fields. When clinicians are uncertain about their professional choices and behaviors, they should look to the ethical standards of their profession for guidance. When clinicians are accused of committing an ethical violation, their behavior is reviewed in light of the ethical code for their profession to determine whether, in fact, they have committed such a violation. Consequences of engaging in ethical violations vary and might include a requirement for supervision, continuing education in a specific area, or even temporary or permanent loss of the license to practice one's profession. Demonstrated knowledge of relevant ethical standards is required for initial credentialing, and many state credentialing boards routinely require mental health professionals to obtain continuing education units in ethics in order to maintain their license or certification. Clearly, social workers, counselors, and psychologists have a strong mandate as well as significant incentives to become knowledgeable about the ethical standards of their profession and make sure that their personal and professional behaviors are consistent with those standards.

General Ethical Principles

The ethical standards of the American Psychological Association (APA) are very similar to those of the American Counseling Association and the National Association of Social Workers. The following five general principles are integral to those standards:

- *Beneficence and nonmaleficence.* Seek to be helpful to others and do no harm. Be aware of the impact and influence that mental health treatment providers have and use those qualities mindfully and for the good of others.
- *Fidelity and responsibility.* Our relationships and actions should reflect ethical standards, appropriate responsibility, and the importance of trust. We collaborate effectively with others and seek to ensure their ethical conduct. We contribute some of our time to pro bono work or other forms of service to the profession.
- *Integrity.* We are honest and truthful in our activities and do not misrepresent ourselves or take advantage of others.
- *Justice.* We recognize that all people have the right to access and benefit from psychological services. We take steps to recognize our possible biases, limitations on our competence, and boundaries of our professional role and avoid practicing in unjust or harmful ways.
- *Respect for people's rights and dignity.* We respect the rights, dignity, and worth of all people and take steps to protect those. We recognize and appreciate diversity, take account of individual differences in our work, and do not participate in or sanction activities that reflect prejudice and discrimination. Although the language is somewhat different, the preamble

to the code of ethics of the National Association of Social Workers advocates the following similar core values: service, social justice, dignity and worth of the person, importance of human relationships, integrity, and competence.

Professional Differences in Ethical Standards

The codes of ethics themselves are divided into broad sections that reflect the specific ethical standards of the profession. A careful comparison of these standards for the three professions of psychology, counseling, and social work reveals that, overall, they attend to the same topics and concerns. However, the code of ethics of the National Association of Social Workers pays a little more attention to the importance of service and somewhat less attention to evaluation, interpretation, and assessment. These discrepancies reflect the differing histories of the three professions. Social work began as a profession that emphasized direct service—working with people who were impoverished and needy—long before social workers moved into the role of therapist. On the other hand, from their inception, psychology and counseling were involved in assessment: psychologists via their role in assessing intelligence and learning abilities in academic, military, and clinical settings; and counselors in assessing interests and aptitudes in schools, rehabilitation settings, and career counseling programs. These differences among the mental health professions continue, although they are lessening over time.

Brief Overview of Ethical Standards

Although a detailed discussion of ethical standards is beyond the scope of this book, a brief overview of those standards is presented here. Particular attention is paid to those standards that are most important in general as well as most relevant to the topic of this book. To organize this overview, the 10 categories of the Ethical Principles of Psychologists serve as the outline for this discussion.

Category 1: Evolving Ethical Issues Clinicians must take an active role in maintaining and safeguarding the ethics of their profession. If we encounter a conflict between the ethics of our profession and the legal mandates of the government or the requirements of our employers, we have a responsibility to address and try to resolve those conflicts. Particularly important is the clinician's role in dealing with ethical violations committed by other mental health professionals. Often, clinicians learn about possible violations from clients who have had previous therapists or we observe violations being committed by our colleagues. I have encountered this several times in my own professional experience. I observed a colleague being driven home by a client after each weekly appointment, and was told by a client that the counselor he saw for marital therapy had invited him and his wife to spend a weekend with her at her beach house. Under such circumstances, ethical standards mandate that we do not ignore the situation but, giving our colleagues the benefit of the doubt, bring up our concerns with them. Perhaps some information and discussion is all they need to rectify a potentially unethical situation and resolve the matter. However, if we become more certain that an ethical violation has occurred and that the colleague will not rectify the situation or stop the unethical practice, we have the responsibility to report the ethical violation to the appropriate professional association, credentialing body, and/or employer. Similarly, we are expected to cooperate fully with all ethics committee investigations as part of the process of maintaining ethical standards.

Category 2: Competence   As mental health professionals, we ensure that any services we provide or have responsibility for are based on "established scientific and professional knowledge of the discipline" (APA, 2002, p. 5). That means that we only practice within our areas of competence and see to it that anyone to whom we delegate work, such as administrative staff and teaching assistants, follow that same guideline. At the same time, we have a mandate to expand on our skills via reading, formal education, conferences, and supervised practice. Through new learning and skill development, we can expand our areas of competence and the range of our practice.

In emergencies, we have the right to offer help, even it if is not in our usual range of competence, but we should make an appropriate referral as soon as possible just as we should do with any clients who require services that we do not have the ability to provide effectively. Should it happen that personal concerns, such as drug or alcohol problems, cognitive impairment, or outside pressures, interfere with our ability to perform our work competently, we are ethically obligated to take appropriate measures, including obtaining consultation, to ensure that our own difficulties do not interfere with performance of our professional duties.

Category 3: Human Relations   This section of the APA code includes many provisions, all designed to clarify our roles and relationships with clients and organizations and protect our clients from any harm that might stem from our negative attitudes and confused and exploitive relationships with them. Overall, we are ethically mandated not to engage in "unfair discrimination, sexual or other forms of harassment, or any other harmful behaviors toward our clients" (APA, 2002, p. 5).

Multiple relationships, formerly referred to as dual-role relationships, are discussed in this section of the ethical guidelines. Previously, professional associations generally prohibited all multiple relationships with a client such as therapist and friend or instructor. However, that stance has been softened, in part out of a realization that, particularly in small communities, mental health professionals must often have such relationships in order to be part of their community. A client may be the town's only actuary or may be a member of the clinician's religious institution or neighborhood organization. These probably are acceptable multiple roles. The key statement in the code of ethics is that "Multiple relationships that would not reasonably be expected to cause impairment or risk exploitation or harm are not unethical" (p. 6). However, clinician and client should discuss all multiple relationships to ensure that any potential issues are identified and addressed. Clients who typically address their therapist as "Dr. [last name]" may not feel comfortable using the person's first name in another context and even minor concerns that may create awkwardness should be resolved. On the other hand, clinicians must avoid potentially harmful multiple role relationships with both clients and people closely associated with or related to clients. This, of course, includes sexual relationships, which are addressed in detail in a later ethical guideline. Other examples of potentially harmful multiple relationships include lending or borrowing money from the family of a client, employing a current client, counseling the child or partner of a member of your own family, and developing a close personal friendship with either a client or a close relative of a client. If we inadvertently find ourselves in a potentially harmful multiple role relationship, we must take steps to modify that relationship as soon as possible.

This section of the ethics code also describes several other ways in which we are expected to protect and respect our clients and colleagues. We do not exploit anyone with whom we have a professional relationship, we cooperate with other professionals in order to help clients, we avoid entering into roles that might create conflicts of interest for us, and we obtain and document informed consent for all of our services. Even when our clients are not legally able to provide informed consent, such as when our client are children, we still are expected to explain the nature of our services and obtain the person's informal approval.

When a third party enters the picture, additional ethical complications can arise that are addressed in the code of ethics. For example, consultants often are hired by management or supervisors to train or assess employees; one result is that consultants' loyalties may be divided between their employers and the employees. A similar conflict of loyalties can arise for a diagnostician who receives a referral from a school district or another clinician to assess a client or for a clinician who is seeing a court-referred client. As often is the case, open disclosure is an important route to preventing such conflicts. Everyone involved should be fully informed about the nature and purposes of the services, who will have access to what information, and any limits on confidentiality.

Finally, this section of the ethical code advises clinicians to plan for any interruptions in services. This entails taking steps to help clients make a transition when we are moving or retiring and also involves having a colleague who can step in to help our clients in the event that we are suddenly incapacitated.

Category 4: Privacy and Confidentiality   Confidentiality is one of the cornerstones of the mental health professions. We are mandated to protect confidential information about our clients, regardless of how it is stored, and discuss with clients the nature and limits on that confidentiality. We can share information when authorized by our clients to do so, but even then we share information only with others who have a reason to know that information and give them only that information that is relevant and germane. We are permitted to discuss clients with consultants and in our teaching and writing, even if we do not have the client's permission, but only if we are certain that we have adequately disguised the identity of those clients. Ideally, however, the clients' written consent should be obtained even under those circumstances. Finally, we can share client-identifiable information without the client's consent when we are legally mandated to do so, when that is necessary to obtain payment for our services, and when we need to break confidentiality to protect the client or others from harm. Again, we disclose as little information as possible and inform clients at the outset of our work with them of these limitations on confidentiality.

Category 5: Advertising and Other Public Statements   The essence of this guideline is that we must be truthful in all information we provide about our experience, training, credentials, publications, fees, affiliations, and other professional qualifications. This mandate extends to our public statements about ourselves, our advertising, and our presentations. Similarly, we provide accurate information about our services, particularly any education programs we provide, being sure to specify clearly the intended audience, learning objectives, presenters, and costs. In addition, we do not solicit testimonials from current clients nor should we solicit uninvited business from actual or potential clients. This guideline is intended to protect people who might be vulnerable and easily influenced.

Category 6: Record Keeping and Fees   Mental health professionals keep accurate records of their services for purposes of facilitating effective treatment, meeting legal and institutional requirements, tracking billing and payment information, and allowing replication of their research. Records are stored and maintained in ways that ensure confidentiality, and provision is made for transfer and protection of records if we no longer practice our profession. Record keeping has become an increasingly important component of the clinician's role and clinicians are generally expected to maintain client records that include, at a minimum, a signed informed consent to treatment form; information on use of third-party payers, dates and charges for services, payments made, a diagnosis and treatment plan, progress notes for each session, and a closing summary.

   Fees are the second important topic of this ethical standard. As early as is reasonable, clinician and client come to a clear agreement as to what fees will be charged and when and how payment will be made (e.g., in full at each session, balance due after payment by insurance companies). We are permitted to use a collection agency in the event of nonpayment of fees, but clients must be informed of this possibility at the outset of treatment and should be offered opportunities and arrangements for paying past due amounts—use of a collection agency is an option of last resort. Bartering has long been discussed by the mental health professions as an alternative to cash payments. The use of bartering can enable people who could not otherwise afford our fees to receive psychotherapy services, but it does raise ethical risks. The APA ethics code allows bartering, but only when the arrangement does not exploit the client or undermine the treatment process. We are not permitted to accept a fee for making a referral; clearly, that could lead us to make referrals that are not in the best interest of our clients.

Category 7: Education and Training   This section of the ethics code is particularly relevant to mental health professionals who provide training, education, or supervision. When we provide these services, we are responsible for ensuring that we give accurate information about the education, training, and supervision, including information on content, goals and objectives, fees and stipends, and requirements. Our syllabi should be accurate and reflect current knowledge and skills, particularly what is needed to meet credentialing requirements or other specific educational goals. Any changes made for educational purposes are communicated to the students quickly and in such a way as to allow them to complete the course requirements. In addition, we should have a timely and specific process for providing feedback to our students and supervisees so that they have a good understanding of their strengths and areas of weakness.

This ethical guideline also addresses the rights of academic programs in relation to students' personal history and development. When students are required to participate in individual or group therapy, they are allowed to select therapists who are unaffiliated with their academic program and who will not be in a position of grading or judging their academic abilities. In addition, students or supervisees should not be required to disclose personal information to their instructors unless that requirement has been stated before the beginning of the learning experience or is needed to evaluate for special assistance those students who may pose a threat to others or who are not competently performing their professional activities. Finally, the code of ethics clearly states that mental health professionals do not engage in sexual relationships with students or supervisees over whom they "have or are likely to have evaluative authority" (APA, 2002, p. 10).

Category 8: Research and Publication This group of ethical guidelines relates primarily to mental health professionals engaged in research and writing for publication and also has relevance to students who are writing dissertations or participating in faculty research. Overall, we are urged to provide accurate information about our research to institutional review boards, participants, and the audience for our publications and presentations. Deception is discouraged in research studies, unless justified by the significance of the study, and then careful protection of participants and rapid debriefing is imperative. When credit is offered to students for participation in research studies, alternatives must also be made available to them.

Researchers studying animal behavior are expected to exert great care in their work. They should ensure that all animals involved in research receive "humane care" (APA, 2002, p. 12).

When research is presented, it must be accurate and its authorship must correctly reflect the relative contributions of those involved. Students are almost always listed as the principal author of articles based on their dissertation. Faculty collaborating with students on other research projects should discuss publication credit with the students early in the process. Needless to say, plagiarism is unacceptable, as is presenting previously published work as original data. To advance research in our field, we share our data with other qualified professionals so that they can expand the knowledge base of our profession. Those who serve as reviewers for journals, funding agencies, or other organizations respect and protect the confidentiality of the authors and do not inappropriately share information about the research studies they have reviewed.

Category 9: Assessment When planning and conducting an assessment, mental health professionals rely primarily on current and appropriate instruments that have demonstrated reliability and validity, and they use those instruments with the population and according to the procedures described in the test manuals. When instruments that have not yet been well supported are used, or when variations in procedures are made, the test report includes this information and limitations are discussed. Informed consent should be obtained from people before administering tests or other assessment procedures. Assessment results are generally shared with and clearly explained to people who have been assessed, as well as with others whom clients have authorized to receive that information. However, test data can be withheld from clients or others to prevent harm or misuse. We are expected to maintain test security. For those who develop tests and assessment procedures, appropriate scientific and other procedures should be followed.

An important aspect of this ethical guideline is the attention it pays to people who may have special needs or whose first language may not be that of the inventory that is used. This guideline speaks to the appropriate use of interpreters and advises that "assessment methods that are appropriate to an individual's language preference and competence" be used (APA, 2002, p. 13).

Category 10: Therapy When we engage in a therapeutic relationship with another person, informed consent is again essential. The processes of clarifying roles and preventing conflicts are addressed repeatedly in this guideline, and they are especially important when conducting couples therapy, family therapy, and group therapy. If you anticipate the possibility of a role conflict, such as counseling a couple who then want you to testify on each of their behalf's in a custody dispute, you should take steps to avoid such conflicts. This guideline clearly states that we do not engage in sexual intimacies with current clients or their relatives or significant others, nor do we accept as clients people with whom we have previously had sexual intimacies. The APA ethics code requires that psychologists refrain from sexual intimacies with former clients for at least 2 years after treatment has terminated and then only under exceptional circumstances, taking steps to ensure that the former client will not be harmed by the experience. Ethical guidelines of the mental health professions differ on this provision, with some prohibiting all sexual intimacy with former clients. We must be familiar with the guidelines for our own profession and keep in mind that, if in doubt, avoiding a potentially harmful and unethical situation is probably the wisest choice. Finally, the ethics code advises care and preparation when therapy is terminated and encourages us to end treatment when the client is no longer benefiting or is even being harmed by the service. We also may terminate treatment when we feel that continuing the relationship would endanger us.

Ethical Decision Making

Even though all of the mental health professions have ethical codes and guidelines, making ethical decisions about real-life situations often is difficult. The following steps will help you make sound decisions (Seligman, 2004):

1. Review the ethical guidelines for your profession regularly to be sure they are fresh in your mind.

Ethical dilemmas can present mental health professionals with difficult decisions

2. When confronted with an ethical dilemma, obtain a full and clear understanding of the situation.
3. Consult the ethical guidelines that have particular relevance to the situation. If your course of action is still unclear, generate alternatives that are available to you and develop a list of the potential drawbacks and benefits of each alternative.
4. If your course of action is still unclear, consult with a trusted colleague or representative of your professional association as to the best option. Decide on the most ethical option and implement your decision.
5. Use this as a learning experience to guide you in making future decisions. The Learning Opportunities section at the end of this chapter offers you the opportunity to consider some challenging ethical situations. These vignettes then enable you to apply what you have learned about ethical guidelines and standards for mental health professionals.

UNDERSTANDING NORMAL AND ABNORMAL HUMAN DEVELOPMENT

Knowledge and understanding of the ethical standards of our profession is only one of the important bodies of knowledge that is important to all mental health professionals. Another is knowledge of normal and abnormal human development. Having a sound grasp of healthy and normal development gives clinicians a perspective from which to view their clients as well as a baseline for identifying when a person's development seems to diverge from what is typical and expected for someone of that person's age group, gender, and background. This is especially important for clinicians who focus their work on children. Early identification and treatment of developmental delays usually result in better outcomes.

However, we should also be knowledgeable about developmental stages and patterns throughout the life span so that we can distinguish, for example, the behaviors reflecting healthy adolescent individuation and separation from those that are symptoms of oppositional or conduct disordered behavior. Similarly, when working with young adults, we need to be able to distinguish age-appropriate efforts at self-discovery, exploration of options, and actualization of one's potential from overinvolvement in romantic relationships and avoidance of commitments and choices. During middle adulthood, too, stages of development provide milestones that help us distinguish healthy and productive relationships and careers from those that reflect emotional barriers and difficulties. Sometimes neglected but also very important is an understanding of development during the later years. Physical difficulties, cognitive deficits, side effects of medication, social isolation and loss, and depression and other emotional disorders often combine to cause impairment, with their intertwining making it difficult to identify both cause and effective treatment for symptoms. Having a clear understanding of normal aging can help clinicians both identify older clients' barriers to effective functioning and take the lead in helping those clients to get the help they need.

Perspectives on Healthy Development

Becoming knowledgeable about healthy and normal human development does not mean that we expect our clients to proceed inflexibly through a series of predictable stages, with little room for individual variation. On the contrary, we should recognize that an essential part of healthy development is exploring our world, expanding our self-awareness, and finding the best way for each of us to actualize our potentials. Our assessment of people's development must allow for individual differences and should take a broad perspective of development that considers a multitude of factors. More will be said on this later in this chapter in the section on diversity and multicultural competence.

Understanding and promoting healthy emotional development is consistent with the current thrust of the mental health professions toward an emphasis on identification and nurturance of people's strengths. Clinicians have embraced the empowering perspective of positive psychology, stemming from the work of Martin Seligman (1999), and attend to emotional intelligence, resiliency, and self-awareness in their work. Clinicians are increasingly de-emphasizing pathology and seeking ways to identify and enhance the qualities that make each of us special and gifted in our own way.

Abnormal Development

Just as mental health professionals need to be knowledgeable about healthy development, so do we also need to be knowledgeable about abnormal psychology and the range of mental disorders. The primary resource on abnormal development is the *Diagnostic and Statistical Manual of Mental Disorders,* Fourth Edition, Text

Revision (*DSM-IV-TR;* APA, 2000). Although published by the American Psychiatric Association, the *DSM* is used by all the mental health professions and provides a common language as well as accepted criteria for defining 17 broad categories of mental disorders, including personality disorders; mood disorders; anxiety disorders; disorders usually first diagnosed in infancy, childhood, or adolescence; and many others.

Two important reasons underlie the need for mental health professionals to be skilled at diagnosis of mental disorders. The most important one is enabling us to provide the best possible help to our clients. Even before beginning your training as a clinician, you could probably recognize the most common symptoms of mental disorders: depression and anxiety. However, are you skilled enough to distinguish between a major depressive disorder and a bipolar disorder or a panic disorder and posttraumatic stress disorder? And are you conversant enough with the criteria for the 10 personality disorders that you can determine whether such a disorder accompanies a person's complaints of an eating disorder or a substance use disorder? These are the sort of challenging diagnostic questions that arise for practicing clinicians. Each of the disorders just mentioned calls for a somewhat different treatment approach. Making an accurate diagnosis, then, can help us choose the treatment approach and strategies that are most likely to be effective, determine whether a referral for a medication evaluation is indicated, and facilitate our efforts to identify familial, environmental, and other factors that can have an impact on the course of the disorder. Although a detailed discussion of the *DSM* is beyond the scope of this book, readers are referred to other books, including *Diagnosis and Treatment Planning in Counseling* (Seligman, 2004) and *Selecting Effective Treatments* (Seligman & Reichenberg, 2007) as well as the *DSM* itself for information on the diagnosis of mental disorders.

A second reason for learning about abnormal psychology and the diagnosis of mental disorders stems from the increasing need for clinicians to be accountable for what they do and to document and justify their work. Accepted practice today requires that clinicians in mental health settings make a diagnosis for each of their clients and then develop a treatment plan that is likely to be effective in treating that diagnosis. In addition, nearly all managed care organizations and health insurance companies require a diagnosis, and often a treatment plan, before they will pay for the clinician's services. Consequently, in order for many clients to receive the help they need and to receive reimbursement for the costs of their therapy, clinicians must provide a diagnosis and treatment plan for those clients.

This requirement may seem burdensome to clinicians and may seem like it is cutting into valuable time that we could better use providing direct services to our clients. Although that is sometimes the case, having a written diagnosis and treatment plan encourages us to think about the most effective way to help our clients, facilitates transfer of clients from one clinician to another, and offers clinicians some protection if they are sued for malpractice.

Clinicians who are employed in academic or career counseling settings or who primarily provide social services, such as housing or aid to dependent children, generally are not required to document diagnoses of mental disorders. However, clinicians in those settings, too, should be familiar with the *DSM* and the major mental disorders so that they know when to make a referral for mental health services and so that they can have a better understanding of any of their clients who do have mental disorders.

THEORIES OF COUNSELING AND PSYCHOTHERAPY

Chapter 1 provided some information on theories of counseling and psychotherapy and indicated that these theories could be divided into the following four broad categories based on their primary focus:

- **Background.** Sigmund Freud/psychoanalysis, Alfred Adler/individual psychology, Carl Jung/analytical psychology, ego psychology, object relations theorists, self psychology, brief psychodynamic therapy
- **Emotion.** Carl Rogers/person-centered counseling, existential therapy, Gestalt therapy, narrative therapy, constructivist therapy, feminist therapy, and others
- **Thoughts.** Aaron Beck/cognitive therapy, Albert Ellis/rational emotive behavior therapy, and others
- **Actions.** Behavior therapy, cognitive-behavioral therapy, reality therapy, solution-focused brief therapy, and others

These four categories, represented by the acronym BETA (background, emotions, thoughts, actions), provide a convenient way to organize and remember the primary treatment approaches. However, keep in mind that treatment approaches have much in common, and nearly all will pay some attention to all four elements of the BETA model.

Clinicians are not expected to have expertise in all of these treatment approaches. Rather, most clinicians have some knowledge of a broad range of theories of counseling and psychotherapy, along with expertise in a few of these approaches. Many factors enter into the choices we make of our preferred treatment approaches, including the models established by our professors, supervisors, and colleagues; the clinical settings and clients of interest to us; and our personal style, background, and beliefs. Typically, as we progress through our career, our clinical orientation shifts to reflect growth and changes in our interest and skills.

In the past, clinicians were more likely than they are now to select one specific treatment orientation as their preference and to present themselves as, for example, an Adlerian therapist or a psychoanalyst or a cognitive-behavioral therapist. Gradually, however, most clinicians have shifted toward a preference for a more eclectic or integrative treatment approach, and today that is how they describe their primary theoretical orientation. However, this should not simply mean that clinicians pull random strategies from a grab-bag. Rather, they should have a logic or system to their theoretical orientation, even if it reflects an amalgam of two or more treatment approaches. The transtheoretical model of Prochaska, DiClemente, and Norcross (Prochaska & Norcross, 2003) provides an appealing and well-conceived approach to integrative psychotherapy, although it is still in a formative stage.

Other useful approaches include Arnold Lazarus's multimodal therapy and developmental counseling and therapy originated by Allen Ivey and his colleagues.

Sound Theoretical Approaches

Although clinicians today have considerable latitude in their ability to combine and mesh treatment approaches, having a clear vision of how we believe we can best help people is an essential attribute of our professional role. A sound theory of counseling and psychotherapy has much to offer clinicians. It typically encompasses a picture of healthy development, an explanation of what causes psychological difficulties, and a cohesive idea of how clinicians can collaborate with their clients to ameliorate those difficulties. It usually includes a variety of treatment strategies that can be adapted to the needs and goals of the individual person or problem. It gives clinicians a road map that they can follow—albeit taking thoughtful detours as needed. Finally, it affords a way for clinicians to evaluate the outcomes of their work and, if they are not helping a person to grow and change in rewarding ways, they can review their work with that person and make changes in the overall treatment approach, as well as the intervention strategies, so that treatment is more likely to be successful. The strategies in this book are organized according to the BETA format previously presented. As you progress through the chapters in this book, think about which of the four elements of this format are most appealing to you, fit best with your natural style of helping, and seem most likely to benefit the sorts of clients and problems that interest you. That should provide you with information that will be useful to you as you seek a clearer picture of your own preferred theoretical orientation.

MULTICULTURAL UNDERSTANDING AND COMPETENCE

Clinicians today are expected to view their clients and their work through a multicultural lens, to think of people in their contexts and environments, and to identify, prize, and nurture diversity. The term *multicultural* is a broad one and refers not only to culture but also to such variables as gender, age, abilities, religious and spiritual beliefs, family and community background, and context. According to Sue (1998), cultural competence is "the belief that people should not only appreciate and recognize other cultural groups but also be able to work effectively with them" (p. 440).

The mental health professions have paid considerable attention to the importance of multiculturalism and diversity since at least the early 1980s. Each of the professions has taken its own route to promoting awareness and appreciation of diversity, but all of the mental health professions seem in agreement that clinicians now need to be cognizant of the impact that multicultural variables have on people, their strengths and difficulties, and their responses to counseling and psychotherapy. Multicultural similarities and differences, particularly those between client and clinician, also need to be considered for clinicians to promote a positive therapeutic alliance and understand their clients as fully as possible.

Guidelines for Multicultural Competence

Arredondo and her colleagues have taken the lead in identifying and describing multicultural competencies (Arredondo, 2003; Arredondo et al., 1996). They identify three dimensions of human diversity that mental health professionals should consider:

Dimension A: age, culture, ethnicity, gender, language, physical ability, race, sexual orientation, social class

Dimension B: education, partner status, current and previous geographic location, military experience, occupation and work history, income, religious and spiritual beliefs, citizenship status, leisure activities and interests

Dimension C: background and historical context.

According to therapists and theoreticians who promote the importance of multicultural competencies, clinicians should assess clients according to all of these dimensions and should use that information to inform their work with them. This means that clinicians should attempt the following:

- Develop their awareness of their own reactions to various types of diversity.
- Seek to understand their clients (as well as themselves and their colleagues) from a holistic perspective.
- Help their clients become aware of their own diverse characteristics, particularly how those features of themselves and their backgrounds have enriched and strengthened them and exposed them to experiences of prejudice and oppression.

It is important for counselors to view clients through a multicultural lens

- Take steps to prevent their clients and others from being discriminated against and disenfranchised because of their multicultural characteristics while helping them to recognize and build on the strengths they have gained from their culture, their age, their religion, and other multicultural aspects of themselves and their lives.

Application of a Multicultural Perspective

The following is a brief description of a boy named Lu. As you read this description, list the multicultural variables under Dimensions A, B, and C that would be important to consider as you get to know and understand Lu.

Lu is a 12-year-old boy who was brought to treatment by his parents. His father is Caucasian American and his mother is Japanese. Lu is the older of two children; his 5-year-old sister is outgoing, athletic, and lively. Lu's parents both have professional careers but seem committed to each other and to their family. The family lives in San Francisco. Lu has been having difficulty at school. He has been diagnosed with a motor deficit disorder, which causes him to have poor coordination and to have great difficulty performing well at most physical activities. Because of this, the other children tease him and avoid including him in many of their activities. Lu has also been diagnosed with a learning disorder although his intelligence is above average. Although usually well behaved, he has recently been acting out and punched a boy who called him names. Lu is receiving help with his learning disorder and is working closely with his school counselor on his behavioral concerns. Lu is very interested in Buddhism but has not been brought up to have clear religious beliefs.

Dimension A: _____

_____

Dimension B: _____

_____

Dimension C: _____

_____

After you complete this exercise, reflect on what you learned from this scenario. Were you surprised at how many multicultural variables potentially had an impact on Lu? Did you view Lu differently than you would have if you have not been focusing on the multicultural variables? You can probably see that, although this is only one of many ways to understand people, taking a multicultural perspective can offer new ideas and insights.

Controversy Surrounding Multicultural Competencies

You may be surprised to know that questions have been raised about the value of multicultural competencies. Some prominent writers in mental health, including

Patterson (2004) and Weinrach and Thomas (2004), suggest that emphasis on these competencies is counterproductive and promotes the very problems the competencies are intended to alleviate. For example, Weinrach and Thomas (p. 81) suggest that attention to diversity promotes, rather than reduces, emphasis on people's race and ethnicity. In addition, they suggest that an emphasis on multicultural competencies politicizes the mental health professions, is unlikely to reduce discrimination, and can persuade clinicians that culture and race are critical issues for all clients when, in fact, that may not be the case. Weinrach and Thomas suggest that clinicians are more likely to think in terms of classifications, problems, and deficits when they are consciously trying to apply multicultural competencies.

Theorists who are critical or questioning of the multicultural competencies do not suggest that clinicians ignore background, race, culture, and other aspects of diversity. Instead, they believe that clinicians who are skilled in their work will attend to diversity just as they attend to all important aspects of clients and their presentation and will advocate an integration of the areas of cultural competence and overall proficiency in clinical skills (Goh, 2005; Patterson, 2004). As Goh states, "Cultural competence and expertise in mental health counseling are conceptually similar and intertwined" (p. 72). He notes that several studies have found the two competencies to be highly correlated and potentially inextricable. Skilled and ethical clinicians have expertise in both general treatment skills and the ability to address multicultural issues through that treatment. In addition, they recognize that, regardless of people's backgrounds, the establishment of a sound therapeutic alliance, the communication of empathy and the other core conditions discussed later in this book, and the attention to similarities among people are essential and universal skills of the effective clinician (Patterson, 2004).

Resolving the Controversy

This controversy may raise questions, and even discomfort, for some of you. The learning opportunities at the end of this chapter afford you the chance to further explore your thoughts about the relationship between multicultural counseling competencies and clinical skills. Whatever your opinions are about this controversy, keep in mind that clinicians should attend to those issues that are important in shaping their clients' lives and should understand their views of the world. Clinicians need to honor clients' reasons for seeking help, and they need to take a strength-based approach to treatment that promotes self-esteem and empowerment while enabling people to make the choices and use the coping skills that will enable them to create and enjoy rewarding lives. In addition, clinicians need to be aware of their own cultural background, in the broadest sense, and the impact it has had on them. They should approach all clients with openness, acceptance, and interest, eager to listen to them and learn about their lives and experiences. Clinicians must guard against judging and stereotyping others, imposing their values on others, and allowing their biases to color the ways they interact with clients and the goals they have for them. Whatever view you take of the importance of specific multicultural competencies, emphasizing the needs of the client, knowing yourself as well as your clients, appreciating diversity and differences, and manifesting the core conditions of empathy, caring, and respect will enable you to demonstrate both multicultural sensitivity and effective clinical skills.

SOCIAL JUSTICE AND ADVOCACY

The emphasis on expanding multicultural awareness and competence seems linked to a parallel growth and interest among the mental health professions in social justice and advocacy. According to Arredondo and Perez (2003), "social justice has always been the core of the multicultural competency movement . . ." (p. 284). Once clinicians became aware of and sensitized to the impact of oppression, social injustice, and disenfranchisement, many recognized that these problems needed to be addressed not only in individual, family, and group counseling, but also in a way that attacked the roots of the problem and tried to effect change at many levels.

Social Justice and Positive Psychology

The emphasis on social justice also is compatible with and grows out of the current emphasis in the mental health professions on positive psychology and strength-based treatment. The thrust of many social justice programs is the empowerment of people who have been disenfranchised, helping them to build on their individual and community strengths and acquire the skills, tools, awareness, voice, and influence they need to both obtain necessary help and services and maximize their ability to help themselves and each other.

Understanding Social Justice and Advocacy

Kiselica and Robinson (2001) describe the emphasis on social justice as "a growing movement to expand the practice of counseling from its traditional focus on the intrapsychic concerns of clients to a broader focus on the many extrapsychic forces that adversely affect the emotional and physical well-being of people. This movement is commonly known as 'advocacy counseling,' 'social action,' and 'social justice' approaches to counseling and psychotherapy" (p. 387). According to Lopez-Baez (2005), "Social justice seeks a process of allowing access to power and influence for all. The goal is to lessen the existing differences of access to power and wealth between individuals. There are those who are systematically excluded from such access due to circumstances beyond their control. They require assistance!" (p. 2). In the book *Counseling for Social Justice*, Lee and others (2007) elaborate on this movement. They discuss the motivations and skills needed for clinicians to take on the important roles of social change agents, advocates for their profession and for underserved populations, and leaders in the promotion of social justice. Social justice has been an integral part of the profession of social work since its inception, and many people in the other mental health professions have long had social justice and advocacy as part of their professional goals and endeavors. What is new is not the involvement of mental health professionals in promoting social justice and certainly not the need for social justice and social advocacy. What is new is the perception that all mental health professionals have an ethical obligation to help humanity by becoming advocates for social justice and taking on proactive and leadership roles.

Approaches to Social Justice and Advocacy

Social advocacy takes many forms (Kiselica, 2004; Lewis & Bradley, 1999). Some ways to promote social justice are as follows:

- Lobby for improved policies related to prevention of emotional difficulties and provision of mental health treatment.
- Write or call government officials to persuade them of the need to initiate or maintain important social and mental health services.
- Facilitate consciousness raising and self-awareness to help people become more aware of both the threats to their power and ways they can use their voices, skills, and strengths to effectively take care of themselves and others.
- Model and share our own power; serving as a mentor is one powerful way to do this.
- Initiate or participate in development of a program designed to reduce inequity and develop strengths and resources in an underserved group.
- Promote interdisciplinary collaboration such as community and university or business and social service agency.
- Serve communities through participation in programs designed to promote leadership, mobilize strengths, develop community cohesiveness, and teach skills that will promote economic self-sufficiency.
- Advocate for universities to integrate social justice work into university curricula and appropriately recognize and reward scholarship that serves communities.
- Advocate for clients, students, and others who are unable to be their own advocates.
- Accept and appreciate both traditional and nontraditional approaches to helping.
- Challenge any unjust practices and systems.

Examples of Social Justice Initiatives

Social advocacy and promotion of social justice can occur in many venues and many levels, ranging from the universal to the individual. The following is a sampling of advocacy activities of mental health professionals described in the recent literature:

- *Developing school-based programs to promote school success for all students.* Examples include the Ecological Developmental Cognitive Framework to expand "understanding of how oppression affects the development of youth from low-income and diverse backgrounds" and the Achieving Success Identity Pathways, offering curriculum guidelines to "help youth become engaged in their own academic success, to improve teacher–student relationships, and to manage oppressive messages and influences in youth's lives" (Howard & Solberg, 2006, p. 286).

- *Intervening on the national government level* to raise awareness of employment discrimination against people who are single and urging legislation to protect the rights of this group (O'Ryan & Whewell, 2005).

- *Writing a booklet* with accurate information on homosexuality, intended for use in schools and other settings, with the primary goal of helping gay and lesbian students gain greater acceptance and better treatment and feel more motivated and valued (Olsen & Riebli, 2005).

- *Presenting educational programs and lectures.* Columbia University's School of Social Work served as a model when it provided information to the public on being LGBT (lesbian, gay, bisexual, transgendered) in the workplace.

- *Establishing a program* to assist women who have experienced domestic violence and sexual assault (Vargas, 2004). One program, Women Escaping a Violent Environment, is a multiservice program that offers emergency shelter for women and children, sexual assault and domestic violence assault teams, legal services, and counseling.

- *Integrating social justice into university curricula.* Faculty at George Mason University, under the leadership of Fred Bemak and Rita Chi-Ying Chung (2005), redesigned the counselor education program. Leadership, social change, advocacy, and social justice became a central mission of the program, equipping students to become agents of social change. One way that Bemak and Chung demonstrated their commitment to social justice was to take a group of students to Mississippi to assist people in need of help because of Hurricane Katrina. Referring to themselves as Counselors Without Borders, the 14 students first received training on skills needed for disaster counseling and then met with approximately 600 clients. Bemak and Chung are hoping to use this experience as a model for other counselors to provide services to people in need.

- *Engaging professional associations in advocacy for meaningful goals.* Advocacy by the American Psychological Association succeeded in preventing significant cuts in Medicare payments.

- *Promoting social justice at the international level.* Lawrence Gerstein, counselor-educator, initiated an international multifaceted campaign to help the people of Tibet, particularly to raise awareness of and reduce the human rights violations in Tibet. His program included development of educational and counseling services for Tibetan refugees, peaceful protest walks, dissemination of information via the media and the Internet, lobbying and letter-writing initiatives, promoting and mentoring school-based chapters of Students for a Free Tibet, and taking other powerful steps to promote the welfare of the people of Tibet (Kiselica & Robinson, 2001).

This list of social justice and advocacy endeavors probably is sufficiently lengthy and varied to provide a sense of the scope and importance of these efforts.

Skills Needed for Promoting Social Justice

Success in social justice requires the following skills:

- Awareness of oneself and one's values
- Concern about a societal issue
- Commitment to make a difference
- Effective communication and counseling skills, particularly multicultural sensitivity
- Collaboration skills
- Ability to access and share power in promoting the strengths and resources of others
- Capacity to set clear and realistic goals, develop a viable plan, and identify and obtain needed resources
- Accountability and assessment skills to determine progress and change the plan if needed

Rewards of Promoting Social Justice

Making a difference by acting as a social change agent can be a very rewarding role. My own advocacy efforts have focused on helping people cope with chronic and life-threatening illnesses. I have sought to effect change and awareness through my writing, talks I have given at hospitals and treatment organizations, training of other professionals to help people cope with serious illnesses, my role on the advisory board of Y-ME (a program to help people cope with breast cancer), my meetings with support groups, and my counseling of people coping with chronic and life-threatening illnesses.

Mental health professionals today have social advocacy as an expected and essential aspect of their professional role. I encourage you to think about what issues in our society are most disturbing to you, perhaps because they have affected you and your loved ones directly or because they conflict so strongly with the values you hold and the life you want to lead. Invest yourself in making a social change and incorporate that commitment into your life, both for your own betterment and for that of our society.

We have reviewed several overriding guidelines, perspectives, and endeavors that are important in today's mental health professions. Another of these is the emphasis on the mind–body–spirit connection. Most clinicians seem to advocate perceiving people holistically. Modern mental health professionals recognize that people are an integration of three important areas (Myers & Sweeney, 2005):

- *The mind,* including our thoughts, perceptions, choices, goals, creativity, cognitive functioning, multicultural identity, organization of our lives, distribution of our time
- *The body,* including physical attributes, appearance, health, nutrition, exercise, self-care and stress management, work and leisure activities, medical difficulties, and medical treatment
- *The spirit,* including our religious and spiritual beliefs, our sense of purpose and direction, our perception of our place in and connection with the universe, the love we feel for others, and our belief in a higher power, whether that involves attending a place of worship and embracing the God of a specific religion or feeling a sense of transcendence through nature or in another way

Example of Mind–Body–Spirit Integration

The following example illustrates the integration of the mind, body, and spirit in both a client's life and the treatment that helps to alleviate his difficulties:

> Don is a 52-year–old, recently divorced Caucasian male. He has two grown children and a full-time job as a business executive. His father died of a heart attack at age 57. Don's mother is still alive but has been incapacitated by heart disease for many years. Don's older brother recently had heart bypass surgery. Don has been diagnosed with high blood pressure, high cholesterol, and atherosclerosis (plaque in his arteries). His physician recommended several medications and advised Don that, in light of his family history and medical risks, he needed to begin an aggressive program of diet and exercise, designed to help him lose 25 pounds and establish an exercise routine. However, Don has not followed these recommendations and believes he will inevitably follow his father's pattern and die of a heart attack when he is in his 50s.
>
> Don describes himself as agnostic. Although he was raised as a Protestant and attended church regularly with his family when he was a child and, again, when his children were young, he has little current interest in formal religion and thinks of it as incompatible with his current beliefs and as having little to offer him.

When we think about Don and his current situation, the mind, the body, and the spirit are clearly intertwined and afford him resources and strengths while, at the same time, causing him difficulties. A picture of the mind, body, and spirit issues related to Don's concerns and his treatment might look like the following:

- *Mind:* Don is an intelligent man who views his business knowledge and financial skills as his greatest strengths. At the same time, he has a dis-

Most clinicians view individuals holistically, as a combination of mind, body, and spirit

torted cognition: the belief that he will inevitably follow in his father's footsteps and die at a relatively young age. This belief may become a self-fulfilling prophecy in that it is contributing to Don's poor self-care and his sense of hopelessness. In addition, the end of his marriage and his perception that his children do not need him anymore now that they are adults have further exacerbated his discouragement and left him without a purpose in life.

- *Body:* Don has many medical concerns, some of them very serious. His atherosclerosis, probably reflecting a genetic propensity toward heart disease in his family, is the most serious. However, because of his pessimistic and fatalistic attitude, Don is not taking good care of his physical health; improvement is needed in his compliance with recommended medical treatment as well as in his nutrition and exercise. Don also is unlikely to be dealing well with stress and this may exacerbate his physical concerns. Don probably also has a negative perception of his body and may mistrust both his own body and the medical system because of his father's early death and the impact of heart disease on his family. On the other hand, Don's physicians are optimistic that, with some improved self-care, Don may be able to reverse or at least stabilize his symptoms. In other areas, especially work, Don is hard working and motivated to succeed; he spends long hours at his office and has been successful in his profession. Some of those qualities may be transferable to Don's efforts at self-care.

- *Spirit:* Don is a practical man who has not seen the value of religion in his life, although he does have knowledge of and experience with formal religion. Right now, he is lonely, has little social interaction, and few leisure activities and is pessimistic about his future. However, he has had enough contact with formal religion to see that it offers the potential of helping him in many areas of his life. The following preliminary treatment plan for helping Don acknowledges his strengths and difficulties in all three areas (mind, body, and spirit) and incorporates strategies from all three areas. Most of these strategies are explained in greater detail in subsequent chapters of this book.

- *Mind:*   Strength-based treatment is important in working with Don. He takes pride in his intellect, his education, his career success, and his occupational skills, including his grasp of research, his clarity of thought, and his ability to make sound decisions. These can all be incorporated into cognitive therapy designed to help Don become more aware of and evaluate his thoughts, ideally modifying those that are unhelpful to him. Engaging Don in a discussion of the importance of meaning and purpose in people's lives might appeal to his curious mind and start him on a path of bringing greater fulfillment into his life.

- *Body:*   Once he has modified some of his distorted cognitions and realizes that his life could evolve differently from that of his father, Don might be more willing to follow medical recommendations and improve his nutrition and exercise. Taking more control of his life seems consistent with Don's independent nature and, because he typically follows through on his work commitments, his clinician can help Don set realistic goals for behavioral change with the expectation that Don will probably follow through on any commitments he makes to behavioral change. Progress in this area of Don's life should enhance Don's self-esteem, improve his mood, and help him move forward in his efforts to make behavioral changes and improve his physical health.

- *Spirit:*   Although Don has previously gotten little benefit from religion and has a narrow and fairly negative view of religion, he is comfortable in formal religious settings. Drawing on his knowledge of research as well as his practical and curious nature may help to engage him more productively in religious and spiritual activities. Reading about the meaning and value that spirituality has for others may raise his awareness of ways he might benefit from nurturing this aspect of his life. Also, visiting various places of worship, especially those that offer considerable flexibility and encouragement for people to find their own higher power and sense of spirituality, may appeal to Don. In addition, emphasis on the social and interpersonal aspects of religious institutions may enhance their appeal for Don. He wants to meet other people in his age group, especially those dealing with divorce, but is apprehensive about venues such as Internet dating and is uneasy about his new role as a single person. A spiritual setting that offers opportunities for socialization may provide a safe setting for Don to meet others with similar goals and concerns. This brief vignette illustrates how much rich and useful information can be gleaned from an exploration of the integration of the mind, the body, and the spirit, and how these three areas manifest themselves in a given person. The Learning Opportunities section at the end of this chapter offers you an opportunity to think further about the mind–body–spirit connection.

OTHER AREAS OF KNOWLEDGE AND COMPETENCE

The areas discussed so far in this chapter include ethical issues, normal and abnormal human development, theories of counseling and psychotherapy, diversity and multicultural competencies, social justice and advocacy, and the holistic mind–body–spirit perspective. These areas underlie all of the helping professions and give mental health professionals a solid foundation and a common perspective on ways to understand and help people.

Many other important areas of learning shape the mental health professional and enable psychologists, counselors, and social workers to provide effective help to a broad range of people and problems and also to develop their own areas of expertise. The following list includes many of these additional areas of learning:

- *History of and orientation to one's profession.* Although the content of this area of learning will, of course, vary depending on the particular profession being studied, the training of mental health professionals almost always involves learning about the development of their profession and its current status.
- *Group dynamics, counseling, and psychotherapy.*
- *Family dynamics, counseling, and psychotherapy.*
- *Assessment.* This areas includes knowledge of intake interviews and both standardized and nonstandardized methods of gathering information about people and measuring change. The social work profession makes far greater use of such subjective tools as exploration of the person-in-the-environment than it does of tests and inventories. However, both counseling and psychology rely heavily on the use of valid and reliable inventories to assess intelligence, abilities, interests, values, and personality. In recent years, the use of brief tools such as the Beck Depression Inventory has become widespread as a way of tracking client progress and maximizing the effectiveness of treatment plans.
- *Career, educational, and lifestyle development.* This is another area that typically receives less emphasis and attention in programs to train social workers than it does in training programs for psychologists and counselors. However, all of the mental health professions pay some attention to these areas of development, and counseling and psychology, which have their roots in vocational psychology and career counseling, typically place considerable emphasis on training clinicians to understand and promote healthy career, educational, and lifestyle development.
- *Research, supervision, and evaluation.* Again, emphasis on these areas of learning varies among training programs. Doctoral programs in all the mental health professions typically pay more attention to these skills, although learning to understand and perhaps conduct research also is incorporated into the learning process at the master's level.
- *Areas of specialization.* Graduate and postgraduate training offers mental health professionals the opportunity to focus their learning, develop expertise in one or two areas of their profession, and specialize in working in

specific settings or with particular client populations. The list of possible specializations is lengthy; the following three represent some of the most popular choices:

- *Services:* private practice, social justice/social welfare, career and educational counseling, family therapy, coaching, consultation, rehabilitation, neurological or other assessment, pastoral/spiritual counseling, employee assistance counseling, conflict resolution and mediation, critical incident stress debriefing.
- *Client populations:* children, adolescents, older people, people with substance use problems, people with mood and/or anxiety disorders, people with severe and chronic mental disorders, people in prison or other forensic settings, people with chronic or life-threatening illnesses, people with dissociative identity disorders, people with concerns about anger management and impulse control, people with behavioral difficulties such as smoking or dysfunctional eating, people with acculturation issues or those from a particular cultural or ethnic background, people in the military, people who have experienced abuse and other traumas.
- *Theoretical orientations:* cognitive-behavioral therapy, psychodynamic therapy, psychoanalysis, solution-focused brief therapy, existential therapy, eye movement desensitization and reprocessing, transpersonal and Asian-influenced therapies, reality therapy, and others.
- *Location:* Specializations also can be defined by the location in which we are employed. Mental health professionals may prepare themselves to work in a broad range of settings including psychiatric and medical hospitals, community mental health centers, group or individual private practice, social welfare agencies, schools, colleges, nursing and other residential facilities, prisons, churches, and other agencies that focus on the needs of a specific client group.

As you progress through the information and exercises in this book, and as you continue the formal and informal education in your field, you will develop a clearer idea of the sort of professional role that is right for you. The preceding list of popular areas of specialization offers you an idea of the many options available to you. Learn about new and interesting opportunities from your peers, supervisors, and teachers, and keep an open mind about your options. Maintaining such an attitude as you continue your learning will help you benefit both personally and professionally from that process.

LEARNING OPPORTUNITIES

This chapter has provided information on the following areas: ethical standards and guidelines, human development, theories of counseling and psychotherapy, multicultural understanding and competence, social justice and advocacy, the mind–body–spirit integration, and other important areas of learning and specialization.

The learning opportunities presented here include written exercises, discussion questions, and personal journal questions. This chapter, unlike Chapters 3 through 10, does not include either a practice group exercise or an accompanying Assessment of Progress form because this chapter focuses on the foundation needed to build effective skills rather than the skills themselves.

Written Exercises

1. You have clear evidence that a colleague in the school or agency or practice where you are employed is acting in unethical ways toward her clients. What are the steps you would take to address this situation? What questions or areas of discomfort does this process raise for you?

2. Although you may have only a limited understanding of theories of counseling and psychotherapy at this point, you have probably already begun to identify a style of helping that is most comfortable for you. This may well change as you gain knowledge and experience. However, describe what you currently believe to be your preferred style of helping others. Indicate whether you gravitate toward an approach that emphasizes background, emotions, thoughts, or actions and, if possible, the specific treatment approach and strategies you find particularly appealing and likely to be effective. Also, write briefly about what seems to have led you to these choices.

3. Today's clinicians are expected to become involved in social justice and advocacy activities. When you entered this profession, did you anticipate that would be a part of your role? How do you feel about the current mandate for clinicians to participate actively in social justice and advocacy activities? Do you believe that this waters down or enhances the clinical role of those in your field? How do you believe that you will channel your social justice and advocacy efforts?

4. Most clinicians acknowledge the importance of taking a holistic perspective of clients and emphasizing the integration of the mind, body, and spirit. What does this really mean and how should clinicians implement these concepts in their work?

Discussion Questions

1. What do you see as the benefits to the ethical guidelines and standards for your profession? What possible drawbacks do you see to these? What should mental health professionals do in their own work to maximize the benefits and minimize the drawbacks of the ethical standards and guidelines?

2. You have had three therapy sessions with a client before you discover that the client is engaged in a romantic relationship with one of your adult children. By now, you have learned that the client uses illegal drugs and is involved in at least two other intimate relationships. What are your options in this situation? What seems like the most ethical choice for you? Are you

experiencing conflicts between your heart and your head, between what you want to do and what you know is the most ethical choice? If so, how will you resolve these conflicts? (If this sounds like a variation on a Hollywood movie, you are correct!)

3. Based on the overview of ethical standards and guidelines presented in this chapter, what do you view as the most important one or two ethical standards and why? The least important one or two ethical standards and why?

4. Both positive psychology and understanding of abnormal psychology via the *DSM* (APA, 2000) currently are key perspectives in the mental health professions. Discuss whether these two perspectives are compatible or in conflict and, if you believe they conflict, identify ways to reconcile the differences.

5. Clinicians today are moving away from adherence to one specific theory of treatment in favor of integrated treatment approaches. How do you explain this trend? Discuss whether you believe this trend will lead to more effective and thoughtful treatment protocols or to less effective and less coherent ones.

6. Discuss the controversy surrounding the need for specific multicultural competencies. Are these redundant skills for effective clinicians or do you see a need to spell out and train clinicians in multicultural competencies? Discuss the rationale for your responses.

7. This chapter has reviewed some important areas of knowledge that underlie and provide the building blocks for developing the skills you will learn in the subsequent chapters of this book. Would you modify the topics covered in this chapter (i.e., ethical standards, human development, theories and strategies to promote change, multicultural understanding and competence, social justice and advocacy, and the mind–body–spirit connection), either by deleting or adding to those topics? If so, how and why?

Personal Journal Questions

1. Have you ever been tempted to engage in unethical or illegal behavior? How did you handle that situation? How do you feel about your decisions and actions? What can you learn from that situation that might help you in the future? If you have never been tempted to engage in unethical or illegal behavior, write about the personal qualities that have distanced you from temptation. Discuss whether these are healthy qualities such as logic and a clear values system or undesirable qualities such as avoidance and fear of risk taking.

2. Compared to what you know about overall standards for healthy and predictable human development, identify a time when you or someone you know well showed early or precocious development and a time when you or someone you know well seemed to be developing slower than the norm. In each case, discuss how you could use that information productively if you were that person's clinician.

3. Sensitivity to and appreciation of diversity has become an essential quality of the skilled clinician. At the same time, nearly all of us of have grown up with

positive and negative images and stereotypes about multicultural groups, both those who are different from ourselves and those who resemble us. Identify two stereotypes or impressions you have about specific multicultural groups, thinking of multiculturalism in its broadest sense to include cultural background, ethnicity, religion, age, gender, sexual orientation, abilities, and other characteristics. If you did not have effective clinical skills and multicultural competence, what impact might these impressions have on your work with clients? What steps can you take to ensure that your work is not adversely affected by your impressions of multicultural groups?

4. Can you identify a time in your own life when you became aware of your mind, your body, and your spirit working together? Describe that experience and what it was like for you. What steps can you take to increase the congruence of your own mind, body, and spirit?

SUMMARY

This chapter paves the way for Chapters 3 through 10, which will present the fundamental skills you will need to become an effective clinician. Chapter 2 reviewed those areas of knowledge that provide the foundation for learning those skills. Theses of knowledge were discussed in this chapter:

- Ethical standards
- Human development
- Theories and strategies to promote change
- Multicultural understanding and competence
- Social justice and advocacy
- The mind–body–spirit connection
- Additional areas of importance and specialization

This chapter provided an introduction to these important areas, as well as some basic information on each area. Other courses, as well as your reading, training, and experience, will provide additional information on each of these areas.

Chapter 3 is the first of the eight chapters in this book that teach the essential and fundamental skills needed by clinicians. Following the BETA format presented in Chapter 1, Chapters 3 and 4 emphasize skills that are used to explore background but also serve many other important functions in the treatment process. The specific focus of Chapter 3 is crafting questions that are likely to elicit important information while, at the same time, promoting client self-awareness, building the therapeutic alliance, and advancing the treatment process to help people reach their goals.

Chapter 3

USING QUESTIONS EFFECTIVELY TO GATHER INFORMATION AND UNDERSTAND BACKGROUND

OVERVIEW

Part 2 of this book encompasses Chapters 3 and 4, which focus on background, the first element in the BETA format. These chapters are designed to teach you to use questions effectively to launch the treatment process, gather important background and other information, establish goals, advance and deepen the treatment process, help people make positive changes, promote people's awareness of their strengths, and, in many other ways, enhance treatment effectiveness.

Questions are emphasized in Chapter 2, a powerful intervention that can encourage self-disclosure and promote the treatment alliance. On the other hand, they also can alienate people and leave them feeling dehumanized and disconnected from their therapist or counselor. The guidelines and strategies presented in Chapter 3 are designed to enable you to use questions in beneficial ways.

Parts 2 through 5 of this book are organized according to the BETA format discussed in Chapter 1. Each of the four parts focuses on one of the four elements of that format: background, emotions, thoughts, and actions. Part 2 presents those skills that are essential to obtaining information on and understanding clients' backgrounds, although questions also have other important functions.

Each of the chapters in Parts 2 through 5 is organized according to the following structure:

1. Learning goals for the chapter
2. List of skills to be learned in the chapter
3. Description of skills to be learned
4. Examples that illustrate and clarify helpful and unhelpful uses of those skills
5. Written exercises to deepen understanding and initiate practice of the skills
6. Discussion topics or questions for use in classes or learning groups to promote thought and deepen knowledge of skills
7. Practice group exercises to provide experience using the skills in role-playing situations
8. Assessment of Progress form for development and review of goals, assessment, and recording of progress
9. Personal journal questions
10. Summary of learning presented in the chapter

Items 3, 4, and 5 will be repeated for each skill presented in a particular chapter.

Although learning is typically an incremental process, people learn best in different ways. The structure described here is designed to provide experiences that will gradually build and strengthen your skills. This structure will also afford you several different ways to learn the material, increasing the likelihood that you will achieve competence in the skills presented.

Effective Use of Questioning

Chapter 3 focuses on using questions, usually the primary way clinicians obtain information about people's backgrounds and histories. Questioning is particularly likely to be an important tool in the repertoire of clinicians who advocate a psychodynamic approach to treatment and who believe that an essential component of treatment is exploration of early childhood experiences that play a key role in determining later emotional and interpersonal functioning. However, all clinicians use questions to a greater or lesser extent. Getting to know clients well and advancing the treatment process is almost impossible without some use of questioning.

Chapter 4, building on the information and skills presented in Chapter 3, offers an array of advanced techniques for obtaining information on clients that draw on, yet go beyond, effective questioning. Among these are use of earliest recollections, genograms, and a lifeline or life chronology.

LEARNING GOALS

As a result of reading this chapter and completing the exercises throughout, you can expect to accomplish the following:

1. Understand the importance of having a clear purpose when asking a question and be able to identify the likely purpose of sample questions.

2. Understand and recognize the appropriate and inappropriate uses of questions in counseling and psychotherapy.
3. Describe the difference between open and closed questions and determine whether a question is open or closed.
4. Determine the appropriate use of open and closed questions.
5. Formulate questions that will help gather important information and promote communication with clients. Become familiar with the use of questions to elicit information on various topics.
6. Know the importance of combining questions with other interventions to promote a smooth flow to the treatment process.
7. Understand the importance of incorporating discussion of background into the treatment process, as well as ways to make that discussion relevant and productive.
8. Become familiar with the nature and purposes of an intake interview.
9. Know the key topics in an intake interview.
10. Be able to conduct an intake interview.

THE IMPORTANCE OF QUESTIONS

One of the most important roles of clinicians is eliciting information on the people they are seeking to help. Imagine that a 12-year-old girl named Angie has been referred to you for help with what her parents refer to as "depression." Many questions probably come into your mind as you imagine ways to help Angie. You might wonder what her family is like, what sort of student she is, what friends and activities she enjoys, what impact puberty may be having on her, what her religious and cultural background is like, how long she has lived in the same community, what might have happened recently to sadden her, and what are the signs and symptoms of her depression. These are only a few of the questions that need to be answered before you can develop an understanding of Angie and her life, determine what factors are contributing to her sadness, and plan effective ways to help her. List a few other questions that you think are important to ask Angie:

1. _____

2. _____

3. _____

The example of Angie illustrates the importance and usefulness of questions. Although questioning is the first important skill presented in this book, readers should be cautious about the use of this intervention. Overuse of questions can turn the treatment session into an interrogation and can make clients feel uncomfortable.

So, how can you obtain the information you need to help Angie while, at the same time, building a positive relationship with her and enabling her to better understand herself and her troubling emotions? The information in this chapter should enable you to accomplish that.

PURPOSES THAT QUESTIONS CAN ACCOMPLISH

Questions are one of the most frequent and powerful interventions that clinicians use. Questions can accomplish the following purposes and perhaps others that occur to you. Following each purpose is an illustration of a question or two that might further that purpose.

- Encourage dialogue.
  - How did you make the decision to seek help?
- Engage people in helping themselves.
  - What have you thought about doing to deal with this situation?
- Help people tell their stories.
  - If you were to summarize the most important moments in your life, what would they be?
- Identify key issues and concerns.
  - What concerns led you to seek some help?
- Assess severity of concerns.
  - What impact were those concerns having on your life?
  - Have you ever felt so badly that you have thought about harming or even killing yourself?
- Facilitate goal setting.
  - How would you like your life to be different at the end of our work together?
- Obtain information on facts, experiences, emotions, thoughts, and actions.
  - What memories do you have of the car accident?
  - What were your first thoughts and feelings after the accident?
- Provide details and examples.
  - What sorts of conflicts have you had with your coworkers?
- Deepen understanding of information presented.
  - What do you think about the possibility that your anger toward your mother is connected to the difficulty you have in relating well to women?
- Obtain clarification.
  - What do you mean when you say that you are being punished for your sins?
- Focus or change the direction of a conversation.
  - So far today, you've talked about your work concerns, your health issues, and your conflict with your sister. What would you like us to focus on first?
  - It sounds like you really enjoyed your trip. How can you use what you learned about having a good time on the trip to help you now that you have returned?
- Move the session forward.
  - We've gone over the details of this issue pretty thoroughly. How would you feel about moving on and looking at some ways to cope with it better?
- Promote thought, introspection, exploration, and elaboration.
  - What connections do you see between your concealment of your abuse as a child and your difficulty in talking about yourself now?

  - What sense do you make of your decision not to go to the birthday party?
- Call attention to contradictions.
  - I'm noticing a conflict here. On one hand, you say you want to get out more and meet new friends and yet when Susan asked you out for dinner, you refused her invitation. How do these fit together?
- Encourage consideration of new possibilities, options, and solutions.
  - What would you think about identifying one or two major goals for each day rather than a to-do list of 10 or 20 items?
  - You believe that your father hasn't visited because he really dislikes you, but could there be other possible reasons for your father's decision not to visit you, such as his health or financial concerns?
- Enrich people's knowledge.
  - What impact do you think puberty might be having on you?
  - Did you know that frequent self-induced vomiting can damage the enamel of your teeth and cause other medical problems?
- Promote people's identification and awareness of their strengths.
  - I can hear that you feel very good about how you handled this. What strengths and coping skills helped you handle it so well?
- Help them feel empowered.
  - What successes have you had this week in using your anger management skills?
  - It sounds like people are noticing the changes you are making. What do you think you are doing differently that is causing that reaction?
  - Can you think of other times when you dealt effectively with that feeling of being overwhelmed that you are having now?
- Encourage clients to synthesize information and consolidate their gains.
  - We covered a great deal of ground in this session. What are the most important ideas that you can take away with you?
  - How can you pull all this information together into a message to yourself about handling stress?

You may have been surprised by the variety and richness of the purposes and questions you just read. Effective questions can greatly enhance the treatment process.

THE IMPORTANCE OF PURPOSE

Having a clear purpose or intention in mind before asking a question is one way to increase the probability that a question will enhance, rather than detract, from treatment. The question then can be phrased so that it is likely to accomplish its purpose.

If you are in the early stages of your training, it may seem impossible to think about the intention of an intervention before making that intervention. It may seem to you that you would have to pause for a few minutes after each client statement to figure out what you should say next. Of course, that would be disruptive to the flow of the session. However, as you gain experience, you probably will find that you can quickly and automatically determine what you hope to accomplish with each intervention and can formulate an intervention that will accomplish your purposes.

One way to develop facility in determining purpose and in formulating interventions that correspond to your purpose is to gain practice by working backward. This entails thinking about an intervention that has already been made and identifying the probable purpose of that intervention. At the end of this chapter, you will be given an opportunity to identify the purpose of some interventions. Having a clear purpose or intention in mind is an important skill for counselors and psychotherapists and usually will determine the nature and impact of your interventions.

Example: Illustrating Purposes of Questions

Consider the probable impact of each of the five clinician questions that follow the client statement below:

> *Client:* I got so angry with my father-in-law, I punched him.
> *Clinician 1:* Don't you know you could get arrested for that?
> *Clinician 2:* What led up to this incident?
> *Clinician 3:* Why did you do that?
> *Clinician 4:* How did you feel after you punched him?
> *Clinician 5:* How did your father-in-law react?

Each of these questions has a different purpose and is likely to have a different impact on the quality and direction of the treatment process. Although it may well be important to help the client consider the possible legal consequences of his behavior, question 1 sounds critical and judgmental. Question 1 is the only closed question of the five. We will learn more about open and closed questions later in this chapter. Closed questions call for minimal and factual responses. Here, the use of a closed question, along with language that is critical, does not allow the client an opportunity to explain his action, and it seems judgmental and precipitous. It is likely to lead the client to feel shame, guilt, and perhaps anger at the clinician.

Question 2 is a neutral response and an open question, encouraging the client to elaborate and provide information that might help make sense of his action. It does not judge, but it draws the client's attention toward the antecedents of the incident, rather than toward his subsequent thoughts and feelings. This might be useful to a person who has difficulty with anger management, helping him understand how his anger builds and is discharged so that he can change that process.

Question 3 is another open question. It asks for explanation and elaboration but is phrased differently than question 2; like most questions that begin with "why," it sounds harsh and critical. Questions beginning with "why," like those beginning with "don't you think," often sound accusatory and generally are not helpful.

Question 4 suggests concern for the client; unlike question 2, it will probably encourage the client to focus on emotions rather than facts. It also differs from question 2 in that it targets the immediate aftermath of the incident rather than its antecedents. Any of those areas of focus may be helpful to the client, but the clinician should choose the focus that is most likely to be productive, based on knowledge of the client, including his background and his typical patterns of feeling, thinking, and acting.

Finally, question 5 shifts the focus away from the client and onto the father-in-law and seems to have the purpose of understanding that person's responses. This is unlikely to help the client process and learn from this experience.

Client Responses to the Questions

Let's see how the client might have responded to each of the five questions from the clinician:

> *Client:* I got so angry with my father-in-law, I punched him.
>
> *Clinician 1:* Don't you know you could get arrested for that?
>
> *Client:* Don't tell me what to do. He deserved it.
>
> *Clinician 2:* What led up to this incident?
>
> *Client:* He was spanking my three-year-old son really hard, just because he spilled his milk.
>
> *Clinician 3:* Why did you do that?
>
> *Client:* I don't know. I just got angry and lost control.
>
> *Clinician 4:* How did you feel after you punched him?
>
> *Client:* I was still really mad but I felt awful too; how could I have done that? My wife will be furious.
>
> *Clinician 5:* How did your father-in-law react?
>
> *Client:* He just gave me a look of disbelief and walked away.

Evaluating the Questions and Responses

Which of these interactions seems to move the counseling process in a positive direction? Both questions 2 and 4 yield important information, the first about the circumstances that prompted the behavior and the second about the client's feelings and his recognition that this behavior was probably not helpful. Usually, there is not only one right question or response but several, such as questions 2 and 4, which might be productive. These two questions might even have been combined, with the clinician asking question 2 first and then question 4, as follows:

> *Clinician 2:* What led up to this incident?
>
> *Client:* He was spanking my three-year-old son really hard, just because he spilled his milk.

Clinician 4: So you had a strong provocation. But how did you feel after you punched your father-in-law?

Client: I was still really mad but I felt awful too; how could I have done that?

Notice that the statement "So you had a strong provocation" was added as a bridge between the two questions. This let the client know that he was heard and that the clinician had some empathy for him. Important information emerged from the client's response to question 2; we know that the client had an understandable reason for his behavior; he was not simply out-of-control and dangerous.

At the same time, part of him realized that, despite the provocation, his behavior was inappropriate. This paves the way for discussion of better ways the client might have handled the situation.

Questions 1, 3, and 5, on the other hand, do not seem to enhance treatment. Question 5 focuses on the reactions of the father-in-law rather than on the client. In general, treatment should focus on the person who is present in the session and is seeking help. Discussion of reactions and behaviors of other people typically is not productive for several reasons. First, the client may or may not report accurately how that person acted. Second, the goal of treatment is not so much to gather the facts, but to help the client learn and change in positive ways; this generally can best be accomplished by focusing on the client. Third, such interventions may give clients the message that the clinician is less interested in them than in other people. Fourth, clients may misinterpret these interventions as a tacit message that focusing sessions on other people is productive; this can encourage clients to spend more time talking about other people and their treatment of the client than on themselves. However, this intervention was not harmful, and so the clinician can quickly recover by shifting the focus back to the client.

Questions 1 and 3 detract from the treatment process. The client reacts defensively and fails to provide useful information. Getting the session back on track after these interventions can be more difficult. The therapeutic alliance may even be compromised by interventions that sound critical and accusatory.

Criteria for Effective Questions

The preceding five questions might be rank ordered according to their helpfulness, using the following criteria:

- *Extremely helpful:* Reflects accurate and insightful listening; moves treatment in a productive direction; promotes client self-awareness, new learning, or positive change.
- *Moderately helpful:* Reflects generally accurate listening; moves treatment in a productive direction, but does not clearly lead to greater self-awareness, new learning, or positive change.
- *Neutral:* Neither contributes to the treatment goals nor harms the therapeutic process; may not accurately reflect what client has communicated.

- *Moderately harmful:* Detracts somewhat from the treatment process or therapeutic alliance; reflects poor listening and perhaps disinterest.
- *Extremely harmful:* Damages the treatment process or therapeutic alliance; perhaps sounds shaming and critical.

The five questions in this example can be evaluated in terms of these categories. They might be rated in the following way:

Extremely helpful: Question 4—How did you feel after you punched him?

Moderately helpful: Question 2—What led up to this incident?

Neutral: Question 5—How did your father-in-law react?

Moderately harmful: Question 3—Why did you do that?

Extremely harmful: Question 1—Don't you know you could get arrested for that?

As you can see from this listing, even a single intervention by the clinician can have a strong impact on the treatment process. This is particularly likely during the first few sessions with people who are vulnerable, fragile, low in self-csteem, and troubled by guilt and regrets or who are angry and reluctant clients. In many clinical settings, attrition is high, with many people terminating treatment prematurely after a session or two. Although some leave because they have gotten what they need, others leave in disappointment or anger, questioning whether treatment can be helpful to them. Now you are probably feeling considerable pressure and are wondering if you can become a skilled clinician. Developing questions that are helpful can go a long way toward meeting your clients' needs and helping them see and experience the benefits of counseling and psychotherapy. The follow sections will provide you more information on formulating effective questions.

Identifying Purpose

To learn more about the purpose of questions, complete the following exercises on identifying purpose. Let's go back to the case of Angie, the 12-year-old who was referred for help because of symptoms of depression. The following are questions that a clinician might ask Angie. Identify the likely purpose of each of these questions and write your responses below each question. Then rate each question as to its helpfulness.

1. Angie, what do you think led your parents to bring you in for some help?

Purpose:

_____

Rating:

_____

2. What do you think your teacher's reaction was when she saw you crying?

    Purpose:
    _____

    Rating:
    _____

3. How have you been sleeping, eating, and performing in school?

    Purpose:
    _____

    Rating:
    _____

4. What do you think is making you feel so sad?

    Purpose:
    _____

    Rating:
    _____

5. You told me that your best friend just moved away and that you didn't get into the private school you wanted to attend, yet you tell me you feel fine. That confuses me. How is it you can feel fine when you have had these two disappointments?

    Purpose:
    _____

    Rating:
    _____

OPEN, CLOSED, AND IMPLIED QUESTIONS

Clinicians have two types of questions in their repertoire of interventions: open questions and closed questions. Both of these have a place in the client–clinician dialogue, but their purposes and functions are different. Clinicians also use implied questions, as discussed in a later section.

Open Questions

Open questions, in contrast to closed questions, usually encourage people to think and explore, to gain awareness and new perspectives, to make connections, and to see patterns. They help clinicians to deepen their knowledge and understanding of their clients and their lives. Open questions are relatively unstructured and allow ample room for clients to provide full responses. They give clients considerable control over the direction of the dialogue and allow clients to determine the focus of their responses. Open questions typically do not have specific right-or-wrong answers but rather welcome whatever response the client makes. Open questions usually begin with such words as *what, how,* and *why.* The following are examples of open questions:

- What led to your decision to leave high school?
- What sort of relationship had you been hoping for?
- How did you feel when your dog was missing?
- How did you support yourself after you lost your job?
- How did you make the decision to refuse the recommended medical treatments?
- What led you to seek treatment at this time?

Clinicians generally make much more use of open questions than they do of closed questions. However, open questions, too, have some pitfalls. Questions beginning with *why* tend to sound accusatory and critical. In addition, clients may not know why they thought or acted in a particular way and so may feel uncomfortable when asked a *why* question. Some people, particularly those who are anxious or fearful or who are experiencing strong guilt and shame, may feel uneasy when any type of open question is asked. They may believe that there is a right answer they are supposed to know and have difficulty with the ambiguous and unstructured nature of open questions. Consequently, clinicians should use open questions, as well as closed questions, with care and sensitivity and should generally avoid *why* questions.

Closed Questions

Closed questions are usually intended to elicit a short, specific piece of information, often facts or figures. They typically begin with *is, are, do, who, when,* and *where.* The following are examples of closed questions:

- Is your mother still alive?
- Are you married?
- Do you have legal custody of your child?
- When did you leave school?
- Who suggested that you seek counseling?

As you can see, these questions are not intended to promote thought or generate learning, but instead usually have the purpose of providing the clinician with some necessary facts. Although some clients will provide lengthy responses to closed questions, most will just respond with the requested information.

Closed questions certainly have a useful role in the treatment process. Closed questions can help to slow down and focus a voluble client and can narrow the scope of a fragmented session. They are especially useful in the first few sessions of treatment to provide clinicians with the details and facts they need to develop a picture of a client's history. Closed questions may also be used productively at other points in the treatment process.

However, excessive use of closed questions can create a negative tone in the session and can give a client an erroneous view of the treatment process. A series of short questions and answers can lead clients to think that the clinician can be relied on to direct the sessions and all they need to do is come up with the right answers. Even worse, clients may feel as if they are being interrogated. This is likely to prevent the establishment of a positive therapeutic alliance and may even lead to premature termination of the treatment process.

Implied Questions

In addition to open and closed questions, clinicians also use implied questions. These are a cross between a directive (discussed in a later chapter) and a question, but they really function as open questions, keeping the focus on the client and encouraging the client to talk. Many clinicians make extensive use of implied questions. Examples of implied questions include the following:

- Could you tell me more about that?
- Please give me more details.
- I wonder how you reacted to that.
- I don't have a clear picture of your feelings at that time.
- Tell me what was happening when you started to cry.
- Perhaps looking at what led up to this would give some clarification.

Implied questions often seem less confrontational and interrogatory than direct questions. As a result, implied questions can effectively promote dialogue and client self-exploration while maintaining a positive atmosphere in the session.

Examples of Dialogue Using the Various Types of Questions

Let's look at three brief dialogues with a self-referred client named David, all reflecting initial sessions. The first relies primarily on closed questions; the second, primarily on open questions; and the third, on a combination of the two, along with implied questions and other interventions.

Dialogue Emphasizing Closed Questions

Clinician: Because this is our first session, I'd like to ask you some questions about your decision to seek treatment. When did you decide you needed help?

Client: Last week, after I had a fight with my girlfriend.

Clinician: And who referred you to me?

Client: I asked my psychology teacher at college for a recommendation, and she suggested you.

Clinician: Have you had any counseling before?

Client: No, never.

Clinician: And is this appointment time convenient for you?

Client: I guess so. (By now, the client may be wondering if he will schedule a second appointment!)

Dialogue Emphasizing Open Questions

Clinician: How are you feeling about being here today?

Client: Well, I'm not sure what to expect. I've never been in counseling before.

Clinician: How did you decide to seek some counseling?

Client: My girlfriend and I have been fighting more and more. She's been getting drunk every night, missing work, and messing up her life. I try to tell her this is no good, but she just tells me to take care of my own problems. I need help figuring out how to get through to her.

Clinician: How do you think I could help you with that?

Client: Well, I guess you could help me understand her better. But I think I know her pretty well. I just can't get her to listen to me. Do you think you could help me with that?

Although this dialogue yields more information about the client's concerns, he is new to counseling and seems uncertain about how it can help him. He is floundering and needs more direction from the clinician. However, the series of open questions, without intervening information or guidance, leave him confused. Let's look at a dialogue that combines open and closed questions with implied questions and other interventions.

Dialogue Integrating Types of Interventions

Clinician: How did you decide to seek some counseling?

Client: My girlfriend and I have been fighting more and more. She's been getting drunk every night, missing work, and messing up her life. I try to tell her this is no good, but she just tells me to take care of my own problems. I need help figuring out how to get through to her.

Clinician: This must be very upsetting to you. How long has this been going on?

Client: Three or four months. We've been together for two years and things were great for most of that time, but not anymore.

Clinician: What have you tried to do to get things back on track?

Client: I told her and told her she was hurting herself, I hid her bottles of wine, and I threatened to move out. Once I even threatened to tell her supervisor why she has been taking so many sick days. Nothing worked.

Clinician: You must feel pretty discouraged. Tell me more about your relationship with your girlfriend.

Client: What do you want to know?

Clinician: You might start at the beginning, when you first met, and tell me about some of the strengths in your relationship then.

What differences do you notice between this dialogue and the two previous ones? Which dialogue seems more likely to get the treatment process off to a good start? What is it about that dialogue that makes it more effective? In general, varying your interventions, gearing your interventions to the client's knowledge of and readiness for treatment, and providing some direction improve the treatment process. However, the previous intervention probably has too many questions and not enough reflections and empathic statements, as discussed later in this text.

Exercises in Creating Open and Closed Questions

Applying what you have read about questions can solidify your learning. To accomplish, that, complete the following brief exercise:

1. Write an open question that you might ask David about his previous romantic relationships.

   _____

   _____

2. Write a closed question that you might ask David about his previous romantic relationships.

   _____

   _____

3. Write an implied question that you might ask David about his previous romantic relationships.

   _____

   _____

4. Write a two-sentence intervention that combines a statement with an open question that you might ask David about his family relationships.

   _____

   _____

5. Write a two-sentence intervention that acknowledges some feelings that David might express about his family and encourages him via an open question to

look at the connection between his feelings about his family and those about his girlfriend.

_____

_____

PITFALLS OF QUESTIONS

Clearly, questions are one of the most important interventions in the clinician's repertoire. They are invaluable for promoting client exploration and self-awareness and for eliciting important information. However, when they are poorly presented or used without a clear purpose, questions can have a negative impact on the therapeutic alliance and on the treatment process. Clinicians should be aware of the following possible pitfalls inherent in the use of questions, some of which have already been mentioned earlier in this chapter:

Multicultural Considerations

Most people raised in the United States, particularly those who grew up in heterogeneous urban areas, seem comfortable with a relatively high level of self-disclosure and are accustomed to being asked questions. We tell the pharmacist about all of the medications we are taking, we share information about our personalities in order to be matched with roommates as college freshmen, and our system of education relies heavily on both teachers and students asking questions. An evening spent watching television programs on forensic medicine, cosmetic surgery, and celebrity interviews leaves little doubt about what some may consider a lack of discretion and privacy in American society.

However, we must not assume that those norms are held by people from other cultures, by people who have not grown up in the United States, or even by many who do live in the United States but choose to maintain the values of their culture of origin. When I lectured in China, for example, I was advised that I could not count on students to volunteer questions that would promote discussion and help me clarify any confusing points. Instead, I distributed cards so the students could anonymously write down their questions for my response.

People from many cultures find questions to be intrusive and inappropriate. In addition, questions may be interpreted as criticism or doubts about someone's truthfulness. Such clients are unlikely to express their dissatisfaction with the clinician's use of questions. Instead, they may leave treatment abruptly, evade or not answer the questions, or provide answers out of politeness and a desire to please rather than out of an effort to increase their self-awareness and help the clinician get to know them fully. Clinicians must be especially carefully in their use of questions with multicultural clients. They are probably wise to ask questions sparingly, carefully noting reactions and replies, and making sure that the questions are promoting rather than hindering treatment goals. Asking people directly about their reactions to questions may be counterproductive because it involves asking a question about asking questions. However, done gently and with great care, this may be another avenue to gather information. Clinicians might say, for example, "Therapists have many ways to help people with their concerns. I want to find a way that is comfortable for you and I wonder how you feel about my asking you questions? It is always fine with me if you would prefer not to answer a question."

Leading Questions

Leading questions generally are closed questions that telegraph to the client the expected answer and counteract the value of questions as a tool to promote exploration. Examples of such questions are "Don't you think you overreacted to his statement?" and "You weren't physically or sexually abused, were you?" Much better would be open questions such as "How do you feel about your reaction to his statement?" and "Could you tell me about any times when you felt that you were being physically or sexually abused?" Be careful to use closed questions almost exclusively for obtaining factual information and be sure that your question is not really a statement or an expression of your own opinion.

Shifting Focus Away from the Client

Sometimes curiosity, inattention, or lack of a clear purpose leads clinicians to ask questions that shift the focus away from the client and onto other people in the client's life or even onto the clinician's own concerns. Although this shift in focus sometimes yields useful information, clinicians cannot be certain that clients are presenting reliable information about other people. Their perceptions of others often are based on incomplete information and are filtered through the clients' own phenomenological perspectives. The result may be distorted and inaccurate information. I have found, for example, that the uncaring or malicious family members described by my clients often turn out to be caring and well-meaning people who just have weak interpersonal and listening skills.

In phrasing your questions about people in a client's life, generally focus on the client's perceptions of that person. For example, rather than asking "What kind of parent was your mother?," ask "How did you experience your mother as a parent?" Most important to the treatment process are the client's memories and images rather than the actual characteristics of the people in the client's life.

Occasionally, even the best clinicians ask questions to meet their own needs or satisfy their own curiosity. I have been guilty of this myself. A new client once mentioned that his father was a famous writer of mystery novels. A lover of mysteries, I lost focus for a moment and asked who his father was and what he had written. Before going too far down that path, I realized that my apparent interest in the father's writing could be undermining my alliance with the client who resented his father's high expectations. Although all clinicians sometimes make interventions that are not helpful, keep in mind that the client's needs are paramount. Of course, we can set limits and guidelines for our sessions, but, in general, we must set aside our own needs and emphasize those of the client. This is essential to developing and maintaining a trusting relationship with our clients.

Interrogation

Inappropriate and excessive use of questions can make clients feel like they are being interrogated rather than participating in a collaborative endeavor. This is most likely to happen in the following situations:

- *Clinicians rely almost exclusively on questions in their interventions.* This pitfall can be counteracted by consciously combining questions with other interventions. The combination of a question with a reflection of feeling or meaning, discussed in Chapter 5, is particularly powerful; it lets clients know the clinician has heard them and it also elicits additional information. An example of this is "It sounds like you feel very angry at your parents (reflection of feeling). How have you dealt with that anger (open question)?"
- *Clinicians use double or triple questions in one intervention,* such as "Do you like school? I mean, what are your favorite subjects? How do you get along with your teachers?" This pattern is particularly common among beginning clinicians who are not sure if their clients understand the first question, so they rephrase it and then rephrase it again. Trust that you will usually make yourself clear and that, if clients are confused by what you have said, they will let you know. Make your interventions brief, clear, and concise. You should almost always limit yourself to one question per intervention. If you find yourself asking a series of questions, take a close look at that. It may well reflect your own self-doubts and insecurity in the clinician role and be confusing to clients.
- *Clinicians ask* why *questions* such as "Why did you drop out of high school?" and "Why were you fired from your job?" These sound critical and blaming and can make people feel uncomfortable. Better questions are "How did you make the decision to leave school?" and "What was your understanding of your supervisor's decision not to keep you on the job?" How and what questions generally are less threatening than why questions. Therefore, they typically elicit a better client reaction and more useful information. View *why* questions as you do multiple questions in one intervention and scrutinize such interventions closely, being sure that the intervention accomplishes your purpose. If that is too difficult right now, the best strategy for novice clinicians is to eliminate why questions and multiple questions from their repertoire.

FORMULATING HELPFUL QUESTIONS

This discussion of helpful questions includes four sections:

1. Opening words of helpful questions
2. Examples of helpful questions
3. Types of helpful questions
4. Brief dialogues, illustrating use of helpful questions

Opening Words: *How* and *What*

Keep in mind that, in asking questions, you have at least three important goals:

- To further the development of a positive therapeutic alliance
- To elicit information that will help you better know and understand a person
- To help that person become more self-aware and better informed on options and circumstances

Making the opening words of questions gentle and exploratory can advance these goals. Using the words *how* and *what* to begin questions can be particularly effective in initiating open questions and encouraging people to talk about themselves without feeling pressured. The following are some examples of questions using these two key words:

- *How:* How are you feeling about that? How did you manage to accomplish that? How do you think you could improve on this? How will you know when you have reached your goals? How can you cope with that more effectively?
- *What:* What led you to seek therapy? What was most rewarding about that experience? What got in your way? What stands out in your mind about your family background? What are the strengths you prize in yourself?

I often precede a *how* or *what* question with "I wonder," which seems to soften the question even further; for example, "I wonder what you can learn from that?"

The opening words *who, when,* and *where* also have a place in the clinical dialogue, as do other opening words such as *do, can,* and *are.* These words typically begin closed questions that yield specific pieces of information. Although some loquacious clients may provide lengthy responses to your closed questions, you are more likely to receive brief factual responses. We often ask closed questions when we want to obtain a piece of information or when we want to help a person who may be anxious and floundering to focus and gain more control. The following questions illustrate both of these purposes.

Obtaining Information

- *Who:* Who suggested that you seek therapy? Who has been your most important role model? Who can you turn to for some help? Who do you know who has accomplished those goals? Who might be able to help you pay for school?
- *When:* When was your illness first diagnosed? When were you last in therapy? When did you marry? When did you separate from your partner? When were you hoping to retire?
- *Where:* Where did you grow up? Where did you attend college? Where is there a place you can envision feeling happy and peaceful? From where did your family immigrate? Where do you like to spend your leisure time?

Focusing the Conversation   The following examples illustrate how you can use closed questions to focus and contain a dialogue. This can help to make a session more productive, facilitate people's efforts to take greater control of their emotions and their treatment, and stop clients' ruminating and feelings of being stuck.

- What would you like to focus on today?
- Do you feel ready to talk about your abuse now?
- Which of the topics you have brought in today is most important to you?
- Is this a good time to work on making that decision?

Although most clinicians favor open, rather than closed, questions, notice that closed questions can serve several important purposes. As long as they are used deliberately and not overused , they can enhance treatment.

Examples of Helpful Questions

When formulating your questions, keep in mind the three goals listed previously and do your best to craft questions that will achieve those goals. Although questions are usually created to fit a specific person and situation, the following are common types of questions—both direct and implied—that can begin or further a dialogue.

Exploratory Questions

- Can you tell me some more about that?
- Can you give me an example of that?
- What seems most upsetting to you about that experience?
- What else do you want to tell me about that?

Questions on Emotions

- How do you feel about that?
- What emotions came up for you when that happened?
- Which feeling was the strongest one for you?
- How would you have liked to feel about that?
- When have you had similar emotions?
- How did you feel about yourself then?

Questions on Thoughts

- What sense did you make of that?
- What did that mean to you?
- What thoughts went through your mind at the time?
- Now that you have had some time to reflect on what happened, I wonder what changes you might have noticed in your thinking about the incident?
- What would be a helpful way for you to think about that?

- How did your thoughts and feelings seem to fit together?
- What was the first thought you had when you got the news?
- How did you make that decision?

Questions on Actions

- What did you do when that happened?
- What steps did you take to cope with that?
- What activities help you feel more confident? More relaxed?
- If you could have changed your behavior, what would you have done differently?

Three Useful Types of Questions

Just as some questions tend to be countertherapeutic, so are some questions likely to advance the treatment process. Several particularly useful types of questions are available to clinicians. These include empowering questions, solution-focused questions, and scaling questions.

Empowering Questions   Some questions can help clients to develop self-confidence and hopefulness and to become more aware of their strengths. Questions such as these assume that people will be effective and they focus on successes and positive exceptions rather than on problems and disappointments. This is a departure from the traditional focus of treatment on pathology and can shift the tone and energy of treatment in a more positive direction. The following are examples of empowering questions:

- What strengths did you draw on in yourself to accomplish that?
- What makes you proud of yourself?
- Which two experiences in your life really reflect your best self?
- What can you learn from this situation that will be helpful to you?
- What would other people say are your greatest strengths?
- How can you apply some of those strengths you have identified to this new situation?
- What will your life be like when you have resolved this difficulty? (assumes success and effectiveness)
- Could you tell me about some times when you did enjoy what you were learning in school? (looks for exceptions)
- It sounds like you and your son got along well yesterday. What did you do to make that happen? (strength-promoting)
- Although you are having difficulty coping with your current situation, you have overcome a great deal in your life. For example, how did you deal with your father's suicide? (identifying effective coping skills),

Solution-Focused Questions   Similarly empowering are questions that help people envision their desired treatment outcome and identify steps they can take toward achievement of their goals. A well-known example of such a question is the Miracle Question, developed by Steve de Shazer (1991): "Suppose that one night there is a miracle and while you were sleeping the problem that brought you to therapy is solved. How would you know? . . . What would be different? . . . What will you notice different the next morning that will tell you that there has been a miracle? . . . What will your spouse notice?" (p. 113). This series of solution-focused questions implies that the problems can be solved and elicits specific evidence of their resolution that can suggest ways to address the problem.

Scaling Questions   Scaling questions are particularly useful in setting goals and assessing whether and how much progress has been made. Although not a precise or scientific measurement, clients usually have little difficulty responding to scaling questions and find them useful to quantify change. Examples of scaling questions are as follows:

- On a 0–10 scale, with 0 representing no fear and 10 representing the highest possible fear, what number would best reflect your current fear of heights? (establishes a baseline)
- When we began working together, you rated your parenting skills as a 2 on a 0–10 scale, with 0 representing a complete lack of parenting skills and 10 representing the best possible parenting skills. Now that you have had the opportunity to learn and practice some new parenting skills, how would you rate your parenting skills on that 0–10 scale? (measures progress)
- On a 0–10 scale, with 0 representing the lowest possible self-esteem and 10 representing the highest possible self-esteem, what would be a realistic number for us to target as a goal as we work on improving your self-esteem? (establishes reasonable goals)

Integrating Questions into a Dialogue

Level 1

You now know the basics of formulating helpful and effective questions. To summarize, these include purpose, phrasing, and pacing. Know why you are asking a question, use language that will accomplish your purpose, and pace the presentation and frequency of questions so they are gentle and enlightening rather than accusatory or pressuring. Integrating questions with other types of interventions, to be discussed throughout this book, is especially effective. Let's look at a few brief dialogues that reflect these points.

Following Up on a Suggested Task

Clinician: How did your plan to talk with your father go?

Client: Not well. I just couldn't do it even though I thought I would be able to.

Clinician: So it turned out to be tougher than you thought. What made it difficult for you?

Client: I was afraid I would say the wrong thing and make our relationship even worse.

Clinician: So you have a clearer understanding of what frightens you about talking to your father. I know you have tackled frightening situations successfully before. How did you go about that?

Client: Well, I really rehearsed what I would say and do and tried to prepare myself for the worst. That seemed to help me.

Clinician: How would it feel to prepare to talk to your father in the same way?

Client: I think that would really help me too.

Talking with a Child About a Behavioral Problem

Clinician: Kiri, I understand you got upset in class this morning. What happened?

Client: Emma tried to take my toy and I got mad.

Clinician: And how did you deal with those feelings?

Client: I didn't mean to do it, but I hit Emma. She shouldn't take my things.

Clinician: You really wanted to let her know that. How did you feel after you hit her?

Client: Not so great. I was afraid the teacher would tell my parents.

Clinician: So hitting Emma didn't really help you to feel better. I wonder if you could think of a different way you might have reacted when she took your toy.

Client: Well, I know I should use my words like the teacher says, but that's hard sometimes.

Clinician: What makes that hard for you?

Client: I was just too mad to talk.

Clinician: How would you feel about our trying to find some ways to help you use your words rather than hit?

Clearly, questions are an extremely useful type of intervention for all clinicians. They are important in promoting dialogue, eliciting information, and advancing the treatment process. Exercises at the end of this chapter afford you the opportunity to practice and improve your questioning skills, and exercises in later chapters will help you learn to combine questions with other interventions.

IMPORTANCE OF BACKGROUND INFORMATION

Questions are especially important early in the treatment process when clinicians are gathering information on their client's histories and background. Theories of counseling and psychotherapy do not all give the same level of attention to clients' backgrounds. For example, most psychodynamic theorists believe that the origins of people's current difficulties lie in early childhood experiences and that those years must be a prominent focus of treatment. Most person-centered, cognitive, and behavioral clinicians, however, de-emphasize the importance of the past and concentrate their work on current experiences.

Despite this difference in emphasis, most treatment approaches in the 21st century take a holistic perspective. They acknowledge the importance of understanding people's contexts, salient early experiences, and multiple perspectives on the world and recognize that early attachments are likely to have an impact on later relationships. Consequently, some attention to background is an essential ingredient of almost all counseling or psychotherapeutic relationships.

Case Example

The following example provides a clear example of the importance of background. Natasha was born in a remote area of the Ukraine more than 50 years ago. Her family was mistreated because of their religious beliefs, and her parents could not earn an adequate living in their native country. When Natasha was about 8 years old, her parents took her and her two brothers, ages 5 and 10, and escaped from their country. The danger and hardship they experienced while fleeing and the death of her younger brother along the way were experiences Natasha would never forget.

After several difficult years, the family immigrated to the United States. They rarely talked about the past, instead emphasizing the importance of looking forward. Natasha graduated from college, became a language teacher, married, and had a son and a daughter. When he was a teenager, her son was severely injured in an automobile accident. For Natasha, this experience felt unbearable, not only because of the injuries to her son, but because it echoed the loss of her brother many years earlier. Those painful memories that had never been discussed or resolved compounded her grief at her son's injuries. Natasha, usually composed and capable, became depressed, inconsolable, and incapacitated. Therapy, initially focused on fear and worry related to her son's accident, had little impact on Natasha. Only when she and her clinician recognized the link between the present situation and her past loss and addressed both experiences was Natasha able to mobilize her resources and move out of her depression.

Benefits of Background Discussion

As you can see from Natasha's story, paying some attention to background can lead to a fuller understanding and appreciation of a person's concerns and difficulties. That, in turn, can lead to more successful treatment. Once again, purpose is key. When clinicians gather background information on clients, their primary goals must be understanding the clients as fully as possible and obtaining information and insights that will enhance treatment effectiveness. Clinicians should not simply gather information to complete an intake form or to satisfy their own curiosity. Instead, they should gather information so that they can understand how the past has contributed to the present, that is, how each person's history and background have shaped them into who they are. Most clinicians do not seek to change or undo the past, but rather to help people make sense of their lives and use background information to enhance treatment of people's current concerns.

Discussion of background can accomplish the following:

- Enable clinicians to view people in context.
- Encourage clinicians to take a holistic and comprehensive view of their clients.
- Facilitate respect and appreciation for the challenges and importance of people's past experiences.
- Provide an understanding of people's worldviews and multiple perspectives.
- Highlight connections between past issues and present symptoms.
- Provide historical information on symptoms so that clinicians can more easily make an accurate diagnosis.
- Reveal relevant issues and concerns that had not yet been presented.
- Reduce clinician biases and preconceptions.

PURPOSES AND NATURE OF INTAKE INTERVIEWS

Although clinicians gather information on background as needed throughout the treatment process, a comprehensive and intensive inquiry into background typically happens early in the treatment process. Whether this process is viewed as a formal intake interview or an introductory phase of treatment, gathering some client history early in the treatment process is essential to launching treatment in a productive direction. The next section of the book discusses the use of intake interviews to obtain background information. Questions are the most useful intervention when clinicians elicit client information during an intake interview. Conducted either prior to the start of treatment or during the first session or two, the intake interview lays the groundwork for successful treatment. An intake interview is generally intended to accomplish the following purposes:

- Clarify the client's presenting concerns and reasons for seeking treatment.
- Orient the client to the treatment process.
- Begin to develop a positive and collaborative therapeutic alliance.
- Obtain relevant information on the client's background, history, and context.
- Identify concerns that seem amenable to treatment.
- Identify the client's strengths and assets.
- Clarify the diagnosis if a mental disorder is present.
- Determine whether the client presents a danger to self or others and, if so, facilitate immediate action.
- Develop a treatment plan that is likely to be effective.

Many resources are available to enhance the intake process. Questionnaires and checklists are often incorporated into that process. This can streamline the intake interview. In addition, some people find it easier to write down personal information rather than to speak about it to a relative stranger. Clients should be offered several ways to present information and should be reassured that, although the intake interview is an important part of treatment, they have the right to disclose as much or as little as they choose. Using the guidelines already presented on asking helpful questions will go a long way toward making the intake process a comfortable and productive experience.

Topics in a Typical Intake Interview

A typical intake interview elicits information on the following topics (Seligman, 2004, pp. 138–140):

- Demographic and identifying information, including age, partner/marital status, family composition, educational background, occupation, and living situation
- Presenting concerns, including reasons for seeking help at the present time, symptoms, onset and duration of difficulties, and the impact of concerns on the person's lifestyle
- Prior psychological and emotional difficulties, treatment history and outcomes
- Current life situation, including important relationships, occupational and educational activities, and social and leisure activities
- Cultural, spiritual, religious, and socioeconomic information
- Family background, including information on composition of current family and family of origin, structure of and relationships within the families, parenting styles, role models, family rules and values
- Developmental history, including important experiences and milestones
- Career and educational history
- Medical history, including significant past and current illnesses, medical treatments, and medication
- Health-related behaviors, including use of drugs and alcohol, exercise, diet, and overall self-care
- Additional information that clients view as important

EXAMPLE OF AN INTAKE INTERVIEW

The following example illustrates a typical intake interview, covering the information categories listed previously. It also introduces Eileen Carter, a hypothetical client who is used to illustrate many of the skills presented in this book. Eileen is a 24-year-old African American woman who sought help at a university counseling center. Assume that Eileen has already been oriented to the treatment process.

As you review this intake interview, pay particular attention to the flow of the interview and the way questions are used, either alone or in combination with other interventions, to gather information. Also notice the development of the therapeutic alliance during this interview. Topics for discussion at the end of this interview will help you see how the questions and other interventions used here further the goals of the intake and treatment processes.

Clinician 1: Eileen, when you called for an appointment, you sounded pretty upset. You talked about your life being "one big mess." Could you tell me about that?

Eileen 1: Yes. I'm a student here at the college, taking my first college course. For years, I thought about going to college and becoming a nurse, and I finally saved up some money and enrolled in English 101. And now I might have to drop out of the course. . . . I feel so discouraged.

Clinician 2: So college represents a sort of dream come true for you. What might interfere with that?

Eileen 2: Well, I'm married, and I have a 4-year-old son, Charles Junior. At first, my husband said he would stay with Junior while I went to class in the evening, but now he's saying that it's my job to take care of our son, that he's too busy, and what do I need an education for anyhow.

Clinician 3: How did you react when he said that?

Eileen 3: I was blown away. I had told him how much it meant to me to start college, and I thought that maybe for once he cared about how I felt. Stupid me! I should have known better.

Clinician 4: So this was very upsetting to you.

Eileen 4: You got that right. I didn't want my husband to know I was upset so I went in the bathroom, turned on the water so he couldn't hear me, and just cried and cried and cried.

Clinician 5: What kept you from sharing your feelings with your husband?

Eileen 5: He would have just laughed at me, and then later he'd use the situation to prove to me what a hopeless mess I am.

Clinician 6: I'm hearing several issues here: concerns about your relationship with your husband as well as about continuing in college. How do you think I can help you?

Eileen 6: I really want to stay in school. I thought maybe some resources here at the college could help me, like child care or financial aid. And I could certainly use some help with my marriage.

Clinician 7: We can work on all that, but before we start to focus on those issues, I would like to put them in context. It helps me to understand your current concerns if I know something about your background. How would you feel about filling me in on your background?

Eileen 7: Fine. Whatever you think would help.

Clinician 8: All right. Maybe you could start by telling me about the family in which you grew up.

Eileen 8: Well, there were my parents, and I had two brothers, one almost four years older and one four years younger than me. And I had two dogs and a cat.

Clinician 9: What was it like for you to grow up in that family?

Eileen 9: Until I was ten or so, it wasn't particularly good or bad. My parents both worked hard; Dad was an electrician and Mom was a beautician. We had to be pretty self-sufficient, just let ourselves in after school, do our homework, and make dinner. We were all like ships passing in the night. I had my pets and that really helped.

Clinician 10: Sounds pretty lonely. And then things changed when you were about ten?

Eileen 10: Yes, my dad died suddenly of a heart attack. I guess he had high cholesterol or something but nobody really knew. My family hardly ever went to doctors. My mom really couldn't handle his death, put us all in foster care for awhile, got a second job. Dad had left her hardly any money, and things were really tough. After about six months, she took us back home but things had gone from bad to worse. She was out dating all the time; I guess she thought that if she got married again, things would get better. She had no time for us. I felt like I was invisible.

Clinician 11: It sounds like you lost both parents in a way.

Eileen 11: Yes, it was pretty awful. I didn't know what to do to feel better. Then one day when I was home alone, I went to the liquor cabinet and started drinking. For a while, I felt better, sort of warm and safe. Of course, by the time my mom got home, I was really sick, but even that wasn't so bad. She didn't know why I was sick, but she put me to bed and fed me toast and tea. That was pretty good, too.

Clinician 12: So you discovered that alcohol made you feel better, at least for a little while.

Eileen 12: Yes, but usually one of my brothers was home with me, so I didn't get much opportunity to raid the liquor cabinet. Then I found another solution. Some of the kids at school were sniffing glue, and I started hanging out with them. Sometimes they would have liquor or marijuana, and we would cut school, go out to the woods, and party.

Clinician 13: How did you feel about that part of your life?

Eileen 13: Now I feel pretty bad about it, but then I was just numb. And when I met Jay, things got even worse.

Clinician 14: Even worse?

Eileen 14: Yeah, I guess I got the message from my mom that you had to have a man in your life. I was about twelve then, and Jay was sixteen and had a car. He wanted to have sex right away, and I thought "Why not?" So we did and that was like the alcohol, helped me feel warm and safe. But it sure didn't last. He started to knock me around, and I knew he was going out with other girls. I don't know why I didn't break up with him, but I didn't. He finally dumped me.

Clinician 15: So what started out feeling good wound up being another loss for you.

Eileen 15: Yeah, but did I learn anything from that? Of course not. So after Jay, there was Mike and then Tyrone. By then, I had dropped out of school and was working in bars, waitressing or dancing or whatever would pay the bills. I moved in with Tyrone when I was seventeen, and he sure wasn't paying for anything. I got pregnant twice when I was with Tyrone, and I had two abortions. It was a terrible choice for me but I just didn't know what else to do; I couldn't support a child and didn't want my child to have Tyrone as a father.

Clinician 16: It sounds like you went through some very tough years. How did you get from that situation to where you are now?

Eileen 16: Well, after Tyrone, there was Charles. He's my husband. He seemed different from the rest; at least he didn't hit me. And then I got pregnant again. I thought it would be okay if I got pregnant by Charles. At least he had a decent job, even though we met in a bar and I knew he drank too much. He said we should get married and so we did. That was four years ago.

Clinician 17: And how have those four years been for you?

Eileen 17: My son has been God's gift to me. He makes it all worthwhile. But marriage sure wasn't what I thought it would be. We don't seem to have any love in our marriage, and I feel very alone.

Clinician 18: I wonder if these feelings remind you of feelings you had as a child?

Eileen 18: You know, they really do. More ships passing in the night.

Clinician 19: You've gone through a great deal to find that warmth and comfort you crave, but it sounds like you still haven't found what you're looking for.

Eileen 19: Except with my son.

Clinician 20: Except with your son. Are there other parts of your life that give you a sense of gratification?

Eileen 20: School does.

Clinician 21: What makes school so special for you?

Eileen 21: I never had any interest in school when I was a kid. But it's so different now. I'm there for me, because I really want to be there. And it makes me feel like I have hope in my life. I even tell my son about the books we're reading, and I read him an essay I wrote. I want him to have a different kind of life.

Clinician 22: School has really helped you make many important changes in your life. What else helps you feel hopeful?

Eileen 22: I did stop drinking, or at least drinking the way I used to. When I was pregnant, I knew that alcohol could harm my son and so somehow I managed to stop drinking. I still smoke and I know that's not good, but I really have alcohol under control. Smoking is next on the list.

Clinician 23: You've taken some big steps to improve your health. Have you had any medical problems or health concerns?

Eileen 23: I do have high cholesterol like my father. It must be genetic because you wouldn't expect someone my age to have that problem.

Clinician 24: That must be frightening, to have the same medical problem that might have killed your father. What are you doing about the high cholesterol?

Eileen 24: It did scare me to get that diagnosis, but the doctor just said to watch my diet; I know I need to do that. And I should exercise more too.

Clinician 25: Perhaps that is another goal you have. What leisure or social activities do you have?

Eileen 25: Not much. Cleaning the house, cooking meals, and running after my son—that's my life. I do enjoy talking with the other women with young children whenever I take Charles Junior out. There's a group of us that all take our kids to the park when the weather is decent. That's how I found out about this college, from one of the other women.

Clinician 26: So you do have some people you socialize with. Are you employed now?

Eileen 26: I do some telephone work from home; I call to see if people are interested in having siding put on their houses and then, if they sound interested, I pass on the lead to this siding company. They pay me for every lead they get an appointment with, and I get a bonus if they make a sale. Nothing else since I got married. Charles wanted me to stay home. I think I'd like to get a part-time job once Junior is in school next year.

Clinician 27: So working for pay isn't a big part of your life right now. What kinds of jobs have you had?

Eileen 27: Just working in bars and nightclubs. I did get my G.E.D., but I don't have any special training. I learned to deal with all kinds of people in the bars, though, and I think I could do pretty well in sales. I even do pretty well on the phone and that's tough; people hang up in your face and even curse at you.

Clinician 28: You see yourself as being pretty good with people, then.

Eileen 28: Yes, I think so. I really like to talk to people.

Clinician 29: So that's a strength you have. One area we haven't talked about yet is your religious beliefs and cultural background. Could you tell me about those?

Eileen 29: Sure. I was brought up with Christian beliefs, even though we never went to church. I always valued my African American heritage and have a strong faith in God. But sometimes I feel so bad about all the mistakes I made in my life, I wonder if even God can forgive me. And yet he gave me my son, so I can't be that bad.

Clinician 30: Your heritage and spiritual beliefs are important to you, but it sounds like you're feeling some guilt and regret.

Eileen 30: That's an understatement. Part of me wants to have a better marriage, to make a good home for my son, to continue my education. But then another part of me thinks that I don't deserve all these good things, that I should be punished for the abortions and the other terrible things I did.

Clinician 31: I hear lots of mixed emotions. What are you feeling now as you talk about this?

Eileen 31: So many regrets, so much guilt. I want to give Junior the love and family I never had, but I'm not sure I can do it. I can't believe I'm telling you all this. I came in to talk about a college course and look where we wound up!

Clinician 32: We did cover a great deal of ground. What reactions are you having to our talk today?

Eileen 32: I'm not sure. It all seems like a big ball of yarn and I don't know where the beginning is.

Clinician 33: It does seem like many parts of your life are intertwined: your family background, your use of drugs and alcohol, your regrets about some of the choices you made, your marriage, your love for your son, and now your feelings about school. We'll want to look more closely at all of these issues and establish some goals, but I wonder how you feel about our continuing to work together?

Eileen 33: I think I feel all right about it. You're really the first person I've talked to about all this. I'd be afraid my women friends would think I'm a terrible person if I told them about my past. Charles knows about all this, but he's not much help. Whenever I mention anything to do with another man, he gets really jealous, so lots of topics are off limits. He says I should just put the past behind me and move on. Maybe he's right. In a way, I'm afraid I'll feel worse if I keep talking about all this.

Clinician 34: I can understand that you wouldn't want to keep feeling pain from those past experiences, and I will do my best to help you deal with those feelings. But I think that counseling might be able to help you find a way to continue your education and also feel better about yourself.

Eileen 34: I would certainly like that. Where do we go from here?

Clinician 35: We do have a little more time before the end of our session. How would it be to look at some of your options for continuing school and then set up an appointment to meet again?

Eileen 35: Sounds good to me.

Discussion Questions

The following questions will help you to examine this intake interview more closely. They also should help you to improve your skills, especially your understanding of appropriate and helpful ways to use questions.

Notice the types of interventions that were used in this interview, particularly the use of questions. Respond to the following questions in terms of your assessment of the interventions used in the interview.

Quality of Interview Questions

- Were the questions mainly open questions or mainly closed questions? What differences, if any, do you notice in the client's responses to the open versus the closed questions?
- Did the interviewer rely too heavily on the use of questions? If so, what might the interviewer have done differently? If not, what did the interviewer do to keep this interview from sounding like an interrogation?
- Which questions seemed particularly fruitful? What made these good questions?
- Were there questions that did not seem to work very well? If so, how might you have improved on these questions?

Goals of the Interview Questions

- Compare this interview with the list on page **101** of the topics that are usually covered in an intake interview. What topics, if any, were omitted? Should they have been included in this session, or are they better left for a subsequent session?
- Did this interview accomplish the important purposes of an intake interview? To determine that, consider the following questions:
  - Was the clinician successful in initiating a positive therapeutic alliance with this client? If so, what made that happen? If not, what might the clinician have done differently?
  - Did the clinician obtain an explanation of why Eileen sought treatment at the present time, as well as a description of her presenting concerns? What led Eileen to seek help?
  - Did the clinician obtain enough relevant information about Eileen's background, history, and context? What information seems especially important to you? What additional information, if any, would have been helpful to the treatment process?
  - What connections do you see between Eileen's history and her current concerns? How might you make use of those connections to help Eileen?
  - What concerns does Eileen have that seem amenable to counseling?
  - What strengths does Eileen have? Consider both stated and implied strengths. How could these help her achieve her goals?
  - Are you able to determine from this interview whether Eileen might present a danger to herself or others? (This information can be inferred from the overall content of the interview or discovered through specific questions.) Would you have done anything differently to assess for dangerousness?

Overall Assessment of Intake Interview

- Overall, how would you assess the quality of this intake interview? What do you see as its strengths? Its weaknesses? How would you have improved on or changed this interview?

- Now that you have some preliminary information about Eileen and her reasons for seeking help, how do you think treatment of this client will progress? What would you want to keep in mind and be sure to address in your work with Eileen? More information will be provided on Eileen's treatment throughout this book.

LEARNING OPPORTUNITIES

As you know, a variety of learning opportunities is included throughout this book to help you develop the skills presented. Learning opportunities at the end of each chapter generally include written exercises, discussion questions, practice group exercises, Assessment of Progress forms, and personal journal questions.

Keep in mind that you are not expected to complete all of the learning opportunities presented throughout this book. Rather, you or your professors or supervisors should select those exercises that are most likely to enhance your professional learning and development, help you reach your goals, and be meaningful to you.

Fundamental Skill: Effective Questioning

The following knowledge and skills have been presented in Chapter 3:

- How questions can enhance the treatment process
- The differences between helpful and unhelpful questions
- Assessing the effectiveness of questions
- Planning the purpose of questions
- Open questions
- Closed questions
- Implicit questions
- Opening words of effective questions
- Key questions
- Formulating effective questions
- Pacing of questions
- Integrating questions with other interventions
- Using questions effectively to gather background information

Written Exercises

1. Determine whether the following questions are open or closed questions:
   a. When will you be home for dinner?
   b. How did you do on your exam?
   c. What was your relationship like with your sister?
   d. Could you tell me more about that relationship?
   e. Have you been in counseling before?

2. Read the following client statements and rate the helpfulness of each of the clinician responses according to the scale, ranging from extremely helpful to extremely harmful:

   a. I asked my daughter whether she minded if I moved next door to her and she said she did. I must have been a terrible mother to her.

      - Where does your daughter live?
      - How did you reach that conclusion?
      - What feelings did you have after your conversation with your daughter?
      - Why did you want to move closer to her?
      - Don't you think that parents should give their adult children some space?

   b. My husband and I really had a wonderful day together for a change.

      - What is your time together usually like?
      - What happened to make that day so special?
      - What did you do to make that day so special?
      - Who took care of the children?
      - How did you spend the day?

   c. My sister still hasn't sent me the money she owes me.

      - How does this affect your feelings about your sister?
      - What impact will this have on your budget?
      - Have you thought about taking her to small claims court?
      - How much money does she owe you?
      - How will you handle this?

3. What characterized the helpful responses in Exercise 2?
4. What characterized the harmful responses in Exercise 2?
5. Write a helpful question in reply to the following client statements:
   a. My mother says that my dog is really sick and it's time to put her down.
   b. How dare my father criticize my marriage! He's been divorced three times.
   c. No matter how hard I try, I just can't get my work done on schedule.
6. Review your responses to Exercise 5. For each response, indicate what your purpose or intention was in the question you formulated.
7. Write an example of a scaling question that you might use with one of the clients in Exercise 5.
8. Write an example of an empowering question that you might use with one of the clients in Exercise 5.
9. Write an example of a solution-focused question that you might use with one of the clients in Exercise 5.

Written or Discussion Questions

Refer to the intake interview of Eileen Carter and respond to the following questions, either in writing or via discussion:

1. What patterns did you notice in Eileen's life?
2. How could you use this information to plan your counseling with Eileen and establish goals with her?

3. How important does it seem to your work with Eileen that you have gathered information about her history?

Discussion Questions

1. Sometimes beginning clinicians feel intrusive when they ask clients personal questions. Have you felt that way? How did you deal with those feelings? What can you do to maximize the likelihood that you will ask helpful questions that are not intrusive?
2. The Miracle Question has become a popular tool for clinicians. How do you explain the popularity of this question? What risks are inherent in using the miracle question? How can you address those risks?
3. What do you see as the most important goals of an intake interview?
4. If you have not yet done the practice group exercises associated with this chapter, discuss your thoughts and feelings about that upcoming experience. How can you allay any apprehensions you might have about that process and prepare yourself to learn from the experience?
5. If you have already done the practice group exercises associated with this chapter, discuss your reactions to that experience. What was the most beneficial aspect of that experience for you? What was the most challenging or uncomfortable aspect of that experience? How can you make future practice group exercises even more rewarding to you?

Practice Group Exercise: *Questions and Intake Interviews*

Divide into your practice groups, as described in Chapter 1. You have probably already had a meeting with your practice group or have discussed the groups in class and so are familiar with the structure and process of the practice group exercises. The practice group exercise presented here will help you gain experience in the two fundamental skills described in this chapter: asking effective questions and using questions to conduct an intake interview.

Each member of the group should have a tape recorder and a blank tape available to facilitate learning from this exercise. Be sure that you record yourself in the clinician role as well as the feedback you receive on your role-play. If the group agrees, I encourage you to tape all of the role-plays and feedback sessions. We can learn a great deal from others' experiences as well as from our own. If possible, allow at least 2 hours for this exercise.

Role-Play Exercise

The primary goal of this role play is for you to conduct a brief intake interview with your partner, making effective use of questions. As discussed in this chapter, you should rely primarily on open questions (particularly those beginning with *what* and *how*) and on implied questions to promote dialogue and information gathering. You should be sure to integrate your questions with other interventions so that your interview builds rapport, puts the client at ease, and sounds like a productive conversation rather than an interrogation. Before beginning this role-play, you might want to review the categories of information usually covered in intake interviews.

Time Schedule and Format

- Allow 15 to 20 minutes for each role-played intake interview. During that time, one person becomes the clinician, one becomes the client, and the other one or two group members become observers and timekeepers.
- As discussed in Chapter 1, when you are in the client role, you will decide whether to be yourself and present accurate information about yourself and your life. Of course, you always have the right not to disclose any particular piece of information that you do not want to share with your group. If you would prefer not to be yourself in this or any other exercise in this book, you can assume the role of someone you know well, being sure to disguise the identity of that person, or you can assume the role of a hypothetical person.
- Following each role-play, take about 10 minutes to provide feedback to the person in the clinician role. Be sure to begin the feedback process with the person in the clinician role, then move on to the person in the client role, and finally to the observers. Focus on strengths first, and offer concrete suggestions for improvement. This should be a positive learning experience, not one that makes people feel criticized or judged. Feedback should emphasize the areas listed in the following Assessment of Progress form. Complete Assessment of Progress Form 3 with a summary of the feedback you received.

  Receiving feedback can be a difficult experience. Try to listen with an open mind to the feedback you receive and ask questions if the information is confusing or unclear. Be sure to play an active role in giving feedback when you are in the client or observer role; those roles, too, can be excellent opportunities for learning.

  After the first round of role-played intake interview and feedback, rotate roles. Continue this process until all group members have had the opportunity to be in clinician, client, and observer roles.

Assessment of Progress Form 3

1. Use of questions
   a. Balance of open and closed questions
   b. Nature of questions (implicit, open, or closed); beginning with *how, what, why,* or another word)
   c. Integration of questions and other interventions
   d. Helpfulness of questions
2. Intake interview
   a. Identification and exploration of presenting concerns
   b. Ability to elicit relevant information on background, history, context
   c. Ability to develop initial rapport
   d. Strengths of intake interview
   e. Omissions or areas needing improvement

3. Summary of feedback
4. Two or three goals that will help you improve your clinical skills

Personal Journal Questions

As discussed earlier in this book, the personal journal questions are designed to promote your self-awareness and personal and professional learning and development. Your responses to these questions should be written in a journal when you have some quiet time and can give thought to your answers to these questions.

1. Listen to the tape recording of the role-played intake interview that you conducted. Respond to the following questions about your role-play:

   - What was your overall reaction when you heard yourself in the role of clinician?
   - Identify the anxieties and rewards you experienced in that role.
   - On the scale presented on page **97**, how would you rate the overall helpfulness of the interview you conducted?
   - List one or two interventions you made that seemed particularly effective.
   - List one or two interventions you made that you think needed improvement. How would you have modified these interventions?
   - Listen to the opening section of the tape and write down the first five interventions that you made. Identify your purpose in using each of these interventions. For each one, note whether you accomplished your purpose.
   - What one improvement will you try to make in your role-plays next time?

2. What is the most important thing you learned from this chapter and its exercises?

SUMMARY

This chapter focused on the fundamental skill of asking effective questions. This skill is especially useful in eliciting background information, although effective questions are used for a wide variety of other clinical purposes. Effective questioning depends on having a clear purpose for the question, phrasing the question in such a way as to elicit an honest and substantive response while enhancing the therapeutic alliance, and pacing questions and other interventions in ways that are helpful to clients. The skill of effective questioning was then applied to the process of conducting an intake interview that is both informative and conducive to developing a positive therapeutic alliance.

The next chapter will present some strategies that draw heavily on the use of effective questions and also promote exploration of background. Particular attention will be paid to helping clients prepare and explore a lifeline and a genogram. Chapter 4 will also present the use effective questions to elicit people's earliest recollections and help them find meaning and self-knowledge in those recollections. In addition, the next chapter will provide information on structuring an initial session and making discussion of the past relevant and meaningful.

Chapter 4

ADDITIONAL SKILLS USED TO GATHER INFORMATION AND UNDERSTAND BACKGROUND: STRUCTURING THE INITIAL SESSION, EARLY RECOLLECTIONS, GENOGRAMS, AND LIFE CHRONOLOGY

OVERVIEW

The use of effective questions and the ability to conduct a successful intake interview, described in Chapter 3, are fundamental skills used by clinicians seeking to better understand their clients and especially to gather information about their histories and backgrounds. This chapter builds on these fundamental skills, providing you with additional knowledge and experience in information gathering as well as several strategies you can use to obtain a deeper, clearer, and more structured picture of your clients' histories.

LEARNING GOALS

As a result of reading this chapter and completing the exercises throughout, you can expect to accomplish the following:

- Understand how to structure an initial session.
- Be aware of pitfalls associated with focusing on the past.
- Help clients elicit and process early recollections.
- Use genograms and lifelines to better learn about clients' pasts.

SKILLS TO BE LEARNED

Six skills that help clinicians gather information and understand clients' backgrounds are presented in this chapter:

- Structuring an initial session
- Making discussion of the past relevant and meaningful
- Eliciting strengths from discussion of background information
- Using early recollections to elicit patterns
- Developing genograms to gather information on background
- Creating lifelines with clients to provide background information

In learning the last four strategies (eliciting strengths, earliest recollections, genograms, and lifelines), you will have the opportunity to apply these tools to yourself as well as to see how they can be applied to clients. This will enhance your repertoire of clinical skills and can also contribute to your own professional and personal development.

STRUCTURING AN INITIAL SESSION

First impressions are powerful and influential, as we all know. That is true in clinical settings as well as in social ones. The first session with a client may well determine the success or failure of the treatment process. In many settings, attrition is high after a first session. Of course, some people leave an initial session having achieved their goals. However, people are more likely to terminate treatment after the first session if they are dissatisfied and do not believe that treatment will be helpful to them. In addition, for people who continue in treatment, that first session may well serve as their prototype of the client–clinician interaction. Clearly, clinicians must pay particular attention to the nature and structure of that first session in order to launch the treatment process in a positive and productive direction.

Important goals to be accomplished in an initial session include the following (Seligman, 2004):

Decide whether the client is likely to benefit from treatment in this setting. Most people seem insightful and knowledgeable enough to seek help from appropriate sources. However, sometimes people do not have a good understanding of their own needs or may be reluctant to acknowledge their most important areas of concern. As a result, they may contact or be referred to a treatment program that does not offer the help they need. Examples include the adolescent having hallucinations who seeks help from her school counselor, the woman with severe drug and alcohol problems who makes an appointment with a psychologist in a general private practice, and the man with career concerns who seeks help from a social worker specializing in helping people with chronic and life-threatening illnesses. Ideally, these mismatches are clarified before an appointment is scheduled and an appropriate referral is made. If that does not happen, clinicians should gently explain the nature of the services they provide and why those services are not likely to meet the client's needs. Providing appropriate referrals to such people, and helping them connect with other sources of help, would now become part of the clinician's role.

Assess and address the urgency of a person's concerns.   Most people seeking mental health services are not in crisis. However, clinicians sometimes see clients who are suicidal, dangerous to others, at risk of being harmed by others, psychotic, or incapable of keeping themselves safe. When clinicians identify such urgent situations, other goals are set aside while these critical issues are addressed. Keeping clients safe and taking steps to prevent harm to anyone become the overriding goals of treatment. Clinicians may need to arrange for hospitalization, help a client find a protected place to live, enlist family and friends in helping keep a client safe, formulate safety plans with a client, or even notify the police or a person who is endangered by the client.

Orient people to the treatment process.   Whether or not people have had previous mental health services, they should be oriented to the treatment process. The nature of this orientation varies greatly; school counselors may present only a brief verbal explanation of how they can help students, whereas clinicians at a mental health agency or private practice typically have a written statement that provides information on their background and training, clinical orientation, and credentials. They also usually present information on their treatment policies including how to contact them, confidentiality, scheduling and cancellation policies, fees, billing, and their participation in managed care organizations.

Although some clinicians view this process as bureaucratic and interfering with the treatment process, clients often are reassured by information on guidelines and limitations of treatment. In addition, today's emphasis on accountability in mental health treatment requires that clinicians provide their clients with information on the treatment process and allow them the opportunity to ask questions and obtain clarification on all policies.

Initiate development of a positive therapeutic alliance and engender hope and positive expectations.   Therapy begins with the first moment of contact, and clinicians should communicate the importance of collaborating and working together from that point onward to help clients achieve their goals. Some clinicians begin the first session with social conversation, trying to put the client at ease with discussion of the weather, the traffic, and other extraneous topics. However, clients are there because they want help; they may be both eager and anxious about the treatment process.

Treatment usually gets off to a better start if clinicians maintain a professional but caring and collaborative role from the outset. Clinicians who are structured yet flexible, who are confident yet able to join with clients, and who are empathic yet do not participate in clients' depression or self-pity are most likely to engender a positive therapeutic alliance and initiate treatment that is productive and helpful. In addition, focusing on strengths as well as problems can give balance to the session and can help people to become more aware of their resources, use them effectively to help themselves, and feel more empowered and optimistic. More will be said later in this chapter on emphasizing and developing people's strengths in treatment.

Provide role induction and help clients quickly learn how they can be effective clients.   Just as being an effective clinician can be learned, so can being an effective client. Emphasizing the collaborative nature of the treatment process, encouraging clients to bring in issues of concern and to talk honestly and openly, and helping them identify and value their strengths and resources all contribute to helping people learn how to help themselves and make good use of the treatment process. To further these ends, clinicians should guard against taking over the session and talking too much. Clinicians may believe that they should be much more active in early sessions, in order to reduce clients' anxiety and provide support. However, this is likely to convey to people an erroneous picture of the treatment process. A more helpful strategy is to engage clients from the outset of treatment, conveying the message that client and clinician are partners in a shared endeavor.

Explore and acquire a preliminary understanding of people's presenting concerns.   People nearly always seek counseling or psychotherapy because they are experiencing distress or impairment or both. They may be depressed or enraged, have difficulty functioning at work or at school, repeatedly conflict with family members, use drugs or alcohol in unhealthy ways, or have a multitude of other concerns. Their primary motivation is almost always to effect a positive change in these presenting concerns. This is the place to begin. Clinicians can start their exploration of people's presenting concerns by asking some of the following questions:

- What led you to seek treatment when you did?
- What sorts of c oncerns brought you into my office?
- What changes would you like to make in your life?
- How are you hoping that our work together will help you?

Some additional questions that contribute to understanding people's presenting concerns include the following:

- How has that issue affected your life?
- Please give me an example of when that concern recently occurred.
- Have you had concerns like this in the past? Please tell me about that.
- How would your life be different if you didn't have to struggle with this problem?
- What reactions have you gotten from other people when this issue presented itself?
- What have you done so far to help yourself deal with this issue? How have those strategies worked for you?

In exploring people's presenting concerns, clinicians should join with their clients in an effort to address their issues, gather information that will help them make a diagnosis and develop a treatment plan, and communicate hope that, together, the client and clinician can effect positive changes in the client's emotions, thoughts, and behavior. Discussing people's presenting concerns both early and late in an initial session can enhance the treatment alliance. Addressing their concerns early conveys respect, interest, and a desire to help them with what is causing them difficulty. Returning to a discussion of presenting concerns toward the end of the session reminds people that clinicians recognize that those concerns are their first priority.

Conclude the session by suggesting a strategy that people might use between sessions to help themselves in order to promote positive action between appointments. This should be a suggestion, not an assignment, and the suggestions should be discussed with clients and modified as needed to ensure that the clients are willing and motivated to follow up on the suggestion. Such a process helps people to feel more in control and powerful, to see that they can take steps to help themselves, and to motivate their return for the next session.

Begin to gather information on context and background. Putting people's presenting concerns in context is essential to truly understanding them and the issues for which they are seeking help. Gathering information on people's backgrounds also is important. That process helps us to look beyond their presenting concerns and to appreciate them from a holistic perspective. It assists us in identifying people's strengths, in recognizing problems or mental disorders that clients may not be aware of or willing to share with us, and helps us to understand developmental, multicultural, familial, interpersonal, and other patterns. This can deepen our understanding of our clients, enable us to develop accurate diagnoses and more effective treatment plans, and increase our ability to help them.

I always explain to my clients that, by gathering some information on their histories, I can better understand their presenting concerns and put them in context. This brief explanation increases people's comfort in discussing their past and encourages their truthful disclosure of important experiences in their backgrounds. They know that I am shifting my attention to the past for awhile, not because I am prying or because I believe that should be our primary focus, but in the service of helping with their presenting concerns. Returning to discussion of those concerns before the session ends further conveys that message.

MAKING DISCUSSION OF THE PAST RELEVANT AND MEANINGFUL

One of the most important reasons why the mental health professions interest us is because nearly all of us reading this book are interested in people and their lives. When our clients present compelling stories of their past, as they often do, we can get caught up in the stories and ask questions out of our own curiosity. Although this may be fine in social settings, it should not provide the purpose for our inquiries during treatment.

The previous chapter discussed the importance of formulating questions with a purpose in mind. Similarly, having a clear and therapeutic purpose in mind is essential when we explore people's histories.

Some clinicians, notably those who practice psychoanalysis or in-depth psychodynamic therapy, dwell at length on the histories of their clients, ferreting out early problems in attachment or in feeding and toilet training that may be worked through via free association, analysis of the transference relationship, and other strategies. However, most clinicians today operate very differently. They appreciate the impact of the past on the present and recognize the need to conduct at least a brief exploration of their clients' histories. However, their ultimate goal is to help people use their knowledge and insights into the past to effect change in the present. This chapter assumes that most clinicians will use past information and patterns to inform and improve on the present.

Pitfalls of Focusing on the Past

Some cautions should be kept in mind as we move on to a discussion of how to make exploration of the past relevant and meaningful:

- Many clients are reluctant to talk about their past. They may find such discussions painful and reminiscent of unappealing stereotypes of Freudian psychoanalysis.
- In addition, people generally seek treatment because they are experiencing impairment and unhappiness in their present lives. When too much of the treatment focuses on the past, people often feel like their current concerns are being ignored and devalued and that therapists are operating according to their own agendas.
- Extensive discussion of past issues and experiences can lead both clients and clinicians to lose sight of the clients' current concerns and get caught up in a compelling story.
- Some people are more comfortable talking about the past than they are about the present. They may have some experiences in their background that are amusing or poignant or shocking and they enjoy telling and retelling stories about these experiences that inevitably elicit concern and interest from others. By focusing on the past, these clients can bypass discussion of their current concerns and the steps they need to take to resolve those concerns. Their emphasis on the past, then, is often a way to avoid making difficult changes in order to alleviate present concerns.
- Discussion of the past can encourage clients to blame others for their difficulties. Extensive exploration of the client's dysfunctional family, childhood bullying, and poverty, although valid and important information, runs the risk of shifting power and responsibility away from the client and onto past experiences that cannot be changed. This can lead the client to feel discouraged and hopeless and can exacerbate depression and other current concerns.

Examples of Dialogues About the Past

Let's look at two client–clinician dialogues about past experiences. Read them carefully, and then respond to the questions about the two examples.

Example 1

Clinician: So you are concerned about your alcohol use and are particularly worried that it may be contributing to your feelings of depression and loss of interest in your family. Often past family patterns program us to develop similar patterns in our own lives. Tell me about your parents' use of alcohol.

Clint: My father did drink a lot and, like me, he didn't make much time for his family. He was a well-known musician and was on the road much of the time. He and his band often performed in bars and nightclubs and so I guess it was easy for him to drink more than he should.

Clinician: Your father was a well-known musician? What was his band?

Clint: They were called the Funky Brother's Band—even had a couple of gold records.

Clinician: Really! Yes, I've heard of them. They were pretty well known when I was in high school. So how did it affect you to have a famous father?

Clint: I don't think I even knew he was famous when I was a kid. He just wasn't around much and I missed him. But then when he'd come home, he'd be drinking and so he was never really much of a father.

Clinician: So you never had a good role model for how a father is supposed to be. It's not surprising that you would have problems much like your father did.

Clint: Yeah, I guess it was sort of inevitable. But at least I don't use drugs like he did.

Clinician: He used drugs?

Clint: Yeah, my dad worked pretty hard to keep that a secret, but one day the cops showed up at our house with a search warrant, looked through my toys and everything. That made the news big time and Dad's music career was pretty much over.

Clinician: So what did he do after his music career ended?

Example 2

Clinician: So you are concerned about your alcohol use and are particularly worried that it may be contributing to your feelings of depression and loss of interest in your family. It might help us to put your concerns in context by spending a little time exploring your own family background. How would you feel about that?

Darren: That would be fine. I've actually thought quite a bit about the parallels between my life now and my family when I was a kid.

Clinician: What thoughts have you had about that?

Darren: Well, my dad had a problem with alcohol, and he wasn't very involved with our family either. Of course, he was a big-time musician with gold records and all. I guess all those performances in bars and nightclubs really set him up to have a problem with alcohol.

Clinician: So even though your career is pretty different from that of your father's, you see the two of you as having similar problems, misusing alcohol and distancing yourself from the family.

Darren: Yeah, I guess I'm just programmed to follow in my dad's footsteps. That's pretty discouraging.

Clinician: Sounds like you see your father as a big influence on you. But I wonder if we can figure out some ways for you to find your own path rather than continuing to follow in your dad's footsteps. What thoughts do you have on that?

Question on Dialogues

1. You have read about the pitfalls of exploration of the past. Drawing on that information, identify three pitfalls in the first dialogue, pinpointing exactly where they occur in the dialogue:

   a. _____

   b. _____

   c. _____

2. We have not yet reviewed ways to help clients make helpful use of past information. However, you may be able to anticipate some of the guidelines in that section. Identify three ways the clinician in the second dialogue guided the

client in making productive use of past information, pinpointing exactly where they occur in the dialogue.

a. _____
b. _____
c. _____

Helpful Use of Past Information

Here are some guidelines for making sound therapeutic use of background information. You may already have identified some of these principles as you analyzed the strengths in the second dialogue.

- Help clients understand why you are shifting attention from current concerns to background. Explain that you and they can probably better understand and address their current concerns by "putting them in context." This makes sense to most people. They are eager to help you understand them better and are generally motivated to provide some relevant past information that helps make sense and meaning of their lives.
- Check out with clients their willingness to talk about past issues and let them collaborate with you in deciding what background information is germane to their current concerns.
- Encourage clients to make frequent connections between their past histories and their current concerns. Examples of questions that facilitate this include:
  - What can you tell me about your background that would help us make sense of the difficulties you are experiencing now?
  - I wonder if there were other times in your life when you had similar difficulties.
  - Does this remind you of any other experiences /symptoms/relationships you had in the past? Please tell me about that.
  - What similarities and differences do you see between your marriage/ career/other variables and those of important family members?
  - Have other people in your family had symptoms such as those you are experiencing?
  - What other questions can you think of that can help you link past and present?
- In general, avoid spending too much time dwelling in the past with a client without referring back to current concerns. If you identify an important topic in the past that warrants further exploration at a later date, you can name the topic and let the client know that you will return to it later. For example, you might say, "It sounds like we want to return to the impact of teasing you experienced as a child, but I do want to spend the last few minutes of our session brainstorming some strategies with you for responding to your supervisor's criticisms. How about if I make a note of this topic and we put it on the shelf to come back to in our next session?"

- Be sure that you always have a clear and therapeutic purpose in mind when delving into past issues. Particularly important is being sure to be guided by the client's best interests, not by your own interest or curiosity.
- Interventions usually are particularly effective when they empower clients and enable them to help themselves. Consequently, rather than jumping in to point out connections or make interpretations, ask questions that will help clients put together the pieces and see patterns. For example, rather than saying, "All the men you looked up to as a child were hurtful to you. No wonder you don't trust your husband," ask, "You've told me about your father who was emotionally distant, your uncle who frequently made fun of your weight, and your favorite teacher who touched you inappropriately. I wonder if you see any connection between those experiences and the difficulty you are having in trusting your husband?"
- Carefully monitor clients' reactions to discussion of the past. Note both verbal and nonverbal messages. If people become uncomfortable with discussion of past issues, you might comment on their reactions and ask if they would prefer to explore the topic at hand further or shift the focus of the session.
- Before the end of the session, bring the focus of attention back to the present, being sure to bring some comfortable closure to the discussion of the past.
- Collaborate with the client in summarizing the session, being sure to highlight gains and strengths and identify ways to continue progress outside of the session.

Of course, the structure of sessions will vary over the course of treatment. However, clinicians should usually begin a session by addressing the client's most pressing concerns, then put those concerns into context while focusing on helpful strengths, and finally bring the session back to the initial concerns of the session, summarizing the progress that was made and suggesting one or more between-session tasks that might continue and solidify gains made during the session.

ELICITING STRENGTHS FROM DISCUSSION OF BACKGROUND

The work of the mental health professional has changed in many ways during the past 10 to 15 years. One of the biggest differences is the shift from a focus on pathology to a focus on strengths. Many clinicians practicing during the 1970s were still closely tied to Freudian psychoanalytic ideology. Their treatment was grounded in the belief that the roots of current concerns lay in the past and that only in-depth work on past issues, particularly those stemming from impaired development in early childhood, could really be effective in ameliorating current concerns.

This perspective changed throughout the 1980s and 1990s and now, in the twenty-first century, most clinicians seem to have adopted a different perspective. Although clinicians continue to recognize the importance of past learning and experiences as formative and meriting exploration, current counseling and psychotherapy typically focus on the present rather than on the past and on strengths as well as on pathology. A strength-based treatment approach helps people to feel hopeful and empowered, to see that they do have effective strategies for coping with their difficulties, and to learn skills that they can continue to use to help themselves deal with future difficulties.

In eliciting strengths, clinicians should cast a wide net, looking at all aspects of a person's life and particularly highlighting assets and coping skills people have used effectively in the past. The quest for strengths should extend, but not be limited, to the following areas and list of potential strengths:

- **Personal:** motivation, decision making, organizational and planning skills, self-confidence, self-awareness, special talents (e.g., art, music, decorating), personal triumphs and successes
- **Intelligence/knowledge:** overall intelligence, specific areas of academic strength (e.g., writing, mathematics, history), educational background, knowledge gained from reading, hobbies, work, leisure activities
- **Physical:** athletic abilities, skill in a particular sport, physical attributes in which the person takes pride, good health, experience in overcoming or living successfully with serious illness or disabilities
- **Interpersonal skills:** empathy and insight into others, communication skills, ability to motivate and inspire others, capacity for warmth and caring toward others, ability to sustain and energize conversations
- **Family and friends:** people who can be relied on to provide support or practical help to clients, role models of healthy relationships and family functioning, people willing to discuss clients' concerns with them or help them implement plans to achieve their goals, relationships that give people a reason to face and overcome their difficulties (such as relationships with children or elderly parents who need help), the gratification clients receive from helping others, a sense of belonging to a family or group of friends, deeply ingrained values
- **Career and work history:** successes, awards, promotions, and other accomplishments throughout clients' career; times when they have effectively handled challenging work situations; financial resources and benefits (e.g., investments, insurance, vacation and sick days, disability insurance); mastery of new and challenging areas of skill and knowledge
- **Religion and spirituality:** belief in a higher power, prayer, guidance from a spiritual leader, practical and emotional support clients receive from their place of worship, traditions and rituals
- **Ethnic and cultural background:** a sense of history, connection to past generations, strength derived from understanding of past challenges such as discrimination and mistreatment faced and overcome by others from the same cultural or ethnic group, cultural beliefs and practices, community resources, pride in one's ethnic and cultural heritage

Helping People Identify and Discuss Strengths

Many people have difficulty identifying and talking about their strengths. This is particularly likely if they are depressed, come from a negative and critical family background, or have not had the opportunity to demonstrate their strengths.

People's cultural and spiritual beliefs also can interfere with their ease in describing their assets; they may view it as self-centered and inappropriate to praise themselves. Be sure to consider factors that may inhibit people's awareness of their strengths when you help them become more aware of those strengths.

The following are prototypes for questions that we can use to help people recognize, appreciate, and draw on their strengths. The questions can be modified so that they target and explore specific areas:

- What do you see as your greatest strengths?
- What do other people see as your strengths? If their perceptions differ from yours, what sense do you make of that?
- What has made you feel especially proud of yourself?
- What do you see as your most important accomplishments so far?
- When have you experienced other challenges in your life that you dealt with effectively? How did you do that?
- Who are the people you admire? Why are you impressed by them?
- If you felt very upset and scared, who would you call first? Who second?
- What helpful resources are available to you in your community? Family? Religious or spiritual organizations? Other?
- What do you see as the greatest strengths in your family of origin? Your current family? Your network of friends?
- What do you see as the contributions you make to your family? Your workplace? Your social group? Your community?
- When you are feeling at your best, what is it that helps you feel that way?
- If you were to describe two or three special days, over the course of your life, that really stand out in your mind, what would they be?

In addition to these questions, what other questions and strategies might you use to help people identify their strengths? List your ideas below.

1. _____
2. _____
3. _____

Becoming more aware of our strengths and recognizing how they have helped us usually is very empowering. This process typically increases people's feelings of control and competence, enables them to see new options, and gives them new ways of dealing with their concerns. A key question that helps people apply their strengths is as follows:

- How can you use this skill or strength to help you deal with the concerns that brought you into treatment?

We are now going to approach the helpful use of background information in a different way by presenting three strategies that can facilitate people's efforts to identify past patterns and apply them to present situations: early recollections, genograms, and lifelines.

The use of early recollections in treatment stems from the pioneering work of Alfred Adler (1963a, 1963b), a Viennese psychoanalyst who wrote and practiced during the late 19th and early 20th centuries. Adler was originally a follower of Sigmund Freud, but Adler eventually broke with Freud and went on to develop his own approach to treatment, *individual psychology*. Although Adler's ideas about human development are less deterministic than those of Freud, Adler, too, emphasized the value of understanding people's early childhood years. This is reflected in the importance he placed on eliciting and exploring earliest recollections.

Early recollections are important in understanding how people make meaning of their experiences and understand their perspectives on their relationships, themselves, and their lives (Deaner & Pechersky, 2005). When asked for significant early memories or for their earliest memories, people typically produce recollections that reflect or embody their orientation toward their lives. The memories they report are not necessarily their earliest or most salient memories and, in fact, the memories may well be reported inaccurately. The veracity of the memories typically is less important from a clinical perspective than are people's recollections and reports of their memories. Selective memory may well have led to changes in the memories so that they are more congruent with how people view their lives, and it is that perspective that is of greatest importance to clients and clinicians.

Eliciting and Processing Early Memories

Early recollections can provide clinicians with a frame of reference for gathering additional background information, deepening their understanding of their clients, identifying underlying patterns and themes, encouraging exploration, and promoting client self-awareness. Usually, clinicians ask for early or earliest memories without specifying topics or time periods. However, the focus of the memories can be narrowed to provide insight into a specific aspect of a person's life. For example, the clinician might request early memories of family conflicts, joyful moments, painful experiences, interactions with friends, or school experiences.

The process of eliciting and processing early memories typically includes the following four steps (Seligman, 2006, pp. 88–89). As you review the steps, notice that, although the early recollections stem from past experiences, they shed light on people's current emotions, thoughts, actions, perceptions, and relationships.

1. **Eliciting the recollections.** People are asked to describe at least three memories that they believe to be their earliest recollections. Clark (2002, p. 92) suggests asking, "Think back to a long time ago when you were little, and try to recall one of your earliest memories, one of the first things that you can remember." These should be memories of incidents in which the person was present. Whether or not these events actually occurred as recalled and whether they are really the person's earliest memories are not important;

what matters are the person's perceptions. The clinician should write down the memories as they are presented.

2. **Processing the memories.** Explore each memory with the teller, gently probing for additional details and inquiring about

- Emotions, thoughts, and actions reflected in the memories;
- Interactions between the client and other people included in the recollection;
- The most important, memorable, or vivid parts of the memory; and
- The meaning each memory has for the client.

3. **Analyzing the memories.** Client and clinician together process the memories, looking in particular for patterns and commonalities in the situations, the client's roles and reactions, and the client's interactions with others in the memories. Clark (2002) suggests that clinicians also assess the memories in terms of dichotomous variables such as active–passive, encouraging–discouraging, alone–with others, confident–fearful, and happy–sad. Identifying strengths that emerge from the memories is an important element in analyzing the memories and can help clinicians build on strengths that clients already possess.

4. **Interpreting and applying the recollections.** Drawing on that analysis of common themes, responses, and dichotomous variables, the clinician develops a hypothesis as to what these recollections reveal about the client's worldview, goals, and lifestyle. The clinician then presents this hypothesis to the client for discussion and clarification. Information obtained through this process often provides considerable insight into people and the impact their perceptions of their early years have had on the way they lead their lives in the present.

Example of Processing Early Memories

The following three recollections were provided by Eileen Carter, the client introduced in Chapter 3:

Recollection 1:   This must have been a really long time ago because I'm in my crib in this memory. I remember feeling bad; I guess I was hungry or needed to be changed or something. But I knew I wasn't supposed to cry. I was just supposed to wait until someone got ready to take care of me. And so I just waited and waited and waited. . . .

Recollection 2:   I remember when my younger brother was born and my parents brought him home from the hospital. My older brother was there and they let him hold the baby. I asked if I could hold him too and my parents said, "No, Eileen, he's too delicate, You might hurt him." They were all together and I was left out. I just went out of the room and played with my dog. That helped me feel a little better.

Recollection 3:   I remember being at a playground with my mom and my two brothers. My mom kept my hair real short then so she could manage it better. A little white girl walked by us and said to her mother, "Why are those boys all so dark?" I knew the girl thought that there was something wrong with us, and I sure didn't like that. And she didn't even know that I was a girl, like she didn't even really look at me! It made me feel ugly and confused about who I was. I looked at my mom but she didn't do or say anything, just kept talking to her friends. I didn't do anything either.

Discussion Questions   Before reading the analysis of these three early recollections, think about your answers to the following questions:

- What patterns of emotions, thoughts, and actions appear in Eileen's three recollections?
- What patterns of reaction and interaction appear in the three recollections?
- When you consider the memories in terms of some dichotomous variables (e.g., active–passive, encouraging–discouraging, alone–with others, confident–fearful, happy–sad), what patterns do you notice?
- What strengths do you see in Eileen, based on the memories?
- What themes emerge from the three recollections?
- What hunches or hypotheses do you have about what these memories tell us about Eileen?

Analysis   In all three recollections, Eileen feels sad, lonely, and excluded. People around her are talking and interacting but she remains passive, no matter how badly she feels. She seems to long for approval, nurturance, and involvement with others. Instead, she is ignored and rejected.

Eileen does not have effective ways of helping herself or of asking others for help. Her low self-esteem and confusion about her identity compound this problem. Withdrawing and playing with her dog help some, but do not really solve the problem or help Eileen feel confident and strong. However, this does suggest a potential strength; involvement in outside activities may be rewarding and comforting to Eileen. Other potential strengths reflected in the memories are her wish for connection with others, her occasional willingness to ask for what she wants (hold her baby brother), her ability to defer gratification, and her awareness of the people around her. The recollections also reflect a maturity and capacity for introspection.

These patterns are reflected in Eileen's adolescence as well as in her adulthood. As a young adolescent, she did not know how to cope directly with the difficulties in her family or how to make good choices for herself. Consequently, she turned away from the family and toward alcohol and destructive relationships in order to have some sense of belonging and importance. However, Eileen's awareness and maturity eventually enabled her to realize the harmful nature of those choices.

As an adult, she has made healthier choices and has somewhat better connections with others. School, perhaps like her childhood dog, gives her comfort and strength. Her relationship with her husband is far less destructive than her earlier relationships with men, and she has blossomed in the role of mother. Nevertheless, Eileen continues to want more out of her life. Although she feels helpless in light of her husband's demands and the needs of her son, she has reached out for help by contacting a counselor at her college and she is hopeful that, with assistance, she can improve her life.

As you can see, early recollections provide clinicians with a rich tool for gaining understanding of both people's backgrounds and their current views of their lives. Most people find the process of exploring early memories to be an interesting and rewarding one and have little difficulty providing useful memories.

Of course, clinicians need to exercise caution when working with people who may have had very painful or traumatic memories. Conducting an intake interview before moving onto early recollections will help clinicians decide if and when this strategy is likely to be helpful to their work with a particular person. The exercises later in this chapter offer readers an opportunity to gain some experience in working with earliest recollections.

GENOGRAMS

Murray Bowen (1974), one of the leading theoreticians and practitioners of family therapy until his death, deserves most of the credit for establishing the genogram as an important tool for clinicians. Bowen believed that patterns in a current family or individual stem from patterns in those people's families of origin and even from patterns in their grandparents' families. He believed that behaviors, personality traits, and family roles and relationships are passed on from one generation to another via a process called *intergenerational* or *transgenerational transmission*. People learn from their families about how they are supposed to feel, think, and act; what relationships should be like; what are appropriate and acceptable male and female gender roles; and how to parent. The genogram is a useful tool, designed to help clinicians gather information on a person's family background and identify important family patterns and messages (Kaslow, 1995). This can be used with individuals, couples, or families and is helpful in highlighting not only family patterns and messages but also career and other patterns.

Developing a Genogram

Based on information provided by the client, the clinician constructs a genogram on a large sheet of paper. Usually, the genogram includes the current person or family, the families of origin, and the grandparents' families, reflecting three generations. The symbols in Figure 4-1 are used to describe family membership, structure, and interactions (McGoldrick & Gerson, 1988).

Once the family members and structure of the family have been mapped on the genogram, the clinician and client complete the genogram with descriptive information on both the families and the people who belong to the families. Generally, at least three generations are included in the genogram.

There is no one right way to elaborate on a genogram. A simple approach is to list years of birth and death as well as occupations for each person, along with three adjectives describing each one. Mottoes can be developed to reflect parental or family messages. In addition, clinicians can ask questions to clarify family dynamics. Examples of such questions include the following:

- Who do you think you are most like?
- Did any of these people have problems with drugs or alcohol? Depression or other emotional difficulties?

Female: ◯

Male: □

Person of unknown gender: △

Marriage (with date, husband on left, wife on right): □ m. 1988 ◯

Intimate cohabitation: □ 1988 ◯

Children (listed in descending order of age from left to right):

□ m.1988 ◯
⑨ ⑧ ⑤

Twins: □ m.1988 ◯
⑦ ⑦

Pregnancy: □ ◯ △

Marital separation: □ s. 1995 ◯

Divorce: □ d. 1998 ◯

Overly close (enmeshed) relationship: □ ══ ◯

Close relationship: □ ══ ◯

Emotionally distant relationship: □ ----- ◯

Conflicted relationship: □∿∿∿◯

Estranged or emotionally cut-off relationship: □—┤ ├—◯

Death: ⊠ d. 1994

Miscarriage: ●

Abortion: ✕

FIGURE 4-1   Genogram Symbols

Creating a genogram can be a useful way to identify important family patterns and messages from one's background

- What were the marriage and partner relationships like in these families? What roles did each partner have? How were decisions made? How were conflicts addressed? What were the strengths of each partner relationship?
- What were parent–child and sibling relationships like in these families? What were the expectations for the children in each of these families?
- How were the children disciplined? Who was in charge of the discipline?
- What differences, if any, existed between the roles of men and women in this family? What messages were given about appropriate gender roles?
- What were the religious, cultural, and spiritual backgrounds, beliefs, and practices in each of these families?
- Who was closest to whom in each of these families? What were the alliances?
- What conflicts or estrangements were present in these families?
- What was the daily life of the family like? What were the joyful aspects of family life? What were the biggest challenges?

Clinicians can be creative when they ask questions about the genogram, tailoring the questions to the client or to a particular issue or pattern.

Example of a Genogram

Figure 4-2 presents a three-generational genogram of Eileen Carter's family. Review the genogram, looking for patterns that provide insight into Eileen and her background. Use the previous questions to help you hone in on important patterns. Then compare your thoughts with the analysis that follows the genogram.

Several family patterns emerge from this genogram that are relevant to understanding Eileen's development and her current situation and difficulties:

- Harmful use of alcohol
- Problems with impulse control (aggressiveness, gambling, use of alcohol)
- Relatively low expectations for the children
- An imbalance in gender roles, with men apparently having more power and economic success than women
- Women predominantly in maternal and nurturing roles
- No involvement in higher education
- Relationship difficulties, reflected in divorces and other behaviors
- Losses through early deaths and divorces

From this genogram and analysis, some of the connections between Eileen's family background and both her past and her current concerns are evident. These include the following:

- Eileen, like others in her family, has difficulty with problem solving, and she used substances, at least temporarily, as a solution to her difficulties.
- Along with others in her family, Eileen has had difficulty with impulse control.

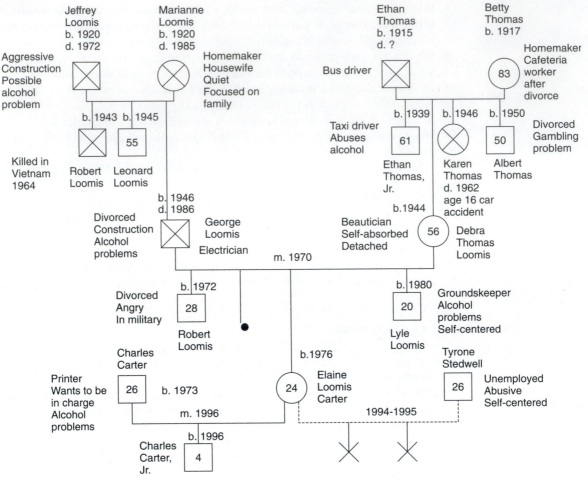

FIGURE 4-2   Genogram of Eileen Carter's Family

- Eileen's family expected little of her, except to avoid causing trouble and burdening her family. This message probably contributed to Eileen's doubts about her ability to succeed in college and in her roles as wife and mother.
- The lack of positive female role models, the apparent dominance of the men in the families, and the lack of family members' involvement in higher education probably also contributed to the difficulty Eileen is having now in believing she has the right and the ability to continue her college education.
- Because relationship problems are common in her family, Eileen apparently lacks models of healthy relationships. She does not have criteria for assessing her marriage, strategies for effectively addressing the issues between her and her husband, or skills for successfully balancing her own needs and those of her husband and son.
- Losses are prevalent in this family and, of course, Eileen lost her father when she was a child. Now that she has her own family, the specter of those

losses may contribute to her fear that if she does not please her husband or be an exceptional mother, she, too, may experience the loss of her family.

Additional Perspectives on the Genogram

Just as early recollections can be obtained and analyzed from both general and specific perspectives, so can the genogram. This is a rich resource that can be developed and processed in ways that will illuminate various aspects of people's lives. Several of these are discussed in the following subsections. Feel free to be creative and think about other ways that genograms can be helpful to you and your clients.

Strength-Based Analysis   Many clinicians easily identify clients' problems and challenges but neglect their strengths. The genogram can help clinicians ensure that they do not overlook clients' strengths, which can be instrumental in helping them make positive changes.

Clinicians can help clients construct a genogram specifically focused on strengths in which clients identify the assets and admirable characteristics of each person and family in the genogram. This can highlight strengths that may have been passed on to the client and also can help identify role models that the client can use to master new skills and acquire new strengths.

In addition, a general genogram such as that illustrated in Figure 4-2 can be used to identify potential strengths. Here are a few that emerge from Eileen's genogram:

- Eileen's rejection of her abusive relationship with Tyrone and her ability to choose Charles, who seems committed to his family and who is not blatantly abusive, are strengths.
- Her mother Debra Loomis, a single parent who raised three children while working as a beautician, might offer some Eileen some ways to blend both parts of her life.
- The men in Eileen's family always succeeded in maintaining employment and supporting their families. Their toughness and pride in their work may have been communicated to Eileen and may help her embrace education and employment as legitimate and rewarding parts of her life.

What other strengths and assets can you identify in Eileen's genogram?

Birth-Order Analysis   Alfred Adler not only promoted the use of early recollections as a way to better understand people, but also advocated an analysis of birth order as a productive source of information about people, their upbringing, their self-images, their roles and aspirations, and their behavior (Adler, 1963a).

The following brief description provides information on some of the most prominent personality traits associated with each birth position:

- **Oldest children:** high achieving, responsible, cooperative and well socialized, often with strong verbal and leadership skills

- **Second-born children:** creative and sociable, typically less traditional than the oldest children, seeking their own paths
- **Middle children:** resemble second-born children, but often need extra nurturing and guidance to help them make lifestyle choices that are right for them
- **Youngest children:** often develop good social skills and sensitivity to others, typically have a spontaneous and innovative nature
- **Only children:** often combine the achievement orientation and cooperative behavior of the oldest with the creativity of the youngest; maturing early is characteristic

Information on birth order can be particularly useful if it is enriched by consideration of gender patterns, abilities and disabilities, and age differences between the children in the family. Sometimes, traditional patterns are altered because of these factors. For example, parents may have expectations for a second-born son that would typically be applied to a first born; however, if the first born is a female, if the age difference between the two children is small, or if the second child seems stronger and healthier than the second, a family may alter the usual patterns in terms of the messages they give their children.

Eileen is the second born and middle child in a family of three children. She has an older brother and a younger brother, with four years difference between her age and each of her siblings. Her family of origin was a traditional one with the highest expectations being placed on Robert, Eileen's older brother. The family was pleased when he enlisted in the military as a teenager, completing high school while in the army. The only messages Eileen recalled related to her future was that she should find a husband with a stable job who could support her and the children they would have. Her gender and birth order, along with her family's traditional views of gender roles, lack of interest and experience in higher education, and strong work ethic for the men, probably all combined to give Eileen the message that being a wife and mother should be her primary role.

At the same time, Eileen's mother is also a second-born and, after the death of her sister, became a middle child with both older and younger brothers. This is the same birth order pattern as that of her daughter. Perhaps this similarity can help Eileen and her mother to better understand each other, lead to a productive conversation, and help Eileen recognize that her career development may have been restricted by factors unrelated to her abilities or interests.

Other Focused Analyses of Genograms   Although other types of genograms and analyses will not be illustrated here, keep in mind that the types and uses of genograms are limited only by the clinician's imagination and creativity. The following are some additional areas of potentially useful focus for genograms:

- **Career-oriented genogram.** This type of genogram focuses on career paths followed by family members, looking at the education required for their occupations, their success and satisfaction with their careers, the integration of their personal and professional lives, and the messages clients received about their abilities and recommended or appropriate career and educational choices. A career-oriented genogram can be particularly useful to people who are having difficulty making career and educational choices or who are floundering and unhappy in their careers but have little understanding of the reasons for these difficulties.

- **Culturally oriented genogram.** A culturally oriented genogram pays particular attention to cultural, religious, and spiritual patterns in families; the impact and messages of those cultural, religious, and spiritual patterns; and messages that clients have received about conforming to or deviating from the belief system in their family of origin. This type of genogram can be especially useful to people from families who have immigrated from one country to another, who have diverse cultural and religious groups in their backgrounds, who have spiritual and cultural beliefs and attitudes that differ from those with which they were raised, who have experienced a significant change in their own spiritual beliefs, or who are struggling to find ways to make their cultural and spiritual backgrounds meaningful for themselves.

THE LIFELINE OR LIFE CHRONOLOGY

The lifeline or life chronology is another tool available to clinicians seeking useful ways to gather background information. The lifeline or chronology can provide a clear and concise overview of a person's history, facilitating identification of high points, disappointments, milestones, hopes, and patterns. The lifeline can be prepared as a list or as a graph. A list is the simplest way to compile this information.

Preparing the Lifeline

After one or two treatment sessions, the clinician might ask the client to complete a form such as the one that follows:

Directions: The purpose of this form is to gather important information about your life so far and your hopes for the future. For each group of ages listed below, provide a brief description of your life during those years, including the following information:

- Primary activities (e.g., attending elementary school, caring for my family)
- Highlights
- Disappointments
- Other milestones or important information

For ages older than your current age, indicate what you hope will be your primary activities and highlights during those years, as well as what problems or disappointments might occur during those years that concern you.

1. Birth–age 4
2. Ages 5–10
3. Ages 11–18
4. Ages 19–24
5. Ages 25–34
6. Ages 35–44
7. Ages 45–54
8. Ages 55–64
9. Ages 65–74
10. Ages 75 and beyond

Additional information can also be incorporated into the chronology. This might include the person's assessment of his or her negotiation of each group of years, one positive and one negative word associated with each age range, and an identification of the one most rewarding and one most disappointing point in the person's life during those years. As with the genogram, clinicians can be creative and adapt the exercise to the particular person.

If client and clinician believe that a graphic representation of the person's life is preferable to a list, the chronological life history outlined previously can serve as the basis for developing a lifeline, using peaks and valleys to reflect the high and low points in a person's life. A solid line reflects the person's life up to the present and a dotted line reflects expectations for future years. Events associated with each peak or valley on the lifeline should be written down to provide clarity.

Example of a Life Chronology

Eileen Carter prepared the following chronology of her life:

1. Birth–age 4

   - Primary activities—Just being a kid, following my older brother around.
   - Highlights—My younger brother was born, I started kindergarten, and I got my first puppy.
   - Disappointments—Not much attention for me with two noisy brothers.
   - Other milestones or important information—My mother had an operation. I was scared.

2. Ages 5–10

   - Primary activities—Attending elementary school, playing with my pets.
   - Highlights—I did well in school and won a good citizenship award.
   - Disappointments—My father died when I was 10.

- Other milestones or important information—I remember wishing for a sister so I would have somebody to play with and talk to.

3. Ages 11–18

- Primary activities—Attended school and then dropped out and went to work in a bar, serving drinks and dancing.
- Highlights—I thought having my first boyfriend was a highlight then, but it sure didn't turn out that way.
- Disappointments—My schoolwork went downhill fast, my mom was always out running around, didn't have much time for us. That was also when I moved in with Tyrone and had the abortions.
- Other milestones or important information—I started using drugs and alcohol; I felt so awful about my life but I didn't know how to change it.

4. Ages 19–24

- Primary activities—Quite a change over these years. Still working in bars at 19 but then met Charles, got married, had my son, raising my son, starting college.
- Highlights—My son and college and finally feeling like I have some hope.
- Disappointments—My marriage hasn't turned out the way I thought it would.
- Other milestones or important information—I'm improving my relationship with my mother and brothers.

Future years:

5. Ages 25–34

- Primary activities—Of course, being a mother. I hope I'll still be married and going to college.
- Highlights—Seeing Junior grow up. Maybe finishing some courses, maybe even getting an A.A. degree. I guess I might have another child if Charles and I stay together.
- Disappointments—I'm worried that my marriage might not make it and that I might not be able to continue school.

6. Ages 35–44

- Primary activities—Being a parent always comes first. I'll probably return to work, hopefully in a decent job, maybe sales or something helping people. I'd also love to work with a vet or a dog breeder and continue writing.
- Highlights—I guess by now Junior would be graduating from high school. That would really make me proud. If I have other children, who knows what wonderful experiences I might have with them.
- Disappointments—My mom might not be doing so well by this time; she may be sick or need my help in some other way. I sure hate to think about losing her now that I've just begun to find her again.

7. Ages 45–54

- Primary activities—The kids will be grown up by now. I'll probably still be working, maybe still married. I'd like to be doing well in a career.
- Highlights—Junior will probably be married. I could even be a grandmother. Maybe Junior will even graduate from college. I'd like to travel, go to Africa and South America.
- Disappointments—I don't suppose I'll like being middle aged much, though maybe I'll feel wise and stable. Nothing could be as bad as being a teenager. I don't know if my mom will still be around.

8. Ages 55–64

- Primary activities—I'd like to see myself with kids and grandkids, still married, still working, maybe even still taking courses.
- Highlights—Knowing that I made it, that I stayed on track and really reached my goals.
- Disappointments—The marriage keeps coming up as the big unknown. I don't want to be alone like my mother.

9. Ages 65–74

- Primary activities—I'm sure I'll be retired by now, maybe doing volunteer work with the Humane Society or an animal rights organization, maybe helping young women who are having trouble getting their lives on track.
- Highlights—You know, I could even be a great-grandmother by this time, one good thing about having Junior when I was young. I hope I'll still be healthy and involved in the community, have enough money to be comfortable.
- Disappointments—Losing people I love, my mom, aunts and uncles, and who knows who else.

10. Ages 75 and beyond

- Primary activities—I just can't imagine that time in my life. My dad died when he was so young. I might be widowed, or that might even happen earlier. I don't even think I'll be around this long.

Analysis of a Life Chronology

Once a life chronology has been completed, analyzing the chronology with the client can be a powerful learning experience. The following questions are some that might be explored during the analysis. The Learning Opportunities section that follows will afford you an opportunity to analyze Eileen Carter's life chronology.

- What patterns did you notice?
- What sorts of highlights are repeated throughout the life history?
- What worries and disappointments keep reappearing?
- What strengths and resources does the client seem to have?

Other questions can be developed to reflect the needs of a particular client and that person's goals, age, and life experiences. Clinicians can then use this information to better understand the client, collaborate with the client to identify meaningful and realistic goals, and plan the treatment.

Learning Opportunities

Here are the learning opportunities for Chapter 4. As in other chapters of this book, this section includes written exercises, discussion questions, practice group exercises, Assessment of Progress forms, and personal journal questions.

Keep in mind that you are not expected to complete all of the learning opportunities presented throughout this book. Rather, you or your professors or supervisors should select those exercises that seem most likely to enhance your professional learning and development, help you reach your goals, and be meaningful to you.

Chapter 4 focused on fundamental skills designed to give you a better understanding of people's backgrounds and histories. The following skills, addressed in the exercises in this section, have been presented in this chapter:

- Structuring an initial session
- Making discussion of the past relevant and meaningful
- Eliciting strengths from discussion of background information
- Using early recollections to elicit patterns
- Developing genograms to gather information on background
- Creating lifelines with clients to provide background information

Written Exercises

1. The following questions and statements focus on people's histories, but do so in ways that are counterproductive. Rewrite each of these clinician interventions so that they are likely to make discussion of the past relevant and meaningful to the client. Be sure that your interventions reflect both what you learned in this chapter and what you learned in Chapter 3 about asking effective questions.

    a. So you were born in Seattle. I understand it rains quite a bit there.
    b. Therapists like to dig into the past so that we can help you work through any early attachment problems you had. Unless we do that, you're unlikely to form good relationships as an adult.
    c. So school was a mixture of highs and lows for you. What are the lows that continue to hold you back now?
    d. You say your mother was a circus performer and walked on the high wire. Did she ever get hurt?

2. Nadia, a 32-year-old single woman, seeks therapy after she was robbed and hit over the head while entering the building in which she lived. She tells you that she is now terrified of being alone and, as a result, has decided to

marry her boyfriend even though he has been abusive to her. She also mentions that she was physically abused by her brother when she was a child. Briefly outline two viable ways that you might structure your initial session with Nadia and explain which approach is preferable and why.

3. List at least five factors that might make people reluctant to talk about the past while they are in treatment. Briefly describe your strategy for addressing at least three of these factors.

Written or Discussion Questions

Refer to the life chronology of Eileen Carter on pages **134–136** and respond to the following questions, either in writing or via discussion:

1. What patterns did you notice in Eileen's life chronology?
2. What categories of highlights are repeated throughout her life history?
3. What sorts of worries and disappointments keep reappearing?
4. What strengths and resources does Eileen seem to have?
5. How could you use this information to plan your treatment of Eileen and establish goals with her?

Discussion Questions

1. Sometimes beginning clinicians feel intrusive when they ask clients personal questions, especially questions about experiences that happened many years ago. Have you felt that way or do you think you might feel that way? What can you do to address your discomfort? What can you do to maximize the likelihood that you will ask helpful questions that are not intrusive?

2. Genograms can be helpful in eliciting information and identifying patterns. How would you integrate genograms into the treatment process? With what sorts of clients or problems do genograms seem especially likely to be helpful? With what sort of clients are genograms contraindicated?

3. Read these three early recollections, presented by Joe, a 43-year-old man. Then answer the questions that follow.

   • I came from a really big family. I remember that when the weather started to get cold, we would all get out our winter clothes and then pass them down to the next youngest child who was the same gender as we were. I was the second youngest of 11 and by the time I got the clothes, they were really in bad shape. I tried to pin the holes so they wouldn't show. What else could I do? At least we never went to bed hungry.

   • I remember once I fell down some steps and cut myself badly. I was bleeding a lot. My older brother went to help me and he got blood all over himself. When my mother came out to see what all the crying was about, she saw blood all over my brother and thought he had been hurt. She took him inside to get him cleaned up and didn't even notice that I was the one who had been hurt. I started to cry, but then I realized how funny it was and started to laugh. My father yelled at me for laughing at my brother, but then we sorted it all out.

- My dad worked in the mines. One day there was an accident and we didn't know if he was dead or alive. I remember how scared I was. But then he came home and he was all right. My mom was so happy, she gave us all ice cream. That was great until the dog knocked mine out of my hand. I just picked up the ice cream and ate it anyhow, dirt and all.

Questions:

   a. What patterns of emotions, thoughts, and actions appear in the three recollections?

   b. What patterns of interaction and reaction appear in the three recollections?

   c. What strengths and coping skills do you see in Joe?

   d. What themes emerge in the three recollections?

   e. What hunches do you have about what these memories tell us about Joe?

   f. Joe is seeking help at the urging of his wife. What would you guess are the difficulties in their marriage? What strengths and difficulties does Joe seem likely to bring to a close relationship?

   g. What multicultural issues are important to keep in mind as you help Joe process his early recollections and better understand his background?

4. If you have not yet done the practice group exercises associated with this chapter, discuss your thoughts and feelings about that upcoming experience. How can you allay any apprehensions you might have about that process and prepare yourself to learn from the experience?

5. If you have already done the practice group exercises associated with this chapter, discuss your reactions to that experience. What was the most beneficial aspect of that experience for you? What was the most challenging or uncomfortable aspect of that experience? How can you make future practice group exercises more rewarding to you?

Practice Group Exercise: *Strength Identification, Early Recollections*

Divide into your practice groups. You have probably already met with your practice group and so are familiar with the structure and process of the practice group exercises. The practice group exercise presented here will help you gain experience in eliciting and identifying strengths and in obtaining early recollections. Each chapter of this book builds on the skills learned in the previous chapters, and that should be reflected in your role-plays. Review and pay attention to the feedback you received during your previous role-plays. I know it is challenging to keep so much in mind, but also remember the guidelines for asking effective questions as you practice strength identification and productive use of early recollections in your practice groups.

As with all of your practice group exercises, each member of the group should have a tape recorder and a blank tape available to facilitate learning from this exercise.

Be sure that you tape yourself in the clinician role and also tape feedback you receive on your role-play. If the group agrees, I encourage you to tape all of the role-plays and feedback sessions. We can learn a great deal from others' experiences as well as from our own. If possible, allow at least 2 hours for this exercise.

Role-Play Exercise

The primary goal of this role-play is for you to elicit three early recollections from your partner, to explore and expand on those recollections as described earlier in this chapter, and then to collaborate with your partner in analyzing the recollections so that they provide useful and meaningful information about that person. Throughout this process, your emphasis should be on identifying strengths and effective coping skills.

When you are in the clinician role, rely primarily on open questions (particularly those beginning with *what* and *how*) and on implied questions to promote dialogue and information gathering. Be sure to integrate your questions with other interventions so that your interview builds rapport, puts the client at ease, demonstrates that you are listening accurately, and the dialogue sounds like a productive conversation rather than an interrogation. Before beginning this role-play, you might want to review the section of this chapter on early recollections, beginning on page **124**.

Time Schedule and Format

- Allow 15 to 20 minutes for each role-played intake interview. During that time, one person becomes the clinician, one becomes the client, and the other one or two group members become observers and timekeepers.
- As discussed previously, when you are in the client role, you will decide whether to be yourself and present accurate information about yourself and your life. You always have the right not to disclose any particular piece of information that you do not want to share with your group. If you would prefer not to be yourself in this or any other exercise in this book, you can assume the role of someone you know well, being sure to disguise the identity of that person, or you can assume the role of a person of your own creation.
- Following the role-play, take about 10 to 15 minutes to provide feedback to the person in the clinician role. Be sure to begin the feedback process with the person in the clinician role giving himself or herself feedback, focus on strengths first, and offer concrete suggestions for improvement. This should be a positive learning experience, not an experience that makes people feel criticized or judged. Feedback should focus on the areas listed in the following Assessment of Progress Form. Complete that Assessment of Progress Form during the feedback process or shortly thereafter, reflecting on the feedback you received.
- After the first round of role-plays and feedback, rotate roles. Continue this process until all group members have had the opportunity to be in clinician, client, and observer roles.

Assessment of Progress Form 4

1. Use of questions
   a. Balance of open and closed questions
   b. Nature of questions (implicit; beginning with *how, what, why,* or another word)
   c. Integration of questions and other interventions
   d. Helpfulness of questions
2. Eliciting and analyzing early recollections
   a. Ability to elicit three early recollections
   b. Ability to help client explore and expand on each recollection
   c. Ability to collaborate with client in identifying themes and patterns
   d. Ability to synthesize themes and patterns and communicate them to the client in helpful ways
   e. Identification and emphasis on strengths, making the role-play a positive and growth-promoting experience
3. Summary of feedback
   a. Strengths of role-play focused on early recollections
   b. Omissions or areas needing improvement
   c. Ability to link past experiences with present issues
4. Two or three goals that will help you improve your clinical skills

Personal Journal Questions

As you know, the personal journal questions are designed to promote your self-awareness and personal and professional learning and development. Typically, they offer you the opportunity to apply to yourself the skills and interventions that have been presented in each chapter. Your responses to these questions should be written in a journal when you have some quiet time and can give thought to your answers to these questions.

1. Write down three of your own early recollections. Then process and analyze them according to the guidelines presented on page **124**.
2. Identify any personal strengths that are reflected in your early recollections and the themes and patterns you have identified. Write briefly about whether and how these strengths are still available to you.
3. Prepare a three-generation genogram of your own family. Then analyze this genogram, looking for patterns such as those presented on page **130**. What did you learn about yourself and your background from this exercise?
4. Develop your own life chronology, using the age categories listed on page **134**. Then analyze this chronology according to the guidelines presented on page **136**. What did you learn about yourself and your background from this exercise?
5. Listen to the tape recording of the role-played intake interview that you conducted. Respond to the following questions about your role-play:

   • What was your overall reaction when you heard yourself in the role of clinician?

- Identify the anxieties and rewards you experienced during and after participating in this exercise.
- List one or two interventions you made that seemed particularly effective.
- List one or two interventions you made that you think needed improvement. How would you have modified these interventions?
- What is the most important thing you learned from this chapter and its exercises?
- What one improvement will you try to make in your role-plays next time?

SUMMARY

This chapter expanded on the fundamental skills of questioning and eliciting background information that were presented in Chapter 3. Additional skills presented in Chapter 4 included structuring the initial session, making discussion of the past relevant and meaningful, eliciting and identifying people's strengths, and use of three structured approaches to obtaining in-depth background information: early recollections, the genogram and its variations, and the lifeline or life chronology. All of these strategies draw heavily on the use of effective questioning to obtain information on people's backgrounds.

The next chapter focuses on the fundamental skill of helping people express, identify, and make desired changes in their emotions. Particular emphasis will be placed on attending skills and reflections of feeling.

PART 3

Chapter 5

USING FUNDAMENTAL SKILLS TO ELICIT AND CLARIFY EMOTIONS

OVERVIEW

Chapters 3 and 4 focused on the first element in the BETA format, background. Chapters 5 and 6 shift focus and address the second element, emotions.

LEARNING GOALS

As a result of reading this chapter and completing the exercises throughout, readers can expect to accomplish the following:

- Understand the importance of emotions in the treatment process.
- Understand the importance, as well as the processes, of attending and following in treatment.
- Learn ways to communicate attending and following.
- Become familiar with types of verbal encouragers.
- Develop your ability to accurately identify emotions and communicate empathy.

Five fundamental skills that help clinicians elicit and clarify clients' emotions are presented in this chapter:

1. Effective attending
2. Tracking
3. Using verbal encouragers (accents, restatements, paraphrases)
4. Summarizing
5. Communicating accurate empathy and reflecting feelings

The following chapter, Chapter 6, presents additional and more specific approaches to helping people express, manage, and change their emotions. That chapter will build on the skills presented in this chapter and will increase your repertoire of interventions designed to address people's unhelpful feelings.

IMPORTANCE OF EMOTIONS

"I'm feeling depressed." "I'm not happy with my life." "I'm feeling lonely and scared." "I can't control my anger." Statements such as these reflect the most common reasons why people seek counseling or psychotherapy: They are unhappy and are experiencing painful, undesirable, and unhelpful emotions. Although treatment may also explore background or focus on modification of thoughts or actions (the other three elements in the BETA format), identifying, understanding, reflecting, and helping to modify people's emotions are essential ingredients in almost all treatment approaches.

Theoretical Perspectives on the Importance of Emotions

The mental health professions have vacillated considerably in the importance given to emotions in the treatment process. Initially, the psychoanalytic therapists, as well as the behaviorists, downplayed the importance of emotions. At best, they were viewed as a secondary source of information and, at worst, a distraction from the business of uncovering the unconscious or modifying behavior.

These attitudes shifted considerably with the arrival of Carl Rogers and his powerful messages about the importance of emotions (Rogers, 1951). Rogers took the position that feelings, especially self-esteem, were the cornerstone of mental health. Consequently, Rogers suggested that clinicians' most important role was helping people express and effect healthy changes in their emotions. According to Rogers, that process alone, facilitated by the context of a positive therapeutic alliance, could lead people to meaningful growth and development.

Although Rogers's person-centered therapy did not replace psychoanalysis or behavior therapy, it was widely accepted and practiced. However, during the 1980s, interest in person-centered therapy waned, probably in response to the growing awareness that it often is not sufficiently flexible or powerful to help the growing numbers of people who presented with such severe concerns as sexual and physical abuse, misuse of drugs and alcohol, self-injurious behavior, and disabling depression

Carl Rogers

or anxiety. Rogers always retained a strong following, but attention shifted away from his work and toward cognitive therapy, which again de-emphasized emotions.

However, the 1990s and the 21st century witnessed a resurgence of interest in Rogers's emphasis on emotions on two important fronts. First, his emphasis on the therapeutic alliance was well supported by both research and clinical experience. Clinicians generally acknowledged that the emotional connection and collaboration between client and clinician, involving the clinician's communication of caring, concern, and support, was an essential ingredient of effective treatment. Nearly all treatment approaches now embrace the need for a positive therapeutic alliance and recognize the importance of using strategies suggested by Rogers and others to build rapport and trust, promote shared goals, and empower and encourage clients. In addition, many clinicians and theoreticians addressed Rogers's strong focus on emotions by developing broader and more integrated versions of person-centered therapy that maintain the essence of Rogers's approach but enhance and expand on treatment options by incorporating into that approach cognitive, behavioral, and other interventions. An example of this is motivational interviewing, developed initially by Miller and Rollnick (2002) for use with people who misuse substances.

In my experience, many students and clinicians embrace this combination of interventions with relief and appreciation. Students, in particular, who are understandably reluctant to stray too far from the guidelines promoted in the texts, often express disappointment with what they perceive as the limitations of cognitive and behavioral treatment approaches and long for permission to ask their clients, "How do you feel about that?" The current thinking in the mental health field is that emotions cannot be neglected in treatment, whether the focus is primarily on those emotions or on background, thoughts, or actions. Clients typically seek help because of their painful emotions and we must respect and meet their needs by attending to those emotions and helping people feel better. Although today's clinicians rarely focus exclusively on emotions, nearly all recognize that, in order to view people holistically, to honor their reasons for seeking help, to connect and collaborate with them effectively, and to address what many see as the most important part of themselves, clinicians must listen to and value people's emotions.

DEFINITION OF EMOTIONS OR FEELINGS

We are constantly experiencing emotions or feelings. Pause for a moment to identify the feelings you have right now. You might be interested in this chapter, eager to learn more, hungry for lunch, bored by your reading, or experiencing lingering joy or sadness from experiences unrelated to this chapter.

Feelings or emotions (terms that will be used interchangeably in this book) are affective states that are accompanied by physiological changes such as tension, warmth, shortness of breath, and perspiration. Among the most basic and frequently experienced feelings are fear, joy, sadness, disgust, and anger. However, we can experience hundreds of different emotions and thousands of subtle variations on those emotions.

Although we have a common language of emotions, that language often fails to capture those subtle differences. For example, you and I might both love our spouse or partner but, if we talked at length about those feelings, the love you experience for your partner is certainly different from the love that I have for my partner. In addition, we may use the same word to describe very different feelings that we have. Our love for our partners is different from our love for our children, which is different from our love for our parents or our closest friends or our pet or our new house. I have often been surprised by clients who describe a painful and even abusive relationship with a parent or partner, but then go onto say that they love that person and so maintain a relationship with him or her. Initially, I thought, "How can you love someone who mistreats you and seems to disregard your wants and feelings?" Now I have come to realize that such an expression of love can have many different meanings, depending on the person and the context. It may reflect a fear of abandonment or a need for financial support, it may reflect a deep appreciation for the good qualities of a complex relationship, it may reflect a person who has unfortunately come to believe that pain is an inevitable part of close relationships, it may be that the person is simply repeating a script or a socially acceptable message, or it may have many other meanings.

Clearly, understanding and communicating empathy for another person's emotions is a challenging task. However, this process is also one of our most important and powerful clinical skills. If we can help people to explore and deeply understand their emotions so that they can express them with greater richness, detail, and accuracy, we have often helped them take some important steps toward positive change. The basic purpose of this chapter and the one that follows is to enhance your skills in dealing with emotions in therapy and counseling.

BENEFITS OF ATTENDING TO AND UNDERSTANDING EMOTIONS

Paying attention to people's emotions can contribute to the treatment process in many ways, including the following:

- *Initiates the treatment process.*   If you have ever had counseling or psychotherapy yourself, or even contemplated contacting a therapist, you may be aware of having conflicting emotions about that prospect. On one hand, knowing that help is available is reassuring, and having someone on your side who is there to listen and join you in your efforts to change is probably appealing. We have few experiences in our lives when our importance and well-being are paramount and the primary goal is to enhance our emotional health and happiness. On the other hand, recognizing that you are having difficulty resolving your own concerns; that you need someone to help you address your problems; that you will probably be disclosing feelings, thoughts, behaviors, and experiences that are embarrassing and uncomfortable to you; and that you may receive a diagnosis of a mental disorder can be daunting. You may have felt flawed and inadequate and even wondered if you were qualified to become a clinician if you could not resolve your own issues without help from a stranger.

Keep in mind that your clients are probably also ambivalent about seeking treatment and may bring with them apprehensions and misconceptions as well as hopes and wants when they come to treatment. Helping to put them at ease and allay some of their reservations are important parts of the treatment process. Carefully attending, and letting our clients know that we have heard and understood them via both words and nonverbal messages, can provide the reassurance they need while simultaneously engendering rapport and conveying an accurate image of the treatment process.

- *Encourages emotional release.* Many people who seek treatment have kept their feelings locked up inside themselves. The process of simply verbalizing those feelings can bring a great sense of emotional release and relief. Paulson, Truscott, and Stuart (1999) found this discharge of emotions to be one of the most helpful experiences in counseling. Through eliciting and reflecting people's emotions, clinicians can gently encourage emotional release.

- *Fosters self-acceptance.* Expressing one's emotions to another person who is attentive, interested, and accepting can be reassuring. People with emotional difficulties often come from backgrounds where their feelings were ignored or denied and where they were told they should have feelings that differed from what they were really experiencing. Children who have been sexually abused, for example, often are told that this is an expression of love and that they should be grateful for the attention and enjoy the experience that will prepare them for adulthood. People who grow up in homes where substance misuse and antisocial behavior are rampant are often told that their home life is a normal and rewarding one, that sudden moves to avoid the police or unpaid bills are exciting changes, and that emotional upheavals and instability in the home are acceptable experiences.

What a relief it is for many people with such backgrounds to have their perceptions validated and to learn that, indeed, those experiences that made them feel so different and even inferior are not the norm and that they may well be able to achieve their vision of a different life. How reassuring it is for people to realize that their feelings are normal and understandable and that others are not horrified by or disapproving of their feelings. This can, in turn, help people to be more accepting of themselves.

- *Promotes the therapeutic alliance.*   Sharing feelings with another person who has empathy for those feelings usually leads to an increased sense of trust, closeness, and caring. People who believe that their clinicians hear and understand them are more likely to be optimistic about the success of the treatment process and to participate more fully in that process. Similarly, once clinicians have heard clients express deep and personal feelings, those clinicians almost inevitably have more caring for and motivation to help those people. This helps clinicians to join with their clients and build rapport. Of course, it also promotes achievement of treatment goals.
- *Establishes direction.*   Even experienced clinicians sometimes feel confused by a client and unsure of the most helpful direction or intervention. Attending to and reflecting about people's feelings can be the best strategy when a clinician feels stuck. Following the client's lead and tracking feelings, when all else fails, usually brings clarity to the conversation and eventually points to a productive direction for treatment. Simply attending to and following people's feelings is an important strategy for clinicians who should remember to move into an attending mode rather than forging ahead in potentially unproductive and even harmful directions when feeling stuck or baffled or even threatened by a client. Active listening, as described in this chapter, can get the treatment process back on track, ground both client and clinician, and allow time for processing and consolidation of insights and experiences. Such an intervention is not just running in place; it can be a powerful therapeutic intervention. Remember that when you feel like you are floundering, simply attend and you may be surprised at the impact of this strategy.
- *Relieves symptoms.*   The expression of emotions can be a healing process. Sharing painful feelings with another person can reduce the discomfort associated with those feelings; help people label, sort out, and understand their feelings; and move toward changing undesirable feelings into emotions that are more rewarding and helpful.
- *Advances treatment.*   Emotions are often the most accessible route to obtaining a full picture of people and their strengths and difficulties, especially for those people who enter treatment with complaints of painful feelings. Expression and exploration of feelings usually leads easily into exploration of background, thoughts, and actions and paves the way for clinicians to formulate specific treatment goals and interventions.

DRAWBACKS TO FOCUSING ON EMOTIONS

Although the benefits of focusing on emotions outweigh the drawbacks, an excessive or exclusive therapeutic focus on emotions can be counterproductive. Consider the following exchange:

Client: I'm feeling pretty discouraged today.
Clinician: Discouraged?

Client: Yes, everything I try at work and at home seems to fail.

Clinician: You're feeling pretty badly about yourself.

Client: Yes, maybe I'm just not cut out for the middle class life. In a way, I felt better before I took on all these responsibilities.

Clinician: Sounds like you're feeling overloaded by your responsibilities.

Client: Yes, they do get me down. I feel like I'm just running in place and getting nowhere.

This is a discouraging interchange that, so far, offers the client no avenues for addressing his concerns. An excessive focus on emotions can lead to a session that is demoralizing and that makes little or no progress. Exploration of emotions, ideally, can pave the way for focusing on thoughts and actions, as well as on ways to modify emotions, giving the session more energy and effecting progress toward clients' goals, rather than reiterating the client's words and apparently going in circles.

GUIDELINES FOR UNDERSTANDING AND ADDRESSING EMOTIONS

Before we move into the specific skills that help clinicians effectively elicit and address people's emotions, we present some guidelines to keep in mind. The following general guidelines can help ensure that emotion-focused interventions are productive and helpful and enhance both the treatment process and the therapeutic alliance:

- Focus on present emotions, especially those that are evident in the session. This is usually more powerful and productive than focusing on past and distant emotions.
- Emotions can be expressed both verbally and nonverbally. Be sure to pay attention to both modes of communication. Especially important in treatment are discrepancies between verbal and nonverbal emotions.
- Do not judge, dismiss, or disparage feelings. Clients need to access and verbalize their feelings, whatever they might be. Clinicians can then help clients determine whether their emotions are helping or hurting them and decide whether they want to work on changing some of their emotions. The clients make these choices with the help of the clinician; they are not made by the clinician.
- Realize that no clinician can always accurately hear and identify people's emotions. Mental health treatment is a dialogue; it is not a quiz game. The goal is not to be right all the time, but to promote exploration and discussion. As long as clinicians afford clients a safe environment and the opportunity to correct and modify what the clinicians say, they are successfully helping clients to become more aware of and in touch with their feelings, as well as more able to express them clearly.
- Keep multicultural factors in mind when using listening skills. The meaning and significance of both verbal and nonverbal communications often

are strongly linked to people's culture, socioeconomic status, gender, age, and ability status. For example, the emotions behind the use of slang and obscenities by a middle-aged woman from an upper class environment are likely to be much stronger than they would be if similar language were used by a young man who grew up in a lower socioeconomic street-wise environment. Similarly, references to spirituality and a higher power are likely to differ, depending on whether someone is Buddhist or Catholic or atheist or a nonreligious member of Alcoholics Anonymous.

EFFECTIVE ATTENDING

Many people enter the helping professions because they view themselves as good listeners. They report that other people confide in them easily, and they seem to have a gift for communicating effectively with others. You may sense this about yourself. However, when I ask students what makes them good listeners, they usually have difficulty figuring out exactly what they do that makes them good listeners. Before reading any further, think about this question and quickly make a list of three qualities or skills that you believe make you a good listener:

1. _____
2. _____
3. _____

Listening involves more than just hearing words. The relevant literature typically speaks of *attending* and *active listening* to communicate the complex task of hearing and understanding what people say and conveying that understanding back to them. Attending is an art that can be learned. Most of the skills presented in this chapter will help you to master effective attending and become a better listener.

Good listeners have the following characteristics:

- They are fully present in the moment and are not distracted or preoccupied.
- They can put their own needs aside temporarily and focus entirely on another person.
- They communicate clearly and concisely.
- They listen intently, not only for the overt content of what is said, but also for the underlying messages and meaning.
- They absorb and respond to both verbal and nonverbal forms of communication.
- They are sensitive to nuances and shifts in speech, including word usage, tone, and pacing of speech and are similarly aware of subtleties and shifts in facial expression and posture.
- They note both congruent and incongruent verbal and nonverbal messages and pay particular attention to mixed or confusing messages.
- They track or follow a person's line of thought and expression of emotions without introducing distracting digressions.

- They keep the focus on the client rather than on other people.
- They convey that they are listening through both verbal and nonverbal means.
- They view their restatements and reflections of feeling as hypotheses and are open to clarification and new information.
- They are aware of their own emotions and recognize when their own responses provide them important information about their clients' feelings.
- They are not afraid to talk about clients' feelings about the treatment process and about their interactions with their clinician and can remain calm, objective, professional, and helpful even when their clients express negative emotions toward them.
- They have a range of skills that effectively encourage people to self-disclose and to understand themselves and their feelings more fully and deeply.

Examples of Effective and Ineffective Attending

Effective attending is not the same as having a friendly conversation, although effective listening can enhance those conversations as well as client–clinician exchanges. Look at the following examples:

Example 1

Helena: I have surgery scheduled for tomorrow and I'm pretty anxious about it.
Diana: I had surgery last year and I was pretty anxious about it, too, but everything worked out fine. You'll be fine, too. I'm hungry. Are you ready for lunch?
Helena: Yes, I guess so.

This dialogue fails to follow many of the guidelines for attending presented previously. Diana focuses only on the overt message, she allows her own needs to preempt those of her friend, she does not encourage further discussion of Helena's apprehension, and she is distracted by her interest in having lunch. Compare Example 1 with the following example:

Example 2

Helena: I have surgery scheduled for tomorrow and I'm pretty anxious about it.
Sandra: What is making you feel anxious?
Helena: Well, it's supposed to be a minor procedure, but my uncle had a minor operation last year and he wound up with an infection and spent two weeks in the hospital.
Sandra: So you're worried that something will go wrong for you, too?
Helena: Yes, but I know my doctors are very good and so probably everything will be fine.
Sandra: It must help to have confidence in your doctors.

Both examples reflect conversations between friends. However, in Example 2, Sandra demonstrates many of the behaviors associated with effective listening. She focuses on Helena and encourages Helena to talk further about her concerns. Sandra concisely rephrases what Helena has said, giving Helena an opportunity to reflect on her own words. In addition, Sandra's own needs are kept out of the dialogue.

Review the additional examples that follow. For each statement, three alternative responses are given. Consider which of the alternative responses best satisfies the criteria for effective attending:

Example 3

Amanda: I was really relieved that I got a C in math.
Response 1: But you're smart. You could do even better than that.
Response 2: Sounds like you were pretty worried about your grade in math.
Response 3: Great!

In Example 3, only the second response is consistent with principles of effective attending. In that response, the speaker is listening for underlying messages and is encouraging Amanda to talk further about her math grade. Although both Responses 1 and 3 are positive and encouraging, they are not in tune with Amanda's feelings of anxiety and relief and might lead her to feel dismissed or devalued.

Example 4

Vanessa: I'm really worried about my marriage. My husband didn't come home until 2 A.M. last night.
Response 1: Where was he?
Response 2: I hope you gave him a piece of your mind.
Response 3: That must have really upset you.

In Example 4, the third response is an example of effective listening. It is concise, keeps the focus on Vanessa, is in tune with Vanessa's feelings, and encourages further conversation. Both Responses 1 and 2 shift the focus away from Vanessa and onto her husband. Respondent 1's curiosity and Respondent 2's anger intrude on the dialogue.

Example 5

Paul: I'm angry that I didn't get a bonus this year. I really need the money for my kids.
Response 1: Sounds like you're upset and worried about finances.
Response 2: I get some great things for my kids at the Salvation Army Thrift Shops. They don't charge very much.
Response 3: How come you didn't get a bonus?

The first response to Example 5 reflects effective attending. That respondent acknowledges Paul's feelings and encourages him to explore his feelings further. Responses 2 and 3, on the other hand, shift the focus away from what is troubling Paul.

Probably all of the responses in these examples would be acceptable in a conversation between two friends, although some seem better than others. However, only those responses that reflect effective listening should be part of counseling or psychotherapy. The therapeutic relationship is distinct from a friendship, not only in terms of its location but, more importantly, in terms of the goals and focus of the treatment process. Every comment or intervention from the clinician should have the purpose of helping clients meet their treatment goals.

TRACKING

One of the most important ways to communicate listening and attentiveness to clients is by tracking or following what they are saying. We begin our discussion with tracking because, in a way, it is the most basic of the listening skills. When tracking, clinicians are not deliberately trying to elicit or analyze or change people's feelings, but simply join them on a path toward communication and understanding. Tracking involves the use of a broad array of effective listening skills. These include the following:

- Verbal encouragers
- Accents/restatements
- Paraphrases
- Summarization
- Reflections of feeling
- Reflections of meaning
- Questions

All of these skills (except for questions, which were presented in Chapters 3 and 4, and reflections of meaning, which are discussed later in this book) are discussed in this chapter. The primary goals of tracking include understanding a person's thoughts and feelings and communicating that understanding to the person. The clinician listens intently and accurately to the client and uses sound clinical skills to demonstrate that. The clinician's interventions are a direct outgrowth of the client's previous statements. The clinician usually is not redirecting or leading the interview, but is instead letting the client set the direction and take charge of the session. At the same time, clinicians contribute to the direction or focus of the session through the nature and wording of their interventions, ensuring that the session is productive.

Benefits of Tracking

Tracking enhances treatment in many ways. This process communicates interest and caring and, thus, it is likely to build trust and contribute to the therapeutic alliance. It encourages people's self-expression and self-awareness and prompts them to broaden and deepen the information they share with their clinicians. Tracking encourages clients to take the lead in the treatment process, which can be empowering and encouraging. This also increases the likelihood that clients' important concerns and treatment goals will surface and will not be deflected by an enthusiastic or hasty clinician who focuses prematurely on a specific topic or issue. Tracking is generally a safe intervention; it affords clinicians the opportunity to gather information, deepen their understanding of their clients, develop rapport with their clients, and identify effective ways to help them before using more active interventions such as probing, challenging, interpreting, or providing suggestions. Exercises in this chapter provide you with the opportunity to practice your tracking skills.

Example of Effective Tracking and Attending

Notice the tracking demonstrated in the following example. The clinician stays with the client, following the client's lead, while demonstrating the principles of effective listening. By the end of this brief excerpt, Olga is not only expressing strong emotions but is also looking at ways to solve the problem she has presented.

Olga: My son really worries me. He'll do fine for awhile and then he'll explode.

Clinician: That must make you feel uneasy, always waiting for the next outburst.

Olga: That's true. It makes it hard for me to enjoy the good times with him because I always have to be on guard. I feel like I'm missing all the best parts of our relationship and soon he'll move out on his own and it will be too late.

Clinician: I hear a real sense of loss.

Olga: Yes, I really wanted to enjoy his last year in high school but I just can't get past this fear that I have.

Clinician: How have you tried to get past the fear?

Olga: I just try to forget about the problem.

Clinician: How has that worked for you?

Olga: Not very well. His outbursts are still so fresh in my mind; I can't forgive him for the damage he's done to our family.

Through tracking and attending, the clinician has helped Olga realize that she cannot push aside her concerns about her son's behavior and that her usual method of coping with his outbursts has been ineffective. Now, Olga is probably ready to collaborate with the clinician in developing new and more successful ways of addressing this issue.

Tracking, like the other effective attending skills presented in this chapter, can help you in your personal and business interactions as well as in your clinical work. For the rest of the day today, try to make a conscious effort to use effective listening and tracking skills in your everyday conversations. Note the responses you receive. You might find that people are more open than usual and that your conversations flow more smoothly. This strategy can work particularly well in tense and conflicted situations.

USING VERBAL ENCOURAGERS

Verbal encouragers are one of the most powerful interventions available to clinicians, especially when they are focused on tracking. These basic interventions help people feel heard and understood. Once people know that they have been heard and understood, they are likely to move forward rather than continue to go over the same ground. Verbal encouragers also help people hear themselves and talk about themselves more openly with others. Verbal encouragers promote dialogue, clarification, self-awareness, and exploration. They keep the focus of the session on the client, while the clinician keeps a low profile. They also contribute to the development of a collaborative therapeutic alliance.

The following three types of verbal encouragers are presented here:

- Accents
- Restatements
- Paraphrases

Accents and Restatements

Accents and restatements underscore an important word or phrase that the client has said and usually can narrow the focus of the session. They encourage further client self-disclosure, particularly about the underscored topic, and indicate that the clinician is interested and attentive.

Accents or restatements are typically very brief, just a word or phrase repeating part of what the client has said. Sometimes accents are just a supportive murmur, accompanied by nonverbal encouragers (discussed later in this chapter). The following are the most common types of accents or restatements:

- *Umm-hmm.* This is the classic minimal encourager; the clinician simply murmurs an encouraging sound that reflects attention and interest and encourages the client to keep talking.
- *Yes, and then? Tell me some more about that.* These, too, are spare and brief comments without much content that encourage the client to continue.

Repetition of a Key Word or Phrase By echoing something the client has said, the clinician underscores it and prompts the client to elaborate further. Accents and restatements are the simplest of the verbal encouragers. They are not intended to add depth or meaning to what the client has said, nor are they intended to identify themes or synthesize information like other verbal encouragers discussed later in this chapter. Because these interventions are so brief and spare, they may seem easy to master. However, their simplicity is deceptive; making helpful use of these verbal encouragers is a skill that needs to be practiced and developed over time. The choice of what word or phrase to emphasize and what to ignore can have a powerful impact on the direction of a session. Even the placement of an "umm-hmm" is likely to have an impact on a client and focus that person's attention. Because of this, clinicians should have a purpose in mind before making an intervention and use phrasing and timing that contributes to that purpose. Having a clear purpose in mind when making an intervention helps clinicians determine what accents used when and where are most likely to be productive.

The Importance of Purpose

Careful listening and clarity of purpose are the keys to effective use of accents and other verbal encouragers. These dimensions of listening have been discussed earlier but, because of their importance, they will be addressed and reviewed several times in this book. Review the following examples. The four interventions in the dialogue between the clinician and Reuben that follow are all examples of accents or restatements. Notice how purpose is reflected in the clinician's use of accents and restatement in responding to Reuben and in the subsequent direction of the discussion.

Example Illustrating Purpose

Reuben: I'm so overwhelmed by my job that I have no time left for my family or even for myself.
Purpose 1: Encourage Reuben to keep talking, without redirecting him.
Clinician: Ummm.
Reuben: Yes, I feel like a cat chasing its tail and getting nowhere.
Purpose 2: Explore Reuben's feeling of being stuck.
Clinician: Getting nowhere?
Reuben: Yes, I feel like I can never meet my supervisor's expectations, no matter how hard I try, and I'm afraid I'll lose my job despite all my hard work.
Purpose 3: Focus Reuben's attention on his own needs.
Clinician: You're working very hard?
Reuben: Yes, I live on fast food, never get to the gym, and haven't had a chance to relax and read a book in months. I don't even have time for my family.
Purpose 4: Explore Reuben's interactions with his family.
Clinician: No time for your family?
Reuben: Yes, my wife and I never have time alone together, and I usually don't even get home until my kids are in bed.

All three of the clinician's verbal encouragers reflect effective attending by keeping the focus on Reuben and prompting him to clarify his statements. Even through single words or brief phrases, clinicians can exert considerable influence over the direction of a session. Because of this, you should be deliberate in your use of all your interventions, have a clear and helpful purpose in mind, and be well grounded in the treatment approaches you are using with each client.

Purpose is reflected by the combination of selective attention and selective inattention to what a client has said. Effective clinicians highlight what they want the client to discuss further and often do not address material that seems counterproductive. That is reflected in the previous dialogue with Reuben.

Notice how, in the following example, the clinician's use of restatement keeps the focus of the session on Petra, the client. This moves the session in a productive direction and discourages Petra from using the session to complain about others.

Example Illustrating Restatement and Purpose

Petra: I can't believe what just happened. I almost got a ticket because I was parked in a no parking zone. The cop could see I was sitting in the car. Doesn't he have anything better to do than harass me? It really made me mad.
Clinician: Mad?
Petra: Yes, the government seems to be falling apart. I can't get any work done with all this bureaucratic mess around.
Clinician: You're having trouble getting your work done?
Petra: Yes, when I went to law school, I had such high hopes but now I feel like a failure. I just can't accomplish anything worthwhile with all these interferences.
Clinician: You're feeling like a failure?

Importance of Varying Interventions

Although this dialogue became more productive as it went on, you probably became tired of the clinician's use of restatement and accents. Indeed, persistent and repetitive use of any type of intervention can have a negative impact on the treatment process. This is particularly likely when clinicians overuse restatements or accents. Clinicians can begin to sound like parrots, and this may lead clients to devalue or ignore the clinicians' input. Sessions may lack energy and fail to hold the interest of both clients and clinicians.

To avoid these pitfalls, clinicians should vary the nature of their interventions. Even if they are relying heavily on encouragers, they can use different types of encouragers, including accents, restatements, paraphrases, and summaries. In addition, interventions sound more natural and spontaneous if clinicians vary the opening of their interventions. For example, consider the following two series of interventions:

Series 1:

Sounds like you were angry with the officer.

Sounds like you are feeling frustrated.

Sounds like you view yourself as a failure.

Series 2:

Sounds like you were angry with the officer.

Could you have been feeling frustrated?

I wonder if you view yourself as a failure.

The first clinician overuses the phrase "sounds like"; as a result, the interventions take on a programmed, almost robotic quality. Although the meaning of the interventions in Series 2 is the same as those in the first series, the second clinician varies the beginnings of his sentences and so avoids sounding like he is on automatic pilot.

Exercise in Accents, Restatements, and Purpose

The following client statement offers many avenues for exploration. Craft an accent or restatement for each of the listed purposes that seems likely to move the session in the desired direction and then write the sort of response you think Annette might make to your intervention. Remember to use a variety of openings in each of your accents or restatements.

Annette: They used to call me the Ice Queen when I was captain of the skating team. I was so talented and so into skating that I think I threatened people and I liked that. Now here I am with a shattered leg full of metal rods and I can barely walk. People talk with me more and joke with me and maybe that's good, but I wish I could still be the Ice Queen.

Purpose 1:   Encourage Annette to keep talking, without redirecting her.
Clinician: _____
Annette: _____

Purpose 2:   Explore Annette's pride in having been a successful skater.
Clinician: _____
Annette: _____

Purpose 3:   Focus Annette's attention on the conflict she is experiencing.
Clinician: _____
Annette: _____

Purpose 4:   Encourage her to talk about the meaning of her disability and loss.
Clinician: _____
Annette: _____

Paraphrases

The purposes of paraphrases are similar to those of accents and restatements. Paraphrases highlight key words or statements, focus the session, encourage client self-expression, and communicate support, interest, and attentiveness. Like accents and restatements, they can enhance the sense of partnership between client and clinician. However, paraphrases also can have the additional purpose of giving clients a new and different perspective on what they have said. This can promote greater self-awareness and give clients an opportunity to reflect on the meaning of their words.

Paraphrases are usually brief, although they usually are longer than accents and restatements. Generally, they should be limited to one or two sentences and should not be longer than the client's original statement.

In a paraphrase, clinicians are not simply engaging in selective repetition of the client's words. Instead, clinicians use their own words to capture the essence of what the client has said.

To illustrate paraphrases, let's refer to the previous example of Petra. This time the clinician will use paraphrases rather than accents or restatements. Notice how the clinician's use of paraphrase enriches the session and gives Petra more to think about and process than did the earlier interaction, which relied on accents and restatements.

Example of Paraphrases

Petra: I can't believe what just happened. I almost got a ticket because I was parked in a no parking zone. The cop could see I was sitting in the car. Doesn't he have anything better to do than harass me? It really made me mad.

> *Clinician:* You felt that the officer was treating you unfairly.
> *Petra:* Yes, the government seems to be falling apart. I can't get any work done with all this bureaucratic mess around.
> *Clinician:* That must be frustrating to you.
> *Petra:* Yes, when I went to law school, I had such high hopes but now I feel like a failure. I just can't accomplish anything worthwhile with all these interferences.
> *Clinician:* You're sounding pretty hopeless.

Although paraphrases typically add more to a session than do accents and restatements, they also present the clinician with more of a challenge and a risk. What if the clinician misunderstands the client and offers a paraphrase that is not on target? Let's see what happens as the dialogue with Petra continues:

> *Petra:* No, I haven't given up hope yet, but I'm just not sure what else to do to make my efforts meaningful.
> *Clinician:* So you are still hopeful that you can find a way to make your work count. What have you done so far to make that happen?

As you can see, no damage was done by the clinician's inaccurate paraphrase. On the contrary, the clinician's statement offered Petra the opportunity to clarify and expand on her statement and opened up a productive avenue for discussion: finding more successful ways for Petra to make her work meaningful. As long as clinicians remain attentive, continue to track the client's statements, and are open to revising their thinking, a misunderstanding can actually contribute to the session by offering clients the opportunity to think through and clarify their points.

The Difference Between Accents/Restatements and Paraphrases

To further clarify how accents and restatements differ from paraphrases, let's look at one more example that illustrates the use of both types of interventions:

> *Jonathan:* This is the fourth time I've tried to stop drinking and I've finally realized I can't do it alone. Three times I failed to stay sober. If I don't get some help fast, my wife is going to take the kids and leave me and then I'll wind up like my father, dying alone in jail.

Purpose 1:   Reinforce Jonathan's decision to get help.
  Accent/Restatement: You realize you can't do it alone.
  Paraphrase: You're hoping that combining some outside help with your own efforts will enable you to stop drinking this time around.

Purpose 2:   Explore Jonathan's previous unsuccessful efforts to change.
  Accent/Restatement: Three times before you failed to stay sober.
  Paraphrase: Your previous efforts to stop drinking didn't work for you and have left you feeling pretty desperate.

Purpose 3:   Explore Jonathan's fear of becoming like his father.
    Accent/Restatement: Without help, you fear you might wind up like your father.
    Paraphrase: Your fear of winding up like your father seems to be a strong motivator for you.

Purpose 4:   Explore John's feelings about his family.
    Accent/Restatement: Take the kids and leave you?
    Paraphrase: Your family seems to be very important to you and you don't want to lose them.

Although accents and restatements, as well as paraphrases, have an important place in treatment, paraphrases typically add depth or a new perspective on what the client has said. This often advances treatment, although at times minimal interventions on the part of the clinician are preferable and allow the client to take the lead.

Let's return to Annette and apply your knowledge of paraphrases and how they differ from accents and restatements. You probably struggled to write restatements for Annette, largely because her situation and accompanying reactions are so complex. You might find it easier to write paraphrases in response to Annette. Keeping the same four purposes in mind, craft a paraphrase that accomplishes each of the four purposes:

Annette: They used to call me the Ice Queen when I was captain of the skating team. I was so talented and so into skating that I think I threatened people and I liked that. Now here I am with a shattered leg full of metal rods and I can barely walk. People talk with me more and joke with me and maybe that's good, but I wish I could still be the Ice Queen.

Purpose 1:   Encourage Annette to keep talking, without redirecting her.
    Clinician: _____

    _____

Purpose 2:   Explore Annette's pride in having been a successful skater.
    Clinician: _____

    _____

Purpose 3:   Focus Annette's attention on the conflict she is experiencing.
    Clinician: _____

    _____

Purpose 4:   Encourage her to talk about the meaning of her disability and loss.
    Clinician: _____

    _____

The process of summarization can be even more challenging than paraphrasing. In formulating a summary, clinicians synthesize a group of client statements to reflect back to the client the essence of what has been discussed. This increases the likelihood that the client and clinician have the same understanding of their dialogue, it reinforces learning, and it effects a transition or closure. Summarization is most likely to be used when client and clinician have finished discussing a topic or issue or when the session is drawing to a close. However, summarization also can be useful when the session feels fragmented and needs a clearer focus or direction. Like paraphrases, summaries are not intended to be interpretive or analytical; they should instead be clear and concise statements of what may have been a lengthy client–clinician interaction.

Examples of Summaries

The following examples illustrate three common uses of the process of summarization:

- *To establish a focus for the session.* You've talked about several things in the first few minutes of today's session: your dissatisfaction with your job, your recent interview for a new job, your thoughts about returning to graduate school, and your desire to revise your resume. Sounds like you have quite a few concerns related to the direction of your career. What would you like to focus on first?
- *To bring closure to one issue and effect a transition to another issue.* You seem to be clear that remaining in your present job would not be a good choice for you. Perhaps we could spend some time looking more closely at the other options that you have. What do you think about that?
- *To bring closure to a session.* Sounds like you have gained quite a bit of clarity on your career direction today. You've decided to apply to graduate school for the fall and, if you are admitted, to resign from your present job in July. Perhaps next week we can continue our discussion of your choice of graduate schools.

All three of these summaries accomplish two goals: They synthesize all or part of a treatment session and they move the session forward. In addition, the second and third summaries probably reinforce and consolidate the client's gains and decisions. In just a few sentences, these powerful interventions can exert considerable influence on the treatment process. However, because making accurate and helpful summaries is more challenging than formulating effective accents, restatements, and even paraphrases, clinicians should usually check the accuracy of their summaries with the client and be ready to modify the summary if it is not on target. Following a summarization with such questions as "How do you feel about what I said?" "How does that fit with your recollection of what we discussed?" "Any ways in which you want to modify what I said?" "How does that sound to you?" or even "Did I get that right?" are all ways to elicit clients' reactions to summaries. Keep in mind that the primary goals of interventions are not to be right or to demonstrate superior listening skills but to understand and be helpful. Clinicians have not failed if they did not hear a client's message accurately; rather, they have succeeded in identifying some confusing communication that client and clinician now have an opportunity to clarify. Once clinicians have additional information from the client, they can revise their summary or other intervention and check it out again with the client to be sure that client and clinician have a shared understanding.

COMMUNICATING ACCURATE EMPATHY AND REFLECTING FEELINGS

Like questions and verbal encouragers, communicating empathy is an essential clinical skill, regardless of the clinician's theoretical orientation. The professional literature provides many definitions of empathy. Gladstein (1983) described empathy as "responding with the same emotion to another person's emotion" (p. 468). According to Kohut (1984), empathy entails "being attuned to the inner life" of another person (p. 84). Carl Rogers (1959), who perhaps more than anyone else made clinicians aware of the importance of empathy, viewed empathy as a process, not a state. He believed it entailed sensing the private world of another person, feeling and thinking "as if one were the other person" (p. 210).

Barett-Leonard (1981) identified three phases of empathy:

• Vicariously experience or resonate to the feelings of another person
• Express accurate empathy to that person
• Person receives the empathy

For empathy to be meaningful and helpful, all three phases must be on target. The clinician feels deeply connected to and caring toward clients and is in touch with both their verbal and nonverbal expressions of feeling. Further, the clinician communicates that emotional awareness in such a way that the clients truly feel heard and understood. This promotes development of a positive therapeutic alliance and creates an atmosphere of safety in the treatment context, enabling clients to take risks and venture into unexplored territory without fear of shame or blame. It also helps them to become more aware of their emotions and to express those feelings with greater comfort and facility. I have found a strong connection between clinicians' effectiveness in experiencing and communicating empathy and the eventual success of the therapeutic process.

Clinicians sometimes confuse empathy and sympathy. Empathy is feeling *with* a person and has an important role in the treatment process. Sympathy, on the other hand, is feeling sorry *for* a person and rarely enters into the treatment process. Sympathy can lead people to feel like helpless victims, while empathy is designed to empower them. Consider the following examples:

Examples of Empathy and Sympathy

Client: You can't believe how much I had to deal with to get here on time! The babysitter didn't show up, my car overheated, and then I got stuck in a traffic jam.
Empathy: You have coped with a lot, and yet you got here on time!
Sympathy: I'm so sorry you had to deal with all of that.

Notice how the empathic response establishes a connection with the client while empowering him and reinforcing his efforts and success. The sympathetic response, on the other hand, brings a note of sadness into the session and is a sort of dead-end, bringing a halt to the discussion.

Sympathy can also emphasize the hierarchy in the therapeutic relationship in that the powerful therapist feels sorry for the unhappy client. Empathy, on the other hand, encourages a partnership between client and clinician and a joining of efforts to help clients meet their goals.

Reflections of Feeling

Empathy is most often communicated through an intervention called a reflection of feeling. Reflections of feeling or emotion focus on people's emotions and use affective language to help them become of aware of their feelings and the nuances of those emotions. As stated earlier in this chapter, simply by naming people's feelings via an accent, restatement, or paraphrase, clinicians can help people to become aware of and express their own feelings more accurately. These strategies communicate effective listening and caring and contribute to the development of rapport between client and clinician. In addition, the clinician's nonjudgmental naming of emotions helps people to accept emotions that may seem undesirable or embarrassing or even shameful to them. This, in turn, enables them to broaden and deepen their expression of emotions.

Reflections of feeling do all this and more. Reflections of feeling provide people with another perspective on their emotions, often presenting them with a deeper and richer picture of their feelings. They encourage introspection and greater attunement to one's own emotions and can lead to the development of new options. Reflections of feeling bring a sense of immediacy to the treatment process and can make sessions more meaningful and relevant. Especially powerful are reflections of emotions that are experienced at that very moment in the session.

Making an Accurate and Helpful Reflection of Feeling A reflection of feeling usually consists of the following three parts:

- An opening
- A feeling word
- A context

Clinicians sometimes add on a fourth part, a phrase to check the accuracy of their reflection. The parts of a reflection of feeling are illustrated in the following examples.

Example 1

Sounds like (opening) you felt terrified (feeling word) when you were riding on the elevator (context). Does that sound like what you were experiencing? (checking accuracy)

Example 2

Being elected president of the junior class (opening) sounds like an overwhelming experience for you. I hear so much joy and excitement (feeling words), but also anxiety (feeling word) about whether you can really handle the job. How does that fit with the feelings you remember having? (checking accuracy)

Example 3

It seemed to me (opening) that you were pretty angry (feeling word) when you came into the office today (context). I wonder if you were feeling abandoned because I was on vacation last week? (checking accuracy)

Including both the emotion and the context helps people reconnect with their feelings. In addition, pairing the stimulus or context with the reaction encourages clients to consider whether the nature and intensity of their emotional response is in keeping with the stimulus and paves the way for discussion of feelings and the impact of the emotion on the client and on others.

Notice how reflections of feeling differ from accents, restatements, and paraphrases. They tend to be longer, they include more information, and, most important, they are not just a repetition or rephrasing of what the client has said. Instead, they seek to add to the client's self-awareness and offer new information and perspectives.

Reflecting Basic Emotions

Ivey, Ivey, and Simek-Morgan (1997) identified four basic emotions: sad, mad, glad, and scared. These four basic feelings can provide a starting place for exploration of people's emotions. However, going beyond the basic emotions to an exploration of the subtle, complex, and sometimes conflicting emotions that people typically experience is important for understanding and addressing people's feelings. Clinicians can help clients find the words they need to capture their emotions as fully and accurately as possible. Consider the following examples of reflections of feeling. The feelings expressed by all of these people might be described as scared. However, the clinician's reflections clarify the distinctions among these scared feelings.

Examples of Reflections of Feeling Scared

Example 1

Client: So there I was on the escalator and all of a sudden I felt scared, my heart started to pound, and I could hardly breathe. I felt so stupid; I knew I wasn't in any danger.
Clinician: It sounds like you were terrified, but also puzzled by your strong reaction to riding on the escalator.

Example 2

Client: When the time came to announce the winner of the math award, I was so scared that I wouldn't get it, but then they called my name. What a relief!
Clinician: You were really worried that you wouldn't be chosen for the award, and that must have made it all the more rewarding when they did call your name.

Example 3

Client: I was scared that I couldn't handle the chemotherapy, but afraid that I would die if I didn't undergo the treatments. So I went ahead with the chemo.
Clinician: What a hard decision for you! Both alternatives were frightening, but you made a choice and moved ahead to get the treatments you needed.

Example 4

Client: Then after I got the math award, I started to feel scared again. Could I live up to this award and keep doing good work?
Clinician: Getting recognition for your good work made you apprehensive about whether you could keep it up.

All four clients use the word "scared," and yet their circumstances and feelings are different. It is the interventions of the clinicians, capturing the specific characteristics of each of the scared feelings, that deepen the client's awareness of those feelings and encourage their exploration.

Exercise on Reflecting Feelings of Anger   Now let's look at another of the four basic emotions, the feeling of anger or being angry. The following four clients all report being angry. However, each one has a distinctive experience of that emotion. Write a reflection of feeling for each of these four clients in which you try to capture the nuances of their feelings. Remember to include both context and one or more feeling words. You might also want to include opening statements as well as statements that check the accuracy of your reflections.

Example 1

Client: I was only 30 or 40 minutes late getting back from the party and it wasn't my fault; we ran into tons of traffic. Of course, my mother wasn't hearing any of that and grounded me for two weeks. I was so mad at her. Now I can't go to the opening football game. You'd think she'd never been my age.
Clinician: _____

_____

Example 2

Client: I couldn't believe it when Sarita got the time-saving award this month. All she did was take the form I developed, change a few words, and submit it under her name. I was so angry at her and at my boss for cheating me out of the award I deserved. I thought they were my friends; how could they have done this to me?
Clinician: _____

_____

Example 3

Client: You know how I've been struggling to lose weight and how slow that process is. Well, yesterday, I'm sitting on the bus and I hear this little kid say to her mother, "Why is that lady so fat?" And her stupid mother says, "I guess she eats too much, honey." I felt so mad at both of them, I felt like screaming at them and telling them what it's really like to be an overweight woman in a world where you're supposed to be emaciated, but that would have only made it worse. Then the mother would probably tell the kid I was crazy too.

Clinician: _____

_____

Example 4

Client: I remember my first day in class, just a week after we arrived from my home country. I knew hardly any English and people kept talking to me, real fast and loud, as though that would help me understand. I felt so angry at the other students and the teacher and even my parents who made me move here. I just wanted to crawl under the desk and hide.

Clinician: _____

_____

After you have completed this exercise, I encourage you to share the interventions you developed with others, comparing your understanding of the different types of anger reflected in the four examples. You may find that your understanding of some of the examples differed from how others interpreted them. Rather than thinking about whether you are right or wrong, I encourage you to view this as another indication of how rich emotions are and how much clients can learn about their feelings with our help.

Exploring the complexity of emotions is important in understanding and addressing people's feelings

Dimensions of Emotion

To make accurate and helpful reflections of feeling, clinicians need not only identify the emotions that are being expressed but also identify other important features
of clients' emotional experiences. By determining the characteristics of a person's
emotional experience and expression, clinicians can understand that person more
fully and find more effective ways to help that person recognize, manage, and perhaps change troubling emotions.

The following eight dimensions or characteristics of emotions have been identified (Seligman, 2006, p. 162). Emotions can be

- Emotional, physical, or a combination;
- Overt, covert, or a combination;
- Positive, negative, neutral, or a combination;
- In or out of awareness;
- Of varying levels of intensity;
- Appropriate or inappropriate to context and stimulus;
- Congruent or incongruent; and
- Helpful or harmful.

Let's go back to the example of Petra, presented on page **156-157** of this chapter, to
illustrate the use of these dimensions in deepening understanding of emotions.
Petra's initial emotion was that of anger at the police officer who threatened to give
her a parking ticket. Her emotional reaction can be described as follows:

- Petra experienced her anger in *both emotional and physical* ways (tearfulness,
tension in abdomen and shoulders). Many people can more easily access
physical manifestations of their emotions than they can the affective ones,
so I often ask where in their bodies they experience their feelings. Be sure
not to neglect nonverbal and physiological signs of emotions.
- Petra's anger toward the officer was *overt, but linked to covert emotions*, including her work-related frustration. Emotions often are additive and the presence of one strong feeling, either positive or negative, makes it more likely
that people will experience other similar emotions. A messy child may seem
cute if we are having a good day or irritating if we are in a bad mood. If a
person's emotional response to an experience seems excessive, look for the
presence of covert emotions that may have kindled the flame of the overt
emotion.
- Her emotion was a *negative* one. Sometimes feelings are clearly positive or
negative, but be on the alert for emotions that combine both positive and
negative reactions. For example, a person may be proud of a brother for his
achievements but envious of his success, or a person may feel overjoyed at
completing graduate school but worried about finding rewarding employment and apprehensive about the responsibility of becoming a therapist.
- Petra was *aware of her anger, but was not fully aware of her underlying feelings*.
Emotions almost always have multiple triggers. People usually focus first on

the immediate context or trigger, but be alert to the possibility that past experiences also contribute to the feelings. Failed relationships are generally disappointing, but reactions will be colored by whether this is the first time this has happened, whether it has happened repeatedly, or whether a long history of failed relationships has led someone to view that as the inevitable outcome to all relationships.

- Her anger was *very intense*. Nonverbal cues often are the best gauge of the intensity of emotions. Tears, smiles, slammed doors, a tight body posture, and angry or affectionate gestures are all nonverbal clues to the intensity of emotions.

- Both the nature and the intensity of Petra's anger seemed *inappropriate* and out of proportion to the situation. Although an emotion itself may be appropriate for a given situation, the intensity of the emotion may be inappropriate and warrant discussion and attention in treatment. This is a clue that other, covert emotions probably are present and may be even more important to identify than the overt emotions.

- Petra's emotional experience of *her anger and her muscle tension were congruent*. However, her *tearfulness added an incongruent element*. Incongruent emotions are red flags; they may reflect emotions that are covert and out of awareness, they may reflect conflicted or mixed emotions, or they may reflect some emotions that are not genuine. Be alert to both verbal and nonverbal messages when assessing congruence of emotional expression. Exploring incongruent emotions usually is important in developing client self-awareness, but timing and language are important in this process to ensure that clients do not feel attacked or humiliated or challenged when conflicting expressions of emotion are pointed out and discussed with them.

- Petra's anger *did not seem helpful* to her. Ideally, clients' emotional responses help them build connections with people, improve their dealing with the demands and challenges of their lives, and move toward achievement of their goals. If their emotions repeatedly get in the way of these ends, then the clients probably need help to either contain their emotions more successfully or modify those emotions. Chapter 6 will provide strategies that can facilitate changing or containing emotions, as well as tolerating strong emotions.

Analyzing Petra's emotions according to the eight dimensions gives a fuller and richer picture of those emotions. This analysis provides a strong indication that Petra's angry reaction to the police officer is probably misdirected anger stemming from other aspects of her life.

Assessing Effectiveness of Reflections of Feeling and Empathic Attunement

Just as the effectiveness of questions can be evaluated (as illustrated in Chapter 3), so can the effectiveness of reflections of feeling. Robert Carkhuff's (1969) pioneering work in this area suggested an approach that has become widely adopted in assessing the communication of empathic understanding. Empathic understanding can be rated on a 1 to 5 scale ranging from level 1 (the lowest level) to level 5 (the highest and most therapeutic level):

Level 1: Clinician statements demonstrate misunderstanding of the client's feelings or miss important aspects of those feelings.

Level 2: Clinician statements respond to the overt emotions of the client, but subtract from the overall feelings.

Level 3: Clinician statements at this level are interchangeable with those of the client. In other words, they are neutral responses, more like restatements than helpful reflections of feeling.

Level 4: These clinician statements add to the client's awareness of his or her feelings, identifying a deeper level of emotion than the client was able to verbalize.

Level 5: Clinician statements greatly facilitate the client's expression of emotion. These statements display true attunement to the client's feelings. They enable the client to gain self-awareness and a broader and deeper understanding of the expressed emotions. They also promote exploration and introspection.

Example of Levels of Empathic Attunement The following example illustrates the five levels of empathic attunement.

Client: I felt such love and closeness, being with Blanca that night, but I was worried that she did not reciprocate my feelings.

Level 1: You found Blanca very attractive and had no thoughts of Marietta. (Misunderstands client's feelings and shifts the focus.)

Level 2: You were very concerned that Blanca did not feel about you the way you felt about her. (Misses the strong love the client felt toward Blanca.)

Level 3: You felt love and closeness toward Blanca but were worried that she would not reciprocate your feelings. (This is an interchangeable response.)

Level 4: Feeling such deep emotions toward Blanca must have felt risky for you. Would she feel the same way toward you? (This statement is in tune with the client's emotions and adds the concept of risk to what the client has said.)

Level 5: I can imagine you feeling such deep emotions for Blanca and yet struggling with what to do with those feelings. It sounds like you were afraid that she would reject you if you took a risk and expressed your emotions. (This reflection is in tune with the client's emotions and adds significantly to his feelings by mentioning the element of risk and the fear of rejection. This statement is most likely to promote introspection and further discussion.)

Exercise in Levels of Empathic Attunement Sometimes, the experience of deliberately writing weak responses can help you learn how to make helpful and effective responses. Following the format of the five levels of empathic attunement just described, write a response at each of the five levels to the following client statement:

Sylvan (14-year-old male): When I lived in the Philippines with my grandmother, she taught me that ghosts lived in our house, both good ghosts and harmful ghosts. She told me that the ghosts could always see what I was doing, so I should be well behaved or the ghosts would play tricks on me. Sometimes I would hear the ghosts, but they never hurt me. Then last week I stole some money from my neighbor and now I am terrified that the ghosts will punish me. I'm afraid to be alone, but I know most people in this country don't believe in ghosts, so I can't talk with anyone about this, not even my mother. I never should have stolen from my neighbor.

Level 1 Counselor Response: _____

_____

Level 2 Counselor Response: _____

_____

Level 3 Counselor Response: _____

_____

Level 4 Counselor Response: _____

_____

Level 5 Counselor Response: _____

_____

How did you feel about doing this exercise? Was it more difficult to write helpful or unhelpful responses? How easily were you able to think about the gradations of helpfulness in your responses?

LEARNING OPPORTUNITIES

This chapter has focused on teaching you the following fundamental skills designed primarily to help people identify and express their emotions as well as to demonstrate that clinicians are actively listening, interested, and involved with their clients:

- Effective attending
- Tracking
- Using verbal encouragers (accents, restatements, paraphrases)
- Summarizing
- Communicating accurate empathy and reflections of feeling

The following exercises offer a broad array of learning experiences that are designed to help you practice and improve your use of the skills presented in this chapter. As with all of the learning experiences in this book, keep in mind that you are not expected to complete all of these exercises. With the help of your professor or supervisor, select those exercises that are most likely to help you develop and improve your skills.

Written Exercises

1. For each of the following client statements, write:
   a. An accent, restatement, or paraphrase
   b. A reflection of feeling
   c. An open question to build on the skills you developed in Chapter 3

Client 1: All my life, I've wanted to be a jazz musician. I taught myself to play and I'm really good, but here I am working as a salesman to support my wife and four kids. I feel pretty hopeless about the future.

Accent, restatement, or paraphrase: _____

_____

Reflection of feeling: _____

_____

Open question: _____

_____

Client 2: My mom thinks I have an eating disorder or something. But all the other girls take laxatives and stuff so they won't get fat. That's the only way I can keep from gaining weight.

Accent, restatement, or paraphrase: _____

_____

Reflection of feeling: _____

_____

Open question: _____

_____

Client 3: I've had three miscarriages and the doctors don't think I'll be able to have a child. My husband doesn't seem to care and won't even talk about it, but I feel like there's a big void inside me without a child.

Accent, restatement, or paraphrase: _____

_____

Reflection of feeling: _____

_____

Open question: _____

_____

2. Review the reflections of feeling you wrote in response to the three client statements in Exercise 1. List your purpose for each of those reflections.

Client 1 purpose: _____

_____

Client 2 purpose: _____

_____

Client 3 purpose: _____

_____

3. Now for each of the three client statements from Exercise 1, list another possible purpose that you might have in mind when responding to the client. After each alternate purpose, write a second reflection of feeling that is consistent with that purpose.

Client 1: Alternate purpose:

_____

Reflection of feeling:

_____

Client 2: Alternate purpose:

_____

Reflection of feeling:

_____

Client 3: Alternate purpose:

Reflection of feeling: _____

4. Review the expanded information provided by 15-year-old Leeza, the second client in Exercise 1. Then analyze her emotional responses according to the eight dimensions of emotion in the list that follows Leeza's comment.

Leeza: My mom thinks I have an eating disorder or something. But all the other girls take laxatives and stuff so they won't get fat. That's the only way I can keep from gaining weight. Last night my parents served this huge dinner; all I ate was salad with no dressing and some carrots, but when I got on the scale this morning, I had gained a pound. I couldn't believe it. I told my mom I was sick and couldn't go to school because I didn't want anyone to see how fat I looked, but she said that I didn't seem sick and I had to go to school. So I put on this baggy sweater so no one could tell I had gained weight, but I just felt gross, like a fat pig.

Eight Dimensions of Emotions:

Emotional, physical, or a combination: _____

_____

_____

Overt, covert, or a combination: _____

_____

_____

Positive, negative, neutral, or a combination: _____

_____

_____

In or out of awareness: _____

_____

_____

Level of intensity: _____

_____

Appropriateness to context and stimulus: _____

_____

Congruence: _____

_____

Helpful or harmful: _____

_____

5. Consider the clinician responses to Leeza's comments in Exercise 4. Rate the helpfulness of each intervention according to the 1–5 scale that follows. Then indicate what distinguishes the helpful responses from the harmful ones.

Level 1: Clinician statements demonstrate misunderstanding of the client's feelings or miss important aspects of those feelings.

Level 2: Clinician statements respond to the overt emotions of the client but subtract from the overall feelings.

Level 3: Clinician statements at this level are interchangeable with those of the client. In other words, they are neutral responses, more like restatements than helpful reflections of feeling.

Level 4:   These clinician statements add to the client's awareness of his or her feelings, identifying a deeper level of emotion than the client was able to verbalize.

Level 5:   Clinician statements add significantly to the client's expression of emotion. These statements display true attunement to the client's feelings. They enable the client to gain self-awareness and a broader and deeper understanding of the expressed emotions and also promote exploration and introspection.

Clinician Response 1:   I can hear that you are very worried about gaining weight.

Rating: _____

Clinician Response 2:   Even gaining one pound brought up strong feelings of shame and disgust with yourself.

Rating: _____

Clinician Response 3:   You look emaciated to me. You really need to eat more.

Rating: _____

Clinician Response 4:   Your mother is probably right. It does sound like you have an eating disorder.

Rating: _____

Clinician Response 5:   You only ate salad and carrots for dinner?

Rating: _____

Differences between helpful and harmful responses: _____

_____

_____

Discussion Questions

1. For many years, helping people express their feelings was considered essential to effective treatment. Some modern approaches to counseling and psychotherapy, however, pay more attention to thoughts and behaviors than to expression of emotions. How do you explain this shift? Do you believe it is beneficial or harmful to the treatment process? Justify your response.
2. What do you view as the most important benefit and most important drawback of focusing on emotions? What can you do in a treatment session to maximize the benefits and minimize the drawbacks of exploring emotions?
3. Review the following statement made by Johnny, a 34-year-old man. Next analyze the client's feelings in terms of the eight dimensions of emotion. You may need to make some guesses as to how Johnny might be expressing his emotions. Then develop an accent or restatement, a paraphrase, a reflection of feeling, and an open question that might serve as helpful responses to Johnny.

Johnny: People don't know what they're talking about when they tell me I'll feel better when I stop drinking. That bottle is my friend, my only friend. It's there whenever I need it. Nobody else is. Nobody else does anything to help me; they just tell me I'm doing everything all wrong. Who needs that!

Eight Dimensions of Emotions:

Emotional, physical, or a combination: _____

_____

_____

Overt, covert, or a combination: _____

_____

_____

Positive, negative, neutral, or a combination: _____

_____

_____

In or out of awareness: _____

_____

_____

Level of intensity: _____

_____

_____

Appropriateness to context and stimulus: _____

_____

_____

Congruence: _____

_____

_____

Helpful or harmful: _____

_____

_____

Interventions in Response to Johnny's Statement:

Accent or restatement: _____

_____

_____

Paraphrase: _____

_____

_____

Reflection of feeling: _____

_____

_____

Open question: _____

_____

_____

4. If you have not yet done the practice group exercise associated with this chapter, discuss your thoughts and feelings about that upcoming experience. How do you feel about sharing your feelings in the role-play session? What did you learn from the previous role-plays associated with earlier chapters of this book that you want to carry with you into the present role-play?

5. If you have already done the practice group exercise associated with this chapter, discuss your reactions to that experience. What was the most beneficial aspect of that experience for you? What was the most challenging or uncomfortable aspect of the experience? How did this role-play experience compare with your earlier one(s)? How can you make future practice group exercises even more rewarding to you?

Practice Group Exercise: *Tracking Emotions*

The practice group exercise presented here will help you gain experience in the skills described in this chapter: using accents, restatements, and paraphrases; summarizing; and reflecting on feelings. It also will help you pay attention to body language (discussed further in the next chapter) and refine your skills in tracking.

Preparing for the Role-Play

Have your tape recorder and a blank tape with you. Be sure to tape the session in which you assume the clinician role as well as the group feedback you receive. Listening to the recording after class will help you to identify your clinical strengths and areas you want to improve. You might find it helpful to record the entire role-play exercise so that you can learn from the role-plays and feedback of others in your group.

The current role-play focuses on tracking emotions. In preparing for this role-play, identify an issue or concern in your life or in that of your role-played client that raises some meaningful emotional responses. This issue will be your presenting problem in the current role-play.

Think carefully about your choice of a concern. Although your practice group has agreed to maintain each other's confidentiality, you will be sharing this issue with other students in a learning, rather than a therapeutic, environment. The person in the clinician role probably is a novice clinician. Because of these factors, I suggest you select an issue that brings up only moderately strong emotions and that does not focus on highly charged or long-standing difficulties in your life or in that of your role-played client. Guidelines for choosing issues to present in the practice group exercises were discussed in Chapter 1. Finally, before beginning your role-play, review the Assessment of Progress form that you completed for the previous chapter. Take particular note of the summary of the feedback you received and the goals you established for yourself. Also review the Assessment of Progress form for this chapter.

Role-Play Exercise

The goals of this role-play are as follows:

- *To help the client express and explore feelings.*   To accomplish this, the person in the clinician role should rely primarily on the following skills that were presented in this chapter: accents, restatements, paraphrases, and reflections of feeling. If it would be helpful to you, you may use the eight dimensions of emotions as a structure for promoting your client's exploration of his or her feelings. You may also include some questions in your interview, demonstrating the skills presented in Chapter 3. In addition, you should conclude the interview with a summary of what has been discussed, being sure to check out the accuracy of the summary with your client.
- *To track what your client is saying.*   When your client is working productively on exploring emotions related to the presenting concern, you should simply follow or track what the client says, using the strategies listed previously. Only if the client seems to go off on apparently unimportant tangents or talks about material that does not seem helpful should you use strategies to refocus the interview.
- *To maintain helpful body language.*   Be aware of your eye contact, your posture, the distance you maintain from the client, your physical gestures and movements, and your voice quality. Try to communicate interest, effective listening, and concern through your nonverbal and verbal messages.

Time Schedule

As in the previous role-play, you benefit most from this experience if you can devote approximately 60 to 80 minutes to the exercise. Spend approximately 10 minutes in each role-play and another 10 minutes sharing reactions and providing feedback to the person who assumed the clinician role during that part of the exercise. Be sure to follow the guidelines for giving, receiving, and recording feedback that were presented in Chapter 1.

Assessment of Progress Form 5

1. *Promoting expression and understanding of emotions.*   What use did you make of each of the following interventions? What strengths were evident in your interventions? How might you have been even more successful in promoting the client's expression and understanding of emotions?
   a. Use of accents, restatements
   b. Use of paraphrases
   c. Use of reflections of feeling
   d. Use of questions
   e. Use of summaries
2. *Tracking.*   How well were you able to follow the client? Did you use any strategies to redirect the discussion? How did they work? Should you have made more or less use of redirection?
3. *Nonverbal messages.*   What impact did the following types of nonverbal messages have on the counseling process? How might they have been improved?
   a. Eye contact
   b. Posture
   c. Proximity to client
   d. Physical movements and gestures
   e. Tone of voice and rate of speech
4. Summary of feedback:
5. Progress in achieving goals from the previous session:
6. One or two additional goals to improve your clinical skills:
   a.
   b.

Personal Journal Questions

1. If you have done the role-play exercise for this chapter, listen to the tape recording of that role-play. Respond to the following questions about your role-play:

   - What was your overall reaction when you heard yourself in the role of clinician?
   - What was it like for you to assume the role of client? How did it feel to share your feelings with your group?
   - List one or two interventions you made that seemed particularly effective.
   - List one or two interventions you made that you think needed improvement. How would you have modified these interventions?

- What was your overall reaction to a session focused on emotions? Did you find the session interesting and productive, or did you find yourself eager to move on to other areas of focus?
- What is the most important thing you learned from this chapter and its exercises?

2. Identify a strong and unpleasant or unhelpful emotion you experienced during the past week. Analyze that emotion according to the eight dimensions of emotions listed on page **167**. What did you learn from that process?

SUMMARY

This chapter focused on fundamental skills associated with helping people identify and understand their emotions and in tracking their expressions of feelings. Particular emphasis was placed on using accents, restatements, paraphrases, reflections of feeling, and summarization. Discussion explored the importance of communicating accurate and helpful empathy via reflections of feeling. Formats for analyzing the eight dimensions of emotions and for rating the helpfulness of reflections of feeling provided structure for systematically assessing and understanding emotions as well as interventions made in response to emotions.

The next chapter builds on this chapter and presents additional ways to facilitate clients' expression and modification of emotions. Specific strategies are presented that clinicians might use to help people express and understand their emotions, contain and manage their emotions, tolerate strong feelings, and change unhelpful feelings. These strategies include analysis of emotions, focusing, using body language, using the imagination, introducing new perspectives, providing reassurance and support, distraction and thought stopping, using language and logic, and rational emotive imagery. Attention also is paid to the nonverbal expression of emotions.

Chapter 6

USING FUNDAMENTAL SKILLS TO CONTAIN AND CHANGE EMOTIONS

OVERVIEW

Chapter 5 of this book introduced you to the important role that emotions play in both our lives and in the treatment process. The chapter presented the fundamental skills of using accents and restatements, paraphrasing, summarizing, and reflection of feeling. That chapter also introduced a model for analyzing emotions and enabling clinicians and clients to look at whether those emotions are congruent, appropriate, and helpful. Chapter 6 continues the focus on emotions and builds on the skills presented in Chapter 5. This chapter has the following learning goals:

LEARNING GOALS

As a result of reading this chapter and completing the exercises throughout, you can expect to accomplish the following:

- Learn additional strategies for making reflections of feeling, especially those that are strength-based.
- Appreciate the importance of positive psychology and strength-based treatment.
- Learn a broad repertoire of skills and interventions to elicit emotions.
- Become aware of some of the barriers and challenges clinicians face in helping people recognize and express their feelings.
- Develop an understanding of nonverbal communication, as well as ways to reflect and respond to nonverbal expressions of feeling.
- Become knowledgeable about ways in which clinicians' own strong feelings can have an impact on treatment and become more able to recognize and deal constructively with those emotions.
- Understand the importance of having ways to contain and tolerate emotions and learn strategies that can accomplish that.

- Gain knowledge and experience in the process of helping people change emotions.

Exercises throughout this chapter, including discussion questions, written exercises, a role-play, and personal journal questions, will facilitate mastery of the material.

SKILLS TO BE LEARNED

This chapter includes a review of the skills presented in Chapters 3, 4, and 5. In addition, eight fundamental skills that help clinicians elicit, contain, and change clients' emotions are reviewed in this chapter:

- Using positive psychology and strength-based reflections of feeling
- Facilitating identification and expression of emotions via accents, restatements, paraphrases, summarizations, and reflections of feeling
- Opening leads that promote expression of feeling
- Developing a repertoire of interventions to elicit emotions through language (clichés, mirroring, solution-focused language, and silence and brevity) analysis, imagery, and new perspectives
- Understanding nonverbal demonstrations of emotions: eye contact, facial expressions, paralanguage, and posture, body position, and movements
- Using focusing and Gestalt strategies to help people access and express emotions
- Understanding clinicians' verbal and nonverbal expressions of emotion
- Helping clients with containing and changing emotions

POSITIVE PSYCHOLOGY

In the late 1990s, Martin Seligman, then president of the American Psychological Association, triggered an important shift in the way clinicians think about their work and their clients. Seligman (1999) stated, "Psychology is not just the study of weakness and damage: it is also the study of strength and virtue. Treatment is not just fixing what is broken; it is nurturing what is best within ourselves" (p. 2). Seligman is now the leading spokesperson for what is called positive psychology. Positive psychology has been defined as "the scientific study of positive experiences and positive individual traits and the institutions that facilitate their development" (Duckworth, Steen, & Seligman, 2005, p. 629). Positive psychology draws on many areas of learning including human development; multicultural understanding; the existential and humanistic work of theorists such as Viktor Frankl, Abraham Maslow, and Carl Rogers; solution-focused and narrative therapies; the literature on risk and prevention; and family and community counseling (Smith, 2006).

Martin Seligman

Because of its multiple roots and its encouraging and empowering messages, the strength-based paradigm of positive psychology is challenging the prominence of the deficit-based paradigm. Positive psychology contends that people have the capacity to heal themselves and to grow in healthy and fulfilling ways. However, this may be difficult, particularly for people who come from toxic environments. According to positive psychology, if clinicians can enable people to recognize and access their inherent and developed strengths, this can buffer them against the impact of emotional difficulties and can build resilience so that they are capable of coping effectively with and rebounding from negative experiences.

Categories of Strength

Martin Seligman and his associates have identified 24 strengths, grouped into the following six broad categories (Peterson & Seligman, 2004):

1. The category of *wisdom and knowledge* goes beyond factual information and includes having an open and curious mind, creativity, and a zest for learning.
2. *Courage* includes not only bravery but energy, perseverance, hard work, and honesty.
3. *Humanity* encompasses the ability to love and be loved and to have close, intimate relationships with others as well as intelligence, caring, and kindness toward others.
4. The construct *of justice* involves such strengths as the ability to collaborate well with others, to demonstrate the characteristics of a good citizen, leadership skills, and an attitude of fairness in perspectives and behaviors.

5. *Temperance* reflects the ability to take care of oneself, to make wise and sound decisions, to be compassionate and forgiving toward others, and to be modest rather than self-aggrandizing.

6. *Transcendence* includes people's spirituality, whether it is expressed through formal religion or a sense of wonder at the beauty of the world. It also encompasses feelings of gratitude, appreciation, and hope along with a sense of humor and playfulness.

Peterson and Seligman have developed an inventory called Values in Action that can be used to assess a person's strengths. Although this may be useful in some cases, having an awareness of positive psychology, the importance of emphasizing strengths, and the previous list of specific strengths probably is sufficient in most cases for clinicians to implement a strength-based perspective through their interventions, especially their reflections of feeling.

STRENGTH-BASED REFLECTIONS OF FEELING

Let's look at some pairs of reflections of feeling so that you can better understand the differences between reflections that emphasize strengths and those that do not.

Client Statement: Rahine was being really mean to me again today. I tried hard not to cry and remembered that book you had given me about bullying. Then I went and sat near the teacher. I knew Rahine wouldn't call me names if the teacher could hear him.

Clinician Response 1: It was very sad and painful for you when Rahine started picking on you again.

Clinician Response 2: Having the teacher nearby helped you handle this situation.

Clinician Response 3: Even though Rahine upset you, you were able to remember what we had talked about. Taking care of yourself by thinking of him as a bully and sitting close to the teacher helped you feel safer.

As you can readily see, the third response identifies the strengths of self-care and attachment and helped this young girl recognize her strengths. The clinician's intervention probably made it more likely that she would use her strengths to take care of herself again next time she felt threatened. Let's look at another example:

Client Statement 1: Work hasn't gotten any better. My supervisor still gives me more work than anyone else, expects me to stay late to finish all of the work, and then makes sarcastic remarks if I leave the office before 8 P.M.

Clinician Response 1: You sound pretty angry and frustrated. How did you handle the situation?

Client Statement 2: I thought about all my choices and tried to figure out what was best. I wanted to tell him off and quit, but this is my first job as a legal assistant and I have a family to support so how would that help me? I'd probably just get fired. I tried to prioritize the work and do as much as I realistically could. Then I went home and asked my wife to help me with my résumé so I could get out of this job as soon as possible. Then I prayed for help and guidance in getting out of this awful situation.

Clinician Response 2a: So you were fearful that you might lose your job and made the decision to do the work but try to leave that job as soon as possible.

Clinician Response 2b: It must feel discouraging to know that, for the time being, you are stuck in this job because you need to support your family.

Clinician Response 2c: Frustrated though you were, you recognized you should not act impulsively but you did enlist your wife's help in taking action to change jobs and drew on your strong spiritual beliefs to help you with that.

Notice that, although clinician responses 2a and 2b do reflect feelings accurately and convey empathy, they center on negative terms—*fearful, discouraging,* and *stuck*—and do not emphasize the client's strengths. On the other hand, response 2c highlights some of the strengths identified by Peterson and Seligman, including prudence, temperance, attachment, perseverance, and spirituality.

Exercise in Strength-Based Reflections of Feeling

Three client statements follow. For each one, compose two reflections of feeling, one that is strength-based and one that is an accurate reflection of feeling but is not strength-based:

Fredericka: When I finally got to the dentist's office ... and that wasn't easy ... this receptionist who looks like she's about twelve years old says to me, "Oh, you're in a wheelchair. You'll have to come through the back door." No, I said, I use a wheelchair; I'm not *in* a wheelchair. "Whatever," she says to me with a look of disinterest. I didn't bother saying anything about the accessibility of the office. I know it's difficult for a young, healthy person to understand my situation; it's not the first time something like this happened to me. But I really need to take some action, join a citizen's task force or something, to help educate people about how to relate to those of us who *use* wheelchairs.

Clinician Response 1 (empathic but not empowering): _____

_____

Clinician Response 2 (strength-based): _____

_____

Marian: My whole family was really in a foul mood last night but, for better or worse, I love them no matter what. They were getting me down too, so I thought I needed to do something. I got out the Halloween witch mask, put it on, and just sat down at the dinner table. They cracked up, called me Mom the Nutcase, and said that my real personality was finally coming thorough. It was all in fun and it sure turned their mood around.

Clinician Response 1 (empathic but not empowering):   _____

_____

Clinician Response 2 (strength-based):   _____

_____

Alfio: My wife told me that my daughter's youngest had colic all week. That must be so tough; she's got three kids under five. I knew she wouldn't ask for help, she doesn't do that, so I just dropped by yesterday. I told her I had a delivery in the neighborhood and took the afternoon off so I could see the grandkids. I made it sound like she was doing me a favor by letting me play with them when she was so busy. I think it really helped her, and it didn't make her look like she couldn't handle the kids herself. Of course, I always like seeing the grandkids.

Clinician Response 1 (empathic but not empowering):   _____

_____

Clinician Response 2 (strength based):   _____

_____

Benefits of Strength-Based Interventions

Formulating strength-based interventions may be a new and possibly challenging way for you to think about responding to people. However, interventions that empower can make a great difference in the effectiveness of the treatment process and in people's ability to identify and access their resources. Emphasizing strengths motivates people to use those strengths in the service of making positive changes. This process helps them to increase their resiliency and to cope with and learn from painful and disappointing experiences. It also can serve as a protective factor in the face of such experiences. Positive relationships and problem-solving ability are particularly important buffering strengths (Smith, 2006). Having one person in our lives who believes in us and loves us no matter what makes it more likely that we will value ourselves, that we can know the difference between healthy and unhealthy relationships, that we will have hope, and that we can mobilize our strengths to improve our lives.

In addition to being encouraging and supportive, strength-based treatment also enhances the client–clinician relationship and accelerates the process of positive change. The terms *encouraging* and *supportive* might suggest that clinicians should say to clients the sort of sentences people often say to friends and family such as "You did a good job," "I'm proud of the way you handled that," "I knew you could do it," and "Congratulations on your accomplishment!" However, statements such as these usually are counterproductive in counseling and psychotherapy because they entail clinicians making judgments about clients. Yes, these are positive statements, but when clinicians take on the role of evaluating clients and their behaviors and choices, they give the message that, although they are making a positive judgment now, the next time around the judgment may be a negative one. This thought may be disturbing because it probably feels natural and caring to praise clients. However, what is most important is that clients evaluate themselves and identify their own successes and strengths. Helping people recognize their successes and strengths by pointing them out without making value judgments is far more likely to effect lasting and internalized changes than is praising clients. This book provides more information about constructive ways to reinforce positive behavior and to help people appreciate themselves in the chapters that focus on behaviors (Chapters 9 and 10).

FACILITATING EXPRESSION AND IDENTIFICATION OF EMOTIONS

Chapter 5 described many of the therapeutic benefits that come from helping people express their emotions. To review, these include

- Promoting clients' self-awareness;
- Developing their awareness of their strengths;
- Building caring, trust, and rapport;
- Helping clinicians to better understand their clients;
- Promoting clients' hope and optimism;
- Helping people to feel heard;
- Promoting their catharsis and emotional release;
- Providing reassurance and normalizing feelings;
- Facilitating problem identification, goal setting, diagnosis, and treatment planning;
- Paving the way for people to subsequently work on assessing, containing, and changing their emotions; and
- Fostering empowerment via increased self-knowledge and self-regulation.

Examples of Fundamental Interventions to Elicit and Explore Emotions

Some of the most fundamental and important strategies for enabling people to express and identify their feelings were presented in the previous chapter and at the beginning of this chapter. These strategies are illustrated in the following examples.

Client: I told my physician about all the worries I have about the children and my husband and my mother, and he just said, "Why don't I give you a prescription for some Xanax." I felt so angry.

Accents
Clinician: Angry?

Restatements
Clinician: It made you angry when he suggested you needed medication.

Paraphrase

Clinician: You sound furious that he thought a pill could solve everything.

Reflection of Feeling

Clinician: You must have felt frustrated and devalued by the physician's offer of medication.

Strength-Based Reflection of Feeling

Clinician: Perhaps you felt you had the inner resources you needed to deal effectively with your worry, but just wanted some direction instead of medication.

Summarization

Clinician: You've talked about incidents in which your husband, your best friend, and even your physician seemed to misunderstand your concerns. It must be very painful and lonely to feel that nobody really understands what you are going through.

ADDITIONAL STRATEGIES TO ELICIT AND IDENTIFY EMOTIONS

With most people and situations, use of these fundamental skills will succeed in helping them to express, identify, and expand on their emotions. Often, however, these fundamental listening skills are insufficient or ineffective. This is particularly likely under the following circumstances:

- Clients are unaccustomed to examining and expressing emotions and lack facility with that process. Such a client might be someone who can be described as *alexithymic;* such a person has a restricted range of emotions and is almost incapable of identifying and verbalizing feelings. On the other hand, this may simply be someone from a background that discouraged and perhaps even mocked or punished emotional expression.
- Clients have confused and conflicted emotions that they are having difficulty clarifying. For example, a person might be worried about having an illness, upset about the pain associated with the illness, yet pleased with the extra attention that people are giving him because he is ill.
- Clients are reluctant to verbalize their emotions, perhaps feeling ashamed of those emotions. Shame is often associated with experiences of sexual abuse and assault, making them particularly difficult topics for discussion.
- People may fear loss of emotional control in a counseling or psychotherapy session. People having strong feelings of rage or sadness may be apprehensive that talking about those emotions will lead them to experience strong anger or cry uncontrollably and they may not want to risk that loss of emotional control.
- The focus of the session is on an issue or experience that clients have blocked from awareness or avoided for many years and are having difficulty retrieving feelings associated with that experience.

- The feelings might relate to the clinician and the therapeutic alliance and clients are uncomfortable with the direct expression of feelings toward another person.
- Treatment may be at an impasse or may have brought closure to a troubling issue and clients are not sure what concern to address now.
- Clients are reluctant to engage in treatment and are not intrinsically motivated to work toward positive change. Perhaps they have been court referred for treatment or pressured into treatment by a supervisor or family member, or clients may be invested in proving that therapy is ineffective.

Even when none of these circumstances are present, people sometimes have difficulty identifying their feelings. You have probably experienced that yourself. This is a common occurrence, but is particularly likely to happen in one of the previous situations.

Because of the difficulty people often have in identifying and expressing their emotions, clinicians need to have a rich and varied array of strategies they can draw on to help people become more aware of and able to verbalize their feelings. In the following sections, we present such an array. Most of these are grounded in and combined with the fundamental interventions of open and closed questions, accents, restatements, paraphrases, reflections of feeling, and summarization but expand on these building blocks in a variety of creative ways that can be adapted to the needs of each person. These strategies will be illustrated with examples, many of which involve Eileen Carter, the 24-year-old African American woman introduced in Chapter 3.

Opening Leads to Elicit Feelings

Clinicians can increase the likelihood of eliciting client emotions if they begin their interventions with words that are carefully chosen to accomplish that purpose. Using a variety of openings that are designed to elicit feelings has several advantages. People may respond differently to different openings and so, by using a range of leads, clinicians are more likely to find one that appeals to a given person. Consciously varying their language keeps clinicians alert and thinking, hopefully preventing them from parroting a script and losing touch with their clients. In addition, clinicians are often parodied for overusing a few standard interventions. Classic are

- I hear you saying …
- What are you feeling now?

These standard interventions are useful ones and that is why they have become classics. Clinicians do not need to banish these from their vocabulary. At the same time, clinicians should avoid overusing these openings so that they do not sound like a broken record. The following list includes other opening leads that are useful in helping people express their emotions:

- I'm hearing a lot of … in what you say.
- When you talked about …, you seemed to be feeling …

- Lots of strong ... inside you.
- Sounds like you were feeling ...
- Sort of feeling ..., but maybe also some ...
- If I understand you right, you're saying you were ... when that happened.
- I'm picking up some ... as you talk.
- I sense a lot of ... in you.
- To me, it sounds like you are experiencing some ...
- That must have made you feel ...
- Right now you're feeling ...
- Sometimes you feel ... but at other times your feelings are very different and you feel ...
- You must have felt ... at that time.
- I wonder if you were sensing emotions like ... and ... at that time?
- As I listen to you, what comes across is ...
- Sitting here now, the emotions you recall are ... and ...
- You appear to be feeling ...
- You feel ... about that.
- As you see it, you reacted with ...
- The strongest feeling that comes across is ...
- It's almost like you are saying you felt ...
- I gather you experienced feelings of ...
- Help me understand your feelings at that time.

This list of more than 20 openers is not an exhaustive one. Feel free to improvise, to use those that are most comfortable for you, and of course to add new openers to the list. Few clinicians probably use such a wide variety of leads, but as you gain experience you will identify your favorites. Just remember to vary your leads to bring a natural, unobtrusive, and encouraging tone to the therapeutic dialogue.

Using Language to Promote Expression of Emotions

Clichés   You have probably been encouraged to avoid the use of clichés in your writing and perhaps also in your speech, especially in a professional context. Now I'm going to give you the opposite advice about your language usage in the treatment setting.

Most people are familiar with clichés and immediately understand their meaning. In addition, clichés capture attention, are not usually threatening because they are so commonplace and familiar, and can have a powerful impact on a person. I find that using clichés deliberately in my sessions is often effective in promoting people's expression and exploration of emotions. Of course, you want to consider your client. Using clichés with the client who has two doctorates may result in a loss of credibility. Even more important, using clichés with someone from another culture may be confusing and may create barriers in the therapeutic alliance. However, judicious use of clichés, as in the following examples, can advance the treatment process and build connection.

Example 1

Client: When they discovered that the figures were incorrect in the final report, everyone looked at me, waiting for an explanation. I didn't know what to do or say.
Clinician: You must have felt like you were on the "hot seat."

Example 2

Client: Often I speculate on what my life would have been like if I had finished graduate school as I had planned rather than leaving college to get married.
Clinician: I wonder if you regret not having chosen that "road not taken" and think it might have been more rewarding for you.

Example 3

Client: I might have been able to get more money for my house if I had waited, but I was scared I wouldn't get another offer, so I took the first reasonable one that came through.
Clinician: It felt safest and most comfortable to you to "strike while the iron was hot."

Mirroring Using language that mirrors that of the client is another way to encourage expression of feelings, as well as to promote the therapeutic alliance and develop trust and a shared understanding between client and clinician. For example, rather than speaking of marijuana, the clinician might use the client's preferred street name for the drug, and rather than referring to "having sexual relations with," the clinician might use the client's preferred term of "hooking up with." Similarly, when clinicians are working with clients who speak with precision and avoid slang, the clinicians might want to match that manner of speaking.

Several cautions are important, however. If the client's language is very different from that of the clinician, it can seem false and even patronizing to adopt that person's style of speech. For example, a middle-aged, middle-class Caucasian female counselor would naturally speak differently from a 17-year-old African American male client who was raised in a crime-ridden lower socioeconomic area and whose language reflects that of his neighborhood. Adopting her client's style of speech is unlikely to impress this client; rather, the counselor is likely to appear foolish and perhaps manipulative. Of course, she should try to use language that is clear and likely to have a shared meaning for both client and clinician, but she should not assume a manner of communicating that is foreign to her.

Clinicians also need to respect themselves and should not use language they perceive as inappropriate. They do not need to adopt slang, profanity, and negative racial and gender terms that are unacceptable to them.

What if we are troubled by a client's use of such language? The usual guideline for mental health professionals is to refrain from criticizing clients. However, a client's repeated use of language that is offensive to the clinician may well interfere with that clinician's ability to establish a sound therapeutic alliance with the client. Before deciding how to handle such a challenging situation, I encourage clinicians to consult with a colleague or supervisor. In addition, clinicians need to phrase their message to the client carefully, focusing on the language and behavior rather than on the person. For example, the clinician might say, "When you use the term ... to refer to the women you date, it makes me uncomfortable. I wonder if we could find another word that works for both of us."

Letting clients know that they are using a term that is troubling to the clinician can actually have benefits for both people. The clients may not have realized that negative reactions could be elicited by their language, they may become more aware of the potential impact of their language both in and out of the treatment room, and they may feel more respect for the integrity and straightforwardness of the clinician.

Solution-Focused Language   Earlier, this chapter discussed the importance of strength-based reflections of feeling. Clinicians can expand on the use of this strategy and further empower people by couching their interventions in language that is hopeful and anticipates a successful and positive outcome. Consider the following illustrative clinician statements:

> *Clinician 1:* What feelings do you think you will have when you find that more rewarding job?
> *Clinician 2:* I can imagine how successful you will feel when you get that license you have been working toward for years.
> *Clinician 3:* What project do you think you will take on next after you have succeeded in clearing out the stacks of magazines?

Notice how each of these interventions anticipates the achievement of a desired goal, accompanied by positive feelings. Statements such as these, especially when used while people are moving toward goal achievement, can be empowering and can help them feel optimistic that they will soon accomplish their objectives.

Silence and Brevity

> *Clinician:* What were you feeling when your neighbor screamed at you for denting his car? I mean, were you feeling angry or embarrassed? You said it wasn't really your fault so I guess you must have had some bad feelings about the way he treated you. I certainly would have felt pretty annoyed at him.

Can you imagine yourself making an intervention like this? Most of us have—particularly when we are working with a client who says little and is reluctant or unable to share feelings easily. Clinicians often try to help such a person by offering many options and openings. Unfortunately, this usually backfires. The client becomes overwhelmed by all the choices the clinician is offering and, rather than fighting for air time or correcting erroneous assumptions, simply says nothing.

When clinicians formulate interventions, less often accomplishes more, and silence is one of the most powerful interventions. This allows clients the time and space to review what they have said so far, summon up their emotions, and find the words to express them. A patient and interested attitude on the part of clinicians lets clients know that they can take their time, that the clinicians are ready to listen whenever they are ready to speak, and that the clinicians are there to help but not to rescue or to speak for the clients.

Of course, silence that goes on for a very long time can be uncomfortable for both client and clinician. The client's body language, discussed later in this chapter, often reflects whether the person is still processing thoughts and feelings or whether that person is edgy and uncomfortable, waiting expectantly for the clinician to break the silence. If the clinician decides that the time has come to interrupt the silence, a brief intervention such as "What thoughts or feelings are you having now?" or "I wonder what emotions have come up for you during this quiet time" is probably best. With all interventions, not just those used to break silence, brevity is desirable. Restating a point to be sure the client understands is typically more distracting than enlightening. Keep interventions brief; allowing the client the opportunity to request clarification or to fine-tune a clinician's reflection keeps the focus on the client rather than on the clinician's words.

Using Analysis to Promote Expression of Emotions

Chapter 5 presented an approach to analyzing emotions that involved assessing eight important characteristics of an expression of feeling. Such an analysis is another effective strategy for helping people identify and explore their feelings. Let's look at an example from Eileen Carter's treatment that illustrates this strategy. In this example, Eileen has difficulty accessing emotions that can be helpful to her. She tends to focus on Tyrone rather than on herself and does not recognize that her investment in her relationship with him was self-destructive.

> *Eileen:* I remember that terrible time when I was living with Tyrone. He would beat me and make me do things ... things I didn't want to do. And then when I was pregnant, he said he would leave me unless I had an abortion.
> *Clinician:* What feelings come up for you when you think about that?
> *Eileen:* I don't really know. I just wish I could have made him love me. I tried as hard as I could to please him but nothing worked. He was always angry.

Analysis of Emotions   Regret is the primary feeling that seems to underlie Eileen's statement. This is probably not the only emotion she is experiencing and does not seem likely to be a helpful emotion for her. To clarify the nature of this emotion, the clinician began by analyzing the feeling of regret according to the eight dimensions presented in Chapter 5. The following analysis can help the clinician identify points where additional or different feelings might be accessed.

- **Emotional, physical, or a combination:** Eileen's feelings were experienced both emotionally and physically. She felt the emotion of regret but also had tightness in her shoulders and abdomen associated with this feeling.
- **Overt, covert, or a combination:** Although some of Eileen's feelings were overt, her clinician suspected that other feelings, more difficult for her to express, lay beneath the surface.

- **Positive, negative, neutral, or a combination:** Eileen's expressed feelings were negative.
- **In or out of awareness:** Eileen had some awareness of her emotions but the clinician guessed that they were only part of her emotional response.
- **Of varying levels of intensity:** Eileen's emotions were very intense.
- **Appropriate or inappropriate to context and stimulus:** Eileen's feelings did not seem appropriate to the context and stimulus. She had been treated abusively, yet channeled her negative feelings toward herself rather than her abuser.
- **Congruent or incongruent:** Eileen's verbalized emotions and her physical experience of her emotions seemed incongruent. Tearfulness, a common correlate of regret, was absent; instead, Eileen experienced muscle tension, which is more likely to be associated with anger.
- **Helpful or harmful:** Eileen's feelings were harmful to her. They led her to blame herself and to feel disappointed that she had not pleased a man who abused her.

A review of the eight-part analysis of Eileen's emotions suggests that points of access to other emotions might be through the following routes:

- Appropriateness
- Congruence
- Helpfulness
- Physical sensations

Questions such as the following, focused on those areas, might help Eileen identify other feelings:

- If your best friend Bettie, whom you admire so much, were involved with a man like Tyrone, how do you think she would feel? (Appropriateness)
- I notice that your words and your physical sensations seem to convey different emotions. What emotions do you sense in your shoulders and abdomen? (Congruence, physical sensations)
- If you had succeeded in maintaining your relationship with Tyrone, what do you think your life would be like now? (Helpfulness)

Exercise in Analyzing the Eight Dimensions of Emotions   Let's try out the process of using analysis to promote people's expression of emotion. Review the following client statement. Then analyze it according to the eight dimensions of emotion. You are then ready to identify points of access to new or elaborated emotions and can formulate interventions based on your analysis and identification of those points of access. This three-step process offers yet another tool that is useful when exploring emotions.

Walter: The doc told me I needed this really pricey medication for my emphysema. I sure can't afford it and Medicare isn't much help at this point. What am I gonna do, run up to Canada for cheap drugs? That's not my style. Oh, well, we all gotta go sometime. The grandkids are all old enough to remember me. (While speaking, Walter looks tearful and tense. He is speaking loudly and at greater length that he usual does.)

1. Analyze Walter's statement according to the eight categories. Use your imagination if necessary to visualize how Walter might present.

   - *Emotional, physical, or a combination*
   - *Overt, covert, or a combination*
   - *Positive, negative, neutral, or a combination*
   - *In or out of awareness*
   - *Of varying levels of intensity*
   - *Appropriate or inappropriate to context and stimulus*
   - *Congruent or incongruent*
   - *Helpful or harmful*

2. Identify at least two of these dimensions that might help Walter gain awareness of and express his feelings more accurately.
   a. _____
   b. _____

3. Drawing on the dimensions that seem to offer access to Walter's underlying emotions, formulate two interventions that might help Walter identify and explore his feelings more deeply and fully.

Using the Imagination to Promote Expression of Emotions

Helping people re-create an emotionally charged scene in their imagination is another powerful tool for eliciting emotions. This strategy, like many of those discussed in this chapter, requires care and sound judgment. Clinicians should not pressure people to retrieve memories or experiences that might overwhelm or terrify them. Clearly, that can be harmful to them and can lead clients to mistrust their clinician or even to terminate treatment prematurely. Clinicians need to let the client take the lead, approach highly charged emotions and experiences with caution, and provide the client a safe and protected environment. Clinicians can break down disturbing experiences, taking one small segment of the experience at a time, and checking frequently with the client to be sure that the client wants to move forward. The reexperiencing of a disturbing experience can be facilitated if it is preceded and followed by a relaxation exercise. The clinician should also help clients to imagine a safe place or repeat a reassuring affirmation when they become anxious. These strategies can enhance people's ability to handle difficult images and memories.

The following example illustrates an imagery exercise designed to access both emotions that are expressed verbally and those that are communicated through the body. Paying attention to the body as a vehicle for communicating emotions affords yet another approach to eliciting people's feelings.

Example of Using Imagery to Elicit Emotions   Following a relaxation exercise and identification of a reassuring affirmation (discussed later in this book), imagery was used as follows to help Eileen retrieve the feelings associated with a painful memory.

Clinician: Eileen, I'd like you to think back to your time with Tyrone and see what images come into your mind.

Eileen: I remember the time right after the abortion. I was in a lot of pain and was trying to take a nap when Tyrone came into the room and said, "You'd better get up and clean this place before the landlord gets here." I had forgotten that the landlord was coming to inspect the apartment before letting us renew our lease. The place was a mess as usual. I dragged myself out of bed and started to empty ashtrays and get the pizza boxes and wine bottles off the floor. Tyrone just sat there, smoking and watching television, even letting the ashes fall on the floor.

Clinician: So there you are, feeling sick, but trying to clean up while Tyrone watches television. You can remember all the details, the messy room, the discomfort you felt, even what you and Tyrone looked like at that time. As you review that scene in your mind, what emotions come up for you?

Eileen: I feel enraged now, at Tyrone and at myself. He treated me like a slave, like a piece of dirt. And I let that happen. How could I have wanted to stay with him?

This brief example demonstrates how imagery can help people access their emotions more accurately, clearly, and deeply. When Eileen first spoke about her relationship with Tyrone, she romanticized their interactions. A loving, forgiving, and hopeful person, Eileen's initial reaction was to fantasize that if she had only done something different, perhaps she and Tyrone could have had a better relationship. However, once the image brought back to her the real nature of their relationship, she recognized that she could not have established a healthy relationship with Tyrone and that he had badly mistreated her. This freed her of some of her guilt about that relationship and helped her to access her anger, an emotion that seems more appropriate and more likely to help Eileen take charge of her life and access her power and strengths. She will probably still need to deal with negative emotions related to the abortion she had while she was with Tyrone, but having a clearer picture of the context and the pressures that led her to have the abortion probably will help her work through her feelings about herself and about having had an abortion.

Using New Perspectives to Elicit Emotions

One of the important guidelines of ethical and effective counseling or psychotherapy is that clinicians should not devalue clients' emotions, nor should they tell clients how they should feel. At the same time, clinicians sometimes can be helpful to clients by offering them new possibilities in their emotional responses or by giving them permission to experience feelings that may, initially, seem unacceptable to them. This must be done carefully. Possibilities are presented but not forced on clients, and whatever feelings they experience are treated with respect and acceptance.

Two helpful ways to offer new perspectives are to suggest how you, the clinician, might feel and to ask the client how someone they admire might respond to a given situation. That admired person might be an actual person in the client's life or it might be an idolized sports figure, actor, writer, or singer. With children, asking for potential reactions of superheroes or television characters can be effective. For example, you might ask, "How do you think Winnie the Pooh would feel if Piglet's favorite toy got lost?" or "How do you think Superman would react if he needed chemotherapy because he had cancer?"

Example of Introducing New Perspectives   In the following example, the clinician suggests some alternate emotions to Eileen.

> *Clinician:* If a man ignored my feelings and tried to force me to engage in behaviors that felt wrong to me, I would feel pretty angry with him. I wonder if you ever felt angry with Tyrone?
> *Eileen:* Yes, now that I think about it, I did. But I was so afraid that if I told him I felt angry at him, he would hit me or even just walk out and never come back. I didn't think I could survive without him.

Notice that the clinician does not tell Eileen how she should feel or dispute or minimize the emotions she has already expressed. Rather, the therapist simply offers another point of view, allowing Eileen to accept, reject, or modify the emotional response described by the clinician.

BARRIERS AND SOLUTIONS TO ELICITING CLIENTS' EMOTIONS

Thus far, this chapter has presented a range of strategies for helping people use both verbal and nonverbal means to express their emotions. However, eliciting feelings is sometimes a difficult process. Not everyone seeking or referred for counseling or psychotherapy is comfortable and willing to freely disclose feelings. If you have had some counseling or psychotherapy yourself, you may be able to recall what your first session was like. You sat across from a stranger who probably expected you to share experiences and feelings that you may never have shared before. That is not an easy process! Particularly for people who have never before met with a mental health professional and for those who are seeking help because of a court order or ultimatum from a supervisor or family member, the process may not be a welcome one and may feel intrusive and uncomfortable.

Other obstacles may also make client self-disclosure difficult. People may be unused to talking about their feelings; they may view doing so as inappropriate or a sign of weakness, and they may have little access to their feelings or language for their emotions. They may fill their sessions by talking about others, reporting the details of their week, or just sitting silently, waiting for the clinician to ask questions or tell them what to do.

Many strategies are available to help clinicians work effectively with people who are unwilling or unable to talk easily about their emotions. Clinicians need to recognize, accept, and view those behaviors as common and understandable reactions to treatment. Such clients need time to develop trust in the clinician and the treatment process. Explaining the treatment process and giving details and examples of how clients can make the best use of their time and help clinicians to help them can promote client openness. Client openness is also encouraged by reassuring people about the guidelines for confidentiality and establishing the privacy and safety of the treatment setting. Clinicians should allow clients to set the pace and choose the topics, especially during the first few sessions. Clinicians also can facilitate progress by listening for common themes and emotionally charged issues and encouraging people to talk about them if and when they are ready.

Some clinician interventions discourage client self-disclosure. These include rescuing clients when they are stuck or experiencing strong emotions, intervening frequently with lengthy statements, making judgments (either positive or negative), finishing people's sentences and telling them what they should feel rather than tentatively offering possibilities, repeating the same intervention again and again, focusing only on emotions rather than encouraging people to also explore thoughts and actions, ignoring or persistently misunderstanding people's feelings, making excessive interpretations about the underlying meaning of people's words, and neglecting to factor in multicultural and background variables. That may sound like a great deal to avoid, but what clinicians need to remember is simpler. They need to create a safe and protective environment that encourages people to share their deepest and most private feelings. They need to accept and understand any and all of their clients' feelings, emphasize client strengths, respond to clients tentatively and with sensitivity, and check out their own perceptions. Clinicians need to listen to clients when they feel misunderstood, and also listen to clients when they say that they finally feel understood and heard. What a satisfying feeling that is for both clients and clinicians! Finally, clinicians need to consciously follow Carl Rogers's advice and communicate empathy, respect, and facilitative genuineness to clients in congruent and appropriate ways.

NONVERBAL EXPRESSIONS OF EMOTION

Both clients and clinicians communicate emotions nonverbally as well as verbally. Although verbal messages tend to receive most of our attention, many researchers have concluded that nonverbal messages are at least as important as verbal ones (Sundaram & Webster, 2000). In light of this, clinicians need to be attuned to clients' nonverbal messages as well as to their verbal ones and to become skilled at using both channels of communication to understand, elicit, and explore clients' emotions. Particularly important are incongruities between verbal and nonverbal messages that can help both clinicians and clients to identify areas of concern, confusion, and conflict.

To be effective listeners and communicators, clinicians also need to be aware of their own nonverbal messages and to use those messages deliberately to enhance the treatment process. Particularly important is making sure that both verbal and nonverbal messages are clear and that the two are congruent, that is, giving the same message.

This section of the book reviews types of nonverbal messages and introduces a variety of ways to use clients' nonverbal cues to promote self-awareness and self-expression. In addition, it also presents information about the clinician's nonverbal messages and ways to use those messages to enhance treatment. Also considered is the interaction between client and clinician nonverbal messages and how to make good use of that process.

Unfortunately, the relevant literature is fairly sparse and relatively few publications are available that help clinicians make effective use of nonverbal communication (Rothman & Nowicki, 2004). Information on this topic, then, comes from both research and clinical experience.

Nonverbal Communication and Multicultural Considerations

When assessing nonverbal messages, clinicians should bear in mind the ethnic and cultural backgrounds of their clients. Also important is the interaction of client and clinician background and gender. Although facial expressions typically vary little from one culture to another, gender, age, ethnicity, and culture often influence other nonverbal cues. The comfortable distance between people, for example, varies considerably depending on culture. People from Middle Eastern or Hispanic cultures, for example, tend to position themselves relatively close to a person with whom they are interacting and are usually comfortable with considerable physical contact in same-gender interactions. On the other hand, people from the United States or from England typically allow more space between people and are less likely to engage in spontaneous physical contact. When I lived in Egypt, I sometimes noticed myself backing away slightly from people from that country, maintaining the distance between us that had become comfortable to me as an American. When counseling people in Egypt, I had to be very careful to honor the use of space that was comfortable for my clients and avoid giving inadvertent messages of rejection by my own need for more space.

Physical space also may be strongly influenced by gender. I have noticed that many of my women clients move closer to me as we develop a rapport, just as they might do with their close women friends. One even began greeting me with a hug, which felt appropriate and reflective of her warm and outgoing personality. (More on client–clinician touch later!) However, I did not notice a similar pattern in my male clients and clinicians would not usually see such a pattern if both client and clinician were male or if one were male and the other female.

Similarly, the significance of certain gestures or words varies among cultures. In some Middle Eastern countries, exposing the feet and the soles of shoes is considered unacceptable, and in some Asian countries, touching people on the head is unacceptable. Several of my older clients dress up for our sessions, wearing business attire as an apparent sign of respect for our work together, and ask permission to eat lunch in session if we meet during their lunch hour. Most of my adolescent clients, on the other hand, feel comfortable wearing their ripped jeans and T-shirts and bringing sandwiches and soft drinks into our sessions.

By now, you may be thinking, "I'm not a mind reader; how can I anticipate and understand the meaning of all these subtle nonverbal messages?" Of course, we cannot understand all of the nonverbal (and verbal) messages of our clients, but we can take steps that reflect our awareness of the importance of and individual variations in meaning of nonverbal messages. The following are some guidelines:

- Exercise considerable caution when interpreting nonverbal cues, especially when clinician and client are from different cultures or differ greatly in terms of age and other variables. Think of culture in broad terms, considering not only ethnicity and the geographic region where a person was born and has lived, but also age, family environment, socioeconomic status, and other hallmarks of culture and background.
- Read about clients' cultures and talk with colleagues and friends from those cultures to educate yourself.
- Encourage clients to verbalize the meaning of their nonverbal messages, particularly if you are confused by a piece or nonverbal behavior and have a sense that you are not joining well with a client.
- Provide a safe atmosphere that encourages open dialogue and ask clients to give you feedback on anything you do or say that is unclear or uncomfortable to them. Repeat this invitation so that clients are likely to believe what you are saying. How else would I have known that one of my clients did not like me to walk behind her and that another wanted me to refer to the man who molested her as her "abuser" rather than using his name? Only by asking questions and encouraging openness can clinicians understand clients' feelings and reactions. This understanding is instrumental for building a positive therapeutic alliance and helping clients achieve their treatment goals.

Nonverbal messages can be communicated through the following four channels, as discussed next:

- Eye contact
- Facial expression
- Paralanguage (sounds, laughs, tone of voice, speech patterns, volume, intensity, silence)
- Posture, body position, and movements including hand gestures and use of space (especially proximity between client and clinician)

Eye Contact

Making eye contact has long been regarded as one of the most important ways for clinicians to build rapport and join with their clients. Eye contact that is natural, that involves neither avoiding the client's gaze nor staring at the client intently, is likely to create a comfortable treatment environment for most clients and clinicians.

Nonverbal messages can be communicated through many channels, such as eye contact

The client's eye contact is, similarly, an important source of information. Some clients have difficulty making eye contact with their clinicians, especially in the early stages of treatment. This can reflect feelings of shame, guilt, shyness, self-doubt, or discomfort. However, cultural background also may lead people to avoid direct eye contact. When clinicians observe a client, they must be sure they consider the person's cultural background before drawing conclusions about the implications of that person's eye contact or lack thereof.

Changes in eye contact and patterns related to those changes can be particularly informative. For example, whenever Eileen, the client presented throughout this book, talked about her son and her rewarding schoolwork, her eye contact was direct and consistent. However, when she talked about her abortions, she leaned her head back to avoid any possibility of eye contact with her therapist. Over time, as she became able to forgive herself for those choices, this shift was reflected in increased eye contact when she discussed her abortions.

I once observed a beginning counselor working with a couple. The counselor was observant and noted that the husband generally made direct eye contact, whereas the wife tended to avert her eyes when she spoke to her husband. Having been taught the importance of eye contact in building rapport, the counselor said to the wife, "I notice that you often look away when you talk to your husband; you should look directly at him when you talk to him and then perhaps your husband will attribute more importance to what you have to say." Although she meant well, the counselor's intervention was a counterproductive one; it made the wife uncomfortable and self-conscious and made it sound like she was to blame for her husband's lack of attention to her words.

This example illustrates the importance of exercising caution when commenting on people's eye contact. Before deciding whether to comment, clinicians should take the time to notice when people maintain or avoid eye contact. They then should try to understand those patterns. Does the client avoid eye contact because of cultural background, a power differential in the relationship, the person's family background, the topic being discussed, or another reason? Once clinicians have formulated a tentative understanding of a person's patterns of eye contact, they can decide whether and how to discuss this with the client, making sure that they have a sound therapeutic reason for addressing this with the client and being careful not to embarrass the client.

Clinicians should not assume that direct eye contact is always the best form of eye contact. Giving people the message that there is a right and wrong way to maintain eye contact may create considerable discomfort and self-doubt. This also could inhibit communication; discussing highly charged topics, particularly those that engender feelings of shame, may be easier for people if they can avoid gazing directly at the clinician or at others who may be present in the session, if it is group or family therapy.

If clinicians do decide to broach the topic of a person's eye contact, they should do so gently, with an accepting attitude that conveys interest and caring. For example, they might say, "I notice that whenever you talk about your brother, you tend to speak more quietly and shift your eyes downward. I wonder if that might reflect some feelings that arise when you think about your brother." A question that is phrased in such a tentative way simply opens a door; the client then has the choice of discussing the topic further or closing the door by saying, "I don't really know" or "I don't want to talk about that right now" or "I wasn't aware of that" and then changing the subject.

Facial Expression

Facial expression is one of the more easily deciphered sources of nonverbal communication, because of the universal meaning of many facial expressions. When photos of people from one culture are shown to people from another culture, they are generally able to identify the expressed emotion, despite the cultural differences.

However, cultural differences do come into play in several ways in relation to facial expression. Levels of expressed emotions and the freedom with which people express emotions via facial changes do seem to vary among cultures. For example, visitors often comment that people in some of the central and eastern European cities seem to smile less than people in some South American cities. Even within the United States, people in large cities where crime is a significant concern seem to communicate less facial warmth and availability than do people from small communities where safety and concern about strangers is less of a concern. Similarly, the topics or situations that evoke emotions can differ among cultures. Religion and spirituality are important aspects of life in many countries in Southeast Asia and the Middle East, whereas in China religion seems to hold little interest, especially among young adults, probably because it was discouraged while they were growing up. As with all of the nonverbal expressions of emotion, clinicians must maintain multicultural sensitivity when reading facial expressions and check out their hypotheses before assuming they are correctly interpreting facial expressions.

Facial expressions, considered in conjunction with verbal statements, eye contact, and posture, often provide particularly good clues to emotions. Clinicians should be sure to note the congruence or incongruence among these ways of expressing feelings and bear in mind that incongruities often reflect experiences or issues that are unresolved and conflicted for people. For example, while talking about her "nearly perfect" childhood, Sue pursed her lips and clenched her jaw. When this was gently pointed out to her, she acknowledged that she had been repeating family messages but that, in fact, she had often felt ignored and neglected in her large, affluent family.

Paralanguage

Paralanguage is another useful source of information on emotions, particularly when juxtaposed against verbal messages. Paralanguage includes an array of vocal utterances and patterns including sounds, laughs, tone of voice, speech cadence, volume, intensity, breathing, and silence. Of course, few clinicians can track all of these indicators of emotion, but they should try to take note of when clients' speech speeds up or slows down, becomes louder or softer, and when they sigh or laugh. As with the other nonverbal indicators of emotion, changes and incongruities are especially important in signaling strong emotions as well as shifts in emotion.

Laughter can be an especially telling response. Of course, people laugh when they are pleased or amused, and bringing humor and joy into treatment sessions can contribute greatly to people's self-confidence and the quality of the therapeutic alliance. However, people also laugh when they are embarrassed or uncomfortable and that sort of response may be especially important to explore.

Speech patterns also can be important clues to people's feelings. Raised voices are often associated with anger; quieter voices with fear or calm; rapid or pressured speech with anxiety; and unusually slow speech with discomfort or difficulty in sorting out feelings. Remember that only clients know with certainty what they are feeling; the use of interventions already presented in this book (e.g., open questions, reflections of feeling) enables clinicians to check their perceptions with clients to be sure they are accurately interpreting changes in clients' nonverbal communications.

Posture, Body Position, and Movements

Posture can be a powerful source of information about a person's readiness to relate to others. When people sit with arms and legs crossed, leaning back in their seats, they typically give a message that they are protecting themselves and avoiding much closeness and intimacy. On the other hand, an open posture in which arms and legs are extended and people are leaning forward is generally inviting and communicates trust and openness. Observing clients' postures can help clinicians determine how best to build rapport and pace the sessions. In general, clinicians should let clients take the lead while they follow. If clients are in what appears to be a closed posture, clinicians need to respect this and move gradually. Perhaps these people will be more comfortable discussing events than emotions, at least until they develop some trust and connection with their clinicians. Of course, cultural background must be kept in mind when assessing posture.

Body movements, especially hand gestures, are other important sources of information on how people are feeling. Interpreting body movements can be challenging. More will be said about this in the discussion of Fritz Perls's Gestalt therapy later in the chapter. Keep in mind that it is difficult to determine, for example, whether a swinging leg reflects anger, anxiety, or boredom or whether a waving hand reflects anger or excitement. Clinicians should not assume that they can definitively translate body movements into clear messages of feelings. What they can do is be alert to changes and patterns in body movement, take note of the corresponding verbal messages, and consider the relationships between verbal and nonverbal messages. They can also gently point out the body movements to clients and ask them to speculate on the messages their bodies are sending.

Personal Space   The posture people assume when interacting with others often is closely related to the space they prefer to maintain between themselves and other people. Early in the treatment process, client and clinician both may be more comfortable with some extra distance between them. However, as treatment progresses and as the therapeutic alliance develops, chairs are often moved closer. By sitting closer to a client and leaning forward to minimize distance, clinicians can add importance to what is being said and communicate listening, caring, and involvement. Again, however, clinicians should be sensitive to clients' needs and be especially attuned to the influence of the client's culture in determining comfortable personal space. People's histories may also exert an influence on their ideas of optimal personal space. People who come from families that are undemonstrative and formal, as well as people who have been abused or neglected, may have a need for considerable space. On the other hand, people who come from affectionate families and supportive and nurturing environments may naturally sit close to their clinicians, even in an initial session.

USING FOCUSING TO HELP PEOPLE ACCESS AND EXPRESS EMOTIONS

Focusing is an experiential strategy designed to help people access and express their emotions by using the body as a source of information on those emotions. This approach can help both clients and clinicians to successfully use the body as a source of information on feelings. Focusing was developed by Eugene Gendlin (1996) and can be incorporated into a broad range of treatment approaches. Gendlin suggests that people experience, in their bodies, what he calls a *felt sense* that reflects their emotions. Accessing these inner emotions can help people move toward change and growth. Gendlin recommends training for clinicians who want to use focusing in their work. However, he also suggests that "even therapists who do not know focusing can markedly improve therapy ... simply by asking [people] how what is being discussed makes them feel *in the middle of the body* and then waiting quietly for the client to sense there" (p. 1). People who have difficulty accessing this felt sense can begin by directing their attention to the big toe on their right foot and then gradually moving their attention up through the body.

The following is an abbreviated illustration of how focusing might be used with Eileen.

Example of Focusing

Clinician: Eileen, I'd like you to focus your attention in the middle of your body, in your abdomen, and just take some time to see what comes up for you.

Eileen: It feels really tight, like a cramping sensation.

Clinician: Just make some space for whatever comes up and pay attention to your feelings.

Eileen: I'm getting more and more tense, all over my body now. It feels like I want to jump out of my skin.

Clinician: What words or images come up that capture the message of these feelings?

Eileen: I feel ashamed, humiliated. And I feel really angry, more now at Tyrone than at myself. How could I have let him treat me the way he did? I didn't deserve that. And how could I have done the terrible things I did to please him?

As illustrated in this example, attending to our physical sensations can help people experience their emotions in more vivid ways, ways that allow them to articulate those feelings that they could not easily name by using only verbal means. Most people seem to respond well to focusing; however, a small percentage derive no benefit from this approach. A few gain great insight that they may not have achieved in other ways.

Consider the use of focusing as an experiment; it can even be presented to clients in that way. If the focusing experience is very difficult for a particular client or is irritating or nonproductive, clinicians can reassure the client that not everyone benefits from this approach and then shift to another approach to access emotions. However, if the client has a positive response to the process, then clinicians have identified a tool they can use again, especially when the person seems stuck or is having difficulty accessing or verbalizing emotions. I have never found focusing to be harmful to clients, probably because they are in charge of the process. Some additional training and reading should enable clinicians to incorporate focusing into their repertoire of skills, providing a structured way to help people use the body to raise their awareness of their emotions.

USING GESTALT STRATEGIES TO HELP PEOPLE ACCESS AND EXPRESS EMOTIONS

Fritz Perls, who developed Gestalt therapy, pioneered the use of the body as a vehicle for communication of emotions (Fagan & Shepherd, 1970). *Gestalt* means viewing parts in terms of a whole and suggests integration and completeness. As the name of his approach suggests, Perls emphasized the importance of wholeness and integration. He believed that many people encounter emotional difficulties because they separate the mind from the body and are guided by the intellect, ignoring the emotions and the messages of the body. As a result, Perls believed that people have a great deal of "unfinished business" in their lives and have difficulty bringing experiences and reactions to a rewarding closure.

To counteract these undesirable patterns, Perls, like Gendlin, emphasized the importance of clinicians paying close attention to clients' body movements and sensations and then using interventions to help those clients give words to the language of the body. In this way, Perls believed that people could understand themselves more fully and bring together all aspects of themselves in a coordinated, balanced, and congruent whole. Particularly important to Perls were present messages and information from the body. Consequently, he emphasized the "here and now" and focused on observing and inquiring about physical expressions of feeling during a treatment session. The following examples illustrate the sort of interventions that Perls might have used to help Eileen access her body language to increase her awareness of her emotions:

- **Giving a voice to the body:** Become your tense shoulders, focus on and feel the tension you have there, and give your shoulders a voice. What feelings would they share with us?
- **Locating verbalized emotions in the body:** You have told me that you are experiencing regret. Where in your body is that located? Go into that part of your body and try to experience the feelings as fully as possible. As you do that, notice what other feelings or experiences come up for you. Describe what you are experiencing and feeling now.
- **Exaggerating bodily sensations and movements:** You described a sensation of tension in your abdomen. I'd like you to tighten your abdomen as much as you possibly can, breathe in, and pull those muscles together with as much pressure as you can tolerate. Exaggerate the tension you are already feeling. Focus on the tightness, the tension, the discomfort, and tell me how the tension feels and what emotions come up for you.

Notice that Perls did not encourage clinicians to analyze emotions and physical sensations, nor did he pay much attention to the link between emotions and earlier life experiences. Rather, by focusing on the "how" and "what" of people's physical and emotional experiences, he sought to help them live more fully and consciously in the moment without the burden of past baggage, incongruent responses, and unfinished business.

THE CLINICIAN'S VERBAL AND NONVERBAL EXPRESSION OF EMOTIONS

Thus far, this chapter has targeted clients' verbal and nonverbal expressions of emotion. Needless to say, clinicians also have emotional responses and also use verbal and nonverbal means to communicate those emotions. However, clinicians have the important responsibility of ensuring that whatever they say and do in their sessions is helpful to their clients while remaining true to their own values and beliefs. This section of the chapter examines some of the challenges and issues that arise for clinicians in relation to this responsibility:

- Clinician's own strong emotions
- Conflicts between client and clinician

- Clinician self-disclosure
- Clinicians' nonverbal messages
- Physical contact between client and clinician

Clinician's Emotions

Although beginning mental health professionals may believe that clinicians should always be neutral and never bring their own issues or personality into the treatment room, I do not believe that is possible. Instead, clinicians need to develop ways to use their feelings and personality both to help clients and to respect their own needs. I will provide some examples of that, but first let's look at some overall guidelines to help clinicians manage their own feelings that may arise about their clients, their interactions with them, and the help they provide to their clients:

- **Be aware of your own feelings.** Clinicians should draw on their intuition, their understanding of themselves, and their past experiences to notice when feelings come up in response to a particular client that are unusual and perhaps troubling.
- **Acknowledge those feelings to yourself.** Clinicians may not always be comfortable with some of the feelings they have in relation to their clients. They may feel angry, or attracted to a client, or bored, or incompetent. Having feelings such as these are not unethical and do not imply that clinicians are ineffective. It is what they do with these feelings that determine their helpfulness to clients.
- **Think about and understand your feelings as well as you can.** In general, strong feelings that clinicians have toward clients come from three sources:

  - **Countertransference.** In this case, clinicians' emotions have more to do with their own background than they do with the client. Perhaps a client reminds them of their punitive father and so they feel anger toward him and are unsympathetic about the conflicts he is having with his children. Or the client might have a learning difficulty similar to one the clinician struggled with as a youth and the clinician feels certain that she knows what would be best for this client.
  - **Current needs and circumstances.** Current circumstances of the clinician's life are driving the emotions. Perhaps his youngest child has just left for college and he is having nurturing feelings toward an adolescent client whose parents have little interest in her academic successes. The clinician might feel protective toward the young woman and even imagine that he could be a better parent to her than her biological parents. Or the clinician might have just ended a romantic relationship and may view a client as someone with whom the clinician would like to feel close and affectionate.

- ○ **Messages and needs of the client.** In this case, the client's behavior and characteristics elicit clinician reactions and would probably elicit similar reactions from most people. Perhaps the client disciplines his child in ways that seem harmful to the child and their relationship. Or perhaps the client spends session after session detailing her efforts to develop a new but incomprehensible mathematical theory.
- **Determine the best strategy for dealing with the emotions.** If clinicians' emotional responses to a client stem from countertransference or from their own needs, those feelings usually should not be brought into the session. Instead, the challenge for clinicians is to find ways to address their own needs and feelings so that they do not intrude on this or future clients. If clinicians need help with this, I encourage them to talk to a trusted supervisor or seek some therapy. One of the best ways for clinicians to improve their own skills is to be a client themselves, working with a skilled therapist. On the other hand, if clinicians' feelings stem from clients' actions, the clinicians should trust and examine their feelings so that they can develop ways to use that information to help clients increase their self-awareness, learn what messages they are giving others, and improve their relationships as well as the therapeutic alliance.
- **Implement the strategy.** Whether it is addressing issues in their own lives or carefully formulating how they will give the client some feedback, this is the time for clinicians to take action. The following is an example of how clinicians might communicate their perceptions to a client.

Example

Clinician: Jack, I know that being a father and helping your children succeed is very important to you, but I felt concerned when you told me you had yelled at your son and taken away his privileges because he got a B on an exam.

Jack: What are you saying, that I'm not a good father?

Clinician: I can hear that what I said bothered you. In fact, I know that you are a very dedicated father and want to be the best father you can for you son.

Jack: Well, my father set high standards for me and I turned out alright. You can't let kids get away with anything or they'll just go downhill.

Clinician: You do have much to be proud of in your own life. But I wonder what your father's rules and discipline were like for you?

Jack: I didn't like it much at the time. He was always on my back.

Clinician: And I know you left home right after high school and moved in with your older brother while you went to college.

Jack: Yeah, I sure didn't appreciate what the old man was trying to do for me. Of course, now he's gone and I can't tell him that I finally understand him.

Clinician: Over the years, you've come to see that he did care about you, but the two of you had little communication for many years. What would it feel like to you if you and your son had that sort of relationship as he matures?

Jack: I'd feel pretty bad if he didn't know how much I love him. But I don't want him to think he can get away with not doing his best. How can I handle this better?

Although the answer to Jack's question may not come easily, Jack now seems ready to engage in a discussion of how he might modify his parenting so that he maintains a close relationship with his son yet upholds the values that are important to Jack.

Conflict Between Client and Clinician

Occasionally clinicians become the target of clients' anger and disappointment. Clinicians' initial reaction to this may well be a negative one. They may feel that the angry client has seen through them and discovered they are not really the effective clinician they pretend to be, or they may feel frustrated that their skilled and well-meaning efforts to help the client were unappreciated. Experiencing negative emotions such as these in response to a verbal attack or criticism from a client is a human and understandable response. However, once again, clinicians need to take time to process their own feelings and craft a response that is helpful to the client.

Probably the first questions for therapists to ask themselves are whether there is some truth to what the client is saying and, if so, how they need to address the client's concerns. For example, are the clinicians often late in starting sessions, did they neglect to return a client's telephone call, did they make a mistake on the client's bill, or did they call the client by the wrong name? These are common complaints about clinicians and do reflect behaviors that clinicians should change. If clinicians identify a need to modify their behaviors and apologize to the client, that should probably be the first step.

However, clinicians next need to think about the nature of the client's reaction, perhaps using the format for analyzing emotions presented in this chapter. Is the client's emotional response appropriate for the situation or does it seem to be an excessive and counterproductive response, probably reflecting other troubling areas in the person's life? If so, this may be another opportunity to increase the client's self-awareness and provide useful feedback.

Example Addressing Client–Clinician Conflict

Clinician: I can see you are very angry that I did not ask about the call to your sister that we had agreed you would make. I apologize for that; I certainly should have asked about that and I do want us to talk about it. However, I do wonder about your decision to cancel our last two sessions because you were so angry at me. What did it mean to you that I neglected to ask about the call?
Client: The call was a disaster even though I did just what we had talked about. My sister just cut me off and you cut me off too by not even asking about what I had been through. How can you help me if you encourage me to do something that turns out badly and then you don't even care, just like my sister!

Although the clinician did make a mistake in this case, the strength of the client's reaction suggested a more complicated issue. By accepting responsibility for making an error, and then encouraging the client to discuss the situation, the clinician opened up several important topics for discussion including the client's difficulty in trusting others.

For most clinicians, dealing with clients' negative feelings toward them is uncomfortable and challenging. Clinicians should not get into an argument with their clients, berate or criticize them, or even engage in an extensive defense of their own behaviors. Again, seeking help from a trusted colleague, supervisor, or therapist can enable clinicians to understand and address their own feelings while finding ways to stay calm and turn the situation into a productive one that can enhance the goals of treatment.

Clinician Self-Disclosure

Although much can be said about clinician self-disclosure, the topic will be discussed only briefly here in order to provide some basic guidelines about the use of disclosure on the part of the clinician. This is an important topic and I encourage additional reading on it.

A survey of the research on clinician self-disclosure suggests that a small amount of self-disclosure can enhance the treatment alliance and build trust between client and clinician. However, self-disclosure must be used judiciously and with a purpose, reflecting the emphasis on purpose discussed earlier in this book. The following are types of acceptable and unacceptable self-disclosures, followed by an example of each:

Usually Unacceptable Types of Self-Disclosure

- *Information on clinicians' own problems and difficulties that is unlikely to help the client, especially when that information is uninvited:* My neighbor sounds just like yours, except the problem with mine is noisy dogs rather than noisy kids.
- *Very personal information about the clinician:* My husband and I had sexual difficulties during our first year of marriage too, so you are not alone.
- *Positive or negative judgments of the client:* I think you did a terrific job of confronting your mother at the party, but you did not do so well at communicating your feelings to your father.
- *Extended casual conversation:* Yes, that was some game last week. My father-in-law gave us tickets so we were lucky enough to be right there when that record-breaking play was made. I'll never forget it. At least you got to see it on television.

Usually Acceptable Types of Self-Disclosure

- *Minimal sharing of neutral factual information:* Yes, I did see that program last night. What were your reactions to it?
- *Gently offering new perspectives based on your own feelings:* I heard you say that it didn't bother you when she spat and cursed at you. I think I would have found that very painful. I wonder if you felt hurt at all?
- *Sharing helpful feelings about the treatment process:* I hope you won't mind if I stop you for a moment. I'm having difficulty figuring out who all these people are at your family reunion and I really want to have a clear understanding of what that experience was like for you. Could we back up so that you could tell me a little about your relationships with the people at the reunion who were most important to you?

Notice that presentation of the acceptable types of self-disclosure is brief and the clinician immediately shifts the focus back to the client. The unacceptable types of self-disclosures, on the other hand, shift the focus of the session to the clinician, lead rather than follow and join with the client, and intrude on the client's work in the session. The exercises at the end of this chapter offer some additional opportunities for you to think about clinician self-disclosure and develop a clearer idea of when you would and would not use self-disclosure.

Clinician's Nonverbal Messages

Just as clients transmit messages and feelings nonverbally, so do clinicians. Consequently, clinicians should be conscious of and purposeful in transmitting both nonverbal and verbal messages. Four types of nonverbal communications that may have a particularly strong impact on the treatment process are discussed next.

Nonverbal Incongruence   The term *nonverbal incongruence* refers to a conflict, either between the clinician's own verbal and nonverbal messages or between the clinician's body language and communications of the client. For example, a clinician might ask a client for more information on his strong emotions while suppressing a yawn and appearing disinterested (incongruence within the clinician), or the clinician might exhibit a tense and angry posture while recalling an argument earlier in the day while the client relates how happy she is that she and her fiancé are planning their wedding (incongruence between client and clinician).

Fidgeting, playing with a pen or paper clip, and similar distracting and extraneous movements also communicate incongruence and detract from the treatment process. Situations such as these can create distance between client and clinician, interfere with the development of trust and empathy, and ultimately sabotage treatment. Being conscious of their thoughts, feelings, and body posture and movements can help clinicians avoid such situations and, instead, convey a sense of calm and confidence that encourages clients to relax and talk openly about themselves.

Nonverbal Complementarity   When clinicians use their body language to convey empathy and concern, leaning forward to show attentiveness, moving closer to convey caring, and maintaining appropriate eye contact, this helps people feel understood and builds a connection between client and clinician.These nonverbal interventions are especially powerful if they are accompanied by parallel verbal statements of empathy and other attending behaviors that reinforce the messages of the nonverbal communication. Although beginning clinicians may need to consciously and deliberately monitor their body language, complementarity will probably become an intuitive process. Skilled and experienced clinicians spontaneously use voice tone, body movements, posture, and eye contact to convey understanding and caring to their clients.

Nonverbal Mirroring or Synchrony   One way to join with people, both in and out of the therapy room, is to mirror their body language. For example, we would cross our legs when they do, smile when they do, relax when they do, and lean forward when they do. This deliberate mirroring of body language is yet another powerful way for clinicians to build a sound therapeutic alliance and engender trust and openness in clients. Matching people's posture, body movements, grammar, and language is a way to connect with them. To some extent, people do this naturally and without thinking when they want to build rapport with someone.

Although this strategy can be obtrusive and even insulting when overdone, occasional and subtle mirroring of clients' words, posture, and gestures can facilitate the process of joining and advance the therapeutic alliance. Next time you are in a conversation, try mirroring the other person's body language; cross your legs when the other person does, and nod your head at the same time. Notice whether it accelerates the development of rapport.

Facial Expressions   Clinicians' facial expressions also play an important part in treatment. I had been counseling a couple, both of whom were dealing with diagnoses of cancer. When they told me that the wife's cancer had returned, tears came to my eyes as they did to my clients'. Although clinicians rarely evidence such strong emotions in their sessions, my sadness made clear to them the empathy and caring I had for them. At the same time, strong emotions evidenced by the clinician can be distracting and can shift the focus from the client to the clinician. Counselors and therapists need to monitor their own emotions in sessions to ensure that they enhance, rather than detract, from the treatment process and give others the message they are seeking to transmit.

Physical Contact Between Client and Clinician

Much has been written about physical contact between client and clinician. The safest policy, especially for beginning clinicians, is to keep physical contact to a minimum, except perhaps for a handshake upon meeting. However, with experience, many clinicians learn when a pat on the hand to comfort a distraught client or even an occasional hug can advance the therapeutic process and build rapport. Physical contact must be offered with extreme care and sensitivity, always respecting the needs of the client and that person's cultural background. Clinicians generally should ask permission before touching a client.

Sometimes clients initiate physical contact with their clinician. This might represent simply a need for comfort, or it might be the beginning of inappropriate and seductive behavior. Dealing with these overtures can be difficult for clinicians who, of course, do not want their clients to feel shamed or rejected.

In deciding how to respond to client-initiated physical contact, clinicians should consider both the ethical standards of their profession and their own instincts. As always, they can confer with a colleague or supervisor if uncertain how to proceed. Many types of concurrent dual relationships, such as client and friend or client and romantic partner, are prohibited by the ethical standards of all mental health professions. Even if the physical contact does not seem unethical, clinicians have the right to set limits on any physical contact that makes them uncomfortable.

Using empathy, reflection of feelings, and gentleness can make this process successful. For example, clinicians might say to the client, "At the end of our past few sessions, you gave me a hug. I can certainly understand your wanting to show caring for me and appreciation of our work together and maybe seek some support and reassurance. I am concerned, however, that this might detract from our work, so I would prefer that we don't hug at the end of our sessions. What reactions do you have to that?"

CONTAINMENT OF EMOTIONS

A favorite intervention of many clinicians is "How does that make you feel?" Usually, clinicians view it as therapeutic for clients to be able to identify and express their emotions. That paves the way for them to modify any unhelpful emotions. Although eliciting emotions is an important component of clinical work, even that can be overdone and may be harmful to some clients. People can become mired in their feelings and may not be able to move beyond crying or raging and into more constructive forms of self-expression. Sometimes clients are so overwhelmed by emotion that clinicians need to take steps to help them curtail their expression of emotions and contain or diffuse the intensity of those emotions so that they become more manageable. This section of the book presents strategies to help people express and contain or modify their emotions.

People may have difficulty tolerating both strong negative emotions and strong positive emotions. Without help, people can become almost consumed by their emotions. In addition, overfocusing on emotions can further entrench undesirable emotions and lead people to feel worse than they did before seeking treatment. The following are some of the interventions that can be used to facilitate containment of emotions.

Reassurance and Support

Offering reassurance and support is an important aspect of the clinicians' role. Just as when clinicians suggest new emotions to clients, they need to be careful not to

Fritz Perls

minimize or devalue people's feelings, to tell them how they should feel, or to judge or disapprove of them. If clinicians keep these cautions in mind, they can make some short, simple statements that can help clients feel safe and supported. The following examples illustrate such reassuring statements.

Examples of Reassurance and Support

- You're doing the best you can.
- You feel overwhelmed by your emotions, but together we can sort them out.
- You have handled this successfully before and you can handle it again.
- Focus on your breathing, and the feelings will gradually lessen.
- You're safe here in this room. You're no longer in danger.
- I'm right here with you.

Distraction and Thought Stopping

Redirecting clients' attention away from overwhelming emotions and onto soothing or distracting stimuli is another strategy to enhance people's efforts to manage their emotions. The following are a few examples of interventions that can accomplish this.

Examples of Distraction and Thought Stopping

- Remember your affirmation. Keep telling yourself, "I am safe and strong now. I am safe and strong now."
- You can choose to turn your attention away from that painful memory and onto the joys you have in your life now. You can replace that memory of Tyrone with your memory of the day you spent in the park with Junior. Remember his laughter, the way he kicked his feet when you pushed him on the swing, the sunshine warming both of you.
- Bring yourself back into this room and notice all of the details: the books on the shelf, the pictures on the wall, the rug on the floor, even the pens on the desk. Focusing your attention on where you are in the present will help you manage troubling emotions from the past.
- When you are fearful that you will become overwhelmed by your guilt, you can tell yourself to stop the emotion. You may need to do this repeatedly before the feeling starts to recede, but gradually you will probably find that you have more and more control over those feelings of guilt.
- I can see that you sometimes become frightened by how much you love Junior. You have had so many losses in your life, you fear that loving him so much will only cause you pain and you may even withhold your love from him. Let's imagine all that love you have for Junior in your heart and know that it is safe there and that you can let out only as much love as you choose. If the love feels too strong, just put it back in your heart for a time when you decide to feel and share it.

Using the Imagination

Just as the imagination can be used to elicit neglected emotions, it can also be used to facilitate containment of overwhelming emotions. The following instructions provide an example. This intervention is designed to give the client a sense of control over her emotions. Using the image of a safe, she can choose to separate herself from her emotions if they threaten to become too painful or overwhelming. On the other hand, if she wants to process and modify those emotions, she can let them out of the safe in small, manageable doses. In this way, she is controlling her emotions rather than allowing her emotions to control her.

> **Example of Using the Imagination to Contain Emotions**
>
> *Clinician:* Eileen, I'd like you to imagine a very large, very strong safe in front of you, as strong as any bank vault. Only you know the combination to this safe. Imagine turning the dial on the safe and opening the door. Now you can put into the safe all those strong feelings that are making you feel so hopeless and discouraged. You can put into the safe all of your anger toward Tyrone, all of the guilt you feel about the choices you made while you were with him, all of the regrets and disappointments you have about that relationship. Imagine yourself putting any or all of those feelings into the safe. Once you have filled up the safe as much as you choose, you can close the door on the safe. Check it to make sure it is firmly shut. Fasten the combination lock and turn the dial a few times to be sure that no one but you can open the safe. You can leave all those troubling emotions in the safe as long as you want, and you can let some or all of those feelings out whenever you want. It is your choice when and how you want to experience those emotions again.

CHANGING EMOTIONS

The interventions described in Chapter 5 and this chapter are not only effective in helping people express and contain emotions, they are also useful in promoting positive changes in feelings. The basic strategies of accenting, restating, paraphrasing, summarizing, and reflecting emotions are often enough to enable people to identify, process, and change their feelings. Specific interventions such as exploring incongruities in emotional expression, suggesting alternate emotional reactions, and using imagery can further enable people to modify their emotions. Additional interventions, such as those discussed next, also are useful in helping people modify their emotions.

Use of Language

Reality therapy, developed by William Glasser (2000) and Robert Wubbolding (2000), emphasizes the importance of people taking responsibility for and recognizing that they can choose their emotions. To encourage clients' belief in their ability to control their emotions, reality therapists use active verbs rather than adjectives to describe emotions. For example, a person would be described as *angering* rather than *angry, depressing* rather than *depressed,* and *anxietying* rather than *anxious.* This gives the message that emotions are not fixed states or conditions but actions that can be changed.

Acting "As If..."

People can often change their emotions by trying on a new emotion, acting as if they feel a certain way, or assuming the persona of someone they admire who would be likely to have the desired emotion. The following examples reflect some ways a clinician might present this strategy.

Example 1: Acting As If a Person Has a Desired Emotion

I know your arthritis has been bothering you lately, but you mentioned that people have been commenting on how unhappy you look and you don't like getting this reaction. How would it feel, just while you are at work today, to act as if you are having a wonderful day and would rather be at work than anywhere else? Push yourself to smile and ask other people about their day. Note the reactions you get from people and let me know in our next session what you experienced through use of this exercise.

Example 2: Trying on a New Emotion

Work has been difficult for you lately because of your supervisor's harsh criticism of you. You have tried a variety of ways to let him know your feelings and effect a change, but have not had much success. How about trying a different strategy today? How about focusing on how pleased you are that your supervisor is not your husband or father or brother and remind yourself that he will be retiring in six months and then you will never have to see him again. Could you find some pleasure in thinking about how soon he will be out of your life?

Example 3: Acting As If You Are Someone You Admire

You've mentioned your admiration for your grandmother who had seven children, was widowed in her thirties, and yet managed to send all of her children to college and complete her own college degree. I wonder if you could take on your grandmother's spirit during this challenging time and act as if you have her energy, fortitude, and determination.

Example 4: Acting As If Today Were an Exception

You told me that some days everything comes together for you, you get along well with people and are very productive in what you do. What if we declare tomorrow one of those exceptional days and, from the time you awaken in the morning, you remind yourself that today is one of those days when everything comes together for you?

Use of Logic

Using logic as part of the process of analyzing emotions often can help people to recognize that their emotions are not warranted and can be replaced with more constructive or appropriate feelings. This is illustrated in the following dialogue.

Example Using Logic to Modify Emotions

Client: I feel so guilty about the kind of father I am. My children don't deserve to have me as a father.
Clinician: I can hear that you have many regrets about your parenting. What is the worst thing you've ever done to your children?
Client: The worst thing?
Clinician: Yes.

Client: One time I was supposed to pick up my daughter at day care and I got so caught up with my work that I didn't notice it was time to pick her up. The day care director had to call me at work and tell me hurry up and get her before they closed.

Clinician: What happened?

Client: I never moved so fast in my life. I'm lucky I didn't get a speeding ticket. I got to the day care center in record time. It was after their closing time and the director was there waiting with my daughter. I felt so terrible.

Clinician: And how was your daughter?

Client: She was fine. She was enjoying having the playroom all to herself.

Clinician: Have you ever physically or sexually abused your children?

Client: No, of course not. I would never do that.

Clinician: Did you ever send them to bed hungry when you had food for yourself?

Client: No, I would always put my children first.

Clinician: So the worst thing you've ever done to your children is arrive late at day care?

Client: Yes.

Clinician: How many times did that happen?

Client: Only once. I felt so terrible, I never let that happen again.

Clinician: If we think of a one-to-ten scale of mistakes parents make, with abusing their children being a ten on the scale, where on the scale would you put forgetting to pick up your daughter at day care on one occasion?

Client: Well, when you put it that way, I guess it's not so bad. Maybe a five. But I should have been more responsible.

Clinician: It does sound like you made a mistake. But I wonder if you expect yourself to be a perfect parent?

Client: I don't know ... maybe.

Clinician: Let's look at this in another way. Can you tell me about some good things you do for your children?

Client: That's easy. I love them, I provide for them, I try to make sure they are safe, I read to them and try to teach them skills as well as values.

Clinician: So you do a great deal to be a good parent.

Client: Yes, I can see that now. I'm not perfect and I've made mistakes, but I really try to be a good parent.

Clinician: When we began this discussion, you felt very guilty about your parenting. I wonder how you feel now?

Client: Well, I know there is room for improvement, but I'm actually starting to feel some pride in the sort of parent I am.

Using Rational Emotive Imagery

Albert Ellis, founder of rational emotive behavior therapy, developed a strategy called rational emotive imagery (REI). REI is designed to help people change unhealthy and inappropriate emotions into healthy and appropriate ones (Ellis & Dryden, 1997). In REI, people are encouraged to visualize a troubling activating event and then experience the unhealthy emotions associated with that event. For example, Eileen might visualize the time Tyrone insisted that she clean the house even though she was recovering from an abortion and then experience the humiliation and guilt she had felt at that time. Once she had allowed herself to feel those emotions for a few minutes, the clinician would encourage her to push herself to experience a change in her feelings. Perhaps she would choose to experience some anger toward Tyrone, accompanied by a sense of relief that she was now safe and could no longer be mistreated by him. Practice of REI and repetition of changing the feelings associated with this activating event would probably lead to a genuine and internalized change in Eileen's feelings about the experience.

LEARNING OPPORTUNITIES

This chapter has built on Chapter 5 by presenting a broad array of strategies that clinicians can use to help clients identify and express their emotions, as well as contain and modify their feelings. In addition, this chapter presented information on types of nonverbal communication and discussed ways to enable clients to better access messages that are conveyed through the body. Discussion also addressed clinicians' own emotional responses to clients and suggested guidelines for dealing with those feelings in therapeutically sound ways.

Overall, this chapter focused on teaching the following skills:

- Using positive psychology and strength-based reflections of feeling
- Facilitating identification and expression of emotions via accents, restatements, paraphrases, summarizations, and reflections of feeling
- Opening leads that promote expression of feeling
- Developing a repertoire of interventions to elicit emotions through language (clichés, mirroring, solution-focused language, and silence and brevity) analysis, imagery, and new perspectives
- Understanding nonverbal demonstrations of emotions: eye contact, facial expressions, paralanguage, and posture, body position, and movements
- Using focusing and Gestalt strategies to help people access and express emotions
- Understanding clinicians' verbal and nonverbal expressions of emotion
- Helping clients with containing and changing emotions

Written Exercises

Consider the following client:

> Wayne, a 44-year-old man, sought treatment with the presenting concern of wanting to find ways to help his family more effectively. His older child Mary, age 14, had been wounded during a shooting in her school. A teacher and two other students were killed in that incident. Mary is currently in the hospital and will probably be unable to walk as a result of her injuries. Wayne, his wife Sarah, and their younger child Joseph have been struggling to make sense of this and to help Mary. The family has strong religious beliefs and a solid support system, both within their family and at their church.

Respond to these questions related to your work with Wayne:

1. Write two strength-based reflections of feeling that you might use with Wayne.
2. List three opening leads that seem likely to help Wayne express his feelings, and briefly explain the reasons for your choice of those interventions.

3. Wayne is having difficulty acknowledging any anger and believes that he must be strong and unemotional in order to best help his family. This is the role model set for him by his father. Remembering to be respectful of Wayne's beliefs and background, how would you address his underlying emotions and the expectations he is setting for himself?

4. While he is talking, you notice that Wayne is clenching and unclenching his fist. Would you address this nonverbal behavior? Why or why not? If yes, how would you address it?

5. What barriers do you think are likely to arise in your work with Wayne? How might you address them?

6. Write two self-disclosure statements that you might make to help Wayne if you were his clinician.

7. Included in this chapter are many strategies for helping people access and express their emotions. Among these are using the imagination, focusing, Gestalt interventions, acting "as if ...," and others. Select one strategy that you think would be especially helpful to Wayne and write out a brief dialogue (approximately five client statements and five clinician statements) that illustrates your use of the strategy you have selected.

Discussion Questions

1. This chapter introduced the idea of providing reassurance and support to clients. Based on what you currently know, what guidelines do you think you should keep in mind when providing reassurance? What pitfalls can you identify?

2. Norms for appropriate nonverbal communication with another person vary from one culture to another. If you were counseling a client from a culture other than your own, how would you ensure that you did not offend that person with your eye contact, posture, body movements, or seating arrangement?

3. How would you describe your typical use of body language? How important a vehicle of communication is your body for you? How has your cultural background influenced your body language?

4. Positive psychology has attracted considerable attention and interest in recent years. How do you explain this? Do you see this as a valuable direction for clinicians or do you think that it is a fad that is detracting from clinicians' real work, alleviating the symptoms of mental disorders? Discuss your response.

5. Some of the common barriers to helping people express and identify their feelings have been presented in this chapter, along with some ways to bypass those barriers. What other barriers can you think of that might make people unwilling or unable to express their emotions freely? What additional approaches can you think of for encouraging people to verbalize their emotions?

6. Assume you have begun to work with a client who occasionally manifests a tremor in his left hand. The client has said nothing about this. You cannot determine whether this is a reflection of strong emotion, a medical disorder, or a combination of the two. Would you bring this up with the client? Why or why not? If yes, how would you approach the client about the tremor?

7. If you have not yet done the practice group exercise associated with this chapter, discuss your thoughts and feelings about that upcoming experience. What did you learn from the previous role-plays associated with earlier chapters of this book that you want to carry with you into the current role-play?

8. If you have already done the practice group exercise associated with this chapter, discuss your reactions to that experience. What was the most beneficial aspect of that experience for you? What was the most challenging or uncomfortable aspect of the experience? How did this role-play experience compare with your earlier one(s)? How can you make future practice group exercises even more rewarding to you?

Practice Group Exercise: *Eliciting and Changing Emotions and Making Helpful Use of Nonverbal Communication*

Divide into your practice groups as you have been doing in conjunction with previous chapters of this book. The practice group exercise presented here will help you gain experience in making helpful use of nonverbal communication and using some of the strategies presented in this chapter to elicit and modify emotions.

Role-Play Exercise

Before beginning this exercise, each member of the practice group should select one of the following interventions, making sure that four different interventions have been selected:

- Using imagery to help people express emotions
- Focusing
- Clarifying emotions by analyzing the eight dimensions of an emotion
- Rational emotive imagery
- Gestalt strategies for accessing nonverbal expressions of emotion

Once each person has selected an intervention, you should choose an issue or situation you will present when you are in the client role. Do your best to be a cooperative partner and select an issue that will facilitate the clinician's use of the strategy he or she selected.

In addition to practicing the use of a specific strategy presented in this chapter, incorporate into your role-play attention to nonverbal communication, both your own and the client's. Try to demonstrate nonverbal complementarity as well as nonverbal synchrony.

In addition, you might also try to incorporate into your role-play one or more of the other concepts presented in the chapter. Particularly useful would be varying your opening leads and using strength-based reflections of feeling.

Your goals for this role-play are as follows:

- To practice and demonstrate one of the specific strategies for eliciting client's emotions

- To develop a better understanding of three or four of these strategies by observing them in action
- To gain additional experience in use of the fundamental attending skills such as encouragers, paraphrase, and reflections of feeling (especially strength-based reflections of feeling) in your dialogue
- To become more aware of your own and your client's nonverbal communication and to find ways to use nonverbal messages to enhance the treatment process

Time Schedule

As in the previous role-play, you will get the most out of this experience if you can devote approximately 45 to 90 minutes to the exercise. If you have 45 minutes, you should have time for two role-plays, which will give each participant the opportunity to assume either the client or the clinician role. If you have 90 minutes, you will have time for four role-plays, with each participant experiencing both client and clinician roles. Spend approximately 10 minutes in each role-play and another 10 minutes sharing reactions and providing feedback to the person who assumed the clinician role during that part of the exercise. Be sure to follow the guidelines for giving, receiving, and recording feedback that were presented earlier in this book.

Assessment of Progress Form 6

1. **Using a specific intervention to elicit emotions.** How successful were you in using the intervention you had selected? What barriers or challenges did you encounter when you made use of the strategy? What strengths were evident in your application of the intervention? How might you have been even more effective in promoting the client's expression and understanding of emotions? In retrospect, do you think a different intervention or strategy would have been more helpful, in light of the concern your partner presented? If so, which one and what are your reasons for thinking it would have been more effective?

2. Assess your use of the following:
   a. Use of a variety of opening leads
   b. Use of strength-based reflections of feeling
   c. Use of other attending skills

3. **Nonverbal messages.** In what ways did you deliberately use nonverbal communication to enhance the role-play? What did you do to demonstrate nonverbal complementarity and synchrony? What impact did these have? What were the strengths in your use of nonverbal communication? How might your nonverbal communication have been improved? Comment on the following behaviors on the part of the clinician:
   a. Eye contact
   b. Posture
   c. Proximity to client
   d. Physical movements and gestures
   e. Tone of voice and rate of speech

   4. Summary of feedback:
   5. Progress in achieving goals from previous session:
   6. One or two additional goals to improve your clinical skills:
      a. a.
      b. b.

Personal Journal Questions

1. Select an hour during the next few days when you will deliberately use nonverbal synchrony and complementarity, concentrating particularly on mirroring the body language of the people with whom you are interacting. After doing that, record what that experience was like for you. What changes or reactions, if any, did you notice in the people with whom you practiced this strategy?

2. Identify a situation in your own life that you want to understand more clearly. Be careful not to select a situation that is highly charged or of which you have only a hazy memory. Review the exercise on page **215** in which the clinician helped Eileen to use her imagination to gain greater awareness of her feelings about Tyrone. Following the model of that exercise, use your imagination to help you become more aware of your emotional reactions to the situation you have identified. Write briefly about what you learned from this experience and what it was like for you to use this strategy to enhance your self-awareness.

3. Assume that you have decided to seek therapy. How do you think you would feel about sharing your emotions with your clinician? What issues or obstacles might make it difficult for you to talk openly about your feelings? What interventions might be most helpful in enabling you to express your feelings?

4. In keeping with the emphasis on positive psychology and strength-based interventions, write three strength-based reflections of your own feelings. I encourage you to remember these or write them down and keep them available to you so that you can use them as affirmations and reminders of your important strengths.

5. Use one of the strategies presented in this book, such as rational emotive imagery, logic, or imagination, to change an unpleasant or unhelpful emotion you are experiencing. What was it like for you to use this strategy on yourself? How successful were you at modifying your emotion?

SUMMARY

This chapter built on the information on eliciting and identifying emotions presented in Chapter 5. It presented an array of specific strategies designed to help clinicians elicit clients' emotions and enable them to contain or change those emotions in healthy ways. Particular attention was paid to ways in which clinicians can vary opening leads, make strength-based reflections of feeling, understand and use nonverbal communications, and bypass barriers to client expression of emotion. In addition, this chapter discussed clinicians' own emotions and ways they can be constructively expressed, both verbally and nonverbally.

Chapters 3 and 4 focused on strategies to address people's backgrounds, whereas Chapters 5 and 6 presented a broad array of strategies and interventions for working with people's emotions. Chapters 7 and 8 shift the focus to the third element in the BETA model, thoughts, and look at some fundamental strategies for eliciting and processing clients' thoughts. Chapter 7 presents a 10-step process to help clients elicit, assess, and modify their emotions, as well as their accompanying actions.

PART 4

USING FUNDAMENTAL SKILLS TO ELICIT, IDENTIFY, ASSESS, AND MODIFY THOUGHTS

Chapter 7

USING FUNDAMENTAL SKILLS TO ELICIT, IDENTIFY, ASSESS, AND MODIFY THOUGHTS AND ACCOMPANYING EMOTIONS AND ACTIONS

OVERVIEW

The previous four chapters in this book presented information and skills linked to the first two elements of the BETA model. Chapters 3 and 4 focused on background and provided information on asking helpful questions and using intake interviews, genograms, early recollections, and other specific skills to gather client information. Chapters 5 and 6 focused on emotions and presented the skills of using accents, restatements, paraphrases, reflections of feeling, summarizations, and other more specific strategies to help people express, analyze, contain, and change their feelings.

The skills presented in Chapters 3 through 6 are essential to all mental health professionals in their work and provide the foundation for Chapters 7 and 8, which focus on thoughts, the third element in the BETA model. Chapter 7 presents fundamental skills that facilitate clinicians' efforts to help people identify, evaluate, and change their thoughts. Chapter 8 continues the emphasis on thoughts and provides additional skills that clinicians can use to help people with distorted, illogical, and self-destructive thoughts to develop healthier and more helpful thought patterns. The specific skills presented in Chapter 8 can be combined with the broad and fundamental skills covered in this chapter to create a powerful treatment package.

Learning Goals

As a result of reading this chapter and completing the exercises, you can expect to accomplish the following:

- Understand the importance of thoughts in people's lives, as well as in the treatment process.
- Learn how thoughts, emotions, and actions form a unit that is amenable to change via cognitive interventions.
- Learn a structured approach to helping people assess and change their thoughts and accompanying emotions and actions.

Skills to be Learned

Six fundamental skills that help clinicians elicit, identify, assess, and modify clients' thoughts are presented in this chapter:

- Eliciting thoughts, emotions, and actions
- Rating belief in the thoughts and the intensity of the emotions
- Analyzing and assessing the validity of thoughts
- Categorizing the nature of distorted thoughts
- Modifying distorted thoughts and accompanying unhelpful emotions and actions
- Understanding the overall process of modifying thoughts, emotions, and actions in combination

To some readers, this may sound simple and straightforward, whereas to others, this may be a new and challenging perspective. Keep in mind that people often are strongly attached to their thoughts and have difficulty reassessing and modifying them. The skills presented in Chapters 3 through 6—open questions, encouragers, reflections of feeling, and others—all are important in eliciting and changing people's unhelpful thoughts. In addition, maintaining a positive therapeutic alliance, as discussed in previous chapters, continues to be an essential component of treatment; having a client–clinician relationship that conveys caring and empathy and that inspires trust and hope in clients greatly facilitates the process of helping people identify, assess, and modify their thoughts.

Albert Ellis   Aaron Beck

THE POWER OF THOUGHTS

Two leading clinicians, Albert Ellis (Ellis & Dryden, 1997) and Aaron Beck (Beck, 1995; Beck & Emery, 1985), have been instrumental in providing counselors and psychotherapists with the tools they need to help people identify, analyze, and modify their thoughts. The writings and research of these authors provide the foundation for the skills presented in this chapter.

Albert Ellis initiated what is now called *rational emotive behavior therapy* in the 1950s. Ellis's work drew attention to the importance of thoughts in determining whether people functioned in healthy, self-affirming ways or developed symptoms and mental disorders that interfered with their ability to live rewarding and successful lives. Challenging his training in psychoanalysis, Ellis concluded that eliciting and modifying people's thoughts were more efficient and effective ways to help them than exploration of background or emotions.

Building on the ideas of Albert Ellis, Aaron Beck and others systematized the use of cognitive therapy. Many research studies have substantiated the effectiveness of treatment focused on changing thoughts, and cognitive therapy now has assumed a prominent place among the established treatment approaches.

In fact, most current theories of counseling and psychotherapy are phenomenological in nature. These treatment approaches recognize that how people perceive and think about themselves, their lives, and their issues have a significant impact on how they feel about those issues and what actions they take to cope with them. Changing thoughts, therefore, usually leads to corresponding changes in emotions and actions.

Examples of the Importance of Thoughts

The following examples illustrate this concept. Hidayah, Selma, and Mona, all women in their 40s, were diagnosed with breast cancer. All three women had mastectomies with reconstructive surgery. All three were diagnosed in an early stage of the disease, and all had an excellent prognosis. That is where the similarity ends.

Example 1

Hidayah had immigrated to the United States from Southeast Asia. She had been raised in the Muslim religion and was married to an American man who was Protestant. Hidayah had only been living in the United States for a few years and had not yet developed a support system here; her parents and sisters still lived in Indonesia. She was devastated by her diagnosis of breast cancer and was certain she would die of the disease. Issues of modesty and privacy, as well as her separation from her family of origin, made it difficult for her to verbalize her concerns and get help. Because she was deeply depressed, her physician prescribed antidepressants and medication to help her sleep. Hidayah rejected the idea of support groups or counseling to help her and remained withdrawn and sad.

Example 2

Selma, an African American woman, was also shocked and frightened by her diagnosis. However, her mother and two women in her church had previously been diagnosed with breast cancer and had survived the disease. She talked with them, gathered information, discussed her condition with several oncologists, and became more hopeful about her prognosis. Her diagnosis even helped Selma to make some positive changes in her life. She had been unhappy in her work and, for many years, had thought about returning to college to obtain a teaching certificate. Her diagnosis with a life-threatening illness led her to realize that she could not postpone her dreams indefinitely and that she needed to take action. She enrolled in a special program to prepare college graduates to become teachers and moved forward toward her goals.

Example 3

Mona, a Caucasian woman, described her diagnosis as a "minor inconvenience." Mona's life was a full one; she had three adolescent children, a supportive marriage, and a rewarding job managing a store. She followed the advice of the first physician she consulted, had her surgery, made a rapid recovery, and resumed her previous activities as soon as possible.

How these women thought about their diagnoses and prognoses had a profound impact on the ways in which they dealt with their disease and the subsequent direction of their lives. This is true of all of us. Our perceptions of our life experiences often are more important than the experiences themselves in determining our responses to those experiences and the impact they have on our lives. Whether people are dealing with a life-threatening illness or a lunch date with a friend, their thoughts are a primary determinant of how they negotiate the experience and its impact on their lives.

This chapter focuses on people's thoughts: how to help people report and identify their thoughts, assess the validity and helpfulness of those thoughts, and, if appropriate, modify those thoughts so that they are more realistic and helpful to them. Changing dysfunctional thoughts can contribute greatly to improving people's moods, helping them make constructive shifts in their behaviors, and enhancing their lives.

TERMINOLOGY

The term *thoughts* is used throughout this chapter. Thoughts can also be referred to as *cognitions, ideas, beliefs, values, attitudes, concepts,* and *perceptions.* Some subtle distinctions differentiate these terms:

- The terms *thoughts, cognitions, concepts,* and *ideas* are basically interchangeable. They are notions about ourselves, our lives, and our world. They are often in our awareness but may also reflect an underlying or core perspective. Thoughts may be trivial and fleeting, such as "I think I'll have a cup of coffee," or they may be enduring and have a profound impact on our lives, such as "I think of myself as an unattractive and unworthy person."
- *Perceptions* typically reflect an awareness or understanding that developed through use of the senses. Examples are "I can barely perceive the ship way out on the ocean" and "I can perceive the difference between right and wrong."
- *Beliefs* usually are deeply held convictions or opinions, generally not amenable to immediate proof. The statements "I believe that we must protect our environment for future generations" and "I believe that men and women should have equal rights and privileges" exemplify beliefs.
- *Values,* like beliefs, typically involve a judgment, with values emphasizing worth or relative merit. An example is "Although that doll has little monetary value, it has great value to me because my parents gave it to me when I was a child."
- *Attitude* is the last term to be considered here. You have probably heard someone say "That person has an attitude." Although this is colloquial speech, it does reflect the nature of an attitude. It is an orientation to the world, perhaps brief and transient or perhaps pervasive and enduring. "She has a negative attitude toward her work" and "She has a good attitude, despite all her difficulties" are statements that illustrate the use of the word *attitude.*

Most clinicians probably do not spend much time and effort distinguishing among these concepts. However, when a client expresses an idea, determining whether that idea reflects a thought, perception, belief, value, or attitude can be useful. Making that discrimination can help clinicians understand the importance the idea has for the person as well as other dimensions of that idea, to be discussed later in this chapter.

ELICITING THOUGHTS

Many clinicians, especially those who view themselves as cognitive or cognitive-behavioral in orientation, believe that identifying, assessing, and modifying people's thoughts are the most effective way to help them make positive changes and cope more successfully with their difficulties. However, even clinicians who do not align themselves primarily with the cognitive treatment approaches developed by Beck,

Ellis, and others typically recognize the therapeutic value of helping people modify their unhelpful thoughts. Often, once thoughts have been modified, emotions and actions change and improve spontaneously.

Before thoughts can be assessed and modified, however, clinicians must help clients identify their thoughts. Once the thoughts have been clearly stated, clinician and client can work together to determine whether the client's thoughts are helpful or harmful and whether the thoughts are valid. However, eliciting thoughts, as well as people's cooperation with the process of cognitive therapy, is sometimes a challenge. This can be particularly difficult if people are overwhelmed by emotion or tend to be motivated more by their heart or their "gut feelings" than by logic and a thoughtful examination of their thinking.

PROVIDING EDUCATION ON COGNITIVE THERAPY

The first step in cognitive therapy is educating people about this process. Knowledge of the concepts and procedures of cognitive therapy helps motivate people to participate fully in that process. It also helps them to better understand how they can contribute to making the process an effective one. In addition, an initial emphasis on education sets the tone for cognitive treatment because this is a structured approach that entails some coaching. An added benefit of educating clients about cognitive therapy is that they typically become more hopeful that treatment can help them. Consequently, clinicians initiate a positive cycle in which knowledge engenders hope, which engenders cooperation and effort, which lead to progress, which, in turn, promotes increased motivation and stronger feelings of hope and optimism.

Education on cognitive therapy generally has the following components:

- **The logic underlying the approach.** Cognitive therapy suggests that thoughts drive emotions and actions and that, by exploring their thoughts and changing those that are unhelpful, people can more easily change their feelings and behaviors and make overall positive changes. Reassuring people that their feelings and behaviors are important and will not be ignored, but that the emphasis of treatment will be on thoughts, can allay apprehension.

- **The research supporting this approach.** Learning that cognitive treatment approaches have received strong support is likely to enhance clients' trust, hopefulness, motivation, and optimism. Whether the extensive empirical support for this approach is mentioned only briefly or discussed in detail and with reference to specific studies depends on the client. Clinicians should gear the presentation to the person, with an extensive description of the relevant research reserved for those clients who are particularly likely to be interested in and persuaded by that information.

- **The importance of the therapeutic alliance.** Although cognitive approaches are relatively structured and cast the clinician in an active leadership role, the therapeutic alliance still has great importance—as it does in almost all treatment approaches. A collaborative working relationship between client and clinician, in which the two join in a process that is important to both of them, is at the heart of cognitive therapy. Clinicians must convey caring, empathy, and genuineness and nurture trust and optimism in their clients, even though the primary treatment focus is on cognition.

- **The hallmarks of thoughts and emotions.** Although most people can identify actions easily, they often confuse thoughts and feelings. I have frequently asked clients questions such as "How do you feel about returning to graduate school?" and received as an answer "I think it's a good idea for me." Notice that I am asking for a feeling but am given a thought in response. Statements of feeling need to include the name of an emotion (e.g., sad, happy, annoyed, grateful), whereas statements of thoughts generally do not include such words. Encouraging people, at least initially, to begin their statements by saying "I think..." and "I feel..." can help them distinguish between the two.

- **The importance of structure in this approach.** Although some people welcome and are reassured by structure, others find it confining and may even feel controlled by the organized, step-by-step process of eliciting, assessing, and modifying thoughts. By preparing them for this in advance and explaining the reasons for the structure, clinicians can probably avoid some initial negative reactions to cognitive approaches. Predicting negative feelings is another helpful way to avoid such feelings and make it more likely that people will discuss them if they do arise. Clinicians may say to a client, "You may be surprised by the structure and organization of this approach and perhaps even feel uncomfortable with it. However, by using a step-by-step process of exploring your thoughts, feelings, and actions, we can understand them more thoroughly and probably do a better job of helping you change those thoughts, feelings, and actions that are not helpful to you. Please let me know if anything about this process does not feel right for you. I want this process to help you reach your goals and so we should talk about anything that isn't working for you or is bringing up negative reactions."

- **The importance of feedback.** Engaging people in a dialogue about the treatment process is important in cognitive treatment. In Aaron Beck's version of cognitive therapy, clinicians are encouraged to request feedback from clients at the conclusion of each session and to use that feedback to shape future sessions in ways that are likely to be more compatible with clients' preferences (Beck, 1995).

- **Respond to any questions.** Because clinicians cannot always know what concerns clients, clients should have the opportunity to ask questions and express any reactions they might have about the treatment process so that clinicians have the opportunity to clarify any misconceptions and make sure that treatment gets off to a good start.

LINKING THOUGHTS TO EMOTIONS AND ACTIONS

When most people come in for an appointment with a clinician, they bring with them an incident or concern that they want to address. After orienting people to the treatment process, the client's presenting issue typically is a good place to start because the client probably is motivated to deal with that situation. If clients do not bring in a concern, clinicians might review the past week with them, looking for an upsetting event or experience that led them to seek treatment. Identification of a specific situation facilitates the process of eliciting thoughts.

Reactions to an experience include not only thoughts, but also emotions and actions. Usually, the three are intertwined. Often, they are congruent or compatible. However, sometimes they are incongruent, leading a person to feel conflicted or fragmented.

To understand a person's thoughts fully, clinicians should obtain information about all three areas of response: thoughts, emotions, and actions. Generally, clinicians should begin with the most accessible of the three, after determining which one a client discusses most easily. The following example of Carrie illustrates the steps in eliciting, assessing, and modifying thoughts and associated emotions and actions.

Example: Carrie's Reactions to Her Mother's Revised Will

Carrie is a 54-year-old woman who is divorced and has no children. She is a music teacher and accompanist who earns a good income from her work and has retirement pay from her earlier career in the military. However, because she is self-employed and single, she worries a great deal about her finances. Carrie has one sibling, a sister, who is married and has three children. Carrie recently learned that her mother has made a new will, leaving only one-fifth of her estate to Carrie and the remainder to her sister and the sister's three children. Review the following three ways that Carrie might react to this situation and notice, for each response, whether thoughts, actions, or emotions are most accessible.

Client Response 1: When my mother told me what she was going to do, I felt really angry at the way she was treating me. Then after I got off the phone with her, I just cried and cried. I felt like I had lost my best friend.

Client Response 2: What she said just didn't seem fair or reasonable to me. My mother has two children, so she should divide the estate equally between us. She must think very little of me to have made this decision.

Client Response 3: As soon as my mother told me what she had done, I said to her, "You've just lost a daughter." I slammed the phone down, and I haven't spoken to her since then.

The first response presents Carrie's strong emotions, the second focuses on her thoughts, and the third emphasizes her actions. Clinicians working with Carrie could begin helping her deal with her mother's decision by focusing on thoughts, emotions, or actions. Clinicians will probably be most successful in joining with Carrie and helping her move forward if they begin with what is emphasized in her initial response (thoughts, emotions, or actions) and then move onto the other two areas for exploration.

Let's begin with the second example, focused on thoughts, and see how a clinician working with Carrie might begin with an exploration of those thoughts and then proceed to gather information on emotions and actions. Notice the clinician's use of many of the skills already presented in this book: questions, restatement, and reflection of feeling.

Example : Eliciting Carrie's Thoughts, Emotions, and Actions

Carrie: My mother called me last week and told me that she was going to leave one-fifth of her estate to me and four-fifths to my sister and her three children. What she said just didn't seem fair or reasonable to me. She has two children so she should divide the estate equally between us. She must think very little of me to have made this decision.

Clinician: It sounds like you had two strong thoughts, "My mother must think very little of me" and "My mother is unfair." What thoughts did that bring up about yourself?

Carrie: Maybe "I'm not lovable" and "I guess my mother doesn't really love me as much as she loves my sister." I also thought, "Now I will have serious financial problems."

Clinician: When you had those thoughts, how did you feel?

Carrie: When my mother told me what she was going to do, I felt really angry at the way she was treating me. Then after I got off the phone with her, I just cried and cried. I felt like I had lost my best friend.

Clinician: I'm hearing a real mix of emotions—anger, sorrow, and rejection.

Carrie: Yes, that pretty much sums it up.

Clinician: And what did you do after your mother told you about the division of her estate?

Carrie: As soon as she told me what she had done, I said to her, "You've just lost a daughter." I slammed the phone down, and I haven't spoken to her since then.

At this point, the clinician has the information she needs to collaborate with Carrie in further exploring her emotions, thoughts, and actions. Client and clinician can assess the helpfulness to the client of those thoughts, emotions, and actions and, if appropriate, work together to develop more helpful responses.

Exercise: Eliciting Devon's Thoughts, Emotions, and Acitons

Before moving onto the next step with Carrie, clarifying and rating her thoughts, emotions, and actions, let's look at another example. Review what Devon, a 19-year-old African American man, has to say and then identify his thoughts, emotions, and actions:

Devon: I spent the first 18 years of my life in Washington, D.C. My neighborhood's becoming gentrified now, but you still hardly ever see a white face there. Everybody knows everybody there, and people look out for each other. It's a tough place, but you always have somebody to turn to, usually somebody's mom. The women there are strong, they have to be, like my mom who raised three kids without much help. I'm used to women being like that, independent, doing what they have to do to get by, no time for games. So now I'm in college. I worked really hard to get here, but I think it may be a big mistake. I don't feel like I belong here. I feel like there's something wrong with me. The guys are okay, I can talk to them about sports and politics, but it's the women I don't get. They're all flirty and superficial, they expect me to pay when we go out, and I don't know how to have a real conversation with them. I didn't know women were like that anymore. The academic part is fine, but in a way I think I learned more in high school where they really pushed the smart kids to do well. The teachers held out the goal of getting a scholarship and going to college. So here I am, but it's not like the teachers said it would be. I thought I would be proud of myself and really happy, but I feel lonely and uncomfortable all the time, worried that I'll do the wrong thing. I'm thinking about dropping out at the end of my freshman year.

Based on what Devon said, identify some of his thoughts, emotions, and actions:

Thoughts:

a. _____

b. _____

c. _____

Emotions:

a. _____

b. _____

Actions:

a. _____

b. _____

We will use the example of Devon again later in this chapter to give you the opportunity to apply what you are learning here.

Identifying and Rating Thoughts, Emotions, and Actions

The first step in the process of modifying people's unhelpful thoughts was illustrated in the previous example of Carrie. This step involves clearly identifying a person's thoughts, emotions, and actions. Usually, people have more than one thought and emotion and they may have taken several actions. Clinicians should explore clients' reactions enough so that they have a clear picture of the range of important thoughts, emotions, and actions that clients have in response to their presenting concern. Particularly important is eliciting thoughts that clients have about themselves.

Clinicians work collaboratively with clients in identifying thoughts, emotions, and actions to be sure that both client and clinician are in agreement and that the language used to convey the thoughts, emotions, and actions feels right to the client. Clinicians should be careful not to rush ahead, no matter how confident they are of their identification of thoughts, emotions, and actions. Any hesitancy on the part of the client should be explored and time taken to maximize congruence between the client's perceptions and those of the clinician.

In the preceding example, after the clinician and Carrie agreed on her thoughts, emotions, and actions, they were written down to facilitate their exploration and rating. Carrie's thoughts, emotions, and actions, as well as her ratings of her thoughts and emotions are reflected in Table 7-1.

Carrie first rated the intensity of her feelings on a 0 to 100 scale in which 0 indicates no experience of the emotion and 100 represents the most intense

TABLE 7-1 Identification and Rating of Carrie's Emotions, Actions, and Thoughts

Identification of Emotions	Rating of Intensity on 0–100 Scale
Anger	95
Sorrow	90
Rejection	97
Identification of Actions	
Slammed down telephone, no further contact with mother	

Identification of Thoughts	Rating of Belief in Thoughts on 0–100 Scale
My mother is treating me unfairly.	100
My mother doesn't love me as much as she loves my sister.	98
I am not lovable.	95
Now I will have serious financial problems.	90

experience of the emotion that a person could imagine. Carrie next rated her belief in her thoughts on a 0 to 100 scale with 0 reflecting no belief in the thought and 100 reflecting complete and absolute belief in the thought. As you can see from the table, Carrie's emotions were very intense and she had a strong belief in the veracity of all her thoughts.

Now list Devon's emotions, actions, and thoughts in Table 7-2 and make some informed guesses as to how he might rate the intensity of his feelings and the strength of his belief in his thoughts

DETERMINING WHETHER THOUGHTS ARE HELPFUL OR HARMFUL

Once the thoughts have been clearly identified and rated, along with their accompanying emotions and actions, clinician and client can work together to determine whether the client's thoughts are helpful or harmful and whether the thoughts are valid. For many clinicians, this is the most challenging part of helping people improve their cognitions. Clinicians must be cautious not to argue with clients or to try to persuade them that their thoughts are erroneous and distorted. Rather, clinicians assume the role of a helpful consultant, offering thoughts and perceptions for review and discussion, but recognizing that the client is the ultimate authority.

TABLE 7-2 Identification and Rating of Devon's Emotions, Actions, and Thoughts

Identification of Emotions	Rating of Intensity on 0–100 Scale
Identification of Actions	

Identification of Thoughts	Rating of Belief in Thoughts on 0–100 Scale

The following are frequent hallmarks of unhelpful thoughts:

- They make us feel bad.
- They block and discourage constructive change.
- They blame other people or the unfairness of the world for our difficulties.
- They are stated in extreme and absolute terms.
- They contain words such as *should* and *must*.
- They reflect an underlying negative self-evaluation.
- They are illogical and irrational.

Although these hallmarks can help clinicians and clients identify thoughts that need modification, they should be used with caution because many exceptions exist. For example, Carrie may have thought, "I am very disappointed that I did not receive a larger inheritance" and "I should treat my mother with respect, even if I feel angry at her decision." The first of these thoughts would probably make Carrie feel sad. However, this is a rational and understandable thought that does not reflect any of the other hallmarks of unhelpful thoughts; it probably does not need to be changed. Her second thought contains the word *should;* however, that thought, too, is rational and does not reflect the other hallmarks of unhelpful thoughts. Both client and clinician should reflect on and assess any thoughts that contain these hallmarks, carefully considering their logic and impact on the client, before concluding that the thought is unhelpful, dysfunctional, and in need of modification.

Carrie's actual thoughts reflect not one, but many, of these hallmarks. They all make her feel badly and do not promote constructive change. They blame another person (her mother) and reflect an underlying negative self-evaluation (I am unlovable). They include the word *should* and are stated in extreme terms (end my relationship with my mother). Consequently, Carrie's initial thoughts about her mother's decision probably are unhelpful, distorted, and dysfunctional and would benefit from some revision.

ASSESSING THE VALIDITY OF THE THOUGHTS

Once clinician and client have agreed that the client has some unhelpful thoughts, the next step in the treatment process is to determine whether those thoughts are valid and accurate. Again, this does not mean that clinicians argue with their clients or tell them to think differently. Rather, evaluating thoughts is a collaborative process of exploring the reasoning behind the thoughts, gathering information to support or refute the thoughts, and using other strategies to determine whether the thoughts are grounded in reality or reflect unwarranted assumptions and faulty logic.

Cognitive therapists have developed many ways to assess the validity of cognitions (Beck, 1995; Ellis, 1995; Moorey & Greer, 1989). Some of the most powerful of these include the following:

- **Testing reality.** This process entails assessing the accuracy of the thought using the client's previous experiences, logic, research, and other sources of information. Carrie might look at the history of her relationship with her mother to determine whether there is any evidence that her mother does not love her, or Carrie might ask her mother directly about her feelings. Carrie might also think about the perceptions she has had over the years of her mother's feelings toward her; if Carrie had previously viewed their relationship as a close and loving one, she might examine whether this incident really outweighs all the loving messages and acts she has received from her mother over the years.

- **Seeking alternative explanations.** Sometimes people see only one explanation for an event or action. However, when client and clinician look for other possible explanations, alternative and more acceptable explanations may emerge. For example, Carrie's mother may have decided to leave less money to Carrie because her mother has so much confidence in Carrie's ability to take care of herself or she might doubt the ability of Carrie's sister to provide appropriately for her children. Alternatively, she might value education above all else and wants to make sure that her grandchildren can afford to attend college. Many possible explanations exist for Carrie's mother's decision, in addition to Carrie's assumption that her mother does not love her.

- **Redefining or reconceptualizing a situation.** When people are not thinking clearly, they tend to overemphasize some pieces of information and overlook others. Obtaining a more balanced picture can help them modify their cognitions. For example, Carrie's parents had paid for her college education. Her sister had not attended college and so had, thus far, received far less money from her parents than had Carrie. Perhaps Carrie's mother was trying to balance out her financial contributions to Carrie and her sister.

- **Decatastrophizing.** When people experience failures or disappointments, they sometimes exaggerate the implications of these experiences and anticipate disaster. Looking at possible outcomes in a reasonable way can be reassuring. When Carrie learned that she would receive only a small inheritance from her mother, her doubts about her competence surfaced and she imagined herself homeless and penniless. In fact, Carrie had always supported herself without difficulty, had adequate savings, and had a sizable pension. Although her disappointment in her mother's decision is understandable, Carrie's careful management of her finances, as well as her pension, meant that, even without an inheritance, she could live comfortably for the rest of her life.

- **Viewing a situation through another person's eyes.** This strategy can help counteract extreme or polarized thinking and provide alternate perspectives. Those perspectives can emerge from asking clients how someone they trust and admire might view this situation, by asking them to put themselves in the shoes of another person involved in the situation, or even by the clinician gently offering another possible viewpoint. Carrie's clinician asked her to temporarily put her own concerns aside and imagine herself as her mother, a woman in her mid-80s who had been widowed for many years and was coping with many serious medical concerns.

Unlike Carrie, she had not had a professional career but had devoted herself to her family. She presently lived close to Carrie's sister, often spent time with the sister and her family, and had close relationships with her grandchildren, one of whom was named after Carrie's father. Carrie was eventually able to understand that her mother might have felt a strong responsibility to her grandchildren, as well as to her children. Carrie also realized that, because she had made her career her first priority and had not had children, she might not fully understand her mother's feelings about her young grandchildren. Carrie was still disappointed but, because of these new perceptions, her rage toward her mother and her feelings of rejection dissipated.

Described here are only a few of the many approaches to helping people assess the logic and validity of their thoughts. Use these strategies as a starting point, but look for other ways to collaborate with clients in determining whether their thoughts are helpful and in keeping with reality or whether those thoughts should be changed.

Example: Disputing Carrie's Unhelpful Thoughts

The following dialogue with Carrie illustrates one way that her clinician might collaborate with Carrie to dispute her unhelpful thoughts. Notice the clinician's use of a variety of interventions, especially open questions and reflection of feeling to convey empathy . Also, notice that the clinician does not argue, debate, or even seek to persuade Carrie, but simply provides information and raises questions for her to consider.

Carrie: I always suspected that my mother loved my sister more than she did me. Now this proves it to me.
Clinician: It must be very painful to you to believe that your mother doesn't love you as much as you want. What other evidence of that have you had over the years?
Carrie: Until now, she's always been pretty fair about money. She and my father paid for my college education, which really helped me out. But she always spends much more time with my sister than she does with me.
Clinician: So finances have not been a problem between you and your parents in the past. However, the extra time she spends with your sister seems to you to mean that she loves your sister more.
Carrie: Well, yes.
Clinician: I wonder if there are other possible explanations for that.
Carrie: Like what?
Clinician: Maybe where you both lived or who needed your mother's help more.
Carrie: My sister has always lived close to my mother. I traveled so much when I was in the military that she didn't get to see me much. But she did come to Japan to visit me. And I guess my sister did need more help; she had three children in the first five years of her marriage, and it seemed like she had at least one sick kid for years. She really did need my mother's help.
Clinician: So it's hard to find any clear evidence that your mother doesn't love you as much as she does your sister.
Carrie: I suppose so, but shouldn't your children come first? I don't want to wind up homeless and penniless.
Clinician: You sound very worried about that. What makes that a worry for you?
Carrie: Well, I'm single and I don't have a husband or children to take care of me.
Clinician: How do you do at taking care of yourself?

Carrie: Actually, pretty well. I've saved quite a bit of money, and I get a pension from the military. I never have trouble getting music students. I've been very careful with my money and work closely with a financial planner.

Clinician: So you have been able to take care of yourself very well financially. Let's look at the worst case scenario for a moment. Suppose you did not inherit any money from your mother and became disabled so that you could no longer teach music. How would you manage?

Carrie: I do have disability insurance, health insurance, and pretty good savings. My townhouse is paid off, and I also own a rental unit. I guess I could still manage.

Clinician: It must be reassuring to know that you can take care of yourself, no matter what happens.

Carrie: Yes, it is. I just always counted on a sizable inheritance from my mother, and it was such a shock when I learned that wasn't going to happen.

Clinician: So it's more the shock and what it might mean about your relationship with your mother that are troubling you than the actual loss of the money.

Carrie: Yes, that's true. But I just can't imagine what was in my mother's mind if it's not that she doesn't love me.

Clinician: You're really puzzled by her decision. How would it feel to ask her how she arrived at her decision to leave you one-fifth of her estate?

Carrie: Ask her? After I slammed the phone down on her and told her I wasn't her daughter any more?

Clinician: You were very shocked and angry when you did that. I wonder how you feel now about your actions.

Carrie: Actually, not too good. You know, my mother is very sick, and that's why she's dealing with her will. It feels like she's expecting to die soon. I've already lost my father, and I don't want to lose her too.

Clinician: I can hear how sad and upset you feel when you think about losing your mother. Have there been other times in your life when you acted out of anger and then regretted what you had done?

Carrie: Of course, hasn't everybody done that at least once?

Clinician: Most everybody I know. What did you do, in the past, when you regretted an action you had taken in anger?

Carrie: Usually I swallowed my pride and apologized. When I didn't do that, I wound up feeling even worse.

Clinician: So apologizing seemed the best strategy in the past. How would it feel to apologize again?

Carrie: Kind of mixed. I really don't want to abandon my mother at this point in her life, but I just can't agree with the way she decided to divide her estate.

Clinician: You don't want her to think that contacting her and apologizing means that you agree with her estate plans.

Carrie: Yes, that's it.

Clinician: Sometimes we love someone, but we don't like a specific behavior or choice that person made. How would it feel to let your mother know that you love and care about her but still don't like her decision?

Carrie: I guess that would be alright. And this way I could explain my thinking to her. She probably doesn't even understand why I got so angry.

Clinician: So I'm hearing quite a few benefits to contacting your mother again.

As is evident in this dialogue, Carrie's thoughts, emotions, and actions are already changing. One more step, labeling her distorted thoughts, should further solidify those changes.

Example: Assessing and Disputing Devon's Thoughts

Before moving onto the next step with Carrie of labeling her distorted thoughts, let's shift the focus back to Devon and look at examples that will help him assess his thoughts. Here are some possible ways to help him take a close look at his thoughts:

- **Viewing his situation through another's eyes.** The clinician might ask Devon how he thinks his strong mother or his supportive and encouraging teachers would view his current situation and what advice they would offer.
- **Redefining or reconceptualizing a situation.** The clinician might suggest that the first year of college, especially when the school is many miles from the student's home and very different from the student's usual environment, is a challenging experience for most people. The clinician then could encourage Devon to do some reading on adjusting to college or ask other students from his high school what it has been like for them to begin college. Another aspect of the situation that might benefit from reconceptualization is Devon's view of the women at the college he is attending; although he perceives them as acting in ways that are foreign and unappealing to him, their behaviors could reflect their interest in getting to know him better. They may feel as awkward as he does, realizing that their apparent flirtatiousness is unattractive to Devon, but are unsure how to get acquainted with him.
- **Decatastrophizing.** Although aspects of the college environment are uncomfortable for Devon, he is doing well academically and has had some satisfying conversations with male students. Whether or not he chooses to continue at this college, part of the experience has been a successful one for him. Perhaps he can shift the balance in his perceptions, building on his accomplishments at the college and finding ways to address or feel less bothered by his disappointments.

Other approaches to helping Devon assess the validity of his thoughts are available. What seem to be the best approaches to helping him assess his thoughts?

_____

_____

_____

CATEGORIZING DISTORTED THOUGHTS

Labeling the types of distorted thoughts that a person has is another helpful step in the process of assessing and changing those thoughts. Labeling the thoughts promotes understanding and awareness of those thoughts. In addition, it enables people to realize that it is not unusual to have thoughts that are confused or self-damaging and that others have had similar thoughts. This can reduce any self-blame and embarrassment that clients may experience as they discover that their thoughts are illogical. Becoming aware of common varieties of distorted cognitions also gives people a tool they can continue to use to help them recognize and change their unhelpful thoughts. Good sources of information on types of distorted cognitions include Judith Beck's (1995) book *Cognitive Therapy* and David Burns's latest revision of his book *The Feeling Good Handbook* (2007).

The following is a list of common types of distorted cognitions, followed by brief descriptions and an example of each (Beck, 1995; Burns, 2007; Seligman, 1996):

- **All-or-nothing thinking** (also called *dichotomous* or *black-and-white thinking*). People think in absolutes, seeing possibilities in only two categories and making judgments based on small pieces of information.
  - **Example:** I didn't even make the finals in the tryouts for the play. I clearly have no acting talent and should just go back to Omaha.
- **Catastrophizing.** People view the future in hopeless and negative terms and cannot consider other options that probably are more likely.
  - **Example:** I feel like I have a dark cloud hanging over my head and no matter what I do, I'll fail. My marriage will be a disaster, my business will go bankrupt, and my children probably won't talk to me when they're adults.
- **Discounting or disqualifying the positive.** Positive experiences and achievements are devalued and do not count.
  - **Example:** Yes, I know my suggestion got an award at work this month, but that was just a fluke. Mine was probably the only one that was submitted.
- **Emotional reasoning.** Decisions and conclusions are based on feelings while facts and contradictory evidence are ignored.
  - **Example:** I know I get lots of calls and e-mails from the other girls at school, but I feel like I just don't fit in. I know they don't really like me. Maybe they just want the answers to the homework questions.
- **Jumping to conclusions.** Conclusions are drawn arbitrarily, based on little or no evidence.
  - **Example:** The doctor didn't return my telephone calls yesterday. My tests probably turned out badly and she just doesn't want to tell me.
- **Labeling.** People place fixed and all-encompassing negative labels on themselves and view themselves in terms of these labels rather than considering any disconfirming evidence. They might also impose similar labels on others.
  - **Example:** I'm such a loser. I don't deserve to live any more. My wife must be an idiot for staying with me all these years.
- **Magnification and minimization.** Negative perceptions and experiences are exaggerated and blown out of proportion while positive ones are minimized.
  - **Example:** I can't believe I forgot to pay the credit card bill this month. Something must be really going wrong with me; I've never done that before. What if I'm developing Alzheimer's disease?
- **Mental filter.** People dwell on negative information and ignore positive information, even though it may greatly outweigh the negative information.
  - **Example:** My daughter's teacher called and said she caught my daughter copying another little girl's homework. What kind of a parent am I? How could she have developed values like this? I've really failed in my role as a mother. My daughter was always a great student and a great kid, but I must have failed her in some way.
- **Mind reading.** People believe they know what others are thinking and fail to consider the evidence and the array of possibilities.
  - **Example:** I saw the way the teacher looked at me when I asked that question. I just knew she was thinking, "How stupid can anyone be? I've already

explained that twice." She must hate having someone in class like me who has attention-deficit disorder.

- **Overgeneralization.** People draw broad negative conclusions that go far beyond the immediate situation.
  - **Example:** I hadn't had a drink in the two months since I got out of rehab, but then I was at that party and everyone was drinking and so I had a beer. I sure wasted lots of time and money in rehab; I've failed again. I'll never be able to stop drinking, no matter how many AA meetings I go to or how much help I get.
- **Personalization.** People blame themselves for a situation that either is not their fault at all or for which they are only partially responsible.
  - **Example:** I had requested a table in the quiet part of the room for our dinner meeting, but the restaurant didn't pay any attention to my request. I got there early to make sure everything was set up properly, but I didn't know how to solve the problem. The good tables were all taken and so we wound up in the middle of the room. We had trouble hearing each other and I'm sure we annoyed the other diners. Why didn't I go to the restaurant in person when I made the reservation? I really spoiled the meeting and everyone must be thinking I'm incompetent.
- **Should and must statements** (also *ought* and *have to* statements). Statements such as these typically reflect rigid and often unrealistic expectations that people impose on themselves.
  - **Example:** I should be a strong person and never let anyone see my weaknesses or know that I feel badly. People don't like a weak, self-pitying person.
- **Tunnel vision.** People take an inappropriately narrow view of a situation, focusing only on negative information.
  - **Example:** Yes, I know that many people noticed that I seem different and my ratings at work have gone up, but I still feel depressed and don't have as much energy as I would like. Last night my son asked me to help him with a school project, and I really had to force myself to stay awake enough to do it. I'll never get myself out of this hole.

These definitions and examples review the major types of cognitive distortions. Clinicians can use this information to help themselves as well as their clients to categorize unhelpful thoughts. The following section illustrates this process, using some of Carrie's cognitive distortions.

Example: Labeling Carrie's Distorted Thoughts

- **My mother is treating me unfairly.** This thought reflects tunnel vision and emotional reasoning. Carrie overlooks the many ways in which her mother has helped her and draws a conclusion based on her feelings of hurt and rejection rather than on logic.
- **My mother doesn't love me as much as she loves my sister.** With this thought, Carrie is jumping to conclusions and engaging in mind reading. Here, too, emotional reasoning leads her to unwarranted assumptions.

- **I am not lovable.** This thought reflects all-or-nothing thinking or viewing a situation in terms of extremes as well as overgeneralization.
- **Now I will have serious financial problems.** Catastrophizing characterizes this thought.

Clinicians can work collaboratively with clients, helping them label their distorted cognitions. This is a delicate process that must be done with support and encouragement so that people do not feel humiliated or blamed for their thoughts. Instead, this can be presented as an interesting process of discovery, reinforcing the concept that thoughts such as those of the client are so common that they have been extensively studied and organized. This process usually enables people to distance themselves from their problems, to gain a sense of control over their thoughts, and to take pride in their subsequent ability to use the tool of labeling on their own.

MODIFYING DISTORTED COGNITIONS

Once distorted cognitions have been identified, assessed, and labeled, clients are probably ready to modify those thoughts. Clinician and client work together to develop replacement thoughts that are both acceptable and more helpful to the client. Thoughts that are acceptable to the client may not always be as positive as the clinician would like them to be; however, imposing the clinician's thoughts on the client is not helpful. This takes power and control away from the client and any new learning is unlikely to endure. The client's acceptance of the new thoughts is essential to their effectiveness.

Example: Carrie's Modified Thoughts

Carrie felt comfortable with the following modified thoughts:

- I don't like the decision my mother made about the distribution of her estate, but I can see that she has made many other decisions that were helpful to me.
- My mother has said and done many things that show that she really does love me.
- I have some close friends who really seem to care about me, so I believe I am a lovable person.
- Although I will not be as financially comfortable as I would have been if my mother divided her estate equally, I will be able to take care of my financial needs.

Exercise: Categorizing and Modifying Devon's Thoughts

Let's return to Devon's unhelpful thoughts and categorize them and also develop some modifications of those thoughts. Of course, we cannot know exactly how Devon would change his thoughts, but try to put yourself in Devon's place as you develop these thoughts. Remember not to make them too positive and unrealistic; rather, think of them as a starting point in helping Devon shift his thoughts as well as his emotions and actions. Following are some dysfunctional thoughts that Devon might have. Categorize each of the thoughts and write a possible replacement thought that seems more accurate and helpful to Devon. The first one has been completed to provide an example.

Thought 1: I'm a failure and a loser. I just can't make it in college.
Category: Labeling, tunnel vision, mental filter, disqualifying the positive
Replacement thought: Although I haven't adjusted as well as I hoped at college, I am passing all my courses and even getting a few A's. Maybe I expected too much too fast from myself.

Thought 2: The women here seem so flighty. They always giggle and flirt. I know they laugh at me behind my back and think about how weird I am.
Category: (*Hint:* This thought can fit at least two categories.)

_____

Replacement thought: _____

_____

Thought 3: I should be getting all A's in college. I had all A's in high school. I must work even harder and sleep less so I can improve my grades.

Category: _____

Replacement thought: _____

_____

Thought 4: I don't feel right being here, I feel like a failure, and so I think the best thing is to leave school at the end of the year.

Category: _____

Replacement thought: _____

_____

If possible, share the categories and replacement thoughts you wrote down with others who completed this exercise. If you did not select the same categories, talk about the reasoning behind your choices. Your replacement thoughts will probably differ considerably; there are many helpful thoughts that might be substituted for Devon's initial thoughts. Just be sure that the replacement thoughts present a more balanced picture, take account of positive as well as negative information, and offer Devon some options that can help him rebuild his self-esteem, recognize his strengths and accomplishments, and think more clearly.

CHANGING EMOTIONS AND ACTIONS

Changing distorted thoughts to more helpful ones usually enables people to change the unhelpful emotions and actions that accompany those thoughts. Again, although clinicians may offer possibilities or suggestions, clients determine which helpful emotions and actions feel acceptable and comfortable to them.

Example: Carrie's Modified Emotions and Actions

Carrie came up with the following modified emotions and actions:

Modified Emotions

- Disappointment in her mother's decision
- Pride in being able to take care of herself without her mother's help

Modified Actions

- Contact mother and reestablish relationship
- Let mother know Carrie's feelings of disappointment with her mother's decision
- Schedule an appointment with her financial planner to review her financial situation and make changes as needed

Exercise: Devon's Modified Emotions and Actions

Based on the new thoughts you have developed for Devon, suggest some realistic and helpful changes in his emotions and actions that might reflect those thoughts and put him on a more rewarding path.

Devon's Modified Emotions

_____

_____

_____

Devon's Modified Actions

_____

_____

_____

RERATING THOUGHTS AND EMOTIONS

Rating the new thoughts and emotions and rerating the earlier unhelpful ones can help you assess progress and solidify gains. This clear measurement of change also can be reinforcing to clients.

When clinicians help clients rerate their thoughts and emotions, their goal is not to bring down the initial ratings to 0 and elicit extremely high ratings for the new thoughts and emotions. Rather, the goal is to effect change, to shift the balance, so that the ratings of the dysfunctional thoughts and emotions drop and, ideally, are below the ratings of the new and improved thoughts and emotions.

Example: Carrie's Revised Ratings

Carrie's revised ratings of her emotions are listed in Table 7.3. Revised ratings of thoughts are included in Table 7-4.

TABLE 7-3   Initial and Revised Emotions and Their Ratings

Unhelpful Emotions	Rating of Intensity on 0–100 Scale
Anger	60 (formerly 95)
Sorrow	85 (formerly 90)
Rejection	52 (formerly 97)
Revised Emotions	**Rating of Intensity on 0–100 Scale**
Disappointment	90
Pride	87

TABLE 7-4 Initial and Revised Thoughts and Their Ratings

Unhelpful Thoughts	Rating of Belief in Thoughts on 0–100 Scale
My mother is treating me unfairly.	65 (formerly 100)
My mother doesn't love me as much as she loves my sister.	45 (formerly 98)
I am not lovable.	20 (formerly 95)
Now I will have serious financial problems.	35 (formerly 90)
Revised Thoughts	**Ratings of Belief in Thoughts on 0–100 Scale**
I don't like the decision my mother made about the distribution of her estate, but I can see that she has made many other decisions that were helpful to me.	95
My mother has said and done many things that show that she really does love me.	99
I believe I am a lovable person.	82
I will be able to take care of my financial needs.	80

The intensity of Carrie's initial emotions, especially her feelings of anger and rejection, declined considerably. To a large extent, pride, a much more positive feeling, and disappointment, a more manageable and realistic emotion, replaced these emotions.

The comparison in Table 7-4 of Carrie's ratings of her initial and revised thoughts indicates that here, too, she has made considerable progress. The degree of her belief in her initial unhelpful thoughts has declined, although the issue of unfairness still troubles her. In contrast, her belief in her revised thoughts is strong although indications are that Carrie is not yet fully convinced of her lovableness and her ability to take care of her financial needs. Continued counseling can address these concerns further.

Exercise: Devon's Revised Ratings

Once again, use your imagination, your understanding of cognitive strategies, and your clinical judgment in revising your ratings of Devon's thoughts. Some negative emotions that Devon has probably been feeling are listed in Table 7-5 and the dysfunctional thoughts attributed to Devon earlier have been listed in Table 7-6. Insert the changes that you would realistically like to see in his ratings of his original thoughts

TABLE 7-5 Devon's Initial and Revised Emotions and Their Rating

Unhelpful Emotions	Rating of Intensity on 0–100 Scale
Hopeless	__(formerly __)
Feeling like a failure	__(formerly __)
Fear and anxiety	__(formerly __)
Revised Emotions	**Rating of Intensity on 0–100 Scale**
	__
	__
	__

TABLE 7-6 Devon's Initial and Revised Thoughts and Their Rating

Unhelpful Thoughts	Rating of Belief in Thoughts on 0–100 Scale
I'm a failure and a loser. I just can't make it in college.	__ (formerly __)
The women here seem so flighty. They always giggle and flirt. I know they laugh at me behind my back and think about how weird I am.	__ (formerly __)
I should be getting all A's in college. I had all A's in high school. I must work even harder and sleep less so I can improve my grades.	__ (formerly __)
I don't feel right being here, I feel like a failure, and so I think the best thing is to leave school at the end of the year.	__ (formerly __)
Revised Thoughts	**Ratings of Belief in Thoughts on 0–100 Scale**
	__
	__
	__

and emotions. Then list the more helpful thoughts that you developed for him earlier in this chapter, along with some constructive emotions, and include some hypothetical ratings for these on the table.

OVERVIEW OF PROCESS OF MODIFYING THOUGHTS

The process of modifying thoughts and accompanying emotions and actions has been illustrated by the example of Carrie and her concerns about her inheritance, as well as by the exercises that applied this information to Devon. This process includes the following 10 steps:

1. Identify key issue or event.
2. Elicit related thoughts, emotions, and actions.
3. Rate intensity of emotions and extent of belief in thoughts.
4. Assess the validity of the thoughts.
5. Categorize any unhelpful and distorted thoughts.
6. Dispute the thoughts.
7. Replace the distorted thoughts with more helpful and accurate ones.
8. Identify new emotions and actions.
9. Rate current intensity of both initial and new emotions.
10. Rate current extent of belief in both initial and revised thoughts.

The following learning opportunities afford you the opportunity to practice the skills you have learned to modify unhelpful cognitions and their accompanying emotions and actions.

LEARNING OPPORTUNITIES

This chapter has focused on teaching the following fundamental skills relevant to eliciting, assessing, and modifying thoughts:

- Eliciting thoughts, emotions, and actions
- Rating belief in the thoughts and the intensity of the emotions
- Analyzing and assessing the validity of thoughts
- Categorizing the nature of distorted thoughts
- Modifying distorted thoughts and accompanying unhelpful emotions and actions
- Understanding the overall process of modifying thoughts, emotions, and actions in combination

Written Exercises

1. For each of the following client statements, list the primary dysfunctional thought, the emotion, and the action.

Client 1: I told my wife that I would like us to drive downtown and look at the holiday decorations. But she says, "I'm tired. Would you take me home?" Well, I wasn't going to let her ruin another holiday for me, so I just ignored her, gunned the engine, and headed downtown.

Dysfunctional thought: _____

Emotion: _____

Action: _____

Client 2: I was really overloaded with work last week, but I didn't want to ask my supervisor for extra help. If she finds out how behind I am, she'll think I can't handle the job and start looking for my replacement. So I worked all weekend and most of the night to get the job done. Even then, I felt pretty bad about what I had produced. I think it's time to check the Want Ads.

Dysfunctional thought: _____

Emotion: _____

Action: _____

Client 3: All the other girls I know have already had a date. I don't know what's wrong with me. Maybe I'm too tall, or maybe the boys don't like me because I get good grades. They call me the Jolly Green Giant. I'm never going to have dates like the other girls. I might as well just give up.

Dysfunctional thought: _____

Emotion: _____

Action: _____

2. Drawing from the list on page 236, categorize the dysfunctional thoughts you identified in Exercise 1.

Client 1's thought: _____

Client 2's thought: _____

Client 3's thought: _____

3. Identify two approaches you might use to help each of the clients in Exercise 1 assess the validity of their dysfunctional thoughts.

Client 1:

Approach A _____

Approach B _____

Client 2:

Approach A _____

Approach B _____

Client 3:

Approach A _____

Approach B _____

4. Write a revised, more helpful thought that might replace each of the harmful and distorted thoughts you listed in Exercise 1.

Client 1: _____

Client 2: _____

Client 3: _____

Discussion Questions

1. Discuss the advantages and disadvantages of focusing on emotions and of focusing on thoughts during the treatment process. (Keep in mind that treatment should always address thoughts, emotions, and actions, even though the emphasis of the treatment process may vary.) Which focus feels more comfortable for you and why? Which focus do you believe will usually lead to a more productive session and why?

2. In recent years, cognitive therapy has gotten a great deal of attention through both research and practice and currently seems to dominate mental health practice. How do you explain this trend? What do you foresee as the relative importance, during the next 10 years, of treatment approaches focused on background, emotions, or thoughts?

3. Consider the following statement made by Isaac, a 46-year-old man. Assume that you are going to follow the 10-step process of eliciting, assessing, and modifying his thoughts. Discuss how each of the 10 steps listed on page **247** might evolve with this client.

Isaac: For the past month, I have been communicating with a fascinating woman named Jeannie whom I met in an Internet chat room. She really seems to listen to me and care about me. This is what I have been looking for all my life. I have finally found happiness. I'm planning to ask my wife for a divorce and move out West to be with Jeannie. My wife and children will be better off without me. They don't really seem to love me the way Jeannie does.

4. Develop helpful cognitions that might replace the following unhelpful or distorted thoughts:

- My husband was furious when he found out I had hidden the credit card bill so he wouldn't see what I had spent on clothes and makeup, but he doesn't understand women. I need to have those nice things so I feel good about myself. I did what I had to do to get what I deserve.
- I told my parents that I really wanted a dog and that I would take very good care of it, but they said we couldn't afford a dog. They could get me a dog if they really wanted to; all my friends have pets and it's not fair that I can't have one too.
- My job at the library is being phased out and my supervisor gave me a month's notice. I'm almost 60 years old. Who would hire me? What am I going to do? Go on welfare or move in with my children? All my years of hard work have amounted to nothing.
- I told my friend that I liked this boy who rode the school bus with us. She told him what I said! I couldn't believe she would do that to me. I can't face either one of them now.
- My son has had behavioral problems all his life. We started getting extra help for him when he was four years old, but I guess that wasn't early enough. I've really failed him.

5. If you have not yet done the practice group exercise associated with this chapter, discuss your thoughts and feelings about that upcoming experience. What obstacles do you expect to encounter? What can you do to try to avoid them? What did you learn from the previous role-play sessions that you want to carry with you into this chapter's role-play, which is focused on thoughts?

6. If you have already done the practice group exercise associated with this chapter, discuss your reactions to that experience. What was the most beneficial aspect of that experience for you? What was the most challenging or uncomfortable aspect of the experience? How did your involvement in this role-play compare with your earlier ones? How can you learn even more from future practice group exercises?

Practice Group Exercise: *Eliciting, Assessing, and Modifying Thoughts*

Divide into your practice groups as described in the previous chapters. The practice group exercise presented here will help you gain experience in the fundamental skills described in this chapter: eliciting, assessing, and modifying thoughts.

PREPARING FOR THE ROLE-PLAY

Once again, you should have a tape recorder and a blank tape with you. Ideally, you have already reviewed one or more tapes from your previous role-play sessions and have some ideas about how you might improve your skills.

By now, you have probably realized what a powerful learning experience it is to hear yourself and others on tape and also to review the feedback you received. You may also have found reviewing the tape-recorded sessions to be a painful experience and cringed as you listened to the sound of your voice and some of the weaker interventions you made. This is a common reaction for both novice and experienced clinicians. Try to view the process as a learning experience, and be sure to focus on your strengths as well as on areas needing improvement. With that perspective, you will probably see that you have already learned a great deal from these sessions. However, one of the exciting aspects of counseling and psychotherapy is that you can always learn more and refine your skills further. These are rewarding professions for people who thrive on learning and growth.

As you approach this next role-played session, keep in mind the strengths you demonstrated in previous sessions and improvements you want to make in your work. Review both the tape recording of your previous session and the Assessment of Progress forms you have already completed to help you identify one or two areas in your work that would benefit from some change. List those here so that they are fresh in your mind:

1. _____

2. _____

Once again, select an issue that you will address when you are in the client role. You may build or expand on issues you presented in previous sessions or you may choose to introduce a new topic. As always, take care of yourself and do not introduce issues that are still very painful to you or reflect deep-seated unresolved issues. Of course, you have the option of acting as if you are someone else or being creative and developing a hypothetical client and situation for this exercise.

Role-Play Exercise

The goals of this role-play are as follows:

- **To build on the skills you have already learned.** Keep in mind what you have already learned about the use of open and closed questions and reflections of feelings, and continue to incorporate those interventions into your role-play.

Use accents, restatements, and paraphrases to track what your client is saying and to encourage self-expression. Monitor your body language to be sure that your facial expressions, posture, eye contact, and tone of voice all reflect effective listening.

- **To help your client express, assess, and perhaps modify thoughts.** To accomplish this, the central goals of the role-play, you should follow the 10 steps in the process of modifying cognitions:

  1. Identify key issue or event.
  2. Elicit related thoughts, emotions, and actions.
  3. Rate intensity of emotions and extent of belief in thoughts.
  4. Assess the validity of the thoughts.
  5. Categorize any unhelpful and distorted thoughts.
  6. Dispute the thoughts.
  7. Replace the distorted thoughts with more helpful and accurate ones.
  8. Identify new emotions and actions.
  9. Rate current intensity of both initial and new emotions.
  10. Rate current extent of belief in both initial and revised thoughts.

During your session, complete the following table with your client:

TABLE 7-7   Eliciting, Assessing, and Modifying Thoughts and Accompanying Emotions and Actions

Presenting Concern or Situation: _____

Identification of Emotions	Rating of Intensity on 0–100 Scale

Identification of Actions

Identification of Thoughts	Rating of Belief on 0–100 Scale
1.	
2.	
3.	
4.	

Strategies Used to Assess Validity of Thoughts:

_____

Categorization of Distorted Thoughts (indicate number of thought from above and nature of distortion):

_____

Rerating:

Unhelpful Emotions	Revised Rating of Intensity on 0–100 Scale
Revised Emotions	Rating of Intensity on 0–100 Scale

Revised Actions

Unhelpful Thoughts	Revised Rating of Belief on 0–100 Scale
Revised Thoughts	Rating of Belief on 0–100 Scale

- **Summarize the session.** Wrap up the session with a brief summary, no more than two or three sentences in length. Be sure to check out the accuracy of your summary with your client.

Time Schedule

If possible, allow at least 15 minutes for each role-play; 20 minutes or even longer would be preferable. In addition, be sure that at least 10 minutes is allocated for feedback to each person in the clinician role.

Assessment of Progress Form 7

1. **Making effective use of skills you have already learned.** What use did you make of the following skills, which were learned in previous chapters? How effective was your use of these skills?

- Open and closed questions:
- Accents, restatements, and paraphrases:
- Reflections of feeling:
- Attentive body language:
- Summarizing:

2. **Helping your client express, assess, and modify thoughts.** How effective were you at guiding your client through the 10 steps in the process? Which steps felt most comfortable for you? Which were most productive? Which presented you with the greatest challenge? How might you have improved on this process?

3. Overall, how would you assess the impact of your session, according to the following rating scale?

- **Extremely helpful:** Moves treatment in a productive direction; promotes self-awareness, new learning, or positive changes.
- **Moderately helpful:** Moves treatment in a productive direction, but does not clearly lead to greater self-awareness, new learning, or positive changes.
- **Neutral:** Neither contributes to the treatment goals nor harms the therapeutic process.
- **Moderately harmful:** Detracts somewhat from the treatment process or therapeutic alliance.
- **Extremely harmful:** Damaging to the treatment process or therapeutic alliance.

4. **Using summarizing to wrap up the session.** How successful was your summarization? How might it have been improved? Did you remember to check out its accuracy with the client?

Personal Journal Questions

1. Listen to the tape recording of your role-play. Respond to the following questions about your role-play:

   - What did you perceive to be the strengths of your role-play?
   - Did you notice any improvement over your previous role-play sessions? If so, what did you do to effect that improvement?
   - What areas needing improvement did you notice? What can you do differently in your next session to effect that improvement?
   - Did you prefer to use interventions that focused on thoughts or on emotions? How do you explain your preference?

2. Identify an experience you had during the past week that bothered you. Be your own clinician and take yourself through the 10-step process of identifying, assessing, and modifying your thoughts. While you are doing that, complete the following table with reference to your own experience.

TABLE 7-8 Eliciting, Assessing, and Modifying Your Own Thoughts and Accompanying Emotions and Actions

Identification of Emotions	Rating of Intensity on 0–100 Scale

Identification of Actions

Identification of Thoughts	Rating of Belief on 0–100 Scale
1.	
2.	
3.	
4.	

Strategies Used to Assess Validity of Thoughts:

_____

Categorization of Distorted Thoughts (indicate number of thought from above and nature of distortion):

_____

Rerating:

Unhelpful Emotions	Revised Rating of Belief on 0–100 Scale
Revised Emotions	Rating of Belief on 0–100 Scale

Revised Actions

Unhelpful Thoughts	Revised Rating of Belief on 0–100 Scale
Revised Thoughts	Rating of Belief on 0–100 Scale

3. As our understanding and mastery of intervention skills develops, we sometimes find ourselves automatically thinking, feeling, and acting differently, as well as perceiving other people in new ways. What spontaneous changes of this kind, if any, have you noticed in yourself? What impact, if any, has that had on your emotional well-being and your relationships? How do these changes feel to you? If you have not experienced any of these changes, how do you explain that?

SUMMARY

This chapter focused on the fundamental skills associated with helping people identify, assess, and modify their thoughts and accompanying emotions and actions. The chapter presented a 10-step process to facilitate those goals.

Chapter 8 will build on the skills presented in this chapter by introducing additional skills that clinicians can use to help people more easily identify, assess, and modify their thoughts as well as solidify the gains they made by changing their dysfunctional thoughts. Among these additional skills are positive self-talk and affirmations, anchoring, identifying a focal concern, meditation, mindfulness, mind mapping, reframing, thought stopping, and journal writing. Information giving, problem solving, and decision making also are presented in Chapter 8 as additional tools that help clinicians encourage people to clarify their thoughts. Highlighted in Chapter 8 is the reflection of meaning intervention, an important strategy to promote awareness of thoughts.

Chapter 8

ADDITIONAL SKILLS USED TO ELICIT, IDENTIFY, ASSESS, AND MODIFY THOUGHTS

OVERVIEW

Chapter 7 presented the fundamental skills clinicians need to help people identify, assess, and modify their dysfunctional thoughts, as well as their accompanying emotions and actions. The 10-step format for this process provides a strong foundation, enabling clinicians to work effectively and constructively with the many people in counseling and psychotherapy who have distorted thoughts.

Unhelpful thoughts almost always underlie the most common symptoms presented in treatment: depression and anxiety. Distorted thoughts also usually play a part in the development and maintenance of many other emotional difficulties including personality disorders, somatic complaints without a medical basis, and even impulsive and self-destructive behaviors such as misuse of drugs, alcohol, and food.

Chapter 8 provides an array of additional skills and interventions that clinicians can use to help people who are troubled by unhelpful thoughts. By enriching their work with these additional skills, clinicians can help people not only to better express, assess, and modify their thoughts, but also to acquire the skills and perspectives they need to take better control of their lives and move forward toward their goals.

LEARNING GOALS

As a result of reading this chapter and completing the exercises throughout, you can expect to accomplish the following:

- Expand your repertoire of strategies for effecting positive changes in cognitions.
- Develop your skill in the use of interventions such as decision making, problem solving, and information giving that empower clients and help them take charge of their lives.
- Promote understanding of the effective use of reflections of meaning and how they differ from reflections of feeling.

- Familiarize yourself with a range of cognitive interventions—positive self-talk and affirmations, anchoring, reframing, thought stopping, meditation and mindfulness, journal writing, and mind mapping—that can help people to use their thoughts in constructive ways, increase their self-awareness, view their lives more clearly, and set meaningful goals and priorities.

SKILLS TO BE LEARNED

Skills that help clinicians elicit, identify, assess, and modify clients' thoughts are presented in this chapter:

- Making helpful reflections of meaning
- Helping people make decisions and solve problems
- Providing clients with useful information.
- Using specific skills to help people change their harmful thoughts and use thinking skills in constructive ways, including the use of positive self-talk and affirmations, anchoring, reframing, thought stopping, meditation and mindfulness, journal writing, and mind mapping

REFLECTIONS OF MEANING

Chapter 5 of this book presented the important skill of reflection of feeling, which is very useful in conveying empathy to clients and in helping them identify, express, manage, and modify their emotions. A similar skill, reflection of meaning, is useful in enabling people to deepen their awareness and understanding of their thoughts and in subsequently assessing and changing those thoughts.

Even the smallest happening in our lives has a personal meaning associated with it. Often, the personal meaning of the event determines its impact on our lives, rather than the event itself. That was illustrated in the Chapter 7 examples of Hidayah, Selma, and Mona, the three women diagnosed with breast cancer. Helping people understand the personal meaning of events and interactions in their lives promotes self-awareness and enables them to better understand their own values, beliefs, and goals. This, in turn, can help them to resolve their difficulties and develop thoughts, emotions, and actions that are more helpful to them.

As discussed in Chapter 7, treatment approaches that emphasize the importance of personal meaning can be described as phenomenological. Such approaches recognize that events usually do not have a universal meaning. Rather, a person's individual life experiences and view of the world determine how that person views and interprets experiences and leads each person to a unique and personal meaning for each experience.

To better understand the concept of personal meaning, assume that you receive a grade of B in a course. If this course has been difficult for you and if you anticipated receiving a C, the B probably will be a relief, a positive experience for you. On the other hand, if you have received A's in all of your other courses, the

B will probably be a disappointment to you because it has marred your excellent academic record.

When we make a reflection of meaning, what we are trying to do is verbalize the thoughts that people have about particular experiences. Making effective reflections of meaning draws on many of the same skills as making reflections of feeling. For both, clinicians need to listen carefully and try to hear not only the expressed content of what a person is saying, but also the message underlying the words. Hearing that message accurately requires insight, strong clinical skills, and the ability to identify with another person and imagine that person's experience.

With both reflections of meaning and reflections of feeling, clinicians should emphasize assets and strengths, seeking to empower people and improve their self-awareness and self-image. In addition, both types of interventions should be made tentatively, allowing clients the opportunity to disagree or clarify if they do not think they have been understood.

Both reflections of feeling and reflections of meaning can greatly enhance the therapeutic alliance and advance the treatment process. These interventions let clients know that their clinicians are tracking what they are saying, that they appreciate and accept their perceptions and emotions, and that they understand them at a deep level.

Where reflections of meaning and reflections of feeling differ is simply that reflections of meaning focus on personal meaning and thoughts, whereas reflections of feeling focus on emotions. Let's look at the following examples to clarify the difference between these two types of interventions.

Examples of Reflection of Feeling and Reflection of Meaning

Experience 1: Anais has given birth to her first child.
Reflection of feeling: You are filled with joy and love at the birth of your daughter.
Reflection of meaning: Now you finally have the family you have wanted for so long.

Experience 2: Jemal's parents discovered illegal drugs in his backpack.
Reflection of feeling: You feel shame and guilt that your parents discovered you have been using drugs.
Reflection of meaning: You believe that you have let your parents down and lost their trust.

Experience 3: Anita's close friend was killed in a car accident.
Reflection of feeling: You feel grief and anger at the death of your good friend.
Reflection of meaning: You have lost a wonderful friend, apparently for no good reason, and are questioning the meaning of life.

Let's practice with some additional examples. After reviewing the experiences that follow, write a reflection of feeling and a reflection of meaning for each:

Experience 4: Melissa had been sexually abused by a teacher when she was in elementary school. For many years, she concealed this experience and blamed herself for it. She recently told her sister Nancy about this experience, the first time Melissa had shared it with anyone. Nancy became cold and distant while Melissa spoke and then Nancy criticized her for allowing herself to be mistreated and not telling her parents about this event when she was a child.

Reflection of feeling: _____

_____

Reflection of meaning: _____

_____

Experience 5: Kara had been sexually abused by a teacher when she was in elementary school. For many years, she concealed this experience and blamed herself for it. She recently told your sister Jackie about this experience, the first time Kara had shared it with anyone. Jackie was very supportive and loving toward Kara and said she wished she had been able to protect her when she had been experiencing the abuse.

Reflection of feeling: _____

_____

Reflection of meaning: _____

_____

Experience 6: Gail has been laid off from her job. She had been unhappy at work for many months but stayed because she needed the income to support her family.

Reflection of feeling: _____

_____

Reflection of meaning: _____

_____

Determining Whether to Use Reflections of Feeling or Reflections of Meaning

Most clinicians use both reflections of feeling and reflections of meaning with their clients. The purpose of the intervention and whether the focus should be on emotions or thoughts determine which of the two is preferable.

Reflections of feeling can be particularly effective when people have trouble identifying or managing their emotions. They also may make emotions more vivid.

Reflections of meaning help people move beyond their immediate and automatic responses to situations and become aware of the deeper underlying significance that those events have for them. Reflections of meaning can also facilitate the identification, assessment, and modification of distorted thoughts. Modification of unhelpful thoughts often is a more direct and effective route to positive change than is a focus on background or emotions, especially in people who do not have good coping skills or who are apprehensive about the treatment process.

Review the six reflections of meaning and reflections of feelings in the previous examples. For each one, consider which would be a more effective intervention, the reflection of feeling or the reflection of meaning. Also, think about what difference each would make in the direction and value of the session. Let's look at the second example again to help you answer these questions and determine the direction the clinician–client dialogue might take, depending on whether you use a reflection of feeling or a reflection of meaning.

Experience 2: Jemal's parents discovered illegal drugs in his backpack.

Dialogue Using Reflection of Feeling

Clinician: Jemal, it sounds like you are feeling considerable shame and guilt that your parents discovered you have been using drugs.
Jemal: Yes, I am. My friends all smoke marijuana and talked me into trying it. I had mixed feelings about it, but they said it was harmless and felt really good. I didn't even enjoy it that much, but I wanted to be like the other kids, to be popular. I usually feel

so different. I've always been a good student and never got into any trouble at school, but now I've really screwed up. I just feel terrible about myself and what I've done.

Dialogue Using Reflection of Meaning

Clinician: You believe that you have let your parents down and lost their trust.
Client: Yes, I really feel like I have lost their respect and I don't know how I'll ever get it back. They've always been so supportive and helpful to me and really trusted me. They couldn't believe it when they found the marijuana in my backpack. I'm not worth all the sacrifices they've made for me. They immigrated to the U.S. to make a better life for our family, and now they find out that I'm using drugs and breaking the law. They must be sorry they ever had a child like me.

As you can see, the two dialogues go in different directions. The first one focuses primarily on emotions and peer relations while the second focuses more on thoughts and the parent–child interaction. Both areas of focus probably are worth exploring with this client. Where would you begin and why?

Evaluating the Effectiveness of Reflections of Meaning

Just as the effectiveness of questions and reflections of feeling can be evaluated (as illustrated in Chapters 3 and 5), so can the effectiveness of reflections of meaning. These, too, can be rated on a 1 to 5 scale, ranging from level 1 (the lowest level) to level 5 (the highest and most therapeutic level), indicating the accuracy of the reflection, its depth, and how much it adds to the person's self-awareness. The following scale can be used to rate reflections of meaning:

Level 1: Clinician statements demonstrate misunderstanding of the client's thoughts or miss important aspects of those thoughts.
Level 2: Clinician statements respond to the overt content of the client's statement but subtract from the underlying meaning.
Level 3: Clinician statements at this level are interchangeable with those of the client. In other words, they are neutral responses, more like restatements than helpful reflections of meaning.
Level 4: These clinician statements add to the client's awareness of his or her thoughts, identifying a deeper level of meaning than the client was able to verbalize.
Level 5: Clinician statements greatly enhance the client's expression of thoughts. These statements display true attunement to the client's meaning. They enable the client to gain self-awareness and a broader and deeper understanding of the personal significance of an experience. They also promote exploration and introspection.

To illustrate the use of this rating scale, review the following responses that a clinician might make to Jemal, the adolescent boy whose parents found drugs in his backpack.

Level 1: You must have thought your parents had no right to go into your backpack.

This statement is not an accurate reflection of the meaning the experience had for Jemal.

Level 2: It must have been quite a surprise to you when your parents showed you the drugs they had found in your backpack.

This statement is accurate in terms of the events but subtracts from the meaning of the experience as presented by the client.

Level 3: You see yourself as having disappointed your parents.

This statement is essentially a paraphrase of what the client has said and does not add insight or depth.

Level 4: Disappointing your parents like this must bring up some negative thoughts about yourself.

This reflection of meaning adds to the client's statement and helps him appreciate the impact this discovery has had on his view of himself.

Level 5: Your wish to be popular and accepted led you to make some choices that you believe have damaged your relationship with your parents and the trust they had in you.

This helps Jemal recognize his motivation to use drugs and the cost that has had for him. More than the other statements listed here, this one helps him see the full picture and the consequences of his choices, as well as several directions for helping himself (e.g., working on his need for peer approval, looking at how to make wiser choices, working on the trust and communication in his relationship with his parents).

To be sure you have a solid understanding of reflections of meaning, let's do one more exercise on this intervention. As the basis for this exercise, use the fourth client statement made earlier in this chapter:

Client experience:

The client, a 32-year-old woman named Melissa, had been sexually abused by a teacher when she was in elementary school. For many years, she concealed this experience and blamed herself for it. She recently told her sister Nancy about this experience, the first time Melissa had shared it with anyone. Nancy became cold and distant while Melissa spoke and then criticized her for allowing herself to be mistreated and not telling her parents about this event when she was a child.

Based on this client's experience with her sister, as well as the meaning that interaction probably had for Melissa, develop five reflections of meaning paralleling the five rating levels on the scale:

Level 1: _____

_____

Level 2: _____

_____

Level 3: _____

_____

Level 4: _____

_____

Level 5: _____

_____

IDENTIFYING A FOCAL CONCERN

One of the benefits of using reflections of meaning with clients is the way this intervention can help clinicians to identify a client's focal concern. When people initially seek treatment, they often are overwhelmed with emotion and have difficulty identifying what they hope to gain from their treatment. They may not understand how to make the best use of that help or they may not have a well-defined picture of how to improve themselves and their lives. They may view their clinicians as simply a source of support in their lives, as someone to whom they can vent their emotions and complain about their lives. Some people bring a crisis into each session and view their treatment as a way to put out fires and help them move from one crisis to the next.

Although at times all of these uses of treatment are appropriate and helpful, if counseling or therapy remains fragmented and if clients and clinicians lack clear goals and direction in their work together, their efforts are unlikely to be productive and unlikely to lead to enduring and meaningful change. Having a focal concern or problem that client and clinician have identified together can serve as a touchstone. Regardless of any temporary digressions treatment might take, both client and clinician know what their primary focus is and can bring the session back to working productively on that concern.

A dialogue with Jemal, introduced earlier in this chapter, illustrates one way that clinicians can help clients identify their focal concern:

Clinician: Jemal, I'm hearing quite a few concerns related to the incident in which your parents found drugs in your backpack, including your need feel accepted by the other students at school; your feelings about yourself and your behavior; making better choices for yourself, especially about drugs; and your relationship with your parents. What do you think about those as issues for us to work on together?

Jemal: Yes, I agree, those all are important issues to me. There are others too. My parents tell me that it is not appropriate for me to be dating or driving at sixteen. I think they're still thinking about what it was like back home when they were young and don't realize what things are like in this country.

Clinician: So this is another concern for us to put on our list. We can talk about all of these important topics eventually, but it might help us to identify a starting point. What seems to be the most urgent of these?

Jemal: I guess working on my relationship with my parents. I'm really scared they're going to lose trust in me because of what I did.

Clinician: Then let's make your relationship with your parents our first priority. What would you see as the goal of our work together on that concern?

Jemal: I need to find a way to talk with my parents about this situation and help them understand how badly I feel about it. I don't want them to think I'm a no-good drug addict. I did make a big mistake, though, in using drugs.

Clinician: Looking at your feelings about yourself after this incident seems important too. Perhaps it would be helpful to take a look at your strengths, as well as the mistakes you may have made, so you have a clear idea of the choices you made that led you into this situation. Then we can figure out how to help you use that information to talk with your parents. How does that sound to you?

Using reflections of meaning to help clients and clinicians identify focal concerns is one of the benefits of this intervention. Making some reflections of meaning and then using the information those reflections yield can give direction to sessions, particularly when clinicians perceive themselves as floundering with a client and lacking a clear direction.

PROBLEM SOLVING

People often seek help because they do not know how to think through a particular problem or because they are having difficulty making a decision. Perhaps they are unsure how to build friendships, whether to make a career change, how to improve their grades, or whether to end a relationship. The use of interventions to help people solve problems can make a great difference in whether or not the clients actually benefit from treatment and can make use of what they have learned in their sessions.

Most clinicians are understandably eager to help their clients achieve their goals. However, that very enthusiasm can lead clinicians to treat clients as though they are helpless and incapable of solving their own problems. Beginning clinicians are particularly likely to rush in to resolve people's problems for them. Clients are likely to learn and benefit more if, instead, clinicians teach them the skills they need to resolve their own difficulties and take the time needed to help them arrive at choices that are right for them.

Consider the following dialogue and, while you read it, think about the weaknesses in the clinician's interventions:

Example of Ineffective Problem Solving

Aja 1: I'm thinking about retiring from the university next year but I'm not sure whether that's the best decision for me. I'm tired of the bureaucracy and all the meetings, but I love teaching and dealing with the students.

Clinician 1: Maybe it's too early for you to retire.

Aja 2: I'll only be sixty-two, but my health hasn't been good and there are other things I want to do with my life.

Clinician 2: Could you cut back to half-time?

Aja 3: I've looked into that, but my university won't allow me to do that.

Clinician 3: Maybe you could retire from your present university and work half-time at another institution.

Aja 4: That would feel like starting all over. I don't want to do that at my age.

Clinician 4: Could you teach as an adjunct professor?

Aja 5: Maybe, but the pay is really low for adjunct faculty.

Although the clinician means well, the session becomes a "yes ... but" sort of interaction in which Aja presents reasons why each of the clinician's suggestions will not work for her. A session like this would probably be frustrating for both client and clinician; the clinician feels blocked at every turn, and Aja fails to get the help she needs. Even if the clinician had succeeded in finding a viable alternative for Aja, she still would not have had the opportunity to learn effective ways to solve problems and make decisions on her own. The immediate problem might be solved, but the treatment process would not lead to growth in Aja's skills and self-confidence.

Now let's examine another sort of interaction with Aja. Notice the differences between this dialogue and the first one, and try to identify what makes this one more successful.

Example of Effective Problem Solving

Aja 1: I'm thinking about retiring from the university next year, but I'm not sure whether that's the best decision for me. I'm tired of the bureaucracy and all the meetings, but I love teaching and dealing with the students.

Clinician 1: Sounds like you have some conflicted feelings about leaving the university.

Aja 2: Yes, I wish I could just teach and advise students and forget about all the rest of my job.

Clinician 2: The student interaction is the most rewarding part of your job for you?

Aja 3: It sure is. I especially like teaching the introductory psychology courses. It's like opening up a new world for the students, giving them an exciting way to think. And many of them make important personal changes as a result of learning about psychology.

Clinician 3: So helping people learn, both personally and professionally, is very fulfilling to you. I wonder if you have thought about other ways to help people grow and develop other than through full-time teaching?

Aja 4: No, I guess I just thought of my job as an all-or-nothing proposition.

Clinician 4: How about if we try to brainstorm some options, just make a list of possibilities, and then we can go back and evaluate them?

Aja 5: That sounds like a good place to start. Let's see ... I guess I could teach as an adjunct professor. I'd like to work half-time but my university doesn't have any half-time employees. Maybe I could go to another university, but that would feel like starting all over again....

Clinician 5: I've jotted down three possibilities so far: adjunct teaching, going half-time, or moving to another university. What others might there be?

Aja 6: That's about all I can think of.

Clinician 6: Could there be some ways to have an impact on people's lives through your profession that doesn't involve a university?

Aja 7: I never thought about that. I guess I could teach adult education or even do volunteer tutoring or mentoring. I've never practiced as a psychologist but, with some more training, that might be an option too.

Clinician 7: I'll add those to the list. Any other possibilities?

Aja 8: I always thought I'd like to be a visiting professor at a college overseas. That would be a real adventure for me! That's about all the options I can think of.

Clinician 8: How would you feel about our taking a close look at each of the options on our list and figuring out their benefits and drawbacks?
Aja 9: That makes sense to me.

What differences did you see between the first and second interviews? Did you notice the following in the second dialogue?

- The second clinician used a wider variety of interventions, including reflections of feeling and meaning and open questions.
- The clinician took the time to understand what it is that Aja finds meaningful about teaching; this facilitates development of new possibilities.
- The clinician encouraged Aja to come up with most of the options rather than suggesting them.
- In intervention 6, the clinician encouraged Aja to think more creatively but does not actually offer suggestions.
- The strategy of brainstorming was used to expand possibilities in dialogue before client and clinician begin to evaluate options.
- Aja and the clinician operated as a team. The clinician did not direct or take charge but instead guided Aja through the process.

Problem solving can offer important learning experiences for clients, teaching them thinking skills they can apply to future problems and decisions. Clinicians who use the strategies illustrated and identified here, in combination with fundamental interventions such as open questions and reflections of feeling and meaning, are more likely to help people find satisfactory solutions to their concerns and to develop important new skills than are clinicians who try to solve clients' problems for them.

INFORMATION GIVING

People are more likely to feel empowered and to take ownership of resolving their difficulties if they generate their own possible solutions. However, sometimes the clinician has useful knowledge, information, or ideas that the client does not yet have. Sharing that information can be a helpful part of the treatment process, as long as the information is presented in a way that broadens the client's thinking and helps the client to make better decisions rather than specifying what the client should do or making the client feel inadequate. Positive use of information giving is illustrated in the continuing dialogue with Aja.

Example of Making Suggestions

Clinician: I wonder if you have considered the option of job sharing?
Aja: No, I never thought about that.
Clinician: I understand that many businesses and institutions nowadays are encouraging job sharing; it can benefit both employers and employees.
Aja: It sounds interesting. I'd like to add that to our list of possibilities.
Clinician: What interests you about the idea of job sharing?
Aja: It would be a way to work half-time and yet collaborate with a colleague to fill a full-time job slot. That could work well, but I don't know if the university is progressive enough to consider that.
Clinician: How could you find that out?

Although the idea of job sharing comes from the clinician, the clinician offers this suggestion tentatively and assesses whether Aja might have some interest in this option. When she is amenable to considering this idea, the clinician shifts ownership of the idea to Aja by asking how she can obtain more information about the viability of the job sharing option. In this way, the information becomes something that Aja can explore, accept, or reject rather than something that the clinician is persuading Aja to do.

Much of my clinical work focuses on helping people nurture their mind, their body, and their spirit and deepening the connection among the three. Both when I am working with physically healthy people who want to improve these aspects of their lives and when I am working with people who have medical or physical concerns that have led them to seek treatment, I often assume an information-giving role. Once again, however, my goal is to empower people via new tools and information and to enable them to assess information and make sound choices for themselves rather than to convince them to change their lives.

Consider the following dialogue on the mind–body–spirit connection and, as you review it, consider its strengths as well as the areas that need improvement.

Example of Giving Information

Patrice: My last appointment with the cardiologist really scared me. She said that if my symptoms worsen much more, I would need bypass surgery. My father had that; it was incapacitating for him and didn't buy him much time. I really want to avoid that surgery and I thought therapy might help me. I know you specialize in working with the mind–body connection.

Clinician: It sounds like you are eager to be proactive in taking care of yourself in the hope of avoiding the surgery that your father had. Many approaches to advancing mind–body–spirit health might be useful to you. What have you done so far to help yourself improve your health?

Patrice: I've been working mainly on my physical health, doing strength training and aerobic exercise according to the guidelines the physician gave me. I read that drinking wine would be good for my heart, but I really don't enjoy alcohol and don't want to develop a drinking problem.

Clinician: So you've made a good start in exercising, following medical guidelines. Diet is another important approach to heart health, but I can hear that you don't want to replace one problem with another. My understanding is that red grape juice has similar heart benefits to alcohol; how would you feel about asking your physician about nonalcoholic drinks to improve your heart health?

Patrice: I can do that. I'd feel much better about drinking grape juice than wine. Where does the spirit come into this mind–body–spirit process?

Clinician: Research has shown us that belief in a higher power, in perceiving a meaning to our existence, can help to reduce stress and give us a sense of belonging and support. How does that concept fit in with your life and your beliefs?

Patrice: Are you saying that I need to go back to church and pray more?

Clinician: You seem uneasy with what I said. What did it mean to you?

Patrice: I'm not sure going back to church is right for me. You know, I always felt guilty in church, like I was a bad girl and didn't measure up.

Clinician: These sound like important feelings for us to talk about, but I didn't mean that you had to go to church to develop your spiritual side. I think of spirituality as a broad concept, reflecting a feeling of being connected to the universe and believing in something greater than yourself, whether it is formal religion or nature or simply a sense of wonder about our world.

Patrice: I can certainly relate to that. But what can I do with those feelings?

Clinician: What brings out your strongest feelings of spirituality?

Patrice: I have those feelings when I'm outside on a beautiful day. I can really feel connected to every plant and animal and I do have that sense of there being something beyond myself that you talked about.

Clinician: You already seem to have found a way to experience and express your spirituality!

This dialogue would continue, further addressing Patrice's spirituality and then moving onto other aspects of the mind–body–spirit connection such as helpful thoughts, positive relationships, and good self-esteem.

Giving Information on the Treatment Process

One of the most common and essential topics about which clinicians provide information to clients is the treatment process itself. At the beginning of treatment, clinicians typically orient clients to that process. This usually is done both in a written format (consent to treatment form) and through discussion. Clients are informed about the ethical aspects of the clinical relationship and such practical matters as fees, scheduling, and contacting the clinician in the event of an emergency. In addition, helping people understand the process of counseling or psychotherapy and how it operates, the anticipated roles of the client and the clinician, and the clinician's usual treatment approach can enable people to make the best use of their treatment.

Acosta, Yamamoto, Evans, and Skilbeck (1983) found that this orientation process, called *role induction,* is associated with greater motivation and optimism in clients and a greater willingness to present and explore their concerns. Transmission of all information provided throughout the treatment process should be done in a way that empowers clients and enables them to understand, ask questions about, discuss, and assume ownership of the information.

Guidelines for Information Giving

Providing information to clients usually is most helpful if clinicians follow these guidelines:

- Presentation of information should be tentative, brief, and concise; clinicians provide details and explanations only if the client shows interest.
- Information is provided one piece at a time, allowing ample opportunity for client responses and for clinicians to attend to and explore the client's reactions.
- The information giving is integrated with other interventions so that the session does not turn into a lecture.
- Clinicians elicit the client's reactions to the information, using reflections of feeling and meaning, open questions, and other interventions to promote exploration.
- Clinicians transfer ownership of the information to the client as soon as possible by encouraging the client to gather additional information and explore the information further.

- Clinicians remain neutral; they don't advocate for their ideas or suggestions, recognizing that they cannot predict what will be best for another person.
- Clinicians monitor their own reactions; if they feel hurt, angry, or annoyed because a client is not interested in their suggestions, they explore and modify their own feelings so they do not undermine the treatment process.
- Clinicians keep in mind that the primary focus of treatment is promoting the client's self-awareness, healthy decisions, and empowerment; information giving is only one of many ways to advance these goals.
- The learning experiences at the conclusion of this chapter afford you an opportunity to practice information giving. Keep these guidelines in mind for that exercise, as well as for times when you decide to provide clients with knowledge and options.

DECISION MAKING

Once clients have delineated their options, gathered information, and evaluated the possibilities, they may still have difficulty making a decision. One strategy to facilitate this is illustrated in the following dialogue with Aja. She has gathered information on job sharing and has learned that 2 years are needed to set up such an arrangement; she had planned to retire in 1 year. She is having difficulty deciding whether to retire as soon as she had planned or to spend an extra year in her full-time position at the university in order to set up a job sharing arrangement with a colleague.

Clinician: Aja, it sounds like you are really struggling with the question of whether to retire in a year or work full time for two more years so that you can then share your job.

Aja: Yes, that is a real dilemma for me. I had anticipated retiring in a year and had already made plans to move into a less expensive apartment. But the job sharing idea really appeals to me.

Clinician: How about if we make up a list of the pros and cons for staying at the university an additional year? Once we have developed the list, we can go back through each item and assign a weight to it, using a zero to ten scale to assess the importance that each item has for you. (See Table 8-1.)

TABLE 8-1 Pros and Cons of Staying at the University an Extra Year

Pros		Cons	
Opportunity to continue teaching	10	Delay of additional leisure time	4
Continued contact with colleagues	6	Bureaucracy, meetings	8
Financial benefits	5	Potential health consequences	7
Total	21	Total	19

A table such as Table 8-1 can be a useful tool, not only to facilitate decision making, but also to increase understanding of what makes the decision a challenging one. The table can promote exploration, clarify choices, and help people generate plans that will contribute to the successful implementation of their decisions. Aja's ratings of the drawbacks to remaining at the university added up to 19, while the ratings of benefits totaled 21. The closeness of the numbers clearly reflected what a difficult decision this was for Aja. A comparison of the totals gave a slight edge to the decision to remain at the university an extra year in order to arrange for job sharing. However, the closeness of the numbers suggested that Aja and her clinician had some more work to do before Aja could make a clear and comfortable decision.

The next step in the decision-making process was for Aja and the clinician to take a close look at the ratings to determine their relative strengths and gain a deeper understanding of the meaning the ratings had for Aja. Clearly, the opportunity to continue her teaching and advising was paramount for Aja and seemed to overshadow the other benefits and drawbacks. Further conversation enabled Aja to become even clearer about the great sense of accomplishment and fulfillment she derived from her teaching.

Following an exploration of the ratings, Aja and her counselor sought to determine whether any of the ratings could be modified to increase the weight of the benefits and decrease the weight of the drawbacks. One important drawback was Aja's concern about her health; she was being treated for osteoporosis, high blood pressure, and high cholesterol. Another drawback was her dislike for the bureaucratic aspects of her job. Through discussion, Aja realized that she could reduce some of the less appealing aspects of her job by resigning from several time-consuming committees. This would afford her additional free time that she could use to begin an exercise program, which might, in turn, ameliorate some of her medical problems. She also decided to have a consultation with her physician about the impact of continued work-related stress on her health. These decisions enabled Aja to make changes in her ratings, as depicted in Table 8-2, leading to a clearer decision to remain at the university for an extra year. The increased gap between the totals of her pro and con ratings affirms the wisdom of Aja's decision to spend another year in her present position.

People who are struggling with complicated and important decisions often have difficulty clarifying their thoughts and articulating their concerns. Tools such as the decision-making grid used in Tables 8-1 and 8-2 can help both client and clinician understand the client's dilemma more clearly, assess the benefits and drawbacks

TABLE 8-2   Rerating of the Pros and Cons of Staying at the University an Extra Year

Pros		Cons	
Opportunity to continue teaching	10	Delay of additional leisure time	4
Continued contact with colleagues	6	Bureaucracy, meetings	5
Financial benefits	5	Potential health consequences	3
Total	21	Total	12

of each choice, modify the strength of those benefits and drawbacks, identify the decision that seems preferable, and find ways to increase the likelihood that the decision will be a rewarding one.

Not all clinicians are comfortable with the structured paper-and-pencil process illustrated in Aja's example. Clinicians can easily modify this procedure by simply using a less structured discussion of the benefits and drawbacks of a particular choice if that approach is more compatible with the clinician's and client's concepts of the treatment process.

SPECIFIC SKILLS RELATED TO MODIFYING THOUGHTS

Cognitive approaches to counseling and psychotherapy are rich sources of intervention strategies that can help people clarify, assess, and modify their thoughts and make changes in emotions and actions as well. The following strategies are reviewed here and illustrated with examples later in this chapter that pertain to Eileen Carter (the client who has been presented throughout this book) and other clients.

USEFUL COGNITIVE STRATEGIES TO CLARIFY DECISIONS

- Positive self-talk and affirmations
- Anchoring
- Reframing
- Thought stopping
- Meditation
- Mindfulness meditation
- Journal writing
- Mind mapping

Positive Self-Talk and Affirmations

Most of us keep up a running commentary of thoughts in our minds, although we are not usually focused on that inner monologue. However, that internal commentary has a powerful impact on how we view and cope with our lives. When we make a mistake at work, for example, we may think, "What a mess I've made. I'm in really big trouble. How could I have been so stupid! I hope my supervisor doesn't find out." Or we might think, "I made a mistake, but I think I can figure out some ways to make it right with some help from my supervisor. I'll have to be more thorough next time." If we can help our clients tune into their inner monologues, assess whether or not those monologues are helpful, and deliberately change the unhelpful messages people are giving themselves, they may well develop improved self-confidence and coping skills. The development of meaningful affirmations can enhance and reinforce this process.

Because she perceived herself as having made some bad choices as an adolescent and young adult, Eileen Carter, the 24-year-old African American woman introduced earlier in this book, had difficulty recognizing her strengths. When anything reminded her of her past, especially her abortions and her misuse of alcohol, she lost sight of all she had accomplished and viewed herself as both helpless and unworthy of happiness.

For example, on a recent visit to the park with her son Junior, Eileen became absorbed in a conversation with a neighbor. While they were talking, Junior fell down and cut his head, requiring a trip to the hospital for stitches. Eileen's internal monologue went something like this: "Junior was injured because of my selfishness. I should have been watching him every second and not talking to my friend. I'm a terrible mother. I just can't seem to do anything right, no matter how hard I try. I can't forgive myself for all the terrible mistakes I made, and it feels like God is punishing me, too, for all that I did wrong." A relatively minor incident sent Eileen into a downward spiral in which she devalued everything about herself.

With her therapist's help, Eileen grew more aware of her inner monologue and was amazed at the way she constantly devalued herself. She learned to interrupt this negative self-evaluation and deliberately replace it with more positive self-talk. Eileen and her clinician worked together to develop some self-talk and an affirmation she could substitute for her negative inner dialogue.

When helping people develop their own positive messages and affirmations, clinicians should help clients use language that is meaningful and believable to them. Although clinicians may prefer clients to think of themselves in strongly positive terms, the clients may have difficulty believing such messages and so may dismiss them or fail to use them in consistent and helpful ways. Clinicians should be sure that any self-talk has language and content that feels right to the client. Even if clients ask for suggestions and encourage clinician input, clinicians should be sure that clients try on and refine their suggestions so that they genuinely take ownership of them. Unless clients can really believe and embrace their positive messages to themselves, those messages are unlikely to be helpful.

Example of Positive Self-Talk and an Affirmation

Eileen's positive messages to herself are included the following:

Positive self-talk: I have made many mistakes but I have learned from them. God loves me and will help me to lead a better life.
Affirmation: I don't have to be perfect to be a good mother and wife.

The positive self-talk acknowledged Eileen's problem-filled background but emphasized the importance of her strong spiritual beliefs and her own determination to change her life. The affirmation reminded Eileen of her most important roles and strengths and helped her minimize her tendency to devalue herself without justification.

Eileen wrote down both the positive self-talk and the affirmation. She agreed to repeat the positive statement to herself many times during the day, especially when she found herself thinking negative and self-deprecating thoughts. She wrote the affirmation on purple note cards and placed them throughout her house so that she would have frequent and eye-catching reminders of her revised cognitions. Both strategies enhanced Eileen's efforts to view herself in balanced and realistic ways and pay attention to her strengths and accomplishments.

TABLE 8-3 Identifying Anchors in Our Lives

Type of Anchor	Specific Anchor	Thought, Feeling, and/or Action Elicited by Anchor
Visual (sight)		
Auditory (sound)		
Kinesthetic (touch)		
Olfactory (smell)		
Gustatory (taste)		

Anchoring

An anchor is a trigger or stimulus that evokes a specific and consistent response pattern from the person using the anchor. Anchors can be visual (sight), auditory (sound), kinesthetic (touch), olfactory (smell), or gustatory (taste).

Think about anchors you have in your own life such as a special food that reminds you of family dinners, a piece of music that leads you to reminisce about a long-ago romance, or an intersection where you had an automobile accident. These are all anchors that arise spontaneously. However, anchors can also be created to further the treatment process. Similarly, self-destructive anchors can be identified and modified.

Because of their strong associations, anchors bring up thoughts, feelings, actions, or a combination of those. Use the following table to identify some anchors in your life. If possible, come up with a mix of positive and negative anchors so that you can see the impact that both have on you.

Anchors can be particularly powerful in both changing undesirable thoughts and in reinforcing helpful thoughts. Through the use of anchors to shape thoughts, associated emotions and actions often will change spontaneously.

When a persistent negative thought has been identified, clinicians can ask about the circumstances in which that thought arose. Zane, for example, reported that after he had put in a hard day at the factory and was walking toward the bus stop, he frequently thought, "I deserve a rest after all I did today. I'll go home, have a cup of coffee, a pastry, and a cigarette, and watch some television." When Zane was diagnosed with a medical illness and was advised to stop smoking and lose weight, this challenging endeavor was complicated by the anchor of leaving work and walking toward the bus, which triggered his desire for coffee, sweets, and smoking. To change his behavior, Zane changed both the anchor (leaving work, walking toward the bus stop) and the thought that he deserved to reward himself with what were unhealthy behaviors. Carpooling to work with a friend and then going to the gym or to his children's after-school sports activities eliminated the harmful anchors or associations and made it easier for Zane to change his thoughts and their associated behaviors. Finding other rewards for his hard work also helped him make the changes he desired.

I often help my clients create positive anchors in conjunction with visual imagery and self-talk. For example, I first lead people through a visualization in which they imagine and review their strengths and assets. When they have a clear picture of those in their mind, I suggest they clasp their hands together. The clasping of the hands now becomes an anchor for the their strengths and assets; by clasping their hands, most people who have established this anchor can easily and quickly retrieve an image of their strengths and assets, especially after some practice. A similar strategy can be used to reinforce and make readily accessible feelings of relaxation, thoughts of empowerment, images of successful goal attainment, and much more. Written anchors, as well as physical ones, can be used as in the following examples.

Examples of Anchoring   The previous section of this chapter described Eileen's use of purple note cards to record her affirmations. For Eileen, the purple note cards themselves became a visual anchor, reminding her of the affirmation she had created. As often happens, stimulus generalization occurred, and Eileen found that the color purple, her favorite color, became an anchor in itself because of its association with her affirmation.

In addition, Eileen and her therapist created a kinesthetic anchor to reinforce her use and internalization of her affirmation. Eileen paired the repetition of her positive self-talk and her affirmation with the act of clasping her hands in prayer. Not only did this remind her of her faith in God and the strength she derived from her religious beliefs, but it quickly brought back the positive thoughts she had developed. All Eileen had to do to remind herself of those thoughts was to clasp her hands. When she felt discouraged or angry, clasping her hands generally calmed her down and helped her modify her upsetting thoughts.

Reframing

Reframing or relabeling is a cognitive intervention in which clinicians help people change the language they use to describe experiences or perceptions. The goal of this process is to modify thoughts, emotions, and actions associated with the experiences or perceptions. This can enable people to view their circumstances in a more positive light and as capable of improvement. In turn, this can increase their hopefulness and motivation, modify the meaning an experience or circumstance has for them, and enhance people's efforts to change.

Examples of Reframing

- A young child who had been labeled as hyperactive is described as having a great deal of energy.
- A therapist suggested to a man who felt hopeless and discouraged that this was his depression speaking and not his usual voice.
- A clinician encouraged a newly married couple, concerned about their occasional arguments, to view the arguments as part of the process of getting to know each other. This not only put the arguments in a more favorable light but externalized the disagreements, making them part of a useful process rather than an expression of negative feelings.
- Concerned about her mother's safety, a woman arranged for her mother to move into a nursing home. When the mother refused to make the move,

the woman felt like a failure. With help, she reconceptualized this as presenting her mother with options and honoring her mother's right to make her own decisions.

- Eileen viewed Junior's fall as evidence that she was a terrible and neglectful mother. Instead, her counselor described it as one of the difficult but inevitable learning experiences of being the parent of a young child.

As these examples illustrate, reframing does not involve arguing with people or telling them their perceptions are inaccurate. Rather, the clinician simply offers a new and different perspective that promotes positive change. This strategy is in keeping with the growing emphasis on phenomenological approaches to mental health treatment that recognize the importance of people's perceptions in determining treatment effectiveness.

Exercise in Reframing   To develop your skill with the intervention of reframing, suggest new ways to conceptualize or reframe the following situations, keeping in mind the importance of encouraging people to make positive changes:

- A man sees his wife as severely troubled ("crazy," as he puts it) and unable to function, either at home or in social and occupational situations.
- The parents of an adolescent child are horrified by their child's lack of interest in religion and believe that she is engaging in sacrilegious thoughts for which she will be punished.
- A young woman was brought up to believe that women's primary role in life is to marry and raise a family. However, she would prefer to go to college and have a professional career. This conflict leads her to view herself as a disappointment to her parents and as having something wrong with her.
- Bill felt aroused when he saw his teenaged stepdaughter in a bathing suit. He now wonders if he is a pedophile and is fearful that he may molest his stepdaughter. He has never engaged in behavior of this kind and seems to have excellent impulse control.
- Lois has started her first teaching job after finishing college. She has had some difficulty maintaining a positive atmosphere in the class. When she sought help from her supervisor, he suggested she did not "have what it takes" to be a teacher. Lois now perceives herself as a failure and is considering quitting her job, which is both challenging and rewarding to her.

What was it like for you to complete this exercise? You probably felt challenged by the process of reframing, but might also have felt empowered by this useful tool. In reviewing your responses, be sure that you emphasized clients' strengths and paved the way for them to make positive changes.

Thought Stopping

People who have few positive feelings about themselves and their lives and feel powerless often are troubled by recurrent negative thoughts. Although this symptom, sometimes referred to as *ruminating* or *perseverating,* is particularly common among people who are depressed or anxious, this pattern also can occur in people without these difficulties. You might even have had this experience yourself.

Ruminating is particularly likely to develop after a situation people believe they have handled badly. Following the incident, people may keep replaying it, dwelling on each thing they did or said and thinking about ways they might have better handled the situation. They tend to magnify their perceived shortcomings, probably exaggerate the negative reactions that others had to them, and have difficulty letting go of the experience. Its meaning is magnified, along with self-blame. As people continue to replay the disturbing scenario, the same words or pictures may keep running through their minds, allowing feelings of being immobilized, powerless, and hopeless to become entrenched.

Affirmations and distraction are ways to interrupt these repetitive thoughts and ruminations. Thought stopping is another strategy.

The first step in using thought stopping successfully is identifying the unwanted recurrent thought or image. Once that has been accomplished, each time people find themselves thinking the upsetting or demoralizing thought, they say to themselves, either aloud or subvocally, "STOP IT!" Like most bad habits, the thought will probably recur before too long but, by teaching clients this simple cognitive strategy, the frequency of the thought is likely to diminish over time.

Meditation

Entire books have been written about the benefits of meditation, so only a brief overview of that process will be provided here. However, with some additional training and experience, clinicians can teach their clients some simple approaches to meditation that promote feelings of calm and self-confidence, increase awareness and insight, and help people let go of troubling thoughts and worries. As Borysenko (1988) stated, "The final goal of meditation is to be constantly conscious of experience so that relaxation and peace of mind become the norm rather than the exception" (p. 47).

Meditation also can be used to help people find answers to perplexing questions. The process of introspection and accessing deeply held thoughts that is encouraged by meditation can give people direction, clarify their thoughts, and help them make wise and helpful choices.

Typically, meditation begins with some brief relaxation exercises, perhaps progressive muscle relaxation or deep, diaphragmatic breathing. Then, according to Smith (1986), "The instructions for meditation can be put very simply: Calmly attend to a simple stimulus. After every distraction, calmly return your attention: again and again and again" (p. 67). When people first begin to meditate, they commonly find that their mind drifts off in many directions and they become concerned that they do not have an aptitude for meditation. However, this experience of losing and then regaining focus is part of the meditation process; over time, maintaining a clear focus and an open, receptive mind during meditation usually becomes easier and more fulfilling.

Meditation promotes feelings of calm and self-confidence, increases awareness and insight, and helps people let go of troubling thoughts and worries

When transcendental meditation first became popular in the United States in the 1970s, students of that process received a special word or phrase to serve as the focus of their meditation. They were sometimes instructed to keep that word secret. Over the years, meditation has lost much of its mystique, and most practitioners recognize that successful meditation does not require a special word or an elaborate process. Rather, any of the following can serve as an appropriate focus for meditation:

- A personally meaningful word such as *peace, hope,* or *love*
- Transcendent images such as a spiritual figure or symbol, the sunrise, or the universe
- Relaxing images such as a pastoral scene or a sleeping child
- Contemplative images such as questions, memories, experiences, or inner guides that can lead to discovery of meaning and direction
- Special objects or burning candles can also serve as meditative images, helping people to concentrate their attention and tune out distractions.

Some people prefer not to focus their attention when meditating but, rather, to approach the process with an open and receptive mind, waiting to see what thoughts, images, and feelings arise for them. Meditation can also be productively combined with action; some types of yoga and even-paced walking can be conducive to the development of a meditative state.

Ideally, meditation should be practiced on a regular basis. One or two 10- to 20-minute meditation sessions per day seem to yield the greatest benefit. However, even shorter and less frequent meditation can be relaxing and can help people to clarify and modify their thoughts and feelings.

Mindfulness Meditation

Mindfulness meditation is a relatively new approach to the process of meditation. Developed largely through the work of Jon Kabat-Zinn (2005), mindfulness meditation encourages people to become more acutely aware of themselves and their surroundings.

Pause as you read this page to have a brief experience in mindfulness meditation. Open your mind and all your senses so that you are present in this moment and take in many of the stimuli both inside and outside of yourself. Begin by tuning into yourself and noticing the physical and emotional sensations you are experiencing:

- Are you feeling warm or cold, tired or alert, hungry or thirsty, or other sensations?
- What are your thoughts? Are you thinking about what you are reading or is your mind focused on the past or the present? Are there messages or recurrent thoughts running through your head or is your mind fairly quiet and ready to absorb new information?
- Notice what you are doing. Are you eating or humming or drinking a cup of tea while you read this book? Perhaps you are manipulating a pen or paper clip or tapping your foot or scratching your head or pulling on a button.
- Then focus outside yourself. What sounds do you notice? What do you see when you look up from your book? Perhaps you are aware of smells or other sensory experiences.
- Now look at the room around you with new eyes, as though you were coming into the room for the first time. What is your impression of the room and the person whose room this is? Is the room neat or cluttered? Well coordinated or homey? Spacious or small? What do the contents suggest about the people who use this room, their tastes, personality, and interests? Avoid making judgments as you absorb this information, but simply tune into your impressions and perceptions.

One of the goals of mindfulness meditation is to help people to live their lives more fully and consciously without acting automatically and being oblivious to their surroundings. People's overly busy and structured lives make it easy for them to go from one chore or appointment to another, without absorbing or noticing the world around them. Mindfulness meditation is yet another cognitive strategy that can increase relaxation, enable people to make more conscious and fulfilling choices, and become more aware of both the strengths and joys in their lives and their difficulties and disappointments.

Journal Writing

Journal writing is another tool that can assist people in identifying and clarifying their thoughts. Many people enjoy keeping journals and find writing in them to be rewarding and meaningful experiences. Other people, however, are reminded of unpleasant and disappointing experiences they had in school and would rather do almost anything than write about their thoughts. Clinicians should be cautious when suggesting this activity to clients and be sure to discuss clients' reactions to the suggestion. Writing will only be productive and worthwhile if people are motivated to make good use of this experience.

Many books are available to help encourage and guide people's use of writing, including *Writing From the Inside Out* (Palumbo, 2000), *In-Versing Your Life* (Gustavson, 1995), and, for adolescents, *Discovery Journal* (Oshinsky, 1994). However, such books are not necessary as long as clinicians use thought and creativity in suggesting writing topics to clients. Particularly useful are topics that are germane to clients' concerns and offer them the opportunity to generate possible solutions to their difficulties. Subjects that are surprising and thought provoking are also appealing to most people.

For example, Chapter 7 and this chapter have discussed Carrie, who was concerned about the distribution of her mother's estate; Jemal, whose parents found drugs in his backpack; Aja, who was considering retirement from a university teaching position; and Selma, who had been diagnosed with breast cancer. This and earlier chapters have discussed Eileen Carter. The following might be useful writing topics for these people:

Carrie

- What makes me a lovable person
- Good memories of my relationship with my mother
- What money means to me

Jemal

- My relationship with my parents
- The benefits and dangers of using illegal drugs
- The true meaning of friendship

Aja

- What I want my life to be like in 5 years
- Life beyond teaching
- Milestones of my career

Selma

- Two losses and one gain from breast cancer
- What I believe caused my cancer
- Cancer as a wake-up call

Eileen

- How my spiritual beliefs can help me
- My transformation
- My ideas about good mothering

Journal writing can be a meaningful and rewarding experience

What topics would you suggest to Devon, the college freshman who is struggling with his adjustment to college?

- _____
- _____
- _____

Of course, the best resource for appropriate writing topics is the person who will be doing the writing. Before suggesting topics, clinicians might ask their clients to propose writing topics they would find helpful.

Clinicians can encourage clients who agree to keep a journal or to write about a specific topic to bring their writing to future appointments. If clients choose to do so, their writing can offer a new perspective on their thoughts and self-help efforts, suggest important topics for discussion in sessions, and reflect progress and barriers to successful treatment.

Mind Mapping

Mind mapping is another creative tool to promote people's awareness of their thoughts and prompt fruitful exploration. In this exercise, people begin the map with a central issue or concept that they have brought to treatment. A circle in the center of the map represents this central issue. People, experiences, or other thoughts related to the central thought are represented as branching out from that

FIGURE 8-1 *Mind Map by Eileen Carter*

thought. The branches may then have branches of their own, reflecting the complexity of a person's thoughts.

The map shown in Figure 8-1 represents Eileen Carter's mind map of the issue that brought her to counseling: her wish to continue her college education. This issue is written in the circle at the center of the map. Discussion of this central issue led Eileen to create five secondary branches, reflecting the major factors that affect whether or not she would continue her education: Husband, My Past, Resources, Dreams, and Junior. Branches extending from each of these reflect the many complex and often conflicted thoughts Eileen has about continuing her education. For example, extending from the circle representing My Past is the positive thought "behind me" as well as the negative thoughts "shame" and "deserve punishment" that present barriers to Eileen's pursuing her dreams.

This rich mind map can help Eileen think through the many factors involved in her decision about whether to continue her education and to make a sound and realistic decision. The exercises that follow this section afford you the opportunity to create your own mind map and to experiment with some of the other cognitive skills presented in this chapter that can help people identify, assess, and change their thoughts.

LEARNING OPPORTUNITIES

This chapter has focused on teaching a variety of cognitive strategies that can be effectively combined with the fundamental cognitive skills presented in Chapter 7 to help clients identify, express, assess, and perhaps change their thoughts. In addition, these skills can be integrated into nearly all treatment approaches to enhance clients' repertoire of skills.

Strategies presented in this chapter include:

- Making helpful reflections of meaning
- Helping people make decisions and solve problems
- Providing clients with useful information.
- Using specific skills to help people change their harmful thoughts and use thinking skills in constructive ways, including the use of positive self-talk and affirmations, anchoring, reframing, thought stopping, meditation and mindfulness, journal writing, and mind mapping

Written Exercises

1. In Chapter 5 you learned about reflections of feeling, and in this chapter you learned about reflections of meaning and how they differ from reflections of feeling. Write a reflection of meaning and a reflection of feeling to respond to each of the following client statements. These may look familiar to you, because you have already gotten to know these clients in Chapter 7.

Client 1: I told my wife that I would like us to drive downtown and look at the holiday decorations. So she says, "I'm tired. Would you take me home?" Well, I wasn't going to let her ruin another holiday for me, so I just ignored her, gunned the engine, and headed downtown.

Reflection of meaning: _____

Reflection of feeling: _____

Client 2: I was really overloaded with work last week, but I didn't want to ask my supervisor for extra help. If she finds out how behind I am, she'll think I can't handle the job and start looking for my replacement. So I worked all weekend and most of the night to get the job done. Even then, I felt pretty bad about what I had produced. I think it's time to hit the Want Ads.

Reflection of meaning: _____

Reflection of feeling: _____

Client 3: All the other girls I know have already had a date. I don't know what's wrong with me. Maybe I'm too tall, or maybe the boys don't like me because I get good grades. They call me the Jolly Green Giant. I'm never going to have dates like the other girls. I might as well just give up.

Reflection of meaning: _____

Reflection of feeling: _____

2. The third client in Exercise 1, a 14-year-old girl, might benefit from some information on adolescent development. The second client might benefit from some information on time management. Write a brief client–clinician dialogue, including some helpful information that you might give to one of these two clients. Be sure to follow the guidelines on helpful information giving.

3. Develop a helpful affirmation for one of the three clients in Exercise 1.

4. Describe how you might use reframing with one of the clients in Exercise 1.

5. Identify two journal writing topics that might be helpful to one of the clients in Exercise 1.

6. You are already familiar with the dilemma presented by Eileen Carter, who wants to continue her college education but is discouraged from doing so by her husband's disapproval. Develop a hypothetical decision-making grid similar to the one given in Table 8-1 on page **269**, complete with ratings, that Eileen might create to help her determine whether to continue school.

Discussion Questions

1. Problem solving and information giving are interventions that clinicians must use with great care. Discuss the possible pitfalls of these interventions. When using these interventions, what steps can you take to avoid those pitfalls?

2. Cognitive interventions can be very structured, such as the decision-making grid; very unstructured such as meditation and mindfulness or something in between. What level of structure is most compatible with your own clinical style? What impact do you think that will have on your sessions? How would you handle the treatment process and the use of structured interventions with a client who has difficulty completing tasks and following through on plans? How would you handle the treatment process and the use of structured interventions with a client who rigidly adheres to plans and has difficulty with spontaneity?

3. Four different clients developed the following affirmations. What are your reactions to each one? Which of these people, if any, would you encourage to revise or rethink their affirmations and why?
   a. Joy, joy, joy!
   b. Life is tough, but the tough keep going.
   c. I will have a full, rich life in spite of what my husband has done to me.
   d. Every day in every way I'm getting better and better.

4. Develop reframes for each of the following:
   a. Franco's father has been diagnosed with dementia. Franco constantly refers to the disease as "this curse that has befallen our family."

b. Everett's wife ended their marriage because she fell in love with another woman. Everett feels humiliated by this and views himself as a "failure" and a "reject."

c. Sari's son has been diagnosed with attention-deficit/hyperactivity disorder. Because of this, he is often careless and tends to drop and break things. Sari refers to him as a "klutz" and punishes her son when he has accidents.

d. Margit is very beautiful, but attributes all reactions she receives from others to her appearance. If people are attracted to her, she believes it is because of her looks and if they are not interested in her, she views them as jealous of her appearance. Her motto is "Beauty is everything."

5. Of the strategies presented in this chapter, which seem the most useful and why? Which seem the least useful and why?

6. If you have not yet done the practice group exercise associated with this chapter, discuss your thoughts and feelings about that upcoming experience. What obstacles do you expect to encounter? What can you do to try to avoid them? What did you learn from the previous role-play sessions that you want to carry with you into the role-play focused on thoughts?

7. If you have already done the practice group exercise associated with this chapter, discuss your reactions to that experience. What was the most beneficial aspect of that experience for you? What was the most challenging or uncomfortable aspect of the experience? How did this role-play compare with your earlier ones? How can you learn even more from future practice group exercises?

Practice Group Exercise: *Reflections of Meaning and Using Cognitive Strategies*

Divide into your practice groups as described in an earlier chapter. The practice group exercise presented here will help you gain experience in using reflections of meaning and supplementing these interventions with some of the specific strategies designed to help people express and modify their thoughts.

Preparing for the Role-Play

Once again, you should have a tape recorder and a blank tape with you. Ideally, you have already reviewed one or more recordings of your previous role-play sessions and have some ideas about ways you might improve your skills.

As you approach this next role-play session, keep in mind the strengths you have already demonstrated in previous sessions and improvements you want to make in your work. Reviewing the Assessment of Progress forms you have already completed will help you identify one or two areas in your work that would benefit from some improvement. List those here so that they are fresh in your mind:

1. _____

2. _____

Once again, select an issue or experience to present when you are in the client role. For this exercise, select an event that was a meaningful experience for you, one in which you learned important information about yourself and made some significant choices and changes in your life. You may build or expand on issues you presented in previous sessions or you may choose to introduce a new topic.

Role-Play Exercise

The goals of this role-play are as follows:

- **Using reflections of meaning.** As discussed earlier in this chapter, helping people grasp the meaning that experiences and interactions have for them is important in enabling them to become more aware of their thoughts, assess the validity of those thoughts, and modify any distorted thoughts. One of your tasks for this session is to deliberately make extensive use of reflections of meaning in order to help the client attain a deeper understanding of the important experience or situation that he or she presents. Of course, you also will use other interventions, particularly reflections of feeling, open questions, and summarization.
- **Using a specific cognitive intervention to reinforce helpful thoughts.** After you have listened to the client, describe the experience and what helped that person gain insight into the meaning of that experience. Conclude your role-play session by helping your client to develop an affirmation or an anchor to reinforce the positive learning and awareness that occurred in the session.
- **Summarizing the session.** Wrap up the session with a brief summary, no more than two or three sentences in length. Be sure to check out the accuracy of your summary with the client.

Time Schedule

The role-play session presented in this chapter is more straightforward than many of the exercises presented in earlier chapters of this book. Consequently, it will require less time. Allow 10 to 15 minutes for each role-play. In addition, be sure that 5 to 10 minutes is allocated for feedback to each person in the clinician role.

Assessment of Progress Form 8

1. **Building on the skills you have already learned.** What use did you make of the following skills, learned in previous chapters? How effective was your use of those interventions?

   - Open and closed questions
   - Accents, restatements, and paraphrases
   - Reflections of feeling
   - Attentive body language

2. **Using reflection of meaning.** If possible, identify two or three examples of your use of reflection of meaning. How successful were these interventions in helping the client clarify the meaning or importance of an experience? What contributed to, or limited, the success of these interventions?

3. Use the following rating scale to assess the overall success of your role-play session, focusing primarily on your reflections of meaning:

- **Extremely helpful:** Moves counseling in a productive direction; promotes self-awareness, new learning, or positive changes.
- **Moderately helpful:** Moves counseling in a productive direction, but does not clearly lead to greater self-awareness, new learning, or positive changes.
- **Neutral:** Neither contributes to the treatment goals nor harms the therapeutic process.
- **Moderately harmful:** Detracts somewhat from the counseling process or alliance.
- **Extremely harmful:** Damaging to the treatment process or therapeutic alliance.

4. **Using affirmations to reinforce helpful thoughts.** Were you able to help the client develop an affirmation to clarify and reinforce the positive impact the experience had on that person? What difficulties, if any, did you encounter in helping the person develop an affirmation? What, if anything, might you have done to improve that process?

5. **Using summarizing to wrap up the session.** How successful was your summarization? How might it have been improved? Did you remember to check out its accuracy with the client?

Personal Journal Questions

1. Listen to the tape recording of your role-play. Respond to the following questions about your role-play:

- What did you perceive to be the strengths of your role-play?
- Did you notice any improvement over your previous role-play sessions? If so, what did you do to effect that improvement and what was the nature of the improvement?
- What areas needing improvement did you notice? What can you do differently in your next session to effect that improvement?
- Did you prefer to use reflections of meaning or reflections of feeling? How do you explain your preference?

2. Reflect back on the past few days. List the first three events you experienced during that time that come into your mind. Then write a reflection of meaning for each of those events.

3. Identify a decision you need to make. Prepare a decision-making grid similar to the one presented in Table 8-1 on page **269** to help you determine the best decision.

4. Prepare a mind map, focused on a concern in your life. Once you have completed the map, write briefly about the information that the map provided and how you might use that information in your life.

5. Write down an example of an affirmation or self-talk that might contribute to your own personal and professional growth.

SUMMARY

This chapter presented reflection of meaning as an important strategy for promoting awareness of thoughts. Additional strategies included in this chapter were identifying a focal concern, problem solving, information giving, decision making, positive self-talk, affirmations, anchoring, reframing, thought stopping, meditation and mindfulness, journal writing, and mind mapping. All of these strategies are useful in helping people to clarify their thoughts and take more control over their lives.

The next two chapters will focus on skills designed to help people describe, assess, and change their actions. A 10-step process to facilitate behavior change is presented that includes information on determining a baseline, goal setting and contracts, using rewards and consequences, addressing obstacles to change, promoting and tracking progress, and teaching change strategies. Emphasis will be placed on useful approaches to behavior change, including reinforcement, suggestions, directives, challenges, between-session tasks, empowerment, behavioral rehearsal, and carefully chosen language, along with other skills to promote progress.

PART 5

Chapter 9

USING FUNDAMENTAL SKILLS TO IDENTIFY, ASSESS, AND CHANGE ACTIONS AND BEHAVIORS

OVERVIEW

The previous six chapters presented skills primarily reflecting the first three components of the BETA model: background, emotions, and thoughts. This chapter and Chapter 10 focus on skills linked to the fourth component of the BETA model, actions and behaviors. This chapter pays some attention to strategies that are useful in effecting behavior change. However, the next chapter provides an expanded and more detailed picture of strategies that are useful to both clients and clinicians who are collaborating to help clients change their harmful and undesirable behaviors. Clinicians also can use many of these strategies to modify their own unhelpful behaviors.

LEARNING GOALS

As a result of reading this chapter and completing the exercises throughout, you can expect to accomplish the following:

- Understand the importance of actions and behaviors in people's lives and in the treatment process.

- Acquire the ability to help people identify their harmful behaviors.
- Become able to develop an effective behavioral change plan to use with a broad range of people and behaviors.

SKILLS TO BE LEARNED

Six fundamental skills designed to help clinicians and clients identify, assess, and change actions are presented in this chapter:

- Describing undesirable behaviors and determining the severity of those behaviors via a baseline
- Setting clear and realistic goals
- Identifying and removing obstacles to goal achievement
- Making effective use of rewards and consequences
- Developing a contract for behavior change
- Tracking and assessing progress

IMPORTANCE OF ACTIONS AND BEHAVIORS

Although people can often conceal their backgrounds, emotions, and thoughts, actions are more difficult to hide. They are often overt and observable by others and give a message about who people are. We probably respond more to people's actions than we do to their backgrounds, emotions, and thoughts, although of course all four elements combine to make us who we are.

On the day I began this chapter, I made a point to note actions that caught my attention en route to and during time I spent in a restaurant. I saw many actions and behaviors; some seemed positive while others appeared negative to me (although I had no knowledge of the determinants of any of these behaviors). Those that seemed negative included:

- A woman who was driving too fast in a residential area
- Two people loudly arguing in a restaurant
- A woman dining alone who consumed an entire bottle of wine, in addition to several mixed drinks
- A man who spanked his child who had crawled under the restaurant table

I also saw examples of what I viewed as positive behaviors:

- A woman helping her parents, one in a wheelchair and one in a walker, have dinner in the restaurant
- The waiter who tried to cheer up a crying child
- A large group of people celebrating the birthday of a friend
- A man engrossed in a book I had enjoyed

As I watched these people and took note of their behaviors, I began to form impressions of them. Of course, my impressions may have been inaccurate, but nevertheless people's actions typically have a great impact on our initial perceptions of them.

In addition, actions themselves usually are the primary determinants of how people lead their lives. How we perform at work, how we communicate love and disapproval to our families, what food and drink we ingest, and how we spend our leisure time all shape who we are, our relationships, and the direction of our lives. Actions, then, are an important focus of our lives and of counseling and psychotherapy.

Advantages of Focusing Treatment on Actions

Focusing on actions in treatment has many advantages (Seligman, 2001):

- People's presenting concerns often target problematic actions such as procrastination, overeating, harmful use of drugs or alcohol, outbursts of anger, and social withdrawal.
- Because changing actions is often people's primary goal in seeking treatment, they are usually willing to discuss their behaviors. In contrast, clients sometimes view discussion of background, emotions, and even thoughts as intrusive and irrelevant to their immediate issues.
- Most actions can readily be described, evaluated, and counted or measured.
- As a result, people rarely have difficulty establishing goals that focus on behavior change.
- Effecting improvement in one behavior often generalizes and facilitates people's efforts to modify other undesirable behaviors.
- Considerable research supports the effectiveness of treatment emphasizing behavior change strategies (Division 12 Task Force, 1996).

DEVELOPMENT OF BEHAVIOR THERAPY

Important research on effective ways to modify actions has been going on for more than 100 years. Many of the early and leading researchers in psychology, such as B. F. Skinner (1969), Ivan Pavlov (1927), John Watson (1925), and Joseph Wolpe (1969), focused their work on behavior change strategies. Prominent modern theoreticians and clinicians who have contributed to our understanding of how to promote behavior change include William Glasser (2000) and Robert Wubbolding (2000) (reality therapy), Donald Meichenbaum (1985, 1993) (cognitive-behavioral therapy), Steve de Shazer (1991), and Bill O'Hanlon and Michele Weiner-Davis (1989) (solution-focused therapy).

Solution-based or solution-focused brief therapy, in fact, is currently one of the most dynamic and efficient treatment approaches available to clinicians. Focusing on a solvable, usually behavioral, complaint, solution-based clinicians establish measurable goals, design interventions, suggest strategic tasks, and anticipate rapid improvement. Although these clinicians draw on a broad range of treatment approaches in formulating their interventions and tasks, they are fundamentally

B. F. Skinner   William Glasser

behavioral in orientation. The hallmarks of brief solution-based or solution-focused brief therapy can be seen in the behavioral skills presented in this chapter.

In addition, theoreticians and practitioners who emphasize cognitive therapy such as Aaron Beck (1995), Albert Ellis (Ellis, 2003; Ellis & Dryden, 1997), and Arnold Lazarus (1989, 1997) (multimodal therapy) also have added greatly to our knowledge of ways to change actions. The combination of cognitive and behavioral treatment interventions is often used in counseling and psychotherapy and makes a powerful treatment package.

DESCRIBING AND MEASURING PROBLEMATIC ACTIONS AND BEHAVIORS

Even when people seek treatment to change harmful and undesirable behaviors, they often lack a clear picture of those actions, their severity, and how to change them. Following are ten typical examples of how people describe their self-destructive behaviors when they seek treatment:

1. I watch too much television. I need to get out and be with people more.
2. I weigh 260 pounds and my doctor has told me to lose weight.
3. I drink too much and my wife says it is hurting our marriage.
4. I'm the only Asian and Buddhist in my company. People seem to ignore me when I talk, so I've just stopped talking. I don't know if they're ignoring me because of how I look or my ideas or something else, but I've just withdrawn from everyone at work.
5. I don't get any exercise and need to change that.

To treat or change harmful behaviors, the specific problem must first be recognized

6. My roommate says I'm too easy, that I party with any guy who comes along. I don't really enjoy it, but that's what guys expect.
7. I don't have any friends at school and don't know how to make friends. I feel so lonely.
8. I procrastinate too much.
9. My teachers say I bully people and always sound mean and angry. I just like to hang with my friends and have some fun. We all do the same things; it's just how we are.
10. My wife had a heart attack two months ago and barely survived. Now I'm afraid to leave her. What if she has another heart attack? She says other people can stay with her and she can even spend time alone and maybe she's right, but I'm afraid to even go to the grocery store.

These statements are all good starting points and can help the clinician and client describe and measure the unwanted actions. However, these presenting problems, in their current form, are too vague to allow client and clinician to clarify unwanted behaviors, establish specific goals, and develop procedures that are likely to effect positive change. In addition, some of these people sound reluctant to make changes. In order to lay the groundwork for changing unhelpful behaviors, the actions first must be described in concrete, detailed, and measurable ways.

Consider the following revisions of some of the presenting problems previously listed:

1. I watch at least four hours of television each day. I see friends no more than once a week. This has gone on since I got divorced six years ago.

2. I consume approximately 3000 calories per day and am 60 pounds over a healthy weight for my height, build, and age.

3. I drink at least 12 beers almost every evening. I have done this since I was in college. I spend no more than 2 hours a week in enjoyable activities with my wife and children.

4. We have weekly office-wide and work group meetings. I haven't spoken up at a meeting in at least 3 months, and I expressed my ideas in my work group only twice in the past 3 months.

5. I walk to and from the parking lot at work and I take the stairs whenever I can. However, I don't get any formal exercise and would like to establish an exercise program.

What changes do you see between the first statement of each problem behavior and the second statement? Notice that in the second series of statements, the behaviors are described in specific terms, with numbers used whenever possible to indicate the duration, frequency, or severity of the unwanted actions.

Now it's your turn to revise the vague descriptions for the last five statements initially presented. Try to craft behavioral descriptions that clearly specify the nature and frequency of the undesirable behaviors so that they are amenable to measurement and change:

6. _____

7. _____

8. _____

9. _____

10. _____

Establishing a Baseline

Helping people describe and assess their unwanted behaviors as specifically as possible is an essential first step in establishing a baseline. However, few people know how many calories they consume, how many hours they spend watching television, or perhaps even how much alcohol they consume. Some data gathering is usually needed to establish an accurate baseline reflecting the current frequency, duration, and intensity at which the behavior is manifested.

Sometimes obtaining baseline information is a relatively easy and straightforward task. However, at other times, it is more challenging and complicated. Let's look at some of those difficult situations before we focus on ways to establish a baseline.

Discrepancies Between Clinician and Client Viewpoints   Establishing a mutually agreed-on description of problematic behavior can be difficult. Clinician and client do not always concur on what actions need to be changed. The people reflected in items 9 and 10 in the previous examples may be unwilling to change their behaviors and may have a different perspective on their behavior than the clinician and other people in their lives. Similar issues and discrepancies are reflected in the following examples.

Examples of Differing Client and Clinician Viewpoints

- Katie is a gifted student who has a D average in her high school courses because she has been cutting classes and doing no homework. Her clinician would like to see her achieve *A*'s and *B*'s, grades that are commensurate with her intelligence. Katie, on the other hand, would be satisfied with *C*'s. However, she does recognize that she must attend classes regularly and is willing to do the homework she absolutely must do to pass her courses.
- Lavinia sought help for career-related problems. Over the course of her sessions, she disclosed to her clinician that she frequently spanks and slaps her children to control their behavior. Her clinician views this as harmful and possibly even illegal behavior and wants Lavinia to learn other ways to discipline her children. However, Lavinia states that she was slapped and spanked as a child, with no adverse effects, and sees no reason to change the way she treats her children.
- Curt has been drinking heavily for at least five years. He has received several DWI (driving while intoxicated) citations and had his driver's license revoked for long periods of time. He entered treatment at the urging of his wife and does not want his marriage to end, but is unwilling to change his consumption of alcohol. His clinician believes that Curt needs to stop drinking alcohol.

These situations are challenging for the clinician. Each one presents a somewhat different dilemma. Katie is the one who is willing to make some change in her problematic behaviors. If her clinician insists on imposing his standards on her, Katie will probably leave treatment and may make no positive changes. The best approach in working with Katie, then, is probably to begin treatment by establishing those goals that seem reasonable to Katie. Perhaps, with some success at school, her motivation will increase and she will subsequently be willing to revise her goals and aim toward *A*'s and *B*'s. Even if that does not happen, Katie has agreed to improve her school attendance and achievement in an effort to graduate from high school, and that is progress.

Lavinia and Curt, on the other hand, are not willing to work on the problems identified by their clinician. Although it may be a matter of opinion whether a bright student has the responsibility to fulfill her academic potential, the laws, as well as public opinion, have determined that Lavinia and Curt's behaviors are harmful and in need of change. Their clinicians, then, cannot simply ignore their problematic behaviors and focus on other goals and issues.

If, indeed, Lavinia's behavior constitutes child abuse, her clinician should inform her of this and may need to report her behavior to the authorities. The clinician should exert great effort to engage Lavinia in changing her treatment of her children, even if her motivation is extrinsic (avoiding legal consequences) rather than intrinsic. Two guidelines probably are important in this process:

- **Recognize and respect the impact of people's backgrounds, role models, and early learning.** Lavinia, herself, was raised with physical punishment. The therapist may gently explore the feelings that Lavinia had during and after being punished as a child, but should avoid discrediting Lavinia's positive feelings toward her caregivers and the way they disciplined her. If she can trust her clinician and feel accepted and supported, she may be able to verbalize some of the anger, fear, and pain she felt when she experienced physical punishment and can then recognize that her children probably have similar reactions to her discipline.

- **Assess the effectiveness of the undesirable behavior** (Lavinia's discipline). The clinician can explore with Lavinia whether her treatment of her children yields the results she desires in terms of their behavior, their relationship with Lavinia, how they interact with other people, and their overall development. Again, with the support and guidance of her clinician, Lavinia may recognize that, although her children may misbehave less at home, they also may have problematic relationships both in and outside of the home and act out increasingly at school. In addition, her clinician can gently provide some information on the emotional impact of physical punishment and the effect it often has on the parent–child relationship.

Although Curt's behavior is not immediately reportable to the legal authorities, the clinician cannot ethically agree to Curt's goals in treatment: Improve his marriage while continuing his misuse of alcohol. That seems like an impossible goal to achieve. Probably the best approach for the clinician is to inform Curt of this, to help him understand the impact his alcohol use has on his family relationships, and to encourage him to set some small goals that address his drinking. Even if Curt is only willing to avoid drinking and driving, that might provide a starting point to treatment, hopefully leading to eventual abstinence. But if Curt is completely unwilling to discuss his alcohol use, extensive treatment focused only on Curt's marriage does not seem like a viable approach. Several additional guidelines emerge from this example:

- **Encourage people to try out small changes or temporary changes as an experiment and then assess their impact.** If Curt agrees not to drive while under the influence of alcohol and succeeds in that effort, his accomplishment may impress his wife and lead to some improvement in their marriage. In addition, even a small success may be empowering to Curt and may encourage him to expand his goals.
- **Clinicians should look for compromises between what they see as ideal and what clients are willing to do.** Imposing clinicians' ideas and values on clients is unlikely to be successful or to result in lasting change. Unless the client's behavior presents a danger, clinicians should support the client in taking small steps toward goal achievement, steps the client is willing to take. Changes are more likely to be effective when a person is motivated and self-directed than when changes are made under duress.
- **Find another important and realistic goal.** Working on Curt's marriage while he continues to misuse alcohol seems destined for failure. In addition, agreeing to collaborate with clients in addressing goals that are unrealistic can be counterproductive. That leads clients to hope for a positive outcome and believe that one is possible. When it does not happen, they may lose

confidence in treatment and feel like a failure. Clinicians are likely to be of more help to clients if they suggest different or smaller goals that are likely to be achieved. For example, Curt might be willing to focus on improving his parenting skills. Again, successes generalize. Helping Curt recognizes that he can make positive changes—by improving the way he communicates with his children and by building a strong therapeutic alliance with his therapist—may pave the way for him to address the more challenging issues of his use of alcohol and his marital difficulties.

The Data-Gathering Process and Its Drawbacks   Let's assume that clinician and client have a meeting of the minds on the undesirable behavior. Even then, establishing a baseline can be difficult. For most behaviors, a period of self-observation and data gathering is needed before an accurate baseline is determined and goals are established. Data gathering may seem to some people to be a tedious and time-consuming process, and it may raise some resistance and negative feelings as people take a hard look at the severity of their unwanted behaviors. They may have underestimated the seriousness of the problem and may feel overwhelmed, discouraged, and ashamed as they tally their actions.

Clinicians can help people gather the information they need to establish a baseline by reducing these barriers. The following strategies can facilitate the process of data gathering:

- **Help people anticipate any negative feelings that can arise.** Although it may seem counterproductive to introduce negative reactions that people are not yet experiencing, in reality preparing people to address troubling feelings that are likely to arise is generally helpful. Then, if they do experience those feelings, they are not caught off guard and can cope with the feelings more effectively. If they do not experience those negative feelings, they can feel especially proud of themselves.
- **Formulate a plan with the client specifying exactly how the behavior will be measured.** This entails determining the following three pieces of information:
  1. **Unit of measure:** Generally, behaviors can be measured in terms of duration, frequency, or intensity. Behaviors such as time per day watching television, time spent completing homework, minutes of exercise per week, and hours of sleep per night can be described in terms of duration. Actions such as the number of beers consumed per day, the number of conversations with another person per day, and the number of times per week someone becomes angry can be measured in terms of frequency. Level of depression or anxiety, degree of rage, and level of self-esteem are variables that can be measured in terms of intensity. This can be done either via a standardized self-report measure such as the Beck Depression Inventory or the Beck Anxiety Inventory or via an informal 0 to 10 rating scale of almost any variable. Although such a scale is not highly reliable or valid, most people find such scales useful in measuring any construct that cannot be counted such as craving for food, level of pain, and strength of social skills. For example, a client may be asked to assess his level of self-esteem

on a 0 to 10 scale in which 0 represents no self-esteem at all and 10 represents the highest possible self-esteem.

2. **Duration of the measurement process:** Determining how many beers or conversations a person has in one day may not be very revealing. However, if a record of those behaviors is kept over a week or two, the data are likely to be more meaningful and reflective of the person's typical behavior. Client and clinician should decide for how long the client will keep track of the target behavior. When determining this time frame, consider both the client's motivation to keep track of the undesirable behavior and the amount of time that is probably needed to obtain an accurate assessment.

3. **Method of recording information:** Two aspects of the process are important: accuracy and ease of recording. Suggesting that a person keep a record of how many sentences he exchanged with a spouse may yield interesting information; however, the most likely outcome is that the person will quickly abandon the recording process because it is so cumbersome. On the other hand, suggesting that, at the end of the week, a person lists all food consumed during that week may entail a relatively brief recording process but memory lapses will probably result in inaccurate information. Clinicians and clients can collaborate in finding a balance between the need for accuracy and the need for an easy system of recording. An accurate baseline is necessary for realistic and meaningful goal setting and subsequent effective use of behavior change strategies.

ESTABLISHING GOALS

Once a baseline has been established, clients are probably ready to establish some goals. Establishing appropriate goals or objectives is an important step in the treatment process, whether the focus is on background, emotions, thoughts, or actions.

Goals reflect the destination of treatment and, as with any journey, the treatment process will be difficult if not impossible if the destination is unknown or unreachable.

Goals that are too ambitious can be discouraging and can sabotage the treatment process. On the other hand, goals that are too easy can limit progress. Given the choice, goals that are too easy are preferable to those that are too difficult; the process of achieving even small, simple objectives can be empowering and can increase people's optimism and motivation to tackle more challenging goals.

Hallmarks of Sound Goals

Sound goals have the following eight characteristics (de Shazer, 1991):

- Important and relevant to the client
- Stated in positive terms
- Clear, concrete, and specific
- Small and incremental

- Measurable
- Realistic and within client's control
- Involving application and effort on the part of the client
- Leading to new learning, skills, or action

Let's use the case of Yoram, age 37, to illustrate the process of formulating sound goals. Yoram immigrated to the United States from Israel about a year ago. He had strong technical skills and had little difficulty finding employment as a web page designer. Although his command of English was relatively good, he felt uncomfortable in his new environment, had difficulty initiating conversations, and had not made any friends since his arrival in the United States. The occasional social contacts he had were with others who had immigrated from Israel and he had difficulty meeting single people about his own age. Baseline information indicated that, after work, Yoram spent approximately 4 hours a day watching television and "surfing the net." He spent most of his time, both at work and away from work, looking at images on a screen.

Yoram was unhappy with this situation and sought treatment to help him make a change. Yoram and his therapist collaborated in the development of the following initial goal statement:

> By one week from today, I will initiate conversations with two people with whom I have not previously had a conversation and will write in my date book the time, place, and person with whom I conversed for each of these interactions. I also will obtain information on one leisure activity of interest to me.

This goal statement met all eight criteria listed previously. It addressed Yoram's need for more rewarding social and leisure activities and was, therefore, *important and relevant* to him. The statement was *positive*, indicating what Yoram would do rather than what he would not do. It was *clear, concrete, and specific,* indicating how many people he would talk to, how many leisure activities he would investigate, and by when these goals would be accomplished. The statement reflected *small and incremental* goals; this initial step would not resolve Yoram's difficulties, but it probably would help him start moving in his desired direction. Future goals would build on this initial goal statement, enabling Yoram to create a more rewarding lifestyle. The goals were *measurable;* the record-keeping process and the information on a leisure activity provided evidence of whether Yoram achieved his goals. Yoram agreed that the activities specified in his goal statement were *within his control* and that he was *capable of reaching the goals*. Finally, *new learning and skills* would emerge from this process. Yoram would identify a potential leisure activity and gather information about that pastime. Discussion with his therapist about strategies for initiating and maintaining conversations and the results of Yoram's efforts to initiate conversations would help him acquire effective skills for beginning conversations.

Having both short-term and long-term goals is helpful in facilitating behavioral change. The long-term goals keep people focused on future possibilities and give them a vision of a different and more rewarding life. However, if they had only long-term goals, months or even years might pass before those goals were achieved, perhaps leading to discouragement and hopelessness. The short-term goals counteract this by offering an opportunity for rapid success and reinforcement. This can be instrumental in maintaining people's motivation and encouraging them to sustain their efforts to make positive changes.

Yoram also established the following long-term goal statement, in addition to his short-term goals:

> By one year from now, I would like to have two people I view as good friends who I see or talk to at least every other week. I would like to have two enjoyable leisure activities in which I participate at least twice a month. I would like to watch no more than 10 hours of television per week.

Yoram's long-term goals also met the previous criteria, except that they presented an ultimate objective rather than small and incremental steps.

Once Yoram met his short-term goals, new short-terms goal statements would be developed, bringing him closer and closer to his long-term goal. For example, a second goal statement, agreed on by Yoram and his therapist after Yoram achieved what his first short-term goal, might be:

> I will identify and gather information about two more leisure activities of interest to me and will identify a first step I might take to become involved in one of the three leisure activities I have explored. I will initiate two more conversations with people with whom I have previously had little or no interaction. I will telephone one person with whom I have already had some interactions at the synagogue I sometimes attend and suggest we meet for coffee. I will accomplish these goals by 2 weeks from today.

Notice how these goals continue to meet the criteria for effective goals and also build on Yoram's initial goals. He will be moving forward both in his involvement in leisure activities and his interactions with others. His skills will be further enhanced as he and his therapist discuss and practice ways for him to invite someone to get together with him. Obstacles to this process, including Yoram's fear of rejection and the unavailability of the person he planned to call, merit attention, helping Yoram prepare for contingencies and develop resilience.

Reformulating Weak Goals

People often present with goals that need to be reformulated. Perhaps the goals are vague or unrealistic or depend too much on other people for their achievement. Here are some examples of these:

Vague Goals

- I want to feel better about myself.
- I want to have a better social life.
- I want to be more successful in my work.

Unrealistic Goals

- I want to win the lottery or find another way to make lots of money quickly.
- I want to write a book (which I have not yet begun) within one month.
- I don't want to ever yell at my child or lose my temper again.

Goals that Depend on Other People

- I want to be married by the end of the year.
- I want my stepfather to treat me with respect.
- I would like my mother to realize that, even though I have a learning disability, I have accomplished a great deal in my life.

When goals such as these are presented, clinicians should recognize that, even though these goals are not expressed in viable ways, they still reflect clients' wants. Understanding those underlying wants, while working with clients to revise their goal statements, can yield a positive outcome.

Clinicians have many ways of helping people modify their goals, including the following:

- Ask people to describe a time in their lives when they had achieved their goals. Details of that description can be used to formulate specific and realistic goals.
- Ask people to describe other people who have achieved similar goals, how they achieved those goals, and what their lives are like.
- Ask people what they have already done to accomplish their goals. This can clarify the goals, as well as suggest new and more effective strategies for goal achievement.
- Use de Shazer's (1991, p. 131) Miracle Question that asks "Suppose that one night there is a miracle and while you were sleeping, the problem that brought you to therapy is solved. How would you know? What would be different? What will other people notice?" Details of people's responses can lead to development of clearer goals.
- Simply explore with clients how they will know when they have achieved their goals. Such a discussion can yield specific information that is useful when revising vague presenting goals.
- Use the 0 to 10 scale described earlier in this chapter to help establish realistic goals. After people use the scale to establish a baseline, clinicians can ask them to select a number on the scale that realistically reflects how they would like to feel or act. Most people have little difficulty with a scale of this nature and typically are realistic in the numbers they select.
- Clients might identify the first step they would take to achieve their goals, thereby clarifying the nature of those goals and what they are willing to do to accomplish their goals.
- To shift attention from another person to the client, the clinician might say, "I wish we could control your mother's attitudes and behavior, but unfortunately we cannot do that. However, sometimes if you make some changes, she will respond differently and, at least, you will feel that you have tried hard to help her understand you better.

Let's take a closer look at three of the earlier goals statements that need revision. For each one, identify a strategy you might use to help that person develop a more viable goal and write down what that new goal might be. Keep in mind the eight criteria of helpful goals.

Goal 1: I want to have a better social life.

Strategy: _____

Revised goal statement: _____

_____

Goal 2: I don't want to ever yell at my child or lose my temper again.

Strategy: _____

Revised goal statement: _____

_____

Goal 3: I want my stepfather to treat me with respect.

Strategy: _____

Revised goal statement: _____

_____

Examples of Effective Short- and Long-Term Goals

Let's look at some additional goal statements for the clients described earlier in this chapter—Katie, Lavinia, and Curt—on pages **295–297**.

Here are examples of short- and long-term goals that might be appropriate for Katie:

- **Initial short-term goals for Katie:** Katie will attend at least 4 of her 5 classes each day next week. She will spend a total of at least 2 hours studying and completing homework this week, ideally spread out over at least three days. She will keep on her computer a record of her class attendance and her study time.
- **Long-term goals for Katie:** By the next quarter of the academic year, Katie will have at least a C+ average and will pass all of her courses. She will attend all her classes unless she has a legitimate medical reason not to go to school. She will spend an average of one hour per school day in studying and homework.

You may think that Katie's short-term goal is too modest and that she should immediately begin to attend all of her classes. Of course, that would be ideal. However, Katie's motivation to change is weak. Phasing in her goals and identifying goals that are acceptable to her are important steps in strengthening her motivation to change and increasing the likelihood that she will actually follow through on plans to meet her goals. Imposing goals on Katie may lead her to mistrust her clinician and view the clinician as just one more adult who misunderstands her. That probably will result in Katie leaving treatment prematurely, making little or no effort to change, and perhaps even deceiving her clinician about her success in reaching her goals.

Here is your opportunity to practice goal setting. Write short- and long-term goals for Lavinia and Curt. Be sure that each goal meets the eight criteria for effective goals, presented earlier in this chapter.

Initial short-term goals for Lavinia: _____

_____

Long-term goals for Lavinia: _____

_____

Initial short-term goals for Curt: _____

_____

Long-term goals for Curt: _____

_____

Sound goals represent a collaboration between client and clinician. Together, the two formulate the goals, fine-tune them, and agree to them. Making sure that clients establish sound goals that meet the eight criteria, believe they can succeed in reaching their goals, and are willing to commit to working toward their goals is essential to a positive outcome.

Although goals receive particular attention in treatment systems emphasizing behavioral change, establishing sound goals is important regardless of the clinician's theoretical orientation or the nature of the desired change. Only when clinician and client have clearly identified desirable treatment outcomes can they plan change strategies that are likely to succeed, assess progress, determine whether interventions need to be modified, and decide when treatment is complete. Goals have become an essential component of most current approaches to treatment.

CREATING A BEHAVIOR CHANGE CONTRACT

Once goals are formulated, they should be written down. They can then be compared to the eight criteria for sound goals and reviewed with the client. Modifications in goals can be made at that time, if needed. This paves the way for creating a behavior change contract. Developing a contract that specifies when and how people will accomplish their goals is the next important step in effecting behavior change.

When formulating behavioral change contracts with clients, clinicians should address the following:

- Determine exactly what effective actions clients will do to move toward their goals.
- Identify and remove obstacles.
- Build rewards and perhaps also consequences into the contract.
- Plan ways to measure and track changes and new actions.
- Identify helpful strategies to facilitate change (this will be discussed in depth in Chapter 10).
- Ensure the client's commitment to change.
- Solidify and affirm the contract.

Determining Effective Actions

Before deciding the actions people will take to begin to make desired changes, review the two important pieces of information already established with them: the baseline or current status of the problem and the short- and long-term goal or outcome people hope to achieve through their efforts. The baseline and the goals can be thought of as the beginning and end of a journey.

The purpose of the contract is to make that journey happen so that people move from baseline to goals. Whether they want to end or curtail undesirable behaviors such as misuse of drugs or alcohol, whether they want to modify a pattern of inaction or ineffective action such as avoiding interpersonal contact, or whether they want to initiate new behaviors such as exercising or completing homework, the treatment approach follows the same steps. Of course, the desired behaviors, the obstacles to the interventions, and the rewards all may differ.

Determining effective actions should be done collaboratively, with both client and clinician participating in that process. Although clients should take the lead as much as possible, clinicians should play an active role in helping people formulate sound and realistic steps that they are likely to accomplish as they move forward toward their goals. To make the process as clear and specific as possible, the steps should be linked to a schedule.

Let's look at how this might be accomplished with Katie, introduced earlier in this chapter.

> *Clinician:* Katie, we discovered that last week you did no homework at all and cut 12 of the 25 classes you had during the week. Your midterm evaluation indicates that you are in danger of failing three of your courses and receiving *D*'s in the other two. (This reviews the baseline.) You have decided that you want to make a change in your homework and attendance so that you can get at least *C*'s in all of your courses by the end of the quarter. (This reviews the goals.)
>
> *Katie:* Yeah, I suppose I'd better do that. I don't want to have to go to summer school or repeat ninth grade. And it will get my parents off my back if I do better in school.
>
> *Clinician:* So you are willing to make some changes. What do you think would be a reasonable first step?
>
> *Katie:* I guess I just need to go to all my classes and do the homework.
>
> *Clinician:* Yes, that would be ideal. But that's a pretty drastic change from what you have been doing. What if we slow down the process a little. How much time do you think it would take to complete all of your homework?
>
> *Katie:* I'd guess maybe an hour, hour and a half, each school day. I do my homework pretty quickly once I decide to get started.
>
> *Clinician:* So that's the eventual goal. How would it be to plan on doing at least 30 minutes of homework each school day? If you decide to do more on some of the days, that will move you toward your goal more quickly, but I'm concerned about too big a change being discouraging for you.
>
> *Katie:* OK, I get the message. That makes sense. I'll do at least 30 minutes of homework Monday through Friday.
>
> *Clinician:* When would be the best time for you to spend on homework?
>
> *Katie:* Most of my friends have after-school activities, but I'm not doing any sports or lessons this semester. I guess I should come home and do the homework right after school, about 3:30, and get it out of the way. Then I can relax for awhile before dinner and have the evening to talk with my friends and write in my online journal.
>
> *Clinician:* Before we talk about a plan for attending class, let's decide how you can keep track of when and how much time you put into your homework.

Katie: I could keep track of it on the computer. I get on the computer every night, so I'll just list homework time on the calendar I have on the computer.
Clinician: So you have a plan for tracking your homework time. Now let's talk about going to classes....

As you can see from the dialogue, the clinician helped Katie establish a reasonable first step for beginning to do her homework. They found a way to help her move forward that would hopefully empower and encourage her rather than demoralize her.

Identifying and Removing Obstacles

The next step in the process of developing a behavioral change contract is identifying and removing obstacles. Potential obstacles to goal attainment should be identified and explored and strategies developed to prevent those obstacles from getting in the way of a successful outcome.

To elicit potential obstacles, Katie's clinician asked her to imagine what might interfere with her homework plan and also to describe what had gotten in the way of her completing her homework in the past. Katie identified two possible obstacles:

- She may not know what the homework assignment is, either because she had not been in class when the assignment was given or she neglected to write down the assignment.
- Her friends might want to get together right after school on days when they had no activities scheduled.

Working together, Katie and her clinician developed several ways to remove these obstacles. Katie developed a convenient place to record her assignments and identified at least two people she could contact if she had missed class or was unclear about an assignment. In addition, her teachers had websites where they generally posted each day's homework assignments and Katie agreed to become familiar with those as soon as possible.

To address the problem of wanting to spend afternoon time with friends, Katie and her clinician agreed that she would complete 2 hours of homework per week, spread out over at least 3 days, giving her some leeway in her plans. In addition, Katie agreed that, if she missed more than one day of homework, she would spend a half hour right after dinner on her schoolwork.

Another example is the situation of Yoram, the man from Israel who was having difficulty building friendships and getting involved in leisure activities. Although Yoram could identify several leisure activities he had enjoyed in Israel, he did not know how to obtain information about those activities in his new community. Following guidelines for information giving discussed in the previous chapter, the clinician provided Yoram with the names of a hiking club and a community recreation center that might offer the leisure activities he had in mind. Yoram and his therapist also identified several people with whom he might initiate conversations and planned some opening comments he could use to begin conversations with them.

Clinicians have a variety of strategies they can use to prevent or eliminate obstacles to people's successful achievement of their plans. Providing people with needed skills and sources of information are often useful in removing obstacles. In addition, planned steps should be under the client's control and should not be dependent on chance or on another person. For example, "I will inform my supervisor about the many projects I have successfully completed, the next time he criticizes me" is not a sound plan. This links performance of the desired actions to the supervisor's behavior and takes it out of the control of the client. A better plan would be "I will schedule a meeting with my supervisor this week to fill him in on the many projects I have completed."

Some clinicians may be apprehensive that focusing on barriers to goal achievement may seem negative and discouraging. On the contrary, it generally empowers people to have ways they can overcome challenges to their goals and increases the likelihood that they will succeed in reaching those goals.

Obstacles to goal attainment can seem particularly insurmountable for people who have experienced long-standing oppression and victimization. Examples might include people who are gay or lesbian, people from ethnic minority groups, people with physical limitations, and people living in abusive or impoverished situations. People like these may be highly motivated to change their behaviors and improve their lives, but may not know how or may feel unable to circumvent the barriers facing them. Clinicians need to collaborate with such clients to make a careful and realistic assessment of the obstacles they face. The use of community resources and support systems, along with the establishment of extremely small goals that take into account the obstacles, can help to break down barriers for these clients, provide them with resources and needed tools, and help them feel more empowered. (Clinicians may also want to address these obstacles on another level via involvement in governmental or social action programs to reduce some of these obstacles.)

Rewards and Consequences

When people make progress toward their goals, that progress will be even more meaningful and motivating to them if it is reinforced or rewarded in some way. Ideally, the chosen reward should be something that will promote further progress. For example, rewarding Yoram's success in achieving his goals with an extra hour of watching television would be counterproductive; on the other hand, treating himself to a new pair of hiking shoes would not only reinforce his accomplishments but would continue to build on those accomplishments.

Rewards should be items or experiences that are personally meaningful to the client. In addition, rewards must be realistic. Yoram might be able to afford a new pair of shoes to celebrate successful achievement of his first short-term goal, but it would not make sense for him to buy a new pair of shoes every week that he reaches his goals. More modest rewards that contributed to his overall goals would need to be established, perhaps a dinner at a special restaurant that would separate him from his television and offer him some interaction with other people.

Rewards can take many forms and need not be material or costly. For Katie, rewards probably will automatically result from her efforts. Her grades will improve and she is likely to receive more praise and approval from her parents and teachers. With Katie's permission, her counselor might contact her parents and teachers, fill them in on Katie's plans, and suggest they recognize and praise her successes. In general, rewards serve as better motivators than negative consequences or punishments. Rewards are more likely to enhance mood, promote optimism and feelings of empowerment, strengthen the therapeutic alliance, and encourage people to work even harder at the next step in their plan. However, consequences do sometimes have a place in behavioral contracting.

Particularly useful is identification of natural or logical consequences. For example, Yoram recognized that if he rarely went outdoors, obtained little exercise, and had few leisure activities, he would probably become less attractive and interesting to others. On the other hand, if he resumed the regular hiking he had enjoyed in Israel and developed additional leisure activities, he would automatically become more physically fit and attractive and have more to talk about with others. Helping people consider the logical consequences of both their current and their desired behaviors can be helpful in encouraging their effort and progress.

Punishments are rarely used in the clinical setting, primarily because they can impair people's self-esteem and create a negative therapeutic environment. However, occasionally, rewards are not powerful enough to change behavior and the addition of some planned negative consequences can be beneficial. For example, Mimi had tried many different strategies to stop smoking with little success. What mattered most to her was the welfare of animals; she was horrified by thoughts of hunting animals for their fur. To motivate herself to stop smoking, she decided that every time she smoked a cigarette, she would put 25 cents into a jar. Each time $5 was accumulated in the jar, she would send a donation to an organization designed to protect the rights of hunters. After painfully sending off a few checks, Mimi finally got control of her smoking, in part because of her love for animals. Although negative consequences have a place in treatment, these should be carefully determined so that they are not shaming or forced on the client but rather have been chosen by client and clinician working in collaboration to enhance the treatment process.

Measuring and Tracking New Actions

To assess progress, clients should keep a record of their efforts toward goal achievement. Only in this way can clinicians determine the success of the plans and whether they need revision. Although some people enjoy the process of documenting their progress, others find it annoying and often forget to keep track of their change efforts. Here, too, clinicians must work collaboratively with their clients to determine the best way for each person to measure and keep track of actions.

The baseline provides a starting point for determining how to track change. It suggests the unit of measure that is appropriate (e.g., time spent, calories consumed, cigarettes smoked, conversations initiated, hours slept, days on time, number of tantrums) and at least one approach to recording that information. Through conversation, clinicians can help people decide whether they would prefer to record information on a computer or in a notebook, on an occurrence basis or on a daily basis, and other aspects of tracking change.

Again, looking for obstacles to recording information and identifying ways to overcome them is essential in obtaining an accurate record of efforts and progress. Common obstacles include forgetting to record information, not having the computer or notebook available, or being too busy. Establishment of a routine, for instance, setting a specific time and place to record information, can bypass some of these obstacles. Additional strategies can be suggested, based on the person and the reasons that the person has had difficulty following through on record keeping. Of course, clinicians should not be blaming or punitive, but should instead view this as just one more piece of the plan that needs to be developed and refined to help people reach their goals.

Once people begin to gather data on changes in their behavior, that process can become rewarding in itself. People can look forward to recording the changes. Building in social rewards for the process also can be helpful. Clinicians can encourage people to congratulate themselves for their careful recording, notice the progress reflected in their records, and emphasize that careful recording is likely to accelerate progress.

Commitment

The likelihood that people will achieve their goals is higher if they make a public commitment to put forth the effort they need to reach their goals. Sharing the goals with people outside of the therapeutic relationship enhances the likelihood that people will achieve their goals. Particularly helpful is sharing the plans and goals with people who are likely to be helpful and supportive. Clients might consider sharing their behavioral change plans with a few people they trust and asking these people to give them some encouragement and praise, to remind them of their commitment in supportive ways, and to serve as good listeners with whom they can discuss the difficulties and challenges of trying to change behavior.

For example, one of Helen's goals was to prepare more healthy meals and, correspondingly, to spend less time and money in restaurants. She decided that she would begin by cooking dinner for herself and her husband at least twice a week. To facilitate this, she shared her goal with her husband and asked him to support her efforts by helping her clean up after dinner and by suggesting some dishes he would like her to prepare. His assistance and enthusiasm for her cooking, as well as the money they were saving, reinforced Helen's efforts to reach her goal.

Putting It in Writing

Just as people "put it in writing" when they buy a house or enter into a business partnership, so is it valuable to put in writing the goals and behavioral change plans clients have established for themselves. A written contract that clients make with themselves and their clinicians has the following advantages:

- The terms of the agreement are clear.
- People can use the contract as a reminder and as reinforcement of their efforts.
- A written contract facilitates making a public commitment.
- Accomplishing change, as well as identifying the successful and the ineffective ingredients of the change plan, is easier if the initial agreement and change procedures are clearly specified in writing.
- People can refer back to this agreement in the future if they need to make other behavioral changes.

A comprehensive written contract can include all of the elements already discussed in this chapter:

- Baseline
- Sound and specific initial and long-term goals
- New actions, what people will do differently
- Ways to overcome obstacles to change
- Rewards and consequences
- Ways to measure and track changes

The contract might also include suggested strategies for accomplishing the goals. This will be discussed further in the next chapter.

Example 1 of Behavioral Change Contracts   Such a contract might resemble the following, a contract made between Katie, the 15-year-old girl presented on page 295 and her counselor. Although she was a gifted student who hoped to graduate from high school and maybe attend college, Katie had not been attending classes regularly or completing her homework on schedule. As a result her grades had dropped from *A*'s and *B*'s to *D*'s and *F*'s in her first year of high school.

- **Baseline:** The contract should include a clear and specific statement of the current severity of the behavior as reflected in frequency, duration, and/or intensity.
  - At present, I am spending less than one hour per week in studying at home. Although I have a study period, I am using that time to read magazines or write notes to my friends. In addition, I am skipping at least half of my classes. I am failing three classes and getting *D*'s in the other two.
- **Short-term goals involving new actions:** The goals should be possitive, important and meaningful, realistic, clear and specific, measurable, small and incremental, within the person's control, involving new skills and learning.
  - I will sign up for a course in study skills by the end of next week.

- ○ I will spend the first 20 minutes of my study period on my homework for at least 3 of the next 5 school days.
- ○ I will spend at least 30 minutes per day or 2 hours per week completing my schoolwork at home, spread out over for at least 3 of the next 7 days.
- ○ I will attend at least four out of 5 of my classes each day.

- **Identifying and removing obstacles:** Plan ahead to determine what might get in the way of people following through on their contracts and identifying ways they can overcome those potential challenges.
  - ○ To allow me some flexibility, I agree that I will spend time on my homework at least 3 days a week. I can choose which 3 school days those will be.
  - ○ If I miss more than one afternoon of homework, I will spend a half hour right after dinner on that day doing my school work.

- **Rewards and consequences:** Rewards are intended to encourage and reinforce progress. Consequences are rarely used but sometimes can help to discourage negative behavior. A statement of reinforcements and penalties for achieving or failing to achieve one's goals, stated in "if/then" terms, clarifies the relationship between behavior and response.
  - ○ I recognize that improving my grades, as well as the approval and positive feedback I will get from my teachers and parents, will be rewarding to me.
  - ○ In addition, if I fulfill my contract for an entire week, then my parents have agreed that they will extend my curfew by 1 hour that weekend so that I will have more time with friends. They told me this is a way of letting me know that, by making better choices for myself, I am showing them that I am mature enough to have additional privileges.

- **Measuring and tracking changes:** This specifies how people will keep track of their agreed-on behavioral changes.
  - ○ At the end of each day, I will list on my calendar in the computer how much time I spent on schoolwork in study period and at home and what classes I attended that day.

- **Helpful strategies to facilitate desired changes:** This includes skills, tools, and ideas generated by client and clinician that will help the client overcome obstacles and successfully achieve short- and long-term goals. (More will be said on this in Chapter 10.)
  - ○ I will learn more about study skills by taking a class and talking to my school counselor.
  - ○ I will plan in advance those days when I will study at home.
  - ○ I will turn off my cell phone when I am studying at home.
  - ○ I will set a timer for thirty minutes when I am studying at home and will focus on my schoolwork at least until the timer rings.

- I will ask my father to make sure I am awake and out of bed before he leaves for work. I also will set two alarm clocks to make sure I wake up as early as needed to get to school on time.

- **Commitment:** A public disclosure of goals makes it more likely that people will follow through on their behavioral change plans and also enables them to obtain support and practical help from others.
  - I will share my goals and strategies with my parents and my two favorite teachers. I will ask them to give me encouragement and remind me of my plans if they see that I am not following through on my agreement.

- **Long-term goals:** This is a statement of the eventual desired outcome that meets the eight criteria for sound goals.
  - I will have established a study schedule that allows me to spend at least four hours per week on my homework. I will improve my grades by the last marking period of this school year so that I have no grades below a *C* and have at least two grades of *A* or *B*. I will attend all classes unless I am ill.

Example 2 of Behavioral Change Contract   Let's look at one more example of a behavioral change contract so that you can develop a good understanding of the process of developing such an agreement. The Learning Opportunities section at the end of this chapter will provide you with additional experience in developing such contracts.

Mario is a 29-year-old Latino male who seeks counseling because of underlying and long-standing feelings of sad or dysphoric mood. Mario grew up in Mexico in a lower socioeconomic family. As the oldest son, he was expected to begin working as soon as possible to help the family financially. He became an apprentice to an electrician, quickly learned that trade, and has been successfully employed for the past 10 years. Mario has now legally immigrated to Arizona, married, and has two children. He sends money to his parents each month and is viewed as a credit to the family.

However, Mario has a beautiful singing voice and, since childhood, has dreamed of becoming an opera singer. The few people with whom he shared this aspiration scoffed at him and he soon learned to keep his dream to himself. He has occasionally sung with local bands, but has felt uneasy even about that expression of his musical interest. Over the years, Mario has become increasingly unhappy with his life and reports feeling unfulfilled and trapped. He has been spending less and less time with his family because of these feelings and wants that to change. However, he believes that no one really knows who he is and that makes it difficult for him even to be around people who care about him.

- **Baseline:**
  - At present, I spend most of my time working at my job where I am successful but unfulfilled. I spend Sundays with my wife and children but never have time alone with my wife. I sing with a band no more than

once every 3 months. I have told no one about my interest in studying music and have taken no steps to fulfill my desire to be an opera singer.

- **Short-term goals involving new actions:**
  - Within the next month, I will tell two people, one of whom will be my wife, about my interest in singing and in opera. I will be sure to let them know how important it is to me that I have their understanding and support in relation to my interest.
  - I will arrange to have a date with my wife within the next two weeks.
  - I will spend at least 30 minutes alone with each of my children during each of the next 2 weeks so that I can start to get to know them as individuals, just as I want people to get to know me.
  - During the next month, I will obtain information on opportunities available in my community for me to begin to study singing.

- **Identifying and removing obstacles:**
  - I will plan the date with my wife in advance to make sure that she is willing and able to spend the time with me, and I will help her arrange for child care while we are out.
  - I will make sure to leave work by 4:30 P.M. at least 2 days a week and will only work in the morning on Saturdays to be sure that I have some time to spend with my children as planned.

- **Rewards and consequences:**
  - I will invite my wife to spend an evening with me at my favorite restaurant where there is music and dancing that I enjoy. That will be rewarding to me.
  - In addition, if I fulfill my initial contract, then I will set aside $50 toward payment for a singing class for myself. I will save this amount each month so that I will be able to begin my training as a singer without negatively affecting my family's financial situation or the help I provide to my parents.

- **Measuring and tracking changes:**
  - I have a list of our short-term goals and when I have agreed to complete them. I will copy this into my computer and, each time I make progress toward one of the goals, I will describe my progress next to the relevant goal on the list. I also will write briefly about any barriers or rewards I encounter during this process.

- **Helpful strategies to facilitate desired changes:**
  - I will rehearse, both with my clinician and by myself, exactly how I will explain to my wife and another person my interest in becoming an opera singer and the support I need.
  - I will plan in advance those days and times when I will spend time with my children and make sure they will be available on those days and times.

○ I will plan in advance my date with my wife.
○ I will limit my overtime hours at work to no more than 8 hours per week.

- **Commitment:**
  ○ I will share my goals and strategies with my wife. I will explain to her that I believe this will enhance our marriage and help our family and will assure her that I will not jeopardize the welfare or financial situation of our family. I will ask her to give me encouragement and support my in my plans.

- **Medium-term (interim) and llong-term (eventual) goals:**
  ○ My interim goal is that I will obtain training as a singer and assess whether I have the ability and persistence to succeed as an opera singer. My long-term goal is to become a successful opera singer if I have the talent or, if I decide that is not a realistic goal for me, at least I will have pursued my dream, gotten training in singing, and will find another way to express my love for music and singing.

REVIEW OF STEPS TO EFFECT BEHAVIORAL CHANGE

This chapter has presented the fundamental skills that clinicians need to effect behavioral change, although more will be said in the next chapter on additional strategies to promote behavioral change. Let's review the steps in the behavioral change process:

1. Describe the undesirable actions as specifically as possible.
2. Establish a baseline, reflecting the current severity, frequency, intensity, or duration of the actions.
3. Determine realistic goals, beginning with short-term goals, and then usually progressing to interim and long-term goals.
4. Identify potential obstacles to goal achievement, as well as ways to eliminate or bypass those obstacles.
5. Provide skills, strategies, and tasks that will promote goal achievement.
6. Determine how the client will track and record progress and facilitate client's plans to keep records of behavior change efforts.
7. Develop a clear contract, specifying goals, steps to take, and any rewards and consequences.
8. Put contract in writing and elicit client's commitment to the contract. If possible, encourage client to make a public declaration of goals and elicit support by sharing the contract with at least one other person.
9. Assess progress toward goals.
10. Implement plans for rewards or consequences, reinforce gains, and, if indicated, revise contract.

This chapter focused on teaching the following fundamental skills needed to help people change undesirable actions and behaviors and develop new and healthier ones:

- Describing undesirable behaviors and determining the severity of those behaviors via a baseline
- Setting clear and realistic goals
- Identifying and removing obstacles to goal achievement
- Making effective use of rewards and consequences
- Developing a contract for behavior change
- Tracking and assessing progress

Written Exercises

1. For each of the clients described here, identify the following:

   - A short-term goal that meets the eight criteria for sound goals
   - A strategy for measuring the undesirable behaviors or actions
   - A viable reward or, if indicated, a consequence
   - A way to track progress

   Client 1: My parents say now that I am in high school, I have to take responsibility for getting my own homework done, but I just don't seem able to do it. I come home from school, sit down with my video games, and before I know it, it's time for dinner. Then my friends start to call and IM. If I spend 20 minutes on homework before I go to bed, it's a lot.

   Client 2: I know it's not good for either me or them, but I always seem to nag my kids. "Pick up your room, wash your hands, do your homework, shut off the television," and on and on. And half the time they don't even listen to me. I think my nagging has just become background noise. I need to find another way to interact with them.

   Client 3: I think I should cut back on my drinking but that's really difficult. It's two or three drinks over a business lunch, then more drinking after work, then there's usually a party or reception and that means more drinking. It's just an accepted part of my work and of my life. But I find I can't drink the way I used to. I'm putting on weight, I feel wiped out at the end of the day, and even my thinking on the job is being affected.

2. Identify an obstacle to positive change that might arise for each of the clients in Exercise 1 and determine a strategy to help them overcome or prevent that obstacle:

   Client 1:
   Obstacle: _____
   Strategy: _____
   _____

Client 2:
Obstacle: _____
Strategy: _____

_____

Client 3:
Obstacle: _____
Strategy: _____

_____

3. Refer back to the examples of Lavinia and Curt presented earlier in this chapter on pages **295–297**. Select one of these people and provide a written description of how you would take them through the entire process of behavioral change according to the following steps:
   - **Description:** Concise picture of unhelpful behavior.
   - **Baseline:** Clear and specific statement of the current severity of the behavior as reflected in frequency, duration, and/or intensity.
   - **Short-term goals:** Statement of goals that are positive, important and meaningful, realistic, clear and specific, measurable, small and incremental, within the person's control, involving new skills and learning.
   - **Identifying and removing obstacles:** Plan ahead to determine what might get in the way of people following through on their contracts and identify ways they can overcome those potential challenges.
   - **Rewards and consequences:** A statement of reinforcements or penalties for achieving or failing to achieve one's goals, stated in "if/then" terms.
   - **Measuring and tracking changes:** This specifies how people will keep track of their agreed-on behavioral change efforts. Include information on what will be recorded when and where.
   - **Helpful strategies to facilitate desired changes:** This includes skills, tools, and ideas generated by client and clinician that will help the client overcome obstacles and successfully achieve short- and long-term goals.
   - **Commitment:** Indicate how the client will disclose the goals to others, making follow through more likely and enabling the person to obtain support and practical help from others.
   - **Medium-term and long-term goals:** These are statements of the interim and eventual desired outcomes that meet the eight criteria for sound goals.

Discussion Questions

1. You have now participated in sessions focusing on background, on emotions, and on thoughts (and perhaps you have already completed the role-play in this chapter that is focused on actions). Which focus felt most comfortable for you and why? Which led to the most productive session and why?
2. Some clinicians believe that sessions focused on actions tend to be superficial and do not result in important or meaningful changes. What is your reaction to that statement?

3. Juanita is an 11-year-old girl who has been diagnosed with attention-deficit/hyperactivity disorder. She is taking medication that is somewhat helpful, but she continues to manifest many behavioral difficulties, including impulsive talking, forgetting to raise her hand before responding to the teacher's questions, getting out of her seat at inappropriate times, and being distracted from her schoolwork. Develop a plan to help Juanita change one of her behaviors. Describe your plan according to the 10 steps to effect behavioral change as listed on page **313**.

4. Consider the following clients' behavioral goals. For each one, develop a realistic and meaningful short-term goal, reflecting the eight criteria for sound goals presented earlier in this chapter, and a possible first step for each person to take toward the desired behavior change:

Client 1: My goal is to lose 50 pounds in 1 year.
Short-term goal: _____

_____

First step: _____

_____

Client 2: I'm 33 years old and I've always been afraid of the water. I want to learn to swim so that I can take my children to the beach.
Short-term goal: _____

_____

First step: _____

_____

Client 3: All my savings are in a bank account, earning about 3 percent interest. I want to learn about investing and make better decisions about my money.
Short-term goal: _____

_____

First step: _____

_____

Client 4: I have an impulse to cut myself and have done so more than half a dozen times. I have had multiple infections and am very ashamed of my behavior, but I don't seem able to stop. Can you help me?
Short-term goal: _____

_____

First step: _____

_____

Client 5: I recently had a leg amputated after an accident and have been fitted with a prosthesis. The doctors tell me that I can learn to walk again, but I am afraid I will fall. Can you help me overcome my fear?
Short-term goal: _____

_____

First step: _____

_____

5. If you have not yet done the practice group exercise associated with this chapter, discuss your thoughts and feelings about that upcoming experience. What obstacles do you expect to encounter? What can you do to try to avoid them? What did you learn from the previous role-play sessions that you want to carry with you into the role-play focused on changing actions?

6. If you have already done the practice group exercise associated with this chapter, discuss your reactions to that experience. What was the most beneficial aspect of that experience for you? What was the most challenging or uncomfortable aspect of the experience? How did this role-play compare with your earlier ones? How can you make future practice group exercises even more rewarding?

Practice Group Exercise

Assessing and Modifying Behaviors

Divide into your practice groups as described in an earlier chapter. The practice group exercise presented here is designed to help you gain experience in some of the fundamental skills presented in this chapter: describing and measuring undesirable actions, goal setting, and contracting. You will also have an opportunity to draw on many of the skills you learned in earlier chapters to enhance the effectiveness of your role-play.

Preparing for the Role-Play

As with all of the practice group exercises in this book, you will probably be more successful and learn more from the role-play if you do some advance preparation, as follows:

- Review the recordings of your previous role-play, along with the feedback you received from your practice group.
- Review your previous Assessment of Progress forms. By now, you can probably identify some patterns in your role-plays. Do you see yourself improving from session to session and adding new skills to your repertoire? Or does it seem like you are stuck and continue to receive the same feedback in one practice session after another? Try to identify the recurrent weaknesses in your work as well as your areas of strength. Don't be surprised if, like many novice clinicians, you tend to talk too much, overlook nonverbal messages, or pay more attention to emotions than thoughts. I have never encountered a beginning clinician who did not have some of these weaknesses. What is important is that you are open to feedback, can identify skills that need improvement, and are taking steps to better your skills.
- Focus your efforts. To avoid feeling overwhelmed by all that you are learning, select one or two skills to work on in this session, jot them down, and think

about ways you can strengthen those skills. Perhaps you would benefit from reviewing relevant sections of this book or doing some extra role-playing with a trusted friend or colleague. List below those skills that you intend to target in your next practice group session and how you plan to improve them.

1._____

_____

2._____

_____

In addition to reviewing your progress and determining ways to improve your skills, you should select an issue to address when you are in the client role. In previous practice group exercises, you talked about background, emotions, and thoughts. In this role-play, your focus should be on actions and behaviors.

Think carefully about your choice so that the session is both beneficial to you and a good learning experience for the other group members. Avoid presenting problematic behaviors that you have struggled with unsuccessfully for a long time or that have a significant negative impact on your life. Behaviors of this type might include a long-standing problem with drug abuse or a serious eating disorder in which you binge and purge. Instead, select a less challenging or volatile behavior that might lead to a more comfortable and productive session for you and your partner. Examples of such actions include the following:

- Drinking less coffee
- Establishing more regular sleeping habits
- Getting more exercise
- Eating more fruits and vegetables
- Spending more time (or less time) on your schoolwork
- Improving your ability to initiate or maintain conversations
- Cleaning out your closets

Role-Play Exercise:

The goals of this role-play are as follows:

- **To build on the skills you have already learned.** Again, remember to review your Assessment of Progress forms to remind yourself of the skills that have already been introduced and what you need to focus on to improve those skills. The use of reflections of feelings and meaning, as well as both open and closed questions, will be especially important to you as you work with your client to assess and change actions. Attending to nonverbal behaviors can also be very helpful in alerting you to signs of reluctance and obstacles to change.
- **To help your client identify, assess, and change undesirable behaviors and actions.** To accomplish this, you should follow the steps in changing behavior that have been presented in this chapter on page 313.

- **To conclude the session by collaborating with your client in determining a viable first step toward change and then summarizing the session.** Be sure to reiterate the contract you made with your client, whether it entails gathering baseline information or making some small behavioral changes. Use language that will reinforce gains and empower and encourage the client. Collaborate with the client in determining a task for the client to completed by the next session; this may be part of the contract that has already been establish. Be sure the client understands and agrees to the task, perhaps modifying it as you discuss it. As you have done in your previous sessions, use the summarizing skill to concisely conclude and describe the session.

Time Schedule

This role-play will probably be most rewarding if it can be extended over two or three sessions, separated by 3 to 7 days. The first session should be used to elicit a specific description of the undesirable behavior and determine ways for the client to assess its severity. The second session can then be used to review the baseline information and establish goals and a written contract. If the schedule allows a third session, that session can be used to follow up on the client's efforts to make positive changes. If it is not possible to spend more than one session on this exercise, complete only the steps suggested for the first and second sessions. These can readily be combined into one session.

Ideally, allow at least 15 minutes for each session if two or three sessions are held and at least 20 to 25 minutes if sessions 1 and 2 are rolled into one session. Of course, also allow time for processing and feedback following each session.

During your session(s), use the following format for taking notes as you and your client complete the steps in the behavioral change process:

Session 1

1. Describe the undesirable actions as specifically as possible.
2. Establish a baseline, reflecting the current severity of the actions.

Session 2

1. Determine sound and realistic goals, beginning with short-term goals.
2. Identify skills and tasks that will promote goal achievement.
3. Address potential obstacles to goal achievement.
4. Facilitate client's efforts to track and record progress.
5. Develop a contract, specifying goals, steps to be taken toward change, and rewards or consequences.
6. Put contract in writing and elicit a commitment to the contract. Goals and contracts emphasize specificity.

Session 3

1. Assess progress toward goals.
2. Reinforce progress, implement plans for rewards or consequences, or, if indicated, revise contract.

Assessment of Progress Form 9

1. **Improving targeted skills.** Review the skills you targeted for improvement in this session. List them here and briefly describe what you did to improve those skills. How successful were your efforts? What do you need to continue to do or to change to maintain or expand on your improvement of the identified skills?

   Skill 1:_____

   _____

   Skill 2:_____

   _____

2. **Building on the skills you have already learned.** What use did you make of the following skills, presented in previous chapters?

   - Open and closed questions:
   - Accents, restatements, and paraphrases:
   - Reflections of feeling:
   - Nonverbal communication:
   - Summarization:
   - Reflections of meaning:

3. **Helping your client describe, assess, and modify actions.** Note whether and how you helped your client progress through each of the steps in this role-play. Which steps felt most comfortable for you? Which were most productive? Which presented the greatest challenge? How might you have improved on your use of the behavioral change process?

4. **Concluding the session.** How successful were you and your client at coming up with a viable first step? How effective was your summarization?

5. How would you describe your overall effectiveness in this session, using the following rating scale?

   - **Extremely helpful:** Reflects accurate and insightful listening; moves treatment in a very productive direction; promotes self-awareness, new learning, or positive changes.
   - **Moderately helpful:** Reflects generally accurate listening; moves treatment in a productive direction, but does not clearly lead to greater self-awareness, new learning, or positive changes.
   - **Neutral:** Neither contributes to the treatment goals nor harms the therapeutic process; may not accurately reflect what the client has communicated.

- **Moderately harmful:** Detracts somewhat from the treatment process or alliance; reflects poor listening and perhaps disinterest.
- **Extremely harmful:** Damaging to the treatment process or therapeutic alliance; sounds ridiculing and critical.

What might you have done differently to improve your self-ratings?

What strengths and improvements did you notice?

Personal Journal Questions

1. Have you had success in the past in changing one of your own undesirable behaviors? If so, briefly describe the behavior and the effective steps you took to modify that behavior. What did you learn from this process about ways to effect behavioral change?
2. Have you tried unsuccessfully in the past to change one of your own undesirable behaviors? What kept you from being successful in this effort? What did you learn from this process about ways to effect behavioral change?
3. Have you ever tried to use behavioral change strategies in your own life to modify the behavior of another person such as a child or a coworker? What was the outcome of your efforts? What strategies did you use that were effective and what strategies did you use that were not effective? What did you learn from this process about ways to effect behavioral change?
4. Identify a behavior you would like to change. Choose a different behavior than the one you discussed in your practice group. Be your own clinician and take yourself through the 10-step process presented on page 313. Write about this process.

SUMMARY

This chapter focused on the fundamental skills associated with helping people identify, describe, assess, and change undesirable actions and behaviors. The chapter presented a 10-step process that is useful in helping people effect behavioral change both in and out of treatment. Particular attention was paid in this chapter to describing behavior in specific terms, establishing a baseline, setting realistic and viable goals, using rewards and consequences, identifying and minimizing obstacles to positive change, recording progress, developing contracts, and assessing progress.

Chapter 10 builds on these fundamental skills by presenting additional strategies that can be incorporated into and enhance treatment focused on behavioral change. These include giving directions and suggesting tasks; promoting feelings of empowerment; using challenge and confrontation to reduce barriers to change; and using visualization, behavioral rehearsal, modeling, skill development, relaxation, and systematic desensitization to help clients change their behaviors.

Chapter 10

ADDITIONAL SKILLS FOR IDENTIFYING, ASSESSING, AND CHANGING ACTIONS AND BEHAVIORS

OVERVIEW

Chapter 9 presented the fundamental skills needed to help people identify, assess, and change their undesirable and unhelpful behaviors. A ten-step format for behavioral change was included in Chapter 9 to provide clarity and structure to the process.

However, as you were reading Chapter 9, you might have felt a need for more strategies to help people succeed at the often challenging process of changing actions and behaviors. Chapter 10 presents you with an array of such strategies that you can use to facilitate behavioral change.

LEARNING GOALS

As a result of reading this chapter and completing the exercises throughout, you can expect to accomplish the following:

- Learn how to suggest tasks and collaborate with clients in determining steps they will take between sessions to achieve their goals.
- Learn specific skills and strategies that are designed to facilitate behavior change.
- Know when and how to use strategies that can increase people's ability to make positive behavioral changes.

SKILLS TO BE LEARNED

Eleven skills that help clinicians promote changes in clients' behaviors and actions are presented in this chapter:

- Between-session tasks to promote goal attainment
- Empowerment

- Challenge and caring confrontation
- Visualization
- Behavioral rehearsal
- Modeling and role-playing
- Skill development
- Breaking down behaviors into small steps
- Possibility or presuppositional language
- Relaxation
- Systematic desensitization

These skills are useful in promoting behavior change not only in people seeking help in mental health settings but also for people in a wide variety of other settings. They can be helpful in schools and colleges, in businesses, and even at home to help you make personal changes.

DEVELOPING BETWEEN-SESSION TASKS TO PROMOTE CHANGE

For many novice clinicians (and unfortunately also for some experienced clinicians), counseling and psychotherapy are synonymous with giving advice or telling people what the clinician thinks they should do. I have interviewed people seeking admission to graduate programs who explain their interest in becoming a mental health treatment provider by saying something like "I didn't get much help when I was growing up, and I want to tell people how to avoid the mistakes that I made" or "I learned so much from my own counseling; I want to pass on what I learned to other people." Although well meaning, such statements reflect the misconception of many clinicians that their role is to tell people how they should lead their lives. One of the most important goals of graduate programs designed to train clinicians is helping them understand how to help people make good choices for themselves. Such programs typically discourage clinicians from giving advice or telling people what to do.

At the same time, giving certain types of advice or suggestions carefully and thoughtfully does have a place in the clinical relationship. Such advice has been referred to as directives, prescriptions, recommendations, suggestions, between-session tasks, or homework assignments. Hill and O'Grady (1985) found that directives, including advice and information giving, constituted one of the main categories of clinician interventions. Scheel, Seaman, Roach, Mullin, and Mahoney (1999) found that many of the suggestions made by clinicians referred to homework or "out-of-session activities suggested during therapy to be performed by the client" (p. 308). The research of Scheel and colleagues concluded that clinicians made an average of 1.85 of these recommendations per session. According to Hay and Kinnier (1998), "Using homework as an adjunct to the work that occurs within the counseling session has been shown to be an effective way to promote therapeutic change in a brief period of time" (p. 122).

Between-session tasks, then, have proven their value. However, the way these are presented and developed has a great influence on how beneficial they are. This section of the chapter discusses the potential benefits of these tasks, as well as ways to maximize these benefits.

Benefits of Between-Session Tasks

Between-session tasks can have the following therapeutic benefits:

- They provide clients an opportunity to practice and apply what they have learned in their sessions.
- This experience, in turn, helps people assess their efforts realistically and identify the strengths and strategies that help them make positive changes as well as any barriers or difficulties that need to be addressed.
- Between-session tasks provide both clients and clinicians with a sense of direction.
- They can enhance and further the work of the sessions by continuing and even accelerating the therapeutic process between sessions.
- They encourage generalization and transfer of new learning and behaviors into a real-life setting.
- These independent efforts promote clients' feelings of self-control, responsibility, self-efficacy, and motivation.

Guidelines for Suggesting Homework or Between-Session Tasks

Although between-session tasks or suggested homework have the potential to advance treatment, they also can be harmful to clients' motivation and to the therapeutic alliance. If poorly planned and presented, such tasks can make people feel pressured, misunderstood, discouraged, and overwhelmed. Failure to perform tasks successfully can lead people to view themselves negatively and even to terminate treatment prematurely.

Following these guidelines can maximize the likelihood that between-session tasks will be beneficial:

- Between-session tasks should be initiated at the first session and made a routine and integral part of treatment.
- The rationale for and potential benefits of between-session tasks should be clearly explained to clients and they should have an opportunity to express their reactions to this aspect of the treatment process.
- Clinicians should clarify that between-session tasks are not homework assignments or mandates and clients' performance of these tasks will not be judged or graded. Between-session tasks are primarily learning experiences, and learning can come from both successes and disappointments.
- Although an activity might be introduced by the clinician, client and clinician collaborate in determining whether or not it is likely to be helpful and in spelling out the details of the task. Clients' perceptions of the activity and

their motivation to attempt the activity seem to be the primary determinants of whether they will follow through on the suggested task and whether it will be helpful.

- The task should be relevant and clearly linked to the work that has gone on in the session. Presenting a rationale for each task helps the client understand how it might be beneficial.
- Whether a client successfully performs a task, has a mixture of positive and negative experiences when the task is attempted, or fails to attempt or accomplish the task should be viewed as helpful information that can improve treatment. Information that emerges from between-session tasks can lead to a revision of goals, the use of different strategies, and the teaching of new skills. Whatever knowledge and insight emerges, clinicians should emphasize and build on clients' strengths, abilities, and interests.
- The level of difficulty of the task should be appropriate to the client. Easily accomplished activities, creating feelings of success, are usually preferable to demanding actions that are likely to lead to failure.
- Any possible obstacles to completion of the task, such as time required for the task, client discomfort with the task, reliance on other people or specific circumstances for the task to be completed, or complexity of the task, should be discussed and, if possible, eliminated. This will increase the likelihood that the task will be performed successfully.
- The suggested task should be written down and reviewed with the client to ensure understanding. Modification, fine-tuning, and clarification of the task might occur at this point.
- The outcome of the task should be discussed in the next session. Of course, clinicians should avoid blaming or shaming clients who have not completed the task as specified. Instead, they should emphasize client choices, self-monitoring, and self-assessment. They can encourage clients who have achieved some success to congratulate themselves and identify the strengths and resources that led to the positive outcome. Clinicians should view any outcome to the process as a learning experience and an opportunity to formulate another, perhaps more appropriate task.

Categories of Between-Session Tasks

Scheel et al. (1999) identified eight categories of clinician recommendations. The following list, in descending order of occurrence, includes examples to illustrate each of those categories. Notice that each suggestion is phrased tentatively, inviting discussion and reactions from the client. The clinicians present themselves as helpers and guides—not all-knowing experts. They are careful not to give orders or to exaggerate the power differential between themselves and their clients.

1. **Validation of internal experience:** It sounds like your intuitions are working well for you. Perhaps this week you could write down two intuitions you have and then list any changes that are suggested by those intuitions.

2. **Social interactions:** How would you feel about introducing yourself to two people you don't know at church this week?

3. **Reframing meaning:** I wonder if your staying home so that you are always available to your children might be a way to protect yourself. Perhaps it would be useful to write in your journal this week about ways that you protect yourself.

4. **Decision making:** What about making a list for our next session of the pros and cons of adopting another child?

5. **Request for action:** Joining Alcoholics Anonymous might help you in your efforts to stop drinking. I can give you a telephone number to call to obtain information on meetings in your area. How do you react to that idea?

6. **Promotion of self-esteem:** Sounds like you are focusing on a few negatives and overlooking many positives in your work. When you make a list of your billable hours for each day, how about also listing your successes for that day?

7. **Referral:** Perhaps some medication might help you with your difficulty focusing and paying attention. Here are the names of three psychiatrists who specialize in treating attention-deficit/hyperactivity disorder, which you have agreed is an accurate label for your difficulties. How would you feel about calling one of them this week to schedule an appointment?

8. **Stress management:** We have reviewed some deep breathing and relaxation exercises in our session today. I wonder if you would be able to find the time to practice them for about fifteen minutes every day.

Formats for Between-Session Tasks

Regardless of the purpose of the task, suggested activities can take many forms. The following are some of the many forms that between-session tasks can take:

- Reading about a topic of interest and benefit, either to oneself or aloud to a friend or family member
- Writing about a topic of interest or about one's background experiences, emotions, thoughts, or actions
- Making lists, perhaps of strengths, successes, or pros and cons
- Thinking in a new way or about a particular topic
- Obtaining information, either through the Internet, the library, or a knowledgeable person
- Joining a support group such as a 12-step program or a group for people coping with a difficult illness or life experience
- Taking a course, such as one on assertiveness skills or parent effectiveness
- Taking carefully planned and gradual risks
- Identifying and engaging in leisure activities and exercise programs
- Communicating with other people in new and better ways
- Observing interactions or experiences
- Planning and scheduling
- Taking a break or establishing a relaxation routine

Although the guidelines generally emphasize the importance of planning task assignments that are nonthreatening, clear, and easily accomplished, several approaches to formulating between-session tasks deliberately violate those guidelines. They can be powerful forces for client change. However, they also have the potential to do harm and so must be used with considerable caution. Although I will describe these strategies here so that you are aware of them, they should be reserved for experienced clinicians who have received training or supervision in these strategies.

Shame-attacking exercises stem primarily from the work of Albert Ellis (1995). The idea behind these experiences is that if people inundate themselves with the very experiences that they most fear, they are likely to get over that fear. For example, as a young man, Albert Ellis was apprehensive about asking women out for a date. To overcome this, he assigned himself the task of asking out 100 women. Although none accepted his invitation, the exercise served the purpose of reducing Ellis's fear.

In *paradoxical interventions,* derived from the writings of Viktor Frankl (1963), clinicians typically suggest to clients a way of thinking or acting that is the opposite of what they have been trying to do. People might be encouraged to schedule arguments with their partners, to assume that the worst will happen, to do less rather than more, and to schedule a relapse. Doing something radically different from what they have been doing unsuccessfully can be beneficial to people. In addition, the surprising nature of these interventions can be intriguing to clients, increasing the likelihood that they will complete the task. Of course, suggestions such as these pose a risk and can be discouraging to clients and harmful to the treatment process. Again, these strategies should be used with care and reserved for experienced clinicians.

Example of Suggesting a Between-Session Task

The following dialogue between client and clinician illustrates a positive and constructive approach to suggesting a between-session task. Notice that, although the task is initially proposed by the clinician, both collaborate in developing the activity to maximize the likelihood that it will be a successful and informative experience for the client. Following the development of the task, a second dialogue illustrates one way in which the exercise might be processed in the next session.

Suggesting the Task

Clinician: Destiny, this week we have been working on ways for you to control your anger at your children and find more effective ways for you to deal with them when they fight or get on your nerves. One approach that seemed to make sense to you was to encourage them to work out their own conflicts rather than drawing you into the middle. This week, how would it be for you to stand back and encourage them to work out their conflicts?

Client: I guess that makes sense, but what can I say to them so they know things are going to be different now?

Clinician: That's an important question. How do you think you could explain the change to them?

Client: I could say that I think they're now old enough to handle some of their conflicts themselves and I'm not going to keep running in to resolve every little argument.

Clinician: That sounds like a clear way to start to explain the change to them. It also gives them the message that you trust them and see that they are maturing. I wonder if they know how to resolve arguments well?

Client: Probably not. They're so used to running to me, whining and complaining, that they may not know what else to do.

Clinician: Could you teach them another way?

Client: Yeah, I could explain what you taught me about working things out with my mother, both of us trying to listen to each other and then find a middle ground. I could even practice that with my children when they're not in the middle of a fight. I could make it sort of a make-believe game; it might be fun for them to practice acting more grown-up.

Clinician: That sounds like a plan. Now let's suppose that you're at home and one of the children forgets what you said. Maybe your younger boy Billy runs in complaining that Teddy won't share his toys with him. How will you handle that?

Client: I could remind him of what we talked about, maybe help him figure out what he wants, but not go into the playroom and take over. I would feel good if I could do that.

Clinician: So you have a goal. What else can you do to help yourself reach that goal?

Client: Well, I know it won't be easy to do this. The children's whining always gets to me and I just run in and try to quiet them down. I don't have to put up with the whining. I could ask Billy to talk in a more grown-up voice and tell me what he can do to solve the problem. Then after he leaves, I could take some deep breaths and turn on some music to help me relax. But what if they start to hit each other? Shouldn't I go in then and break things up?

Clinician: What do you think?

Client: Yes, I do need to be sure they don't hurt each other. That doesn't happen much, but it wouldn't be the first time.

Clinician: So that would be an exception to the plan. If either of the children becomes physically aggressive, you will go in and break up the fight. Now this is the first time you are trying this new strategy. How about if we think of this as a learning experience? Let's see how it goes and if we need to change our strategies next time, based on what we learn, we can do that. How does that sound to you?

Client: Yes, I know it won't be so easy to change the way I've been for years.

Clinician: So it makes sense to see this as a work in progress. What could you do to keep track of your efforts to change how you deal with your children this week so we can more easily learn from your experiences?

Client: It's hard to find time to write things down. I'm not sure.

Clinician: If you have a small tape recorder, perhaps you could just keep it handy and talk into the tape recorder about your efforts to change how you interact with the boys when they argue.

Client: Yes, that's an idea. I could keep it by the bed and spend just a few minutes every night talking about how I did at this. It's worth a try.

Processing the Task

Clinician: Destiny, how did your efforts to stay out of the boys' arguments go this week?

Client: Kind of mixed. I did what we talked about and explained to the boys that I thought they were big enough now to work out their own conflicts and I suggested some ways they could do that. The first time Billy came in whining about Teddy being mean to him, I just reminded him of what we talked about and sent him back to the playroom to work things out. No problem! I turned on some music and congratulated myself. A little too soon.... Next day, same thing, but this time Billy comes back in again and he's crying. He says Teddy called him a name we don't allow in our house, so I went charging in to tell Teddy off. I got into yelling at them, Billy kept crying, and Teddy started yelling back at me. Bad as ever! I really messed this up.

Clinician: I can hear you sound pretty disappointed, but let's not forget that you did get off to a good start. You know, it's not easy to change children's behaviors. Often, their undesirable behaviors will get worse before they get better. Maybe when Billy couldn't engage you in his argument with his brother the first time, he tried harder the second time.

Client: That makes sense. He did get to me when he came in crying.

Clinician: So what might you have done differently the second time?

Client: I could have just done what I did the first time and sent Billy back in to deal with Teddy. But don't I have to let Teddy know that he can't call his brother bad names?

Clinician: That part bothered you. I wonder if there is another way you could have given Teddy that message without getting in the middle of their argument?

Client: I guess I could have talked to him alone afterwards and let him know that language is not acceptable in our home.

Clinician: How would that have worked for you?

Client: That would be okay. I just don't want him to think that it's fine to talk to his brother that way.

Clinician: So talking with each child alone after the argument would be a way for you to make sure their behavior doesn't get out of hand. How would it be to try this again next week, following your new strategy?

Client: I'll give it a go. Things did seem a little better this week, at least at the beginning, and it did make me feel good to have a plan for handling the boys' fights and whining.

Clinician: So it started to build your confidence as a parent. Let's see if we can keep that trend going.

Notice that the process of formulating and processing the between-session task is a collaborative one. Learning, empowerment, progress, and the development of new skills and strategies are emphasized, as is transfer of learning the client has already acquired. Learning opportunities at the end of this chapter afford the opportunity to practice developing and presenting between-session tasks.

POTENTIAL BARRIERS TO CHANGE

Clinicians sometimes encounter clients who are reluctant to take steps to change unhelpful behaviors. They may be willing to talk about their lives and perhaps even express their emotions and analyze their thoughts, but they are reluctant to take actions that are likely to help them. Many factors can contribute to this lack of movement, including these (Carlock, 1999):

- **Low self-esteem:** People may view themselves as incapable of even the smallest positive change and are certain they will fail at any undertaking.
- **Anxiety and apprehension:** People become comfortable with the known, even if it is replete with problems, and they may fear venturing into new areas.
- **Perfectionism:** People are afraid that if they take on new challenges, they may not have immediate success and are reluctant to risk looking bad in their own eyes and in those of others.
- **Procrastination:** People may have difficulty getting started and following through on their plans. They put things off and miss deadlines in many areas of their lives, and that pattern carries over to their treatment.
- **Depression and inertia:** Taking a small step forward and trying something new may appear impossible to people who are depressed. They typically feel as though they are in a dark hole from which there is no escape. Hopelessness and lack of energy keep them trapped.
- **Benefits of the unhelpful behaviors:** Even though people have been told, and may believe, that their behaviors are harmful to them, those behaviors may also offer some immediate rewards and gratifications. Overeating, getting high from drugs or intoxicated from alcohol, watching television for many hours, and avoiding work offer temporary rewards to some people. The pleasure they derive from those activities can deter them from making changes that may eventually lead to a more rewarding life but may take away some short-term pleasure.
- **Anger and resentment:** Negative behaviors sometimes are used to punish others. People who engage in angry and violent outbursts, for example, may believe that others deserve their wrath and feel justified in their behavior, despite legal and relational consequences.
- **Conflicts:** People sometimes become immobilized when they are in conflict and experience competing forces pushing them in opposing directions. They may want to stop drinking but fear their friends will reject and ridicule them. They may want to earn a higher salary but are apprehensive that working harder will cut into their family and leisure time. They may want to become involved in sports at school but worry that their anxiety and inexperience may cause them to fail.

- **Cultural messages and disenfranchising experiences:** People from disempowered groups such as women, people with disabilities, and those from other than mainstream cultural backgrounds may come to believe that they have few options and little power. This perception can lead them to underestimate themselves and to believe that positive change is impossible. They may also be discouraged from making changes by restrictive cultural messages about their gender, ethnicity, and expected roles.

People often present with a combination of these factors, such as depression and low self-esteem or anger and feelings of being disenfranchised. People with multiple barriers to change can pose a particular challenge in treatment.

GENERAL GUIDELINES FOR PROMOTING BEHAVIORAL CHANGE

Clinicians can help people to make change by promoting their awareness of their strengths, nurturing their desire for and belief in a more rewarding life, helping them view themselves as competent and likely to succeed, enabling them to see that mistakes and even failures are inevitable and acceptable, and giving them ways to overcome obstacles. Clinicians can accomplish these goals in many ways. Clinicians' overall orientation to the treatment process can make a difference in people's motivation to make changes in their actions. Forming a strong, supportive, and accepting therapeutic alliance is essential to helping people overcome barriers to behavioral change. The development of such an alliance is essential in all treatment approaches, including those focused on changing actions. The following strategies can promote such an alliance and encourage people to make positive changes:

- **Listen to people's stories.** Take time to really get to know clients. Ask about their families, their work, their joys and regrets, and their dreams for the future.
- **Make sense of the unhelpful behaviors.** Look beyond the manifestations of the harmful behavior, and try to understand the development and purpose of that behavior. What maintains it and what benefits does it bring?
- **Emphasize collaboration in the therapeutic alliance.** People are unlikely to change to please their clinicians. The motivation toward change, of course, needs to come from within the person. However, having a clinician who can accompany them on the risky and unpredictable path of change can smooth that path and encourage progress.
- **Pay attention to and make use of nonverbal messages.** People's nonverbal messages may reflect emotions and attitudes that cannot be verbalized. Clinicians can gently identify and explore those messages to help people better understand their own barriers to change and how to circumvent them. Also, clinicians can mirror body language to communicate understanding and support and to strengthen the therapeutic alliance.

- **Maintain a stance that is hopeful and optimistic yet realistic.** Use language that conveys the message that positive change is possible and even likely, although achieving that change may require effort.
- **Help people focus on positive outcomes.** Motivation is critical in effecting behavioral change. People benefit from having a clear vision of how their lives will be improved if they do make desired changes and from noticing and taking credit for even small changes.
- **Encourage but do not pressure people to change.** Remain the client's ally, supporting but not insisting on change. Guide people in the right direction, present an array of options for initiating change, and help clients carefully consider and make the choices that are right for them.

In addition to this overall orientation to the treatment process, clinicians have a broad range of strategies they can use to encourage client change. Most of the rest of this chapter is devoted to the presentation and illustration of some of these strategies.

EMPOWERMENT

Although clinicians' support, encouragement, optimism, and suggestions can contribute to clients' feelings of empowerment, they often are not enough. Feelings of worth, power, and competence need to stem primarily from the insights and actions of the client rather than from judgments of the clinician.

As tempted as clinicians might be to say to a client, "I know you can do it if you just give it a try," this can do more harm than good. Statements like this can contribute to the tendency of many clients to base their self-evaluation on the views that others have of them. Instead, clinicians should promote clients' intrinsic feelings of worth and competence. In addition, if clinicians assure people that they will succeed and that does not happen, they may lose faith in the treatment process and the therapeutic alliance. Some clients even deliberately fail at tasks that are initiated by clinicians in order to sabotage treatment and demonstrate that it will not help them. Clinicians should keep in mind, then, the importance of empowering people from within rather than telling them what they should feel, think, or do differently.

Fortunately, many strategies are available to facilitate people's efforts to empower themselves so that they can take constructive action to improve their lives. The following list includes some of the most useful ones, but feel free to develop your own approaches to helping your clients build up their feelings of worth and competence.

Lists of Strengths and Accomplishments

Asking people who feel powerless and discouraged to identify their strengths or list their admirable qualities is not likely to be successful. Inherent in most people with low self-esteem is the tendency to exaggerate their flaws and ignore their strengths.

However, with some coaching, even these clients can develop a list of strengths and accomplishments. Questions such as the following can facilitate this process:

- If your child (or partner or best friend or employer) were telling someone about you, what would you like them to say about you?
- Tell me about one or two of your accomplishments in your work? Your relationships? Your home management activities? Your leisure activities? Your fund of knowledge? Your contributions to society?
- What qualities about you do you think led your employer to hire you? Your partner to be with you? Your friends to spend time with you? Your customers to seek you out again and again? Your teacher to give you an award?

Once people have begun to list accomplishments and strengths, clinicians can suggest additions to the list, based on what they have learned about the clients. Clinicians should keep in mind that they are not assessing the worth of the person, but rather simply identifying that person's positive qualities and achievements. Clinicians should try to be specific and give examples to promote the clients' awareness of their assets, emphasizing what the clients have said about themselves. In other words, rather than saying, "I think you are a very intelligent person," the clinician might say, "You have two master's degrees and a doctorate in philosophy. What does that say about your abilities?" Of course, clients always have the right to reject or rephrase any suggested additions; clients must believe in the list and view it as an accurate reflection of themselves if it is to be meaningful.

Drawing One's Strengths

Especially for children or early adolescents, drawing and other creative methods can be used to elicit strengths and accomplishments. For example, clinicians might suggest that the children pretend to be medieval knights, creating a shield to represent their power and scare off enemies. The shield would depict words, symbols, or pictures that represent the person's strengths and accomplishments. Similarly, a collage with drawings and pictures cut from magazines can be used to create an image of a person's strengths and accomplishments. Some adults also might enjoy these activities and find them less constricting than using only words to describe themselves. Affirmations can be developed to go along with the positive images in order to solidify and reinforce clients' recognition of their strengths.

Proudest Moments

A popular career counseling strategy is to have people write brief vignettes in which they describe times when they felt happy and successful in their work. This strategy can be broadened and adapted to almost any treatment setting. Clinicians can suggest that people write or talk about times in their lives when they felt competent and proud of themselves. Identifying behaviors and perspectives that contributed to those good feelings can help people replicate them and create other sources of pride.

Task Accomplishment

Earlier in this chapter, we discussed the value of between-session tasks. Successful completion of such tasks can be empowering and can encourage people to take on increasingly greater challenges.

Refocusing Attention

People who experience low self-esteem and who feel immobilized typically focus on information that supports their negative views of themselves rather than incorporating disconfirming information. Clinicians can help people reverse this process via discussion in sessions as well as via between-session tasks that shift the client's focus of attention. For example, clinicians might suggest that clients notice and write down two accomplishments and one action to be changed during the previous week. Allowing people to identify both positives and negatives seems to make it easier for them to develop a realistic picture of themselves without leaning too far in either direction. Negatives, however, should be presented as something that can be improved upon, not a defect or fixed limitation.

CHALLENGE AND CARING CONFRONTATION

This book has stressed the importance of empowering people and helping them make choices that seem best for them. Clinicians sometimes believe that clients are making harmful choices and are acting in ways that are inconsistent with their goals and values. This was illustrated by the cases of Katie, Lavinia, and Curt presented in Chapter 9. At such times, clinicians usually need to encourage clients to look at and evaluate the choices they are making and help them see that other options would be more helpful to them.

This process has been described by many terms. *Confrontation* is probably the best known of these terms. However, in recent years, this term has fallen out of favor because of its negative connotations. Clinicians have come to realize that people often have strong reasons why they are reluctant to move forward and need support, information, and direction rather than pressure to change. Clinicians today are more likely to speak of *challenging clients* or using *caring confrontations*. Just as the name has changed, so has the nature of this process. Challenges, like other interventions in the clinician's repertoire, should be delivered with caring and sensitivity to ensure that they are helpful and enlightening rather than critical and shaming. An effective challenge can promote insight and awareness, reduce resistance, increase congruence between clients' goals and their behaviors, promote open communication, and lead to positive changes in people's emotions, thoughts, and actions.

Ten Types of Client Discrepancies

When people present for treatment of unhelpful behaviors but make little or no progress toward modifying those behaviors, they are experiencing a conflict or discrepancy in their point of view. Helping them recognize this can enable them to think through and resolve the conflict so that they can make progress. Generally, the best way to accomplish this is to calmly and gently point out the discrepancy to the client. The following list includes 10 types of discrepancies that people may present. Each is accompanied by the sort of statement a social worker, counselor, or psychologist might make to help people become aware of their conflicts (Hill & O'Brien, 1999).

1. **Discrepancy between two verbal statements:** Sometimes you tell me how much you love and value your parents, but at other times you tell me that you can't stand being around them and refer to them as toxic.

2. **Discrepancy between words and actions** (probably the most common type of discrepancy): Although you have made a commitment to sobriety, you went to a party where you knew there would be a great deal of drugs and alcohol.

3. **Discrepancy between two actions:** You teach courses on ways to promote children's self-esteem, and yet you tell your own children they are ignorant and clumsy.

4. **Discrepancy between two emotions:** You long for some close friends, yet your fears and shyness keep you from taking steps to make friends.

5. **Discrepancy between reported emotion and implicit emotion:** You have told me that it doesn't bother you that your girlfriend ended your relationship, and yet I see tears in your eyes when you talk about it.

6. **Discrepancy between values and behaviors:** One of your important values is maintaining the financial security of your family and yet you have lost so much money through high-risk investments that your home might be repossessed.

7. **Discrepancy between perceptions and experience:** Although you describe Sheryl as a loyal and trustworthy friend, you know that she has repeatedly spread false rumors about you and tried to prevent you from getting a promotion.

8. **Discrepancy between ideal and real self:** I know that you have a dream of going to Harvard like both of your parents, but your school records suggest that it would be difficult for you to gain admission to that institution.

9. **Discrepancy between viewpoints of client and clinician:** You tell me that you view cancer as a "minor inconvenience" and yet I perceive a life-threatening illness like cancer as an experience that has a profound impact on most people.

10. **Discrepancy between client and outside world:** You have told me that you are not planning to pay your taxes on schedule. I wonder if you are aware of the financial penalties that the Internal Revenue Service can levy against people who don't meet tax deadlines?

Guidelines for Effective Challenges

Just like advice giving, the use of challenges or messages about discrepancies presented in treatment poses risks. They may lead clients to feel hurt, attacked, angry, ashamed, confused, scared, insulted, or defensive. However, careful delivery of this information in the context of a sound therapeutic alliance can increase the likelihood that the challenges will be well received by clients and will lead them to new ways of feeling, thinking, and acting. The following guidelines can improve the delivery of challenges:

- Use careful listening to be sure of the accuracy of the challenge.
- Use reflections of feeling and meaning, as well as empathy and support, to demonstrate understanding and caring.
- Time delivery carefully; challenges are most likely to be effective after the development of a positive and trusting therapeutic alliance.
- Use challenges infrequently, generally when no other interventions seem likely to help.
- Be clear and specific when presenting a challenge, citing meaningful examples or statements.
- Be cautious, gentle, and tentative when presenting a challenge. The goal is to promote dialogue and exploration, not to prove the client wrong.
- After making a challenging statement, process the challenge. Elicit the client's involvement and reactions by asking such questions or statements as "What do you make of that?" "What is your reaction to that?" "How does that sound to you?" "Help me understand this," and "Had you noticed that?"
- Take into account the cultural background of the client. Challenges may be so hurtful and offensive to people from some cultural backgrounds that they should not be used at all.

VISUALIZATION

Many successful athletes and performers use visualization or imagery to enhance their success. This strategy can be used to increase the likelihood of success in almost any endeavor, including counseling and psychotherapy.

With the guidance of the clinician, clients imagine themselves effectively coping with obstacles and performing desired actions. These might be inviting a friend for lunch, cleaning out a closet, beginning an exercise class, spending a day without consuming alcohol, or almost any other action.

The visualization process typically begins with a brief relaxation exercise (discussed later in this chapter). Then the client imagines a scene, presented by the clinician, that includes the desired behaviors. The clinician should present a rich and detailed picture, vividly describing the client effectively performing the targeted behaviors, overcoming obstacles, and concluding with an image of the client feeling pride and satisfaction. The image should be a realistic one, including descriptions of difficulties that are likely to arise and negative emotions such as fear and anger that the client might experience. However, the visualization should also present the client addressing those difficulties and feelings and overcoming them. Anchoring, discussed in Chapter 8, can be used to install a positive image of the client achieving success, allowing ready access to that image in the future.

The following script illustrates the application of these principles. It reflects the use of visualization with Jack, a 17-year-old male who has been chosen to play the lead in his high school's production of Hamlet. He is surprised and pleased to have been chosen for the part, but is apprehensive that he will do poorly and will embarrass himself. The script begins after a brief relaxation exercise.

Clinician: Jack, it is now opening night and you are ready to play the part of Hamlet. You have attended all the rehearsals, studied and practiced your part again and again, and know that you are well prepared for this role. And yet you are feeling anxious. As you wait in the wings before the play starts, you recognize that your anxiety is normal and understandable; this is a big event for you. You take some slow, deep breaths to calm yourself and then you walk onto the stage, looking directly at the audience. You feel comfortable in this role that you have practiced so much, and your words come to you easily and automatically. Imagine yourself going through important scenes of the play with confidence and skill. Perhaps there is a time or two when you feel uncertain of what to do or say next; you know your teacher is right behind the curtain, ready to prompt you, and the other actors will all help you too just as you would help them. Now it's time for your most challenging scene, your confrontation of the queen. You have thought carefully about how Hamlet would feel about this scene and you can reach inside yourself and bring up the emotions you have rehearsed, even though that has been draining for you. Now the play is drawing to a close; you are proud of how well you did and know that any minor mistakes were unimportant and were evident only to you. It is your accomplishment of this challenge that is important. You can see your parents in the audience and know that they are so proud of your hard work in the play. The audience is applauding and you're smiling so much that your face hurts. Continue to imagine the applause, the pride of your parents, your pride in yourself, and how far you have come in the past year. Smile now as a reminder to yourself of how good you will feel when you have succeeded in this endeavor and how much you have accomplished. Know that a broad smile can help you to bring back these feelings and remind you of all you have and will accomplish.

BEHAVIORAL REHEARSAL

The old cliché, practice makes perfect, has a great deal of truth to it. When people practice a new or challenging behavior, they can try out a variety of approaches to the behavior, assess and refine their performance, develop new skills and strategies if necessary, and gain confidence through experience and success. Visualization is a sort of rehearsal or practice. In the previous example, Jack and his therapist would probably follow the visualization with a discussion of what Jack imagined and experienced during that process, what helped him to feel more optimistic and prepared, and what still made him anxious. The therapist would probably use additional interventions to alleviate the remaining anxiety and then perhaps engage Jack in another visualization to help him prepare for the performance.

Helping clients find ways to practice desired behaviors can increase the likelihood that they will be relaxed, confident, and prepared and that the actions will be performed effectively. Practice can happen in a variety of ways:

- Behaviors that involve a transaction between two people can be practiced in a treatment session via a role-play involving the client and the clinician. Such transactions could include discussing work-related issues with a supervisor, extending an invitation to a friend, expressing dissatisfaction with someone's behavior, and even proposing marriage. In the role-play, clients generally play themselves while clinicians assume the role of the other person in the interaction. Here, too, realism is desirable; when clinicians engage in the role-play, they should present clients with some issues or challenges that may arise so that they have the opportunity to try out ways to handle them. If clients have difficulty engaging in the role-play and would benefit from a role model, the roles can be reversed initially with the clinician assuming the client's role to demonstrate possible strategies for handling the situation. Reversing the roles can then afford clients the opportunity to try out what they have learned and adapt it to their own styles. The role-play can be tape recorded to facilitate discussion and feedback and then reviewed to identify strengths and strategies for improvement.

- Trying out a behavior in a safe setting can afford practice and learning. For example, assume that Jamie typically has difficulty expressing his needs and wants to practice some new assertiveness skills he has learned. Rather than practicing with his supervisor or even with his partner, which might be too risky, he might be wiser to try out his skills at the supermarket or auto repair shop. In that way, he will have few repercussions if the practice is not successful. In fact, in planning such a behavioral rehearsal, the clinician can emphasize that, whatever the outcome of the practice, it can provide an opportunity for learning and skill development.

- Using a video or audio tape recorder and practicing in front of a mirror can help people to take a relatively objective look at their performance and identify ways to make improvements. Asking a trusted friend or family member to review and comment on the performance can provide another source of useful feedback.

- Practice can also be internal or covert. Similar to the visualization exercise discussed earlier, people can review in their minds the details of a desired behavior. They can also try out, in their minds, various ways of performing the behavior to determine which feels most comfortable and is most likely to succeed.

Clinicians and clients may develop their own ways to incorporate practice into their work on changing behaviors. Whatever approach to practice is used, clients and clinicians should process and learn from the experience, viewing it as a source of information on the client's strengths as well as on sources of help, skills, and information that may be useful.

MODELING

The purpose of modeling is to provide clients with examples of desirable behaviors to facilitate their learning of these new behaviors. Seeing helpful actions performed by others can be encouraging to clients; at least someone can accomplish what they are trying to do! The use of an admired model is particularly inspiring to clients.

Like behavioral rehearsal, modeling can take a variety of forms. Clinicians themselves can serve as models, demonstrating to their clients new and useful types of behaviors such as initiating a conversation, making a request, and expressing anger. Alternatively, clients might be able to identify people they know who manifest the desired behaviors; clients can then observe these people and learn from them. The following are some additional approaches to modeling.

Using the self as a model is a strategy that is particularly useful and empowering. Clients practice a new behavior until they are satisfied with their performance. Then they record themselves exhibiting the desired behavior and watch or listen to it again and again until they believe they have mastered it. People with communication difficulties or social discomfort usually find this approach especially helpful because it is not threatening, does not require them to take risks until they feel ready to do so, and is empowering and reinforcing. Similarly, people who have trouble managing their emotions and who are worried about crying at inappropriate times or becoming angry and blaming are likely to benefit from this approach. They might tape record or read descriptions of situations that are likely to elicit unhelpful emotions and behaviors and then practice responding in different ways. In addition to the value of practice, the repeated exposure to disturbing scenarios can help them get used to such stimuli and, consequently, become less reactive and more deliberate in their responses.

Acting "as if…" is another variation on modeling, one that is particularly useful for young people. In this approach, clients select someone they admire who they believe could successfully perform a desired behavior. They might select a superhero, a well-known athlete, or a famous singer or actor. They might also select an admired friend or family member. Then, when clients are performing the desired behavior, they act as if they are the admired person. The process of identifying with someone who represents competence, power, and success to clients can enable them to take on some of those feelings vicariously and enhance their self-confidence and success. I have seen clients use this strategy successfully when they were preparing to deal with painful medical procedures; standing up to aggressive colleagues, students who bullied them, and abusive family members; and dealing with anxiety-provoking social and performance situations. Jack, described earlier in this chapter, might have acted as if he were his favorite actor when he gave his performance as Hamlet.

Similarly, people can act as if they have a particular trait or ability such as good social skills, assertiveness, extroversion, or a calm and cheerful mood. This strategy may seem simplistic. However, pretending to feel, think, and act in desired ways facilitates people's acquisition of desired traits or skills and helps them manifest them with greater comfort than they would otherwise.

SKILL DEVELOPMENT

Often the biggest barrier to people modifying their behaviors is that they have not learned the skills they need to implement the new behaviors and so continue to use unhelpful behaviors. Part of the clinician's role is helping people acquire those skills. The clinicians can teach the desired skills or they can be learned via reading, films, or workshops that might be useful to clients. These learning experiences might focus on such skills as effective communication, especially active listening, assertiveness, anger management, successful parenting, time management, decision making, and organization. I have even coached clients on how to plan a trip, write college applications and essays, make professional telephone calls, and select what to wear for business and social events. The skills needed vary from one person to another. Clinicians can make an important contribution to clients by helping them identify and acquire the skills that will help them make positive behavioral changes. As you have probably discovered for yourself, having the skills you need to deal with the people and experiences you encounter contributes greatly to your feelings of empowerment and self-confidence.

BREAKING DOWN BEHAVIORS INTO SMALL STEPS

Sometimes the enormity of a goal can be daunting, discouraging people from even beginning to work toward goal achievement. Think about yourself as a junior in high school. Assume that your career goal is to become a licensed social worker, counselor, or psychologist. Consider how many years and how much effort you have spent in achieving that goal. Had you known, when you were 16 or 17, how demanding it would be to achieve your career goal, you might have given up and focused your efforts on a more readily attainable goal. However, the process of becoming a clinician can be broken down into many steps that, in themselves, do not seem overwhelming. You have probably already completed many of those steps and are glad you have taken this journey, lengthy though it may be.

For the high school student aspiring to a career in human services, initial steps might include the following: achieving good grades in high school, taking a course or doing independent reading in the social sciences, identifying colleges with strong undergraduate programs in psychology or social work, and applying to college. Even these actions may seem overwhelming but they, too, can be broken into small steps. For example, the process of applying to college usually entails obtaining and completing applications, writing essays, requesting letters of recommendation, scheduling interviews, visiting the colleges, and making final decisions.

How might you help the following people to break down their goals into small steps?

- The newly married couple with no savings and low-paying jobs who want to purchase their own home
- The young boy who wants to play football in high school

- The woman who wants to write a book about her experience of successfully overcoming a history of abuse
- The man who is recovering from a heart attack who has been advised to stop smoking, improve his diet, begin an exercise program, increase his relaxation practices, and lose 25 pounds

Although keeping their final goal in mind can be useful to people, the process of identifying the steps to attain that goal and taking them one at a time can be far more empowering and more likely to motivate people toward continued action. Clinicians should keep this strategy in mind when working with clients who seem overwhelmed by how much they need to do to achieve their goals.

POSSIBILITY OR PRESUPPOSITIONAL LANGUAGE

Derived primarily from solution-based therapy (O'Hanlon & Weiner-Davis, 1989), possibility language used by clinicians can help people believe that they can act more effectively and that positive change can actually happen. In talking with clients, clinicians assume that the desired changes will certainly happen and that difficulties are only temporary. They use language that reflects those assumptions, creating the expectation of a positive outcome. Clinicians using possibility language might make statements or ask questions such as the following:

- You have not *yet* been able to take the steps you need to resolve this.
- *When you take those steps,* what do you think it will feel like?
- What will your life be like *when you have achieved your goals?*
- You can be fearful, *and you can move forward* to change your actions.
- What differences will your family notice *when you have made those changes?*
- You can clearly see the possibility that *you can improve your life.*

Language such as this promotes optimism and helps people feel more confident and capable of making positive changes. This, in turn, can reduce their apprehension about behavioral change and can motivate them to move forward in realistic ways.

RELAXATION

Relaxation strategies can reduce people's fears and barriers about attempting new behaviors and can enable them to perform those behaviors more confidently and effectively. In addition, acquiring and using relaxation strategies can be empowering, increasing people's conviction that they can learn and use helpful new behaviors.

Many strategies are available to clinicians who are helping their clients to reduce stress and increase relaxation. Among these are meditation (discussed in Chapter 8), diaphragmatic breathing, biofeedback, exercise, yoga, visualization, and progressive muscle relaxation. Combinations of strategies (e.g., diaphragmatic breathing, progressive muscle relaxation, and visualization) can be particularly powerful. Describing all of these strategies is beyond the scope of this book, but many resources such as *The Relaxation & Stress Reduction Workbook* (Davis, McKay, & Eshelman, 2003) can provide this information to both clients and clinicians. Clinicians also can make tape recordings during sessions in which they teach clients techniques such as deep breathing and progressive relaxation. Then the recordings can be given to clients with the suggestion that they listen to the recordings and practice the exercises frequently.

Many studies of both emotional and physical well-being suggest that all of us are likely to benefit from having a relaxation strategy that we use most days of the week. Do you have such a practice in your life? If not, or if you have not been using your relaxation strategies frequently, perhaps this is an opportunity for you to develop such a practice. This is not only likely to be of personal benefit to you, but it will allow you to be a role model for your clients and to experience firsthand the process and benefits of regular relaxation so that you can use that learning in your work with clients.

SYSTEMATIC DESENSITIZATION

Systematic desensitization is a powerful strategy for helping people reduce fears. This, in turn, can eliminate some of their barriers to behavioral change. Systematic desensitization gradually exposes people to their fears while they are in a state of relaxation. Exposure may occur in the imagination (imaginal desensitization) or in reality (in vivo desensitization).

Careful planning is needed to ensure that the person is ready for each exposure and that the exposure is maintained until the fear has diminished and is under control. Stopping the exposure prematurely can increase, rather than decrease, fears. Because the use of systematic desensitization poses some risk, clinicians should acquire training and supervision in this strategy before using it with their clients.

Systematic desensitization is illustrated here via its use with Eileen Carter, who has been discussed throughout this book. Eileen had a fear of taking exams. Although she was enthusiastic about her course work and eager to continue her education, her self-doubts and inconsistent academic history led her to become tense and anxious whenever she had an in-class exam. As a result, despite lengthy preparation for the exams, she did not always do her best on tests. Systematic desensitization was used as follows to help Eileen overcome this fear.

1. **Teach client an effective relaxation strategy.** An array of relaxation strategies was discussed with Eileen, and she was encouraged to do some reading on that subject. She decided that diaphragmatic breathing would be the best strategy for her; because of its simplicity, she was not likely to forget how to use this technique.
2. **Describe the feared experience or behavior as clearly as possible.** Eileen explained that her fear began when she sat down to study for an exam. It gradually worsened, becoming acute when she entered the classroom, and

Physical and emotional well-being benefits from having relaxation strategies

was almost debilitating when the exams were distributed. Her greatest fear was that, when she read the exam, she would discover that she was unable to answer any of the questions.

3. **Establish an anxiety hierarchy.** Eileen's clear description of her fear facilitated the development of an anxiety hierarchy, a list of fears presented in order from the mildest fear to the most severe. Rating each element in the anxiety hierarchy according to the amount of distress it raised on a 0 to 100 Subjective Units of Distress Scale (SUDS) ensured that the items were in the proper order. Eileen's anxiety hierarchy is presented in Table 10-1.

4. **Provide controlled exposure to the anxiety hierarchy.** Because the actual test-taking process could not be re-created in the treatment room, Eileen's clinician used imaginal desensitization. The clinician helped Eileen use deep

TABLE 10-1   Hierarchy of Eileen's Test-Related Fears

Stimulus	SUDS Rating
Putting my books and notes out on the desk so I can begin to study	45
Thinking about the exam while I study	55
Running out of time to study	65
Packing up my book bag to go to the exam	70
Driving to school	73
Walking into the exam room	80
Waiting for the exam to be distributed	85
Reviewing the exam	92
Taking the exam	95
Turning in the exam	99
Listening to the other students talk about their answers	100

breathing to relax and then began the desensitization process with the first item on the anxiety hierarchy. While Eileen relaxed, the clinician described Eileen gathering her study materials and putting her books and notes out on her desk so that she could begin studying. Eileen imagined the scene until she became more comfortable with it and her SUDS score began to decline. This experience was repeated until Eileen and her clinician believed that she had reduced her fear of the first item to a low and manageable level. They then progressed through the list, repeating this process with each item.

5. **Practice to solidify and reinforce gains.** Eileen practiced the relaxation and desensitization between sessions, imagining some of the first few items on the list that no longer raised much anxiety for her. When she began to study for her next exam, she once again used deep breathing to overcome her apprehension about test taking. Affirmations and progressive muscle relaxation further enhanced her efforts to relax. Gradually, Eileen's fear of taking tests lessened enough so that it did not impair her performance on the examinations.

LEARNING OPPORTUNITIES

Clinicians have many strategies they can use to facilitate clients' efforts to change unrewarding and self-destructive behavior. Thoughtful integration of one or more of these strategies into the behavioral change process, presented in Chapter 9, can result in a powerful treatment package.

This chapter has focused on teaching the following strategies that can help people change undesirable actions and behaviors:

- Between-session tasks to promote goal attainment
- Empowerment
- Challenge and caring confrontation
- Visualization
- Behavioral rehearsal
- Modeling and role-playing
- Skill development
- Breaking down behaviors into small steps
- Possibility or presuppositional language
- Relaxation
- Systematic desensitization

Written Exercises

1. For each of the clients described here, identify the following:
   - A useful between-session task
   - A specific strategy you will use to promote behavioral change and how you will use that strategy

   Client 1: I know I appear to be an ordinary middle-aged wife and mother, but my life revolves around video games. I spend at least 5 hours a day playing fantasy games and they have become the most important thing in my life. My husband and children don't seem to matter to me anymore.

A useful between-session task: _____

_____

A specific strategy you will use to promote behavioral change and how you will use that strategy: _____

_____

Client 2: I wish I had friends like the other kids, but I avoid people whenever I can. I go out to the bus stop at the last minute, I don't look at anyone or talk to anyone, and I sit alone on the bus and at lunch. I never volunteer in class and, if I think the teacher is going to call on me, I fake a coughing fit or take the pass to go the restroom. It's too late for me to change now; everyone will notice and make fun of me.

A useful between-session task: _____

_____

A specific strategy you will use to promote behavioral change and how you will use that strategy: _____

_____

Client 3: I started using pain killers when I had my back surgery and discovered how good I felt when I was taking them. Now I get prescriptions from three or four doctors so I'll always have the pills I need, even though my back is fine. I hate the lying and manipulation, but by now I must be physically addicted to the pain killers and I'm afraid to even try to stop using them.

A useful between-session task: _____

_____

A specific strategy you will use to promote behavioral change and how you will use that strategy: _____

_____

2. How might you strengthen feelings of empowerment in each of the three clients in Exercise 1?

   Client 1: _____

   _____

   Client 2: _____

   _____

   Client 3: _____

   _____

3. How might you use modeling or acting "as if…" to help one of the clients presented in Exercise 1?

4. Identify one of the clients in Exercise 1 who seems likely to benefit from skill development. Identify the skills that probably would be useful to that person. Briefly describe how you would go about teaching him or her the desired skills.

5. Write a statement using possibility language that you might use to help one of the clients presented in Exercise 1.

6. Develop a series of small steps that one of the clients presented in Exercise 1 might take to change his or her behavior. Remember to break the process down into incremental steps that are likely to lead to success and feelings of empowerment.

7. Many people are reluctant to take steps to change their unwanted behaviors. Using caring confrontations may help them to overcome their reluctance. Consider each of the following client statements. Identify the type of discrepancy that is present when you compare the two statements made by each person (see page **336** for a list of types of discrepancies). Then write a challenging statement or caring confrontation you might use to help each client become aware of the discrepancy and move forward.

Client 1: I have a new girlfriend and she really seems to like me. She must call me six or seven times a day. We just talk for hours every day; it really makes me feel special. So I haven't had a chance to follow up on our homework plan. I feel stuck; I don't want to have to repeat this grade or go to summer school but I don't want to lose my new girlfriend.

Type of discrepancy: _____

_____

Challenging statement: _____

_____

Client 2: I really wanted kids so much and I was so happy when they were born. I love them more than anything in the world and want them to know how wonderful they are. But sometimes I find myself treating them just like my mother treated me, yelling and belittling them. It seems to get their attention, so maybe it's just what I need to do.

Type of discrepancy: _____

_____

Challenging statement: _____

_____

Client 3: (Client smells of alcohol and appears unsteady.) I did just what we agreed. I haven't had a drink all week. No problem!

Type of discrepancy: _____

_____

Challenging statement: _____

_____

Discussion Questions

1. Clinicians are sometimes uncomfortable with the need to confront or challenge clients who are reluctant to change harmful behaviors. Discuss your thoughts

and feelings about this process. Under what circumstances do you think it is particularly important to challenge clients? What steps can you take to maximize the likelihood that this will be a helpful process for both client and clinician?

2. Consider the following people's behavioral goals, which were presented in the previous chapter. For each one, identify a specific intervention that might promote change, and a suggested between-session task.

   Client 1: My goal is to lose 50 pounds in 1 year.

   Specific intervention: _____

   _____

   Task: _____

   _____

   Client 2: I'm thirty-three years old and I've always been afraid of the water. My goal is to learn to swim so that I can take my children to the beach.

   Specific intervention: _____

   _____

   Task: _____

   _____

   Client 3: All my savings are in a bank account, earning about 3 percent interest. I want to learn about investing and make better decisions about my money.

   Specific intervention: _____

   _____

   Task: _____

   _____

   Client 4: I have an impulse to cut myself and have done so more than half a dozen times. I have had multiple infections and am very ashamed of my behavior, but I don't seem able to stop. Can you help me?

   Specific intervention: _____

   _____

   Task: _____

   _____

   Client 5: I recently had a leg amputated after an accident and have been fitted with a prosthesis. The doctors tell me that I can learn to walk again, but I am afraid I will fall.

   Specific intervention: _____

   _____

   Task: _____

   _____

3. Clients often find it useful for their clinicians to role-play with them interpersonal interactions that they anticipate will be difficult for them. Three pairs of

volunteers are needed for the following exercise. One person in each pair will demonstrate effective communication in the specified situation while the other person assumes the second role.

- A student with a learning disability informs her teacher of this and asks for accommodations while taking examinations. The teacher is unsympathetic and is reluctant to grant the accommodations. The person in the student role should demonstrate effective communication.
- An 85-year-old woman with Parkinson's disease has been living with her married son and his family. She is unable to live alone. However, she feels that her daughter-in-law resents her presence in the home and speaks to her in rude and insulting ways. The son has avoided involvement in the situation. The person playing the 85-year-old woman should demonstrate effective communication skills. The person in the other role can play either the son or the daughter-in-law (or two role-plays may be developed from this vignette).
- A woman has just learned that her husband has been having a sexual relationship with the man who is in charge of renovating their home. She is shocked and upset by this, but has decided to discuss the situation with her husband. The person playing the woman should demonstrate effective communication skills.

4. Most of us have tried to make behavioral changes in our lives. Discuss your own behavioral change efforts, including successes and disappointments. Focus particularly on the ingredients that contributed to the successes, as well as those that led to the disappointments.
5. If you have not yet done the practice group exercises associated with this chapter, discuss your thoughts and feelings about that upcoming experience. What obstacles do you expect to encounter? What can you do to try to avoid them? What did you learn from the previous role-play sessions that you want to carry with you into the role-play focused on changing actions?
6. If you have already done the practice group exercises associated with this chapter, discuss your reactions to that experience. What was the most beneficial aspect of that experience for you? What was the most challenging or uncomfortable aspect of the experience? How did this role-play compare with your earlier ones? How can you make future practice group exercises even more rewarding?

Practice Group Exercise: *Using Advanced Strategies to Modify Behaviors*

Divide into your practice groups. The practice group exercise presented here will help you to gain experience in at least two of the strategies presented in this chapter that can enhance a plan to change behaviors. The strategies that you might use in this role-play include these:

- Giving directives and suggesting between-session tasks
- Challenge/confrontation

- Empowerment
- Visualization
- Behavioral rehearsal
- Modeling and role-playing
- Skill development
- Breaking down actions into small steps
- Possibility or presuppositional language
- Relaxation
- Systematic desensitization

Preparing for the Role-Play

As with all of the practice group exercises in this book, you will probably be more successful and learn more from the role-play if you do some advance preparation as follows:

- Review the tape of your previous role-play, along with the feedback you received from your practice group.
- Review your previous Assessment of Progress forms. Identify patterns of strengths and recurring areas of difficulty so that you can keep those in mind as you engage in this role-play.
- Focus your efforts. Select one or two skill areas that you want to work on in this session, jot them down, and think about ways you can strengthen those skills. List below those skills that you intend to target this week and how you plan to improve them.

    1. _____
    2. _____

In addition to reviewing your progress and determining ways to improve your skills, you should select a behavior that you would like to work on changing when you are in the client role. Remember that this does not need to be a behavior that really is of concern for you; you always have the option of assuming a persona (acting as if you are someone else or creating a character for your role-play).

Role-Play Exercise

The goals of this role-play are as follows:

- **To build on the skills you have already learned.** Again, remember to review your Assessment of Progress forms to remind yourself of the skills that have already been introduced and what you need to focus on to improve those skills.
- **To facilitate your client's efforts to change undesirable behaviors by using at least two specific interventions.** Use two or more of the specific strategies presented in this chapter to promote change.

- **To gain experience in concluding the session with a summarization and suggested between-session task.** As you have done in your other sessions, use a summarization to concisely conclude and describe the nature of the session. In addition, suggest a task for the client to complete by the next session. Process the suggested task with the client to be sure the client understands and agrees to the task, perhaps modifying it as you discuss it.

Time Schedule

Allow 15 to 20 minutes for each session. As usual, be sure that at least 10 additional minutes are allocated for feedback to each person in the clinician role.

Assessment of Progress Form 10

1. **Improving targeted skills:** Review the skills you had targeted for improvement in this session. List them here and briefly describe what you did to improve those skills. How successful were your efforts? What do you need to continue to do or do differently?

   Skill 1: _____

   Skill 2: _____

2. **Using two specific interventions to promote behavior change:** Were you able to use two of the specific interventions presented in this chapter to facilitate your client's efforts to change behavior? If not, what got in the way of your using these interventions? If yes, what interventions did you use and how effective were they? Do you think that another type of specific intervention would have been even more helpful?

   Intervention 1: Name of intervention and assessment of effectiveness, highlighting what worked well and what needed improvement _____

   _____

   _____

   Intervention 2: Name of intervention and assessment of effectiveness, highlighting what worked well and what needed improvement _____

   _____

   _____

   Alternative interventions: _____

   _____

3. **Concluding the session:**

   - How successful were you at coming up with a between-session task that was acceptable to your client?
   - How successful was your summarization?

- Did you remember to check out both the suggested task and the summarization with the client?
- How might you have improved on the conclusion of your session?

4. How would you describe your overall effectiveness in this session, using the following rating scale?

- **Extremely helpful:** Reflects accurate and insightful listening; moves treatment in a very productive direction; promotes self-awareness, new learning, or positive changes.
- **Moderately helpful:** Reflects generally accurate listening; moves treatment in a productive direction, but does not clearly lead to greater self-awareness, new learning, or positive changes.
- **Neutral:** Neither contributes to the treatment goals nor harms the therapeutic process; may not accurately reflect what the client has communicated.
- **Moderately harmful:** Detracts somewhat from the treatment process or alliance; reflects poor listening and perhaps disinterest.
- **Extremely harmful:** Damaging to the treatment process or therapeutic alliance; sounds ridiculing and critical.

What might you have done differently to improve your self-ratings?

Personal Journal Questions

1. Identify a current situation that provokes anxiety in your life. Then identify someone you admire who you believe could handle that situation well. As you think about the anxiety-provoking situation, act, think, and feel as if you are that person. Monitor your reactions, including your emotions, thoughts, and actions. What changes, if any, did you notice in your usual reactions to the anxiety-provoking experience? Write briefly about using the acting "as if..." strategy to help yourself.

2. Using that same situation or another challenging situation in your life, engage in a behavioral rehearsal to help yourself handle the situation. You can either record what you might say in the situation or mentally rehearse the process of successfully dealing with the situation. Write briefly about using the strategy of behavioral rehearsal to help yourself.

3. List three strategies that you might use to empower yourself. Then implement at least one of the three strategies and write briefly about that experience.

4. Identify a fear you have or have had. Develop an anxiety hierarchy that reflects the levels of that fear that you might use if you were going to use systematic desensitization to help yourself overcome that fear.

5. Identify a situation, problem, or task in your life that seems overwhelming to you. Write down a series of small steps that you might take to gradually make inroads in tackling this situation.

SUMMARY

This chapter focused on the specific skills and strategies associated with helping people modify undesirable actions and behaviors. These skills included between-session tasks, empowerment, challenge and caring confrontation, visualization, behavioral rehearsal, modeling and role-playing, skill development, breaking down behaviors into small steps, possibility or presuppositional language, relaxation, and systematic desensitization.

This chapter concludes the presentation of fundamental skills and strategies that are essential to all mental health professionals, whether they are psychologists, counselors, social workers, psychiatric nurses, or others. The final chapter in this book provides a review of the skills you have learned and includes additional opportunities for you to apply those skills.

PART 6
SOLIDIFYING FUNDAMENTAL SKILLS

Chapter 11

REVIEWING, INTEGRATING, AND REINFORCING LEARNING

OVERVIEW

This chapter consists of three major sections. The first section presents the checklist of clinician strengths, initially presented in Chapter 1. Rerating your abilities on this checklist will help you identify the progress you have made by using this book to develop fundamental clinical skills. The first section of this chapter also presents an overview of some of the research on the process of becoming an expert clinician and the important characteristics of such a clinician.

The second part of this chapter presents an intake interview with a man who has both immediate and long-standing difficulties. A series of learning opportunities follows that interview, enabling you to review and apply many of the skills presented in this book to that case.

The third section includes additional learning experiences. Most important is a presentation of all the Assessment of Progress forms you have used throughout this book. This affords you another opportunity to assess your skills, identifying strengths as well as areas that continue to need attention. Use of these forms should give you an even clearer picture of yourself as a clinician and help you target your continuing efforts to improve and refine your skills. A final series of personal journal questions concludes this chapter, enabling you to further reflect on and synthesize the material you have studied and learned.

LEARNING GOALS

The purpose of this final chapter is to help you accomplish the following goals:

- Reevaluate your clinical strengths.
- Gain understanding of the transition from novice to experienced clinician and assess your progress along that path.
- Review the learning you have acquired through the information and exercises provided in this book.
- Raise your awareness of how much you have learned through your study of this material.
- Reinforce, enhance, and increase the learning you have acquired.
- Take another opportunity to practice your skills.

CHECKLIST OF CLINICIAN STRENGTHS

Chapter 1 presented a list of clinician strengths. You were asked to assess yourself, using that checklist. For each item, you used a plus (+) to indicate a strength, a minus (–) to reflect a weakness or a quality you have not yet developed, or a question mark (?) to indicate uncertainty about whether or not an item describes you. Before you look back at your self-ratings from Chapter 1, complete the following checklist using the same scoring method. As was suggested in Chapter 1, you might also ask a trusted friend, colleague, supervisor, or family member to identify those items on the list that he or she perceives as your strengths.

Checklist of Clinician Strengths

_____ Able to ask for help

_____ Able to deal with ambiguity and complexity

_____ Able to express oneself clearly, both orally and in writing

_____ Able to give credit to others for their accomplishments

_____ Aware of own political, spiritual, interpersonal, and other values

_____ Can draw on and learn from past experience

_____ Can see details as well as the big picture

_____ Caring

_____ Comfortable with networking and collaboration

_____ Creative

_____ Emotionally stable

_____ Empathic and able to identify emotions in self and others

_____ Ethical and respectful of laws, rules, standards, and boundaries but also able to exert efforts to change harmful standards

_____ Flexible and resourceful

_____ Hard working

_____ High frustration tolerance

_____ Insightful and psychologically minded

_____ Intelligent

_____ Interested, curious; an eager learner

_____ Maintains balance in own life

_____ Maintains own physical and emotional health

_____ Manifests good interpersonal skills and has some close relationships

_____ May have own concerns, but is addressing them and does not impose them on others

_____ Objective

_____ Open minded

_____ Respectful and appreciative of others and their differences

_____ Self-aware and honest with oneself

_____ Serves as a role model and inspiration to others

_____ Sound capacity for attention and concentration

_____ Willing to listen to feedback and make changes as needed

Once you have completed and reviewed the checklist, compare it with the checklist you completed on pages **6 & 7** in Chapter 1. What similarities do you see in your completion of the two checklists? What ratings have changed? Have you now marked more items with a plus sign and fewer items with a minus sign or question mark? Rerating the list will give you a good indication about the progress you have made in developing your skills.

If you find that you have even more items marked with a minus sign or question mark, don't let that discourage you. As we take a closer look at our skills and acquire a better understanding of the skills of the effective clinician, we may recognize that our skills are not as strong as we originally believed they were. This is a painful, but common, step in the process of becoming an expert clinician and probably does not mean that your skills have really declined. This can actually be viewed as progress because, now that you can more accurately assess the quality of your skills, you can more easily find ways to improve them.

Look at the three steps you identified to help you minimize your weaknesses, build on your strengths, and get to know yourself better. What progress have you made on those steps? What results have come from your efforts? Should you continue to work on those same steps, or do you now recognize other steps that would promote your professional growth? Keep the answers to these questions in mind as you continue reading and complete the exercises in this chapter, providing you even more information on your progress thus far and ways to continue your professional development.

CHARACTERISTICS OF THE EXPERT CLINICIAN

Although you probably do not yet think of yourself as an expert clinician, you may find it useful to learn how the literature describes such a clinician. That should give you a better understanding of the evolution you may experience as you develop from novice to skilled or even expert clinician and provide you with some ideas of ways to accelerate your progress toward increasing your clinical expertise.

Etringer, Hillerbrand, and Claiborn (1995) have taken an in-depth look at the transition from novice to expert clinician. They list the following as specific qualities of expert clinicians:

- Can develop and use strategies to monitor and regulate their own cognitive activity.
- Have a good awareness of what they do and do not know.
- Have a knowledge base that is not only broad and deep but also detailed and well integrated.
- Are able to organize information into abstract, problem-relevant structures and categories.
- Have good memory skills in their areas of expertise and can use them to recognize patterns.
- Can use existing knowledge to solve new problems.
- Are able to generate, assess, and either accept or reject hypotheses and then use those hypotheses to move toward conclusions.
- Can engage in forward reasoning and analysis and synthesis.
- Can start with existing information and then move toward a future-oriented goal or can start with a series of problems and move toward a diagnosis.

These findings can be summarized as follows:

> The expert clinician is characterized by being able to process and synthesize information, noting discrepancies and highlights along the way, and can then use theoretical and conceptual frameworks to make sense of that information and generate diagnoses, goals, and treatment plans to help people resolve issues and solve problems.

Sawatsky, Jevne, and Clark (1994) provide another useful study on the process of becoming an expert clinician. They refer to expert clinicians as "empowered" and offer an interesting view of the process of becoming empowered or expert. According to Sawatsky et al., clinician development is a cyclical process of seeking and experiencing dissonance, responding to that dissonance, and learning from the process. Dissonance can come from many sources, including realizing that we have weaknesses in our knowledge or skills, encountering challenging clients and problems, and receiving feedback from supervisors, colleagues, and clients. Using dissonance as a learning experience often entails some risk taking as we acquire and experiment with new skills and strategies. Anxiety is inherent in this process and, unless at disabling levels, usually is a promoting rather than an inhibiting factor.

The journey from novice to expert clinician is often an erratic and gradual one that continues, and usually accelerates, long after formal coursework has been completed (Skovholt & Ronnestad, 1992). Over time, learning comes increasingly from interpersonal encounters rather than from data, from clients rather than from mentors, and from within rather than from without.

Although I have been a professor, therapist, supervisor, mentor, and writer for many years, I continue to learn more about my profession and constantly improve my skills. My learning now comes primarily from my clients, the people I supervise, and my own reading rather than from classroom learning. However, the rapid growth of knowledge in the helping professions and my own desire to remain up to date in my field and help others as much as possible fuel my ongoing and rewarding quest for increased knowledge and understanding of my profession.

Successful negotiation of the cyclical process described here, as well as a quest for knowledge and skill development, ultimately leads effective clinicians to develop the following characteristics (Leach, Stoltenberg, McNeill, & Eichenfield, 1997; Sawatsky et al., 1994; Skovholt & Ronnestad, 1992):

Self-Awareness

- A sound capacity for self-reflection
- Awareness of own motivations, needs, attitudes, values, personalities, and perceptual styles

Self-Efficacy

- Eagerness to engage in continual self-reflection and growth
- Empowerment
- Professional individuation, reflected in an integration of professional and personal selves
- Reasonable confidence in their own judgment
- A sense of control over their responses
- Ability to welcome dissonance as a learning experience
- Consistency and congruence between both their beliefs and values and their theoretical framework and strategies
- Flexibility and psychological health reflected in emotions, thoughts, and actions
- Awareness of ethical standards

Strong Knowledge Base and Conceptual Skills

- A broad and deep knowledge of events, concepts, and skills in their field
- Ability to use that knowledge base to construct their own knowledge and to organize information
- Ability to acquire and apply new learning and skills from many sources, including role models, clients, and the professional literature
- Acceptance and appreciation of human diversity

Think about yourself in relation to these profiles of expert clinicians. Try to be honest with yourself. You will probably find that you already possess many of the qualities of the expert clinician and that you need further learning and development in some of these areas. As part of the process of continual self-evaluation that characterizes advanced clinicians, the personal journal questions at the end of this chapter afford you the opportunity to assess yourself in relation to the previous descriptions of the expert clinician.

Now that you have reviewed some of the characteristics and abilities of the skilled and expert clinician, you have the opportunity to apply and demonstrate some of your skills. The following exercise includes an intake interview and a series of questions related to the client presented in the interview. This affords you the opportunity to use many of the skills presented in this book and document your progress on the Assessment of Progress forms that have been included at the end of the chapter. Begin by carefully reading and thinking about the case of Samuel Gold.

Intake Interview of Samuel Gold

The client, Samuel (Sam) Gold is a 34-year-old Jewish man who is self-referred for treatment. He is about 5 feet 7 inches tall, and slender. He has dark hair and a beard and is dressed casually in a T-shirt, jeans, and running shoes. Sam appears tense and talks rapidly but clearly.

Clinician 1: What brings you in for treatment, Sam?

Client 1: Do you want the long story or the short story?

Clinician 2: Which would you prefer to tell me?

Client 2: Let's start with the short one, and I'm sure we'll get to the long one soon. About 3 weeks ago, I was diagnosed with lymphoma. Now I'm facing months of chemotherapy and other treatments and who knows what the outcome will be. I'm only 34. I should be dealing with raising a family like all my friends, not with thoughts about dying.

Clinician 3: This must be very frightening and upsetting to you.

Client 3: Yes, it sure is. But then, in a funny way, it isn't.

Clinician 4: So your feelings about this are really mixed?

Client 4: Yes, you might say that. I guess I always knew I'd get cancer or some terrible disease.

Clinician 5: What made you think that?

Client 5: A couple of things. First, I had been feeling lousy for 6 or 8 months—tired, run-down, just not myself. I'm not a real high-energy person but this was worse than usual. And the one thing I do on a regular basis is run; that's been part of my life for years. I couldn't even get myself to do a mile or two, let alone my usual 5 or 10. Something had to be wrong. I went through a bunch of docs and then finally found one smart enough to figure it out.

Clinician 6: So you hadn't been feeling well for quite a few months and suspected you had a medical problem going on.

Client 6: Yeah, but that wasn't all. . . .

Clinician 7: It wasn't all?

Client 7: Yeah. This might sound strange, but I'm just not a lucky person. Bad things keep happening to me. So it really wasn't such a surprise when they told me I had cancer. I guess we got into the long story even faster than I thought.

Clinician 8: It probably would be useful to put your diagnosis with cancer in context, so how would you feel about giving me some background information that is probably part of the long story?

Client 8: Sure. I know we only have 45 minutes but I'll try to make a very long story short, even though I have to start with my great-grandparents. All four sets of great-grandparents came to the United States from Eastern Europe, Poland, or whatever it was then, in the early 1900s. Came through Ellis Island. Jews had been treated pretty badly in that part of Europe, so they came here to get away from the persecution. I guess the men came first, hooked up with relatives who were already here, found jobs and places to live and then sent for the women and children. I think a couple of the grandparents came over as very young children and the other two were born here. They settled in urban areas in the northeast United States—New York, Philly, Hartford. They were poor when they got here, couldn't bring much with them. But I guess they were pretty industrious. The great-grandparents became merchants of one kind or another and tried to make a decent home for the kids, get them a decent education.

Clinician 9: It sounds like you believe they had quite a struggle but tried hard to realize their values of family and education.

Client 9: Yes, that's really the Jewish tradition, of religion, family, and education all being important. And you can see this pattern of each generation doing a little better than the last one—until they got to me. But I'm getting ahead of myself, and I really want to tell you the whole story. The grandparents did a little better than their parents. My mother's father became a pharmacist and his wife was an elementary school teacher. My father's father was an accountant. His wife never worked for pay, but she did lots of volunteer work in New York City. So then we get to my parents. When they met, my father was a medical student at Columbia University, and my mother was a graduate student in social work. She was spending the summer in New York, taking some courses but really getting away to sort out her life. A perfect match except for one little problem: She's already married and has a husband and baby back in Connecticut. She's miserable; her husband's abusive and she can't stand him. So she starts seeing my father and gets pregnant. Sounds like a soap opera, doesn't it?

Clinician 10: It's a pretty complicated story. How does all of this affect you?

Client 10: Now we get to the part about me. I'm the little surprise, the pregnancy that messes up this great romance. This was back in the late sixties when everybody is having sex but you're still not supposed to. Hard to hide when you get pregnant. So my parents move in together, my mother gets a quick divorce, and they get married as soon as they can. They don't tell my father's parents about my mother's first marriage, just make believe it never happened. My father's parents, the rich accountant and his wife, make them a big party to celebrate the marriage. Nobody mentions the ex-husband and kid in Connecticut, and now my parents are supposed to live happily ever after. Of course, my mother gives up custody and all contact with her daughter and never talks about any of this to anyone except my father. And by now he's doing his residency and is never home.

Clinician 11: This was certainly a hard way to start a marriage.

Client 11: Yeah, too difficult. Now, remember that I'm making a long story short. My mother gets very depressed, tries to kill herself, and is put in a psychiatric hospital. I get farmed out to my father's parents who have no time for a kid, and so I'm in child care before I can even walk. Well, the story keeps going downhill. After a couple of tries at reconciliation, my parents get a divorce, my mother never really recovers and has been in therapy, on medication, and in and out of the hospital her whole life. My father finishes medical school, becomes a top New York City cardiologist, gets married again, has a few more kids, and only remembers me long enough to call me and ask how my grades are.

Clinician 12: You must have felt pretty alone through all this and yet you survived. How did you cope with this?

Client 12: How did I cope? Not very well. I felt a lot of pressure on me to bring something good out of this mess. I guess I was pretty precocious as a child, played the piano and the violin when I was very young, wrote music. The next Mozart, they thought. Send him to special schools, put even more pressure on him. So I started causing trouble, not doing my homework, not practicing my music, then cutting class, smoking pot, running away, having sex with anybody I could. Then they started in with the therapists who were supposed to fix me. The only one who did me any good was the one who just sat there and played chess with me for the whole time. I didn't want to be fixed, so I wouldn't say a word.

Clinician 13: Perhaps you were working very hard to be your own person and to be noticed for yourself.

Client 13: I'm sure that was at least part of it. But now I'm 34 years old and I'm still doing it. I dropped out of high school, made some money off of some pyramid schemes, got a GED, tried a couple of colleges. Bard was too unstructured, City College was too structured, and the community college was too boring. Finally, after many years, I put all the pieces together and got a college degree. And I do the same thing with women and jobs. Just go from one to another and when the going gets tough, I get going.

Clinician 14: For many years, then, you've been looking for a niche that fits you, but you haven't been able to find it. How has that made you feel?

Client 14: Like a real loser. Dad keeps paying the bills and bailing me out when I get into trouble; at least he does that for me. But that almost makes things worse. Each time he bails me out, he says, "Samuel, I hope you can learn something from this. I hope the next time will be different." But it never is. I know he's disappointed in me. His other kids, younger than I am, are these great successes. His son is a lawyer and his daughter is in an M.D./Ph.D. program. And then there's Samuel, the failure.

Clinician 15: You sound disappointed with many of the choices you have made in your life.

Client 15: You can say that again. I've always felt pretty bad about myself. I don't know if I inherited my mother's depression but I've felt depressed most of my life too.

Clinician 16: What is your depression like for you?

Client 16: I have trouble falling asleep. It's so bad, I hate to even try to go to sleep, so I stay up watching late-night television, commercials interspersed with a few minutes of programs. Sometimes it makes me sleepy enough so I drift off but usually it just leaves me so tired in the morning that I can't get much done. I worry a lot, ruminate about all my past failures and the ones I know are still to come. I feel guilty about the mess I've made of my life but I haven't been able to change it. I feel pretty hopeless. I guess I'm not as bad off as my mother. I've never tried to kill myself and, most of the time, I have a job, but it still feels like I'm trapped in a tunnel with no way out.

Clinician 17: It does sound like you have been very depressed. What has your life been like lately?

Client 17: I hesitate to say this; I don't want to jinx myself. But actually things were getting slightly better before I was diagnosed with cancer.

Clinician 18: How so?

Client 18: I've been dating a decent woman for a change. Vicki is her name. She's a history teacher, very bright with lots of interests. We can actually carry on a conversation, a first for me with women. She's never been married either. And she's even Jewish, which makes all the relatives happy. I've been in the same job now for over a year, working in publicity for an arts complex. It's pretty creative and they put up with me wearing whatever I want and making my own schedule.

Clinician 19: So both personally and professionally, you have made some positive changes in your life. What impact did your medical diagnosis have on all that?

Client 19: I figured Vicki was going to drop me as soon as I told her, but she's hanging in with me. She even went to a couple of doctor's appointments with me. The people at work have been pretty supportive, too, giving me time off and helping me figure out my medical coverage. Even my father came through. He told me which oncologist to see, he read my medical reports, and he helped me make some decisions about my treatment. His name really opened doors for me and I've gotten in to see the top docs at Sloan-Kettering. I guess my dad figures if I die, there's no hope I'll ever amount to anything.

Clinician 20: You sound surprised that people have tried to help.

Client 20: Yeah, I guess I am. You know, the thought of marrying Vicki even crossed my mind. The docs told me my treatments might make me sterile and suggested I bank some sperm in case I ever wanted to have children. A few years ago, I wouldn't have cared, but now I'm going to do it. I sure can't imagine myself as a husband and father, though. How would I even know how to be a decent husband and father?

Clinician 21: You sound pretty doubtful about your ability to handle those roles, and yet I hear some excitement about that, too. Sometimes dealing with a life-threatening illness can lead us to reevaluate our lives and make some important changes in our goals and priorities.

Client 21: Really! I guess that's what happened. Now if I can just survive this, there may still be some hope for me. Before, I never felt like I had much hope or reason to go on. Now, I think I do. I don't want to die, and I want to see if I can do something more with my life after I'm through with all my treatments.

Clinician 22: I'm hearing some goals there. Sounds like you want to use your new perspective on your life to try to make some positive changes.

Client 22: You got it.

Clinician 23: Our time is just about up. We've covered quite a bit of ground and still have lots more to talk about in future sessions but I wonder if there is anything else you want to be sure to mention before we wrap up for today?

Client 23: Not right now. It looks like I did tell you the short story as well as the long story after all.

Clinician 24: And they both fit together. You've been through a great deal in your life, and something inside you kept you alive and still fighting. Even though you will probably have even more to deal with as you cope with cancer and its treatments, I think it is important for us to remember how much you have dealt with, along with the sense of hopefulness you are feeling now.

Client 24: Yeah, I guess I do have some things going for me even now. Let's schedule another appointment.

LEARNING OPPORTUNITIES

The case of Samuel Gold is a lengthy and complex one. To understand Sam as fully as possible, you need to consider many factors, including:

- The content of this dialogue
- Sam's presentation and style of talking
- His cultural and religious background
- The intergenerational messages and models he received
- The backdrop of the times in which he and his family members grew up
- His life history
- His immediate presenting concern (his diagnosis with lymphoma)

Consider all of these factors as you complete the following exercises. The exercises are organized according to the sequence of chapters in this book. You can focus on those discussion questions and exercises that are particularly interesting or challenging to you or you can work your way, systematically, through the discussion questions and exercises as they are presented. This approach will provide you with a review of the skills and concepts presented in this book.

Chapter 1:

Establishing the Foundation for Skill Development: Becoming an Effective Clinician

1. Chapter 1 introduced the BETA framework. For each of the four components of that model, list relevant information about Sam:

    a. Background
    b. Emotions

      c. Thoughts

      d. Actions

2. Which of these areas is emphasized in this interview? Which are de-emphasized? Would you have changed this emphasis? If so, how and why?

3. How important is it that Sam and his clinician have a strong and positive therapeutic alliance? What has led you to that conclusion? Based on what you currently know about Sam, what steps would you take to build a strong therapeutic alliance with him? What obstacles seem most likely to arise in your work with Sam and your efforts to work collaboratively with him? What steps might you take to address those obstacles?

Chapter 2:

Laying the Groundwork for Skill Development: Antecedents to Effective Skill Development

1. What elements of diversity and multiculturalism are important in your understanding of Sam? How have those elements contributed to Sam's development? What steps would you take to demonstrate your sensitivity to and appreciation for the multicultural elements in Sam's history?

2. How well do you think Sam has integrated his mind, body, and spirit? How might you help him achieve a better integration of these three areas?

3. What ethical concerns, if any, do you have about your treatment of Sam?

Chapter 3:

Using Questions Effectively to Gather Information and Understand Background— Open and Closed Questions, Intake Interviews

1. Identify the open questions used by the clinician in the interview with Sam. Which seem particularly helpful? Do any of the questions seem neutral or harmful? If so, write a replacement intervention that seems more helpful.

2. Identify the closed questions used by the clinician in the interview with Sam. Which seem particularly helpful? Do any of the questions seem neutral or harmful? If so, write a replacement intervention that seems more helpful.

3. Look at the first three questions asked by the clinician in this dialogue. What seemed to be the clinician's purpose in asking each of those questions?

4. How would you assess the clinician's ability to combine questions with other interventions to build rapport and elicit the involvement and cooperation of the client in the intake process?

5. Page **101** of Chapter 3 list the topics usually covered in an intake interview. How well was each of these topics covered in this intake interview? Which topics, if any, warranted more attention and why?

6. What do you see as the strengths and weaknesses of this initial interview? How might it have been improved?

Chapter 4:

Additional Skills Used to Gather Information and Understand Background—Structuring the Initial Session, Early Recollections, Genograms, and Life Chronology

1. What is your assessment of the structure of this initial session with Sam? What suggestions, if any, do you have on how the structure might have been improved?
2. Create two early memories that you think might reflect Sam's history and his perspective on the world and his life. What themes emerge from these memories and what do they reveal about Sam?
3. Draw a genogram of Sam Gold's family, including brief hypothetical descriptions of each family member, as was done for Eileen Carter on page **130**. What important pieces of information do you think would probably emerge from Sam's genogram?
4. Draw a lifeline for Sam Gold. Feel free to determine specific dates that are not provided in the interview, as long as your dates are consistent with the information provided.

Chapter 5:

Using Fundamental Skills to Elicit and Clarify Emotions—Understanding the Importance of Emotions, Attending and Following, Using Verbal Encouragers, Communicating Empathy, Addressing and Using Nonverbal Communication and Silence

1. What is your assessment of the effectiveness of the clinician's listening skills in the dialogue with Sam? What strategies did the clinician use to convey effective attending?
2. What might the clinician have done to demonstrate even more effective listening?
3. Identify at least three places in the dialogue when the clinician used a verbal encourager. For each, identify what type of verbal encourager was used (accent, restatement, paraphrase, summarization).
4. How well did the clinician track or follow what Sam was saying? Can you find places in the dialogue when the clinician changed the focus of discussion or did not respond to important comments Sam made? Was each of these interventions helpful, or did it detract from the interview?
5. List the emotions that Sam reported. Analyze at least one of these emotions according to the eight dimensions of emotion, listed on page **167**.
6. What other emotions do you sense that Sam was experiencing?
7. Identify at least three places in the dialogue where the clinician used reflections of feeling.
8. Would you have made more or less or the same use of reflection of feeling? Explain your response.
9. The clinician paid little attention to Sam's nonverbal communications. Drawing on the picture of Sam that you have in your mind, write three reflections of nonverbal communication that the clinician might have used with Sam.

Chapter 6:

Using Fundamental Using Fundamental Skills to Contain and Change Emotions—Additional Strategies for Eliciting and Promoting Understanding of Emotions, Making Constructive Use of Our Own Emotions, Strategies for Containing and Modifying Emotions (Focusing, New Perspectives, Distraction, Thought Stopping, Imagery, Use of Language)

1. As you became acquainted with Sam through the initial interview, what feelings did you develop toward him? If you had any negative feelings, how would you deal with those so that they do not adversely affect your work with Sam? If you had positive feelings, how could you use those to enhance your work with Sam and help him feel more empowered and positive about himself?
2. What strengths can you identify in Sam? What interventions did the clinician make to help Sam become more aware of his assets? How might the clinician have called greater attention to Sam's strengths?
3. Consider use of the following strategies with Sam to help him control and modify his emotions:

   - Focusing
   - Introducing new perspectives
   - Containment
   - Distraction or thought stopping
   - Reassurance and support
   - Guided imagery

Which of these strategies do you think would be most effective with Sam and why? How would you go about using this strategy with Sam? Which do you think would be least effective with him and why?

Chapter 7:

Using Fundamental Skills to Elicit, Identify, Assess, and Modify Thoughts and Accompanying Emotions and Actions—Understanding the Nature and Importance of Thoughts, Identifying and Disputing Distorted Cognitions as Well as Accompanying Emotions and Actions

1. As you read the dialogue with Sam, you probably noticed that, at many points, Sam's thoughts seemed distorted or unrealistic. Imagine that you are going to help Sam clarify his distorted and self-critical thinking after he is unsuccessful in his efforts to obtain a job that requires an advanced degree he does not have. Add information to the case as needed, as long as it is consistent with what you already know about Sam.

   - Identify the emotions Sam is likely to experience.
   - Estimate the intensity of those emotions on a 0 to 100 scale.
   - Identify two to four distorted thoughts that Sam is likely to have in response to his unsuccessful job application.

- Estimate the degree of belief he has in each of those thoughts on a 0 to 100 scale.
- Identify actions Sam is likely to take in response to his distorted cognitions.

2. Describe two ways in which Sam's clinician might collaborate with him to dispute his thoughts.
3. Suggest replacements for Sam's emotions, thoughts, and actions that are more likely to be helpful to him.

Chapter 8:

Additional Skills Used to Elict, Identify, Assess, and Modify Thoughts—Reflection of Meaning, Decision Making and Problem Solving, Information Giving, Additional Strategies to Help People Change Thoughts

1. Develop a reflection of meaning you might use with Sam to help him understand the significance the following experiences have had for him:

- His diagnosis with cancer
- Vicki's commitment to stick by him as he goes through his treatments
- His father's disapproval of Sam's academic difficulties

2. Sam tells you he is reluctant to tell his mother he has been diagnosed with cancer; he views her as very fragile and does not want to upset her. Discuss or role-play how you might help Sam with this issue. In your dialogue or role-play, be sure to make use of problem-solving and decision-making strategies presented in Chapter 8. In addition, incorporate information giving into your plan, providing Sam some knowledge of the often negative impact of secrets in families.
3. Suggest an affirmation that might help Sam.
4. How might you use anchoring to help Sam deal with his anxiety about chemotherapy and its side effects?
5. Sam views himself as a failure because of his many unrewarding jobs and relationships. How might you use reframing to help Sam take a more positive and empowering perspective on those experiences?
6. How do you think Sam would respond to the suggestion that he use meditation to help himself relax and focus? What sort of meditation seems most likely to minimize any resistance he might have to that process?
7. Develop a mind map of how Sam feels about himself and his life. At the center, should be Sam's Life. Second level branches might include My Father, My Mother, Relationships, My Career, Cancer, My Strengths, and My Concerns. Feel free to add other second-level branches. Then extend the mind map to least one more level.

Chapter 9:

Using Fundamental Skills to Identify, Assess, and Change Actions and Behaviors— Understanding the Importance of Actions and Behaviors, Establishing a Baseline,

Promoting Behavior Change Goal Setting and Contracting, Using Directives and Suggesting Tasks

1. Sam reported that one of the job-related problems he had was submitting work on schedule. He was critical of the reports and projects he prepared and would often spend many hours reviewing and revising them, trying to make them as perfect as possible. The result was that he missed deadlines. Develop a behavioral change plan to help Sam with this problem. Your plan should include the following elements:

   - Establishing a baseline
   - Formulating goals that meet the eight criteria listed on page **298**
   - Developing skills to facilitate goal attainment
   - Identifying obstacles and ways to overcome them
   - Establishing meaningful rewards
   - Planning record keeping
   - Creating a contract

2. Suggest two between-session tasks that might help Sam cope with deadlines more successfully. Be sure that, although you may be drawing on your own experiences with this issue, you follow the guidelines for giving clients advice and do not impose your recommendations or learning on Sam.

Chapter 10:

Additional Skills Used to Identify, Assess, and Change Actions and Behaviors—Stages of Readiness, Confrontation and Challenge, Specific Skills to Promote Behavioral Change

1. As is evident in the dialogue, Sam tends to feel hopeless and discouraged. This gets in the way of his making good use of his considerable abilities. Identify one strategy you might use to empower Sam to take effective actions.
2. How might you use visualization to help Sam resolve his difficulties and move forward with his life?
3. How might you use behavioral rehearsal or modeling to help Sam?
4. Write a statement using possibility or presuppositional language that might be helpful to Sam.
5. Systematic desensitization can help people cope with anticipatory anxiety associated with chemotherapy. Plan how you would use this strategy to help Sam cope with his medical treatments. Your plan should include development of a hypothetical anxiety hierarchy, based on what you know about Sam.

OVERVIEW OF SELF-EVALUATION

This section presents all the self-evaluation forms that are included throughout this book. This material can be used in the following ways:

- As you learn the material and complete the exercises in earlier chapters, you can look ahead to this section for a preview of the learning and exercises to come. This can help you put in context the information presented in earlier chapters.

- You can use these forms for a final class exercise. Divide into your usual practice groups. Ample time should be allowed for this exercise so that each person has the opportunity to role-play both client and clinician. Allow at least 30 minutes for each role-play plus at least 30 minutes for processing. If necessary, the processing time can be shortened by ensuring that each session is tape recorded for later review and analysis. If that is done, participants in the exercise can then complete their self-evaluation forms alone, with their role-played clients, or with the entire group either outside of class time or in a subsequent class session.

- The role-played session should represent an initial meeting between client and clinician, with clients presenting different concerns or issues than they have addressed in earlier role-played sessions. Other than that, the focus of the session should be determined by each client. The session simulates an actual treatment session in that clinicians may have little or no information about their clients and their concerns at the initial meeting.

- To provide feedback, individuals, dyads, or the entire group of three or four people can review each person's final role-play in terms of each of the ten Assessment of Progress forms. This should provide a comprehensive picture of each group member's current level of skills and facilitate identification of areas of strength, areas of competence, and areas still in need of attention.

- Yet another approach to using these evaluation forms is as a stimulus for reflecting on the growth in clinical skills you achieved while you engaged in the learning provided in this book. Review your initial self-evaluations in earlier chapters and think about improvements you have made in your skills. Also identify those skills that you believe still need improvement. Recalling specific examples of strength, growth, and shortcomings in your skills can help you to prepare specific and meaningful self-evaluations. Based on your reflections, complete this second set of forms, providing a written record of your progress.

Compilation of Self-Evaluation Forms to Assess Progress

The Assessment of Progress forms that follow appeared at the end of each chapter, as indicated. Complete these forms again, as described previously, based either on a final role-played exercise or on your own assessment of your progress.

ASSESSMENT OF PROGRESS FORMS

Assessment of Progress Form 1

1. List three clinical skills that you believe are strengths for you:

   a.

   b.

   c.

2. List three clinical skills that you believe you need to develop or improve:

   a.

   b.

   c.

Assessment of Progress Form 3

1. Use of questions

   a. Balance of open and closed questions
   b. Nature of questions (implicit, open, or closed); beginning with *how, what, why,* or another word)
   c. Integration of questions and other interventions
   d. Helpfulness of questions

2. Intake interview

   a. Identification and exploration of presenting concerns
   b. Ability to elicit relevant information on background, history, context
   c. Ability to develop initial rapport
   d. Strengths of intake interview
   e. Omissions or areas needing improvement

3. Summary of feedback
4. Two or three goals that will help you improve your clinical skills

Assessment of Progress Form 4

1. Use of questions

   a. Balance of open and closed questions
   b. Nature of questions (implicit; beginning with *how, what, why,* or another word)
   c. Integration of questions and other interventions
   d. Helpfulness of questions

2. Eliciting and analyzing early recollections

   a. Ability to elicit three early recollections
   b. Ability to help client explore and expand on each recollection
   c. Ability to collaborate with client in identifying themes and patterns
   d. Ability to synthesize themes and patterns and communicate them to the client in helpful ways
   e. Identification and emphasis on strengths, making the role-play a positive and growth-promoting experience

3. Summary of feedback
   a. Strengths of role-play focused on early recollections
   b. Omissions or areas needing improvement
   c. Ability to link past experiences with present issues

4. Two or three goals that will help you improve your clinical skills

Assessment of Progress Form 5

1. **Promoting expression and understanding of emotions.** What use did you make of each of the following interventions? What strengths were evident in your interventions? How might you have been even more successful in promoting the client's expression and understanding of emotions?

   a. Use of accents, restatements
   b. Use of paraphrases
   c. Use of reflections of feeling
   d. Use of questions
   e. Use of summarizing

2. **Tracking.** How well were you able to follow the client? Did you use any strategies to redirect the discussion? How did they work? Should you have made more or less use of redirection?

3. **Nonverbal messages.** What impact did the following types of nonverbal messages have on the counseling process? How might they have been improved?

   a. Eye contact
   b. Posture
   c. Proximity to client
   d. Physical movements and gestures
   e. Tone of voice and rate of speech

4. Summary of feedback:
5. Progress in achieving goals from the previous session:
6. One or two additional goals to improve your clinical skills:

   a.
   b.

Assessment of Progress Form 6

1. **Using a specific intervention to elicit emotions.** How successful were you in using the intervention you had selected? What barriers or challenges did you encounter when you made use of the strategy? What strengths were evident in your application of the intervention? How might you have been even more effective in promoting the client's expression and understanding of emotions? In retrospect, do you think a different intervention or strategy would have been more helpful, in light of the concern your partner presented? If so, which one and what are your reasons for thinking it would have been more effective?

2. Assess your use of the following:
   a. Use of a variety of opening leads
   b. Use of strength-based reflections of feeling
   c. Use of other attending skills

3. **Nonverbal messages.** In what ways did you deliberately use nonverbal communication to enhance the role-play? What did you do to demonstrate nonverbal complementarity and synchrony? What impact did these have? What were the strengths in your use of nonverbal communication? How might your nonverbal communication have been improved? Comment on the following behaviors on the part of the clinician:
   a. Eye contact
   b. Posture
   c. Proximity to client
   d. Physical movements and gestures
   e. Tone of voice and rate of speech

4. Summary of feedback:
5. Progress in achieving goals from previous session:
6. One or two additional goals to improve your clinical skills:
   a.
   b.

Assessment of Progress Form 7

1. **Making effective use of skills you have already learned.** What use did you make of the following skills, which were learned in previous chapters? How effective was your use of these skills?

   • Open and closed questions:
   • Accents, restatements, and paraphrases:
   • Reflections of feeling:
   • Attentive body language:
   • Summarizing:

2. **Helping your client express, assess, and modify thoughts.** How effective were you at guiding your client through the 10 steps in the process? Which steps felt most comfortable for you? Which were most productive? Which presented you with the greatest challenge? How might you have improved on this process?

3. Overall, how would you assess the impact of your session, according to the following rating scale?

   • **Extremely helpful:** Moves treatment in a productive direction; promotes self-awareness, new learning, or positive changes.
   • **Moderately helpful:** Moves treatment in a productive direction, but does not clearly lead to greater self-awareness, new learning, or positive changes.
   • **Neutral:** Neither contributes to the treatment goals nor harms the therapeutic process.

- **Moderately harmful:** Detracts somewhat from the treatment process or therapeutic alliance.
- **Extremely harmful:** Damaging to the treatment process or therapeutic alliance.

4. **Using summarizing to wrap up the session.** How successful was your summarization? How might it have been improved? Did you remember to check out its accuracy with the client?

Assessment of Progress Form 8

1. **Building on the skills you have already learned.** What use did you make of the following skills, learned in previous chapters? How effective was your use of those interventions?

   - Open and closed questions:
   - Accents, restatements, and paraphrases:
   - Reflections of feeling:
   - Attentive body language:

2. **Using reflection of meaning.** If possible, identify two or three examples of your use of reflection of meaning. How successful were these interventions in helping the client clarify the meaning or importance of an experience? What contributed to, or limited, the success of these interventions?

3. Use the following rating scale to assess the overall success of your role-play session, focusing primarily on your reflections of meaning:

   - **Extremely helpful:** Moves counseling in a productive direction; promotes self-awareness, new learning, or positive changes.
   - **Moderately helpful:** Moves counseling in a productive direction, but does not clearly lead to greater self-awareness, new learning, or positive changes.
   - **Neutral:** Neither contributes to the treatment goals nor harms the therapeutic process.
   - **Moderately harmful:** Detracts somewhat from the counseling process or alliance.
   - **Extremely harmful:** Damaging to the treatment process or therapeutic alliance.

4. **Using affirmations to reinforce helpful thoughts.** Were you able to help the client develop an affirmation to clarify and reinforce the positive impact the experience had on that person? What difficulties, if any, did you encounter in helping the person develop an affirmation? What, if anything, might you have done to improve that process?

5. **Using summarizing to wrap up the session.** How successful was your summarization? How might it have been improved? Did you remember to check out its accuracy with the client?

Assessment of Progress Form 9

1. **Improving targeted skills.** Review the skills you targeted for improvement in this session. List them here and briefly describe what you did to improve

those skills. How successful were your efforts? What do you need to continue to do or to change to maintain or expand on your improvement of the identified skills?

Skill 1: _____

_____

Skill 2: _____

_____

2. **Building on the skills you have already learned.** What use did you make of the following skills, presented in previous chapters?

- Open and closed questions:
- Accents, restatements, and paraphrases:
- Reflections of feeling:
- Nonverbal communication:
- Summarization:
- Reflections of meaning:

3. **Helping your client describe, assess, and modify actions.** Note whether and how you helped your client progress through each of the steps in this role-play. Which steps felt most comfortable for you? Which were most productive? Which presented the greatest challenge? How might you have improved on your use of the behavioral change process?

4. **Concluding the session.** How successful were you and your client at coming up with a viable first step? How effective was your summarization?

5. How would you describe your overall effectiveness in this session, using the following rating scale?

- **Extremely helpful:** Reflects accurate and insightful listening; moves treatment in a very productive direction; promotes self-awareness, new learning, or positive changes.
- **Moderately helpful:** Reflects generally accurate listening; moves treatment in a productive direction, but does not clearly lead to greater self-awareness, new learning, or positive changes.
- **Neutral:** Neither contributes to the treatment goals nor harms the therapeutic process; may not accurately reflect what the client has communicated.
- **Moderately harmful:** Detracts somewhat from the treatment process or alliance; reflects poor listening and perhaps disinterest.
- **Extremely harmful:** Damaging to the treatment process or therapeutic alliance; sounds ridiculing and critical.

What might you have done differently to improve your self-ratings?
What strengths and improvements did you notice?

Assessment of Progress Form 10

1. **Improving targeted skills:** Review the skills you had targeted for improvement in this session. List them here and briefly describe what you did to improve

those skills. How successful were your efforts? What do you need to continue to do or do differently?

Skill 1: _____

Skill 2: _____

2. **Using two specific interventions to promote behavior change:** Were you able to use two of the specific interventions presented in this chapter to facilitate your client's efforts to change behavior? If not, what got in the way of your using these interventions? If yes, what interventions did you use and how effective were they? Do you think that another type of specific intervention would have been even more helpful?

Intervention 1: Name of intervention and assessment of effectiveness, highlighting what worked well and what needed improvement

_____

_____

Intervention 2: Name of intervention and assessment of effectiveness, highlighting what worked well and what needed improvement

_____

_____

Alternative interventions: _____

_____

3. **Concluding the session:**

   • How successful were you at coming up with a between-session task that was acceptable to your client?
   • How successful was your summarization?
   • Did you remember to check out both the suggested task and the summarization with the client?
   • How might you have improved on the conclusion of your session?

4. How would you describe your overall effectiveness in this session, using the following rating scale?

   • **Extremely helpful:** Reflects accurate and insightful listening; moves treatment in a very productive direction; promotes self-awareness, new learning, or positive changes.
   • **Moderately helpful:** Reflects generally accurate listening; moves treatment in a productive direction, but does not clearly lead to greater self-awareness, new learning, or positive changes.
   • **Neutral:** Neither contributes to the treatment goals nor harms the therapeutic process; may not accurately reflect what the client has communicated.
   • **Moderately harmful:** Detracts somewhat from the treatment process or alliance; reflects poor listening and perhaps disinterest.

- **Extremely harmful:** Damaging to the treatment process or therapeutic alliance; sounds ridiculing and critical.

What might you have done differently to improve your self-ratings?

Assessment of Progress Form 11

Now that you have reviewed and revised your evaluations on the Assessment of Progress forms in light of your overall clinical development, you should be ready to respond to the following questions to bring closure to the training you acquired through use of this book.

1. Page **358** of this chapter presented information on qualities of the expert clinician. List three of those qualities you believe you currently possess:

   a.

   b.

   c.

   Now list three of those qualities that you have not yet fully developed and that you want to work toward developing in yourself:

   a.

   b.

   c.

1. Develop a plan to address each of the clinical skills or qualities you have identified as needing improvement, either in your Assessment of Progress forms or in your response to the previous question. Your plan might include, but need not be limited to, the following:

   - Additional reading on particular skills
   - Additional practice, with feedback and supervision
   - A conference with your professor or supervisor or with a trusted colleague
   - A specific change in your clinical work
   - Discussions with colleagues and coworkers

2. Assume that you have read an advertisement for a position as a clinician that sounds exactly like what you are seeking.

   - Write the advertisement, describing the job.
   - Write your letter of application for the position, describing yourself as a clinician and highlighting your strengths.

Personal Journal Questions

1. Describe your overall reactions to the information and learning experiences provided in this book.
2. What were the most important skills this book provided to you?
3. How will you plan to use those skills in your work as a mental health professional?

4. What parts of this book were especially challenging for you? How do you explain that? How did you deal with those challenges?
5. What parts of this book were least interesting or important to you? How do you explain that?
6. How would you improve this book?
7. In three sentences or less, describe the positive changes you have made in your skills as a result of your work with this book.

REFERENCES

Acosta, F. X., Yamamoto, J., Evans, L. A., & Skilbeck, W. M. (1983). Preparing low-income Hispanic, black, and white patients for psychotherapy: Evaluation of a new orientation program. *Journal of Clinical Psychology, 39*(6), 872–877.

Adler, A. (1963 a). *The practice and theory of individual psychology.* Paterson, NJ: Littlefield, Adams.

Adler, A. (1963b). *The problem child.* NY: Putnam.

American Psychiatric Association. (2000). *Diagnostic and statistical manual of mental disorders, fourth edition, text revision (DSM-IV-TR).* Washington, DC: Author.

American Psychological Association. (2002). *APA ethics code.* Washington, DC: Author.

Arredondo, P. (2003). Evolution of the multicultural counseling competencies: Background and context. In G. Roysircar, P. Arredondo, J. M. Fuertes, F. G. Ponterotto, & R. L. Toporek, (Eds.), *Multicultural counseling competencies 2003: Association for multicultural counseling and development.* Alexandria, VA: ACA Press.

Arredondo, P., & Perez, P. (2003). Expanding multicultural competence through social justice leadership. *The Counseling Psychologist, 31,* 282–289.

Arredondo, P., Toporek, R., Brown, S., Jones, J., Locke, D., Sanchez, J., et al. (1996). Operationalization of multicultural counseling competencies. *Journal of Multicultural Counseling and Development, 24,* 42–78.

Barett-Lennard, G. T. (1981). The empathy cycle: Refinement of a nuclear concept. *Journal of Counseling Psychology, 28,* 91–100.

Beck, A. T., & Emery, G. (1985). *Anxiety disorders and phobias.* New York: Guilford Press.

Beck, J. S. (1995). *Cognitive therapy: Basics and beyond.* New York: Guilford Press.

Bemak, F., & Chung, R. C. (2005). Advocacy as a critical role for urban school counselors: Working toward equity and social justice. *Professional School Counseling, 83,* 196–202.

Black, L. L., & Magnuson, S. (2005). Women of spirit: Leaders in the counseling profession. *Journal of Counseling and Development, 83,* 337–342.

Borysenko, J. (1988). *Minding the body, mending the mind.* New York: Bantam Books.

Bowen, M. (1974). Theory in the practice of psychotherapy. In P. J. Guerin, Jr. (Ed.), *Family therapy: Theory and practice.* New York: Gardner Press.

Burns, D. D. (2007). *The feeling good handbook.* New York: Penguin.

Carkhuff, R. R. (1969). *Helping and human relations.* New York: Holt, Rinehart, & Winston.

Carlock, C. J. (Ed.). (1999). *Enhancing self-esteem.* Philadelphia, PA: Accelerated Development.

Chambless, D. L., Baker, M. J., Baucom, D. H., Beutler, L. E., Calhoun, K. S., Crits-Cristoph, P., et al. (1998). Update on empirically validated therapies, II. *Clinical Psychologist, 51,* 3–16.

Clark, A. J. (2002). *Early recollections: Theory and practice in counseling and psychotherapy.* New York: Routledge.

Davis, M., McKay, M., & Eshelman, E. R. (2003). *The relaxation and stress reduction workbook.* Oakland, CA: New Harbinger Publications.

de Shazer, S. (1991). *Putting difference to work.* New York: Norton.

Deaner, R. G., & Pechersky, K. (2005). Early recollections: Enhancing case conceptualization for practitioners working with couples. *The Family Journal, 13,* 311–315.

Division 12 Task Force. (1996). An update on empirically validated therapies. *Clinical Psychologist, 49,* 5–18.

Duckworth, A. L., Steen, T. A., & Seligman, M. E. P. (2005). Positive psychology in clinical practice. *Annual Review of Clinical Psychology, 1,* 629–651.

Ellis, A. E. (1995). *Better, deeper, and more enduring brief therapy.* New York: Brunner/Mazel.

Ellis, A. E. (2003). Early theories and practices of rational emotive behavior therapy and how they have been augmented and revised during the last three decades. *Journal of Rational-Emotive & Cognitive-Behavior Therapy, 21,* 219–243.

Ellis, A. E., & Dryden, W. (1997). *The practice of rational emotive behavior therapy* (2 nd ed.). New York: Springer.

Etringer, B. D., Hillerbrand, E., & Claiborn, C. D. (1995). The transition from novice to expert counselor. *Counselor Education and Supervision, 35,* 4–17.

Fagan, J., & Shepherd, I. L. (1970). *Gestalt therapy now.* New York: Harper & Row.

Fong, M. L., Borders, L. E., Ethington, C. A., & Pitts, J. H. (1997). Becoming a counselor: A longitudinal study of student cognitive development. *Counselor Education and Supervision, 37,* 100–114.

Frankl, V. E. (1963). *Man's search for meaning.* Boston: Beacon.

Gendlin, E. T. (1996). *Focusing-oriented psychotherapy*. New York: Guilford.

Gladstein, G. A. (1983). Understanding empathy: Integrating counseling, development and social psychology perspectives. *Journal of Counseling Psychology, 30,* 467–482.

Glasser, W. (2000). *Counseling with choice theory*. New York: Harper & Row.

Goh, J. (2005). Cultural competence and master therapists: An inextricable relationship. *Journal of Mental Health Counseling, 2005,* 71–81.

Gustavson, C. B. (1995). *In-versing your life*. Milwaukee, WI: Families International.

Hay, C. E., & Kinnier, R. T. (1998). Homework in counseling. *Journal of Mental Health Counseling, 20,* 122–132.

Hill, C. E., & O'Brien, K. M. (1999). *Helping skills: Facilitating exploration, insight, and action*. Washington, DC: American Psychological Association.

Hill, C. E., & O'Grady, K. E. (1985). List of therapist intentions illustrated in a case study and with therapists of varying theoretical orientations. *Journal of Counseling Psychology, 32,* 3–32.

Howard, K. A. S., & Solberg, V. S. H. (2006). School-based social justice: The achieving success identity pathways program. *Professional School Counseling, 4,* 278–287.

Ivey, A. (1971). *Microcounseling: Innovations in interviewing training*. Springfield, IL: Charles C. Thomas.

Ivey, A. E., Ivey, M. B., & Simek-Morgan, L. (1997). *Counseling and psychotherapy*. Boston: Allyn and Bacon.

Jennings, L., & Skovholt, T. M. (1999). The cognitive, emotional, and relational characteristics of master therapists. *Journal of Counseling Psychology, 46,* 3–11.

Kabat-Zinn, J. (2005). *Wherever you go, there you are*. New York: Bantam Dell.

Kaslow, F. (1995). *Projective genogramming*. Sarasota, FL: Professional Resources Press.

Kiselica, M. S. (2004). When duty calls: The implications of social justice work for policy, education, and practice in the mental health professions. *The Counseling Psychologist, 32,* 838–854.

Kiselica, M. S., & Robinson, M. (2001). Bringing advocacy to life: The history, issues, and human dramas of social justice work in counseling. *Journal of Counseling and Development, 79,* 387–397.

Kohut, H. (1984). Introspection, empathy, and the semicircle of mental health. In J. Lichetenberg, M. Bornstein, & D. Silver (Eds.), *Empathy I* (pp. 81–102). Hillsdale, NJ: Erlbaum.

Lambert, M. J., & Bergin, A. E. (1994). The effectiveness of psychotherapy. In A. E. Bergin & S. L. Garfield (Eds.), *Handbook of psychotherapy and behavior change* (4th ed., pp. 143–189). New York: Wiley.

Lambert, M. J., & Cattani-Thompson, K. (1996). Current findings regarding the effectiveness of counseling: Implications for practice. *Journal of Counseling and Development, 74,* 601–608.

Lazarus, A. A. (1989). *The practice of multimodal therapy (update)*. Baltimore, MD: Johns Hopkins University Press.

Lazarus, A. A. (1997). *Brief but comprehensive psychotherapy*. New York: Springer.

Leach, M. M., Stoltenberg, C. D., McNeill, B. W., & Eichenfield, G. A. (1997). Self-efficacy and counselor development: Testing the integrated developmental model. *Counselor Education and Supervision, 37,* 115–124.

Lee, C. C. (Ed.) (2007). *Counseling for social justice*. Alexandria, VA: American Counseling Association.

Lewis, J., & Bradley, L. (1999). *Advocacy in counseling: Counselors, clients, & community*. Greensboro, NC: ERIC Clearinghouse.

Little, C., Packman, J., Smaby, M. H., & Maddux, C. D. (2005). The skilled counselor training model: Skills acquisition, self-assessment, and cognitive complexity. *Counselor Education and Supervision, 44,* 189–200.

Lopez-Baez, S. (2005, August). "It was the best of time; it was the worst of times": Reflections. *CSJ Activist, 6,* pp. 2–3.

Luborsky, L., McLellan, A. T., Woody, G. E., O'Brien, C. P., & Auerbach, A. (1985). Therapist success and its determinants. *Archives of General Psychiatry, 42,* 602–611.

Luborsky, L., Crits-Cristoph, P., McLellan, A. T., Woody, G., Piper, W., Liberman, B., et al. (1984). The nonspecific hypothesis of therapeutic effectiveness: A current assessment. *American Journal of Orthopsychiatry, 56,* 501–512.

McGoldrick, M., & Gerson, R. (1988). Genograms and the family life cycle. In B. Carter & M. McGoldrick (Eds.), *The changing family life cycle* (pp. 164–189). New York: Gardner Press.

Meichenbaum, D. (1985). *Stress inoculation training*. Elmsford, NY: Pergamon.

Meichenbaum, D. (1993). Changing conceptions of cognitive behavior modification: Retrospect and prospect. *Journal of Consulting and Clinical Psychology, 61*(2), 202–204.

Miller, W. R., & Rollnick, S. (2002). *Motivational interviewing: Preparing people for change* (2nd ed.). New York: Guilford.

Moorey, S., & Greer, S. (1989). *Psychological therapy for patients with cancer: A new approach*. Washington, DC: American Psychiatric Press.

Myers, J. E., & Sweeney, T. J. (2005). *Counseling for wellness*. Alexandria, VA: American Counseling Association.

O'Hanlon, B., & Weiner-Davis, M. (1989). *In search of solutions: A new direction in psychotherapy*. New York: Norton.

Olsen, J. A., & Riebli, A. (2005, March). Developing better justice in our schools. *CJS Activist, 5,* 1, 3, 5.

O'Ryan, L. W., & Whewell, K. K. (2005, August). The sociopolitical nature of singlehood: Implications for the counseling profession. *CSJ Activist, 6,* 1, 6–7.

Oshinsky, J. (1994). *Discovery journal*. Odessa, FL: Psychological Assessment Resources.

Palumbo, D. (2000). *Writing from the inside out: Transforming your psychological blocks to release the writer within*. New York: John Wiley.

Patterson, C. H. (2004). Do we need multicultural counseling competencies? *Journal Of Mental Health Counseling, 26,* 67–73.

Paulson, B. L., Truscott, D., & Stuart, J. (1999). Clients' perceptions of helpful experiences in counseling. *Journal of Counseling Psychology, 46,* 317–324.

Pavlov, I. P. (1927). *Conditioned reflexes* (G. V. Anrep, Trans.). London: Oxford University Press.

Peterson, C., & Seligman, M. E. P. (2004). *Character strengths and virtues: A handbook and classification*. Washington, DC: American Psychological Association.

Prochaska, J. O., & Norcross, J. C. (2003). *Systems of psychotherapy: A transtheoretical analysis*. Pacific Grove, CA: Brooks/Cole.

Rogers, C. R. (1951). *Client-centered therapy: Its current practice, implications and theory*. Boston: Houghton Mifflin.

Rogers, C. R. (1959). A theory of therapy, personality, and individual relationships as developed in the client-centered framework. In S. Koch (Ed.), *Psychology: A study of a science* (pp. 184–256). New York: McGraw-Hill.

Rogers, C. R. (1967). The conditions of change from a client-centered viewpoint. In B. Berenson & R. Carkhuff (Eds.), *Sources of gain in counseling and psychotherapy*. New York: Hold, Rinehart & Winston.

Rothman, A. D. & Nowicki, S. (2004). A measure of the ability to identify emotion in children's tone of voice. *Journal of Nonverbal Behavior, 28,* 67–92.

Sawatsky, D. D., Jevne, R. F., & Clark, G. T. (1994). Becoming empowered: A study of counselor development. *Canadian Journal of Counseling, 28,* 177–192.

Scheel, M. J., Seaman, S., Roach, K., Mullin, T., & Mahoney, K. B. (1999). Client implementation of therapist recommendations predicted by client perception of fit, difficulty of implementation, and therapist influence. *Journal of Counseling Psychology, 46,* 308–316.

Seligman, L. (1996). *Promoting a fighting spirit*. San Francisco: Jossey-Bass.

Seligman, L. (2001). *Systems, strategies, and skills of counseling and psychotherapy*. Upper Saddle River, NJ: Merrill/Prentice Hall.

Seligman, L. (2004). *Diagnosis and treatment planning in counseling*. New York: Kluwer Academic/Plenum Publishers.

Seligman, L. (2006). *Theories of counseling and psychotherapy: Systems, strategies, and skills*. Upper Saddle River, NJ: Pearson Merrill/Prentice Hall.

Seligman, L. (2008). *Conceptual skills for mental health professionals*. Upper Saddle River, NJ: Pearson Merrill/Prentice Hall.

Seligman, L., & Reichenberg, L. (2007). *Selecting effective treatments*. San Francisco: Jossey-Bass.

Seligman, M. (1988). Positive social science. *APA Monitor, 29*(4), 2, 5.

Seligman, M. (1999). Teaching positive psychology. *APA Monitor on Psychology, 30*(7). Available from www.apa.org

Sexton, T. L. (1995). Outcome research perspective on mental health counselor competencies. In M. K. Altekruse & T. L. Sexton (Eds.), *Mental health counseling in the 90 s* (pp. 51–60). Tampa, FL: National Commission for Mental Health Counseling.

Sexton, T. L., & Whiston, S. C. (1991). A review of the empirical basis for counseling: Implications for practice and training. *Counselor Education and Supervision, 30,* 330–354.

Skinner, B. F. (1969). *Contingencies of reinforcement: A theoretical analysis*. New York: Appleton-Century-Crofts.

Skovholt, T. M., & Ronnestad, M. H. (1992). Themes in therapist and counselor development. *Journal of Counseling and Development, 70,* 505–515.

Smith, E. J. (2006). The strength-based counseling model: A paradigm shift in psychology. *The Counseling Psychologist, 34,* 13–79.

Smith, J. C. (1986). *Meditation*. Champaign, IL: Research Press.

Sue, S. (1998). In search of cultural competence in psychotherapy and counseling. *American Psychologist, 53,* 440–448.

Sundaram, D. S., & Webster, C. (2000). The role of nonverbal communication in service encounters. *The Journal of Service Marketing, 14,* 378–391.

Vargas, L. (2004). The emergence of a counselor for social justice. *CSJ Activist, 5,* 1, 3.

Walborn, F. S. (1996). *Process variables*. Pacific Grove, CA: Brooks/Cole.

Watson, J. B. (1925). *Behaviorism*. New York: Norton.

Weinrach, S. G., & Thomas, K. R. (2004). The AMCD multicultural counseling competencies: A critically flawed initiative. *Journal of Mental Health Counseling, 26,* 81–93.

Whiston, S. C., & Coker, J. K. (2000). Reconstructing clinical training: Implications from research. *Counselor Education and Supervision, 39,* 228–253.

Wolpe, J. (1969). *The practice of behavior therapy*. New York: Pergamon.

Wubbolding, R. E. (2000). *Reality therapy for the 21st century*. Briston, PA: Accelerated Development.

PHOTO CREDITS

Chapter 1

Page 02 Getty Images, Inc.—Photodisc; **30** Scott Cunningham/Merrill.

Chapter 2

Page 56 Photodisc/Getty Images; **61** Getty Images, Inc.—Digital Vision; **69** Photodisc/Getty Images.

Chapter 3

Page 128 Patrick White/Merrill.

Chapter 5

Page 145 National Library of Medicine; **166** Photodisc/Getty Images.

Chapter 6

Page 183 Martin E.P. Seligman; **201** Anthony Magnacca/Merrill; **213** Gestalt Journal Press.

Chapter 7

Page 227 Institute for Rational-Emotive Therapy/Aaron T. Beck, M.D.

Chapter 8

Page 277 Laima Druskis/PH College; **280** SW Productions/Getty Images, Inc.—Photodisc.

Chapter 9

Page 292 Dawn E. O'Day/Craig Ferre Photography/The William Glasser Institute; **293** Getty Images, Inc.—Stockbyte.

Chapter 10

Page 344 James Carroll/PH College.

INDEX

Note: Locators in italics indicate figures or tables.